The Battle for the Presidency

By the same author

American Freethought
Farthest Frontier: The Pacific Northwest
The President as World Leader
The American President (ed.)

The Battle
for the
Presidency

by
Sidney Warren

J. B. LIPPINCOTT COMPANY
Philadelphia and New York

A portion of the last chapter of this book was first published in the July
4, 1964, issue of *Saturday Review* under the title "How to Pick a President" and is reprinted here by kind permission.

*To My Father and to
the Memory of My Mother*

Preface

Presidential election campaigns have greatly influenced and even altered the course of American politics and the nature of the Presidency. They have contributed to the development of a clearly defined party system. Concomitantly, the presidential office was strengthened as its occupant became the acknowledged leader of his party. And, among other things, a national consensus of political values was achieved.

These contests also illuminate a number of basic characteristics of the nation's political system: the qualities Americans look for in leadership, the position of the Chief Executive in the constitutional scheme, the difference between presidential and congressional constituencies, and the relative weight assigned to domestic and foreign policy.

Not all campaigns, of course, have been equally consequential. I have selected the ten which I believe best illustrate significant aspects of presidential politics or whose results have had an impact on national affairs. In this descriptive and analytical study of those contests, I have explored such factors as the role of party and of party organization in electing a President, the changing pattern and style of presidential campaigns, the uses and abuses of campaign propaganda, the distortion or oversimplification of vital national issues, the influence of personality, the effects of money and the mass media, the merits and deficiencies of the primary system and the national convention, the politics and problems of the electoral college, and criteria for recruiting political leadership.

To the American Philosophical Society my sincere thanks for the research grant awarded me. My profound gratitude to Professors Allan Nevins and Thomas A. Bailey for their careful reading of the manuscript and for their many helpful comments and suggestions. Any errors of fact or interpretation are naturally my own. Many friends and colleagues offered me advice and encouragement when I first undertook this study. I want to especially thank Professors James MacGregor Burns, Louis Koenig, Clinton Rossiter, and Martin Ridge.

I am obligated to Miss Betty Armstrong and her staff at the California Western University library for their generous cooperation. My thanks also to the staffs of the libraries of San Diego State College and the University of California at Los Angeles for their assistance.

My wife's contribution in the preparation of this book was truly indispensable. Nothing I can say here could adequately express my profound indebtedness.

Sidney Warren

San Diego, Calif.

Contents

The Battle for the Presidency

1. An Elective Kingship

A S Thomas Jefferson was about to retire from the White House, he confided to a friend, "Never did a prisoner, released from his chains, feel such relief as I shall in shaking off the shackles of power." Similar disenchantment was expressed by other Chief Executives. John Adams wrote, "If I were to go over my life again, I would be a shoemaker rather than an American statesman." On the day he left office, President Polk declared, "I am sure I shall be a happier man in my retirement than I have been during the four years I have filled the highest office in the gift of my countrymen." And James Garfield groaned to his diary, "My God, what is there in this place that a man should ever want to get into it!"

Most Presidents, however, have not regarded their tenure as so onerous or so dismal an experience. The incomparable power and prestige of the office have more than compensated them for the heavy responsibilities, the frequently crushing burdens, the fishbowl existence, the scurrilous public attacks, even the jeopardy to their lives.

From its inception, the American Presidency has been a unique institution. At the Constitutional Convention in Philadelphia in 1787, more time was spent deliberating over the office of the executive than about any other element of the governmental structure. Should it be unitary or plural? Some shared Madison's view that a single executive would

3

"savour too much of a monarchy," but James Wilson's contention that it would give the "most energy, dispatch, and responsibility to the office" ultimately prevailed.

A basic issue was the status of the Chief Executive in relation to Congress. If he were merely to execute the laws, then his tenure, his selection and removal, and the nature of his power would have to be different from what they would be if he were to function as a countervailing force upon legislative authority. If subordinate to Congress, then logically the legislature should be empowered to elect and remove him; if not, another method would have to be devised for putting him in office. At the core of the problem was the nature of the governmental structure. The framers of the Constitution, in considering a number of alternatives, made a unique contribution to statecraft when they decided in favor of equal and coordinate branches of government.

When vigorously debating the method of selecting a President, the lawmakers gave scant consideration to the idea of direct election by the people. Nurtured for the most part in an aristocratic tradition, the Founding Fathers believed that the head of state should be a product of the "natural aristocracy" of men endowed with the qualities of birth, wealth, virtue, talent, and superior intellect. Direct election by the people, one of the methods proposed, accordingly received the least support. "It would be as unnatural to refer the choice of a proper character for the chief magistrate to the people as it would be to refer a trial of colors to a blind man," George Mason said. "The extent of the country renders it impossible that the people can have the requisite capacity to judge of the respective pretensions of the candidates." Others felt that the people would be hoodwinked by schemers or by those with special interests, so that direct election would be little better than choice by lot.

All the other plans proposed—selection by the House of Representatives, by the state governors, by the state legislatures—met with one objection or another. The formula finally adopted was the product of compromise. It combined the advantage of independence from the legislative branch with that of indirect popular participation. Concessions were made to all interests, the large states and the small, the advocates of national government, and the state "particularists." An electoral college, whose numbers would be equal to the number of representatives and senators from each state, was to be appointed in such manner as the legislatures of the states considered appropriate.* Intended to comprise the most capable individuals, it would meet every four years and presumably have the wisdom to choose the ablest man. A majority vote was required to elect the President, but if none of the candidates received it, the House of Representatives would select the man from among the three who obtained the highest number. The one who received the second highest vote would be Vice-President. It had been expected that electors would exercise independent judgment in their selection of a President. As soon as political parties developed, however, they functioned as instruments of their parties and only very rarely has any elector voted contrary to his instructions.

When the Committee on Detail, assigned to prepare a draft constitution, submitted its results, the Convention spent five weeks in the humid, sweltering heat of a Philadelphia summer debating it almost word for word. Then, on September 8, a Committee on Style was appointed to put the draft into final shape. Article II, dealing with the Presidency, began: "The executive power shall be vested in a President of the United States of America." Broad constructionists among the delegates, and broad constructionists ever since, have interpreted this clause as permitting a large grant of discretionary and residual power. Regarded as an additional source of "residual" authority is the simple statement which follows that "he shall take care that the laws be faithfully executed. . . ."

The President created by the members of the Convention

---

* Various methods for choosing electors were later employed: selection by the state legislature, election by the people on a district basis, and popular election by state-wide general tickets.

was invested with two characteristics of an ideal executive
—strength and responsibility. He was commander in chief
of the armed forces, required to approve or veto congressional bills, and, with the consent of the Senate, empowered
to make treaties, appoint ambassadors, Justices of the Supreme Court, and other high officials. Envisioning the Chief
Executive as being above factionalism and not anticipating
the formation of political parties, they naturally could not
foresee that yet another of his major roles would be that
of party leader.

With the emergence of political parties, the manner in
which presidential candidates were selected changed radi-
cally from the original design. As early as 1796, the nation
was already divided between Federalists and Jeffersonian
Republicans. To unite the members of the electoral college
behind a slate of first and second choices, candidates for the
highest office were selected by informal party caucuses in
Congress. Open nominations by a congressional group
seemed to be the most expedient method. Soon, however,
the Federalists, whose representation in Congress steadily
dwindled, resorted to other methods. In 1808 and in 1812,
Federalist leaders selected in a variety of ways assembled in
secret to choose a candidate.

By the 1820's the caucus had lapsed into disfavor. Secretary of State John Quincy Adams recorded in his diary in
1819 that the congressional caucus encouraged ambitious
men to curry favor with senators and representatives, that it
made the President subservient to Congress, and that it
gave rise to cabals and corrupt deals in Congress. But the
most potent factor was the steadily increasing democratiza-
tion of political life. A number of state constitutions had
been changed to extend the suffrage, and presidential electors were chosen directly by the people in most of the
twenty-four states. The caucus was now regarded as inadequate to reflect the popular will, champions of democracy derisively referring to it as "King Caucus." To be endorsed by one was virtually the kiss of death, and the last
one was held in 1824. The demise of the caucus was of

much significance to the Presidency, for the successful aspirant to the office would no longer be indebted to the members of his party in the legislature.

The creation of a new third party, the Anti-Masons, before the election of 1832, provided the occasion for a novel method of nominating presidential candidates. Since its followers were concentrated mostly in western Massachusetts and New York and only a few of its members held public office, to achieve success it would have to become more widely known. Toward that end it was decided to hold a national nominating convention in 1831 and to make the proceedings public. State organizations were to select delegates in any manner they considered appropriate. The number of votes for each delegation would be equal to its state's congressional representation, and a three-fourths' majority was required for the nomination. In September, 116 delegates gathered at Baltimore, where they nominated a former United States Attorney General for the Presidency. A national committee was designated to direct party affairs between conventions.

The National Republicans (later known as Whigs), seeking cohesion for their fragmented party in which each state or section claimed leadership, held a public convention in December. Henry Clay was nominated, and in May 1832 a group meeting in Washington adopted resolutions setting forth the party's position.

That same month, the Democratic Republicans (or Democrats) also held a national convention in an effort to resolve one of their problems. While the popular Andrew Jackson's renomination was undisputed, the administration was split between supporters of Vice-President Calhoun and Secretary of State Van Buren for the second place. Jackson wanted the latter, but Calhoun had strong backing in Congress. A convention held after the legislature adjourned would enable the President to obtain broad support for his choice. Calhoun was defeated.

By 1840, nominating conventions every presidential year had become the established practice in American politics.

Among the methods for selecting and recruiting political leadership in democratic nations, the nomination system of the American party convention is unique. Outside the United States, wherever the parliamentary system prevails, experience in government and service to the party are considered indispensable. Great Britain, for example, requires a long period of apprenticeship and distinguished service in the House of Commons before a politician is recognized as a party leader and prospective prime minister. Leaders cannot emerge full-blown; they are chosen through internal party processes, generally by members of the party's executive or central committee after years of testing as party leader in Parliament. In the United States, on the other hand, a man may become a serious contender without having had to climb the rungs of the political ladder.

As most parties abroad are centralized, they have the advantage of being more immune to outside influences and pressures than the American parties, each of which is in reality a combination of fifty autonomous organizations. Their disadvantage is that dissent from the official party position is discouraged, so that leaders who disagree with basic policy can promote their viewpoints only by founding a splinter party. American parties have provided stability and avoided the proliferation of parties characteristic of many other nations by being able generally to encompass a diversity of views, thereby providing representation for all segments of the population.

Both the single member district system in congressional elections and the electoral college have encouraged a two-party system. Each party vies for votes across sectional, class, and ethnic lines, a process which encourages broad coalitions of heterogeneous interests rather than cohesive and disciplined organizations. As the electoral system does not provide for proportional representation, minor parties are relegated to the status of peripheral groups.

Ideological parties have never succeeded in gaining any appreciable strength because adherence to doctrine results in fragmentation, which is fatal for victory. Furthermore, the necessity for dealing with the President, whose influence and power place him at the core of the party system, demands cooperation and a working relationship among factions within the party. What the President advocates today may become an explosive issue tomorrow. Whether active or not, he sets the pace and determines the tone. The focus, accordingly, is on the man in the White House and the character of his leadership rather than on the doctrinal expression of the party.

The nominating convention is both the end of one campaign and the beginning of another. In the months preceding the gathering of delegates, and even after they have assembled, factional lines within the party may be drawn and redrawn. In some instances one man or one group may dominate the party, leaving the convention with a *pro forma* ratifying function, but almost always at least one of the two major parties is compelled to engage in complicated political maneuvers until the final ballots are cast. However, fierce as the in-fighting may be among the aspirants during the preconvention period, once a candidate is chosen the party closes ranks and erstwhile opponents embrace each other for a common objective—victory over the opposing party.

Coalition politics is also reflected in the party platform, one object of which is to unite the competing and clashing elements within the party. The platform has often been derided as a meaningless and useless compilation of platitudes, designed to say nothing by saying everything to placate all elements and offend none. Moreover, with each congressman free to vote as his interests and preferences dictate, the majority party cannot always translate platform promises into legislation. Even presidential candidates have sometimes taken positions at variance with the platforms of their parties. Yet platforms are significant because they say, as Herbert Agar put it, "not what a party will do but who is pushing and pulling for what, and with how much success." They reveal where the center of gravity, comprising the dominant forces and tendencies within the party, is located.

The convention has been criticized on many counts: that

it is unrepresentative of the party and of the national electorate; that the crucial decisions are made by a relatively small number of men without regard to the wishes of the hundreds of delegates who attend presumably to share in decision-making; that it often fails to select the man best qualified; that it lacks dignity, being conducted more like a Shriners' gathering than a deliberative assembly.

Much of this judgment is valid. Although delegates on the whole reflect the broad currents of American life, they are generally chosen because of their position in local and state politics, so that their political contacts rarely extend beyond the party workers with whom they have been associated. Unfamiliar with the national political scene and thereby dependent on key members of their state delegations to provide essential information, they are in no position to perform individual roles. Moreover, from a sheer physical aspect, the size of the convention does not allow for a town-hall type of gathering. The plenary meetings, as well as those of the subcommittees, are little more than ratifying sessions. Even a floor debate rarely persuades the delegates to alter a decision arrived at in caucus, though the outcome of the issue may have serious implications for the party.

Strong leaders, some maintain, are still passed over in favor of men less qualified or not clearly committed to definite policy positions. Yet the acid test of an aspirant's capacity for presidential leadership may be his facility to survive the intricate negotiations and maneuverings that bring about his candidacy. He demonstrates considerable political skill by satisfying the leaders who support his nomination, placating the heads of the factions who had backed the defeated aspirants, and reconciling opposing objectives and positions by achieving compromise programs.

The convention itself is an extraordinary phenomenon. "The more I see of conventions," wrote H. L. Mencken, "the more I marvel that anyone can be induced to attend them. The oratory is bad almost beyond description . . . [the work] is carried on in the most tedious and wasteful way imaginable [and] the whole thing is simply an elaborate scheme for wasting time and money." Yet several thousand delegates, assembled in a cavernous hall for their quadrennial ritualistic exercise, manage to settle disputes over credentials, adopt rules for carrying on their business, choose temporary and permanent officers, draft a party statement of principles, and, finally, select the man who may lead the nation during the next four years. The convention reinforces party loyalty and galvanizes followers into active support. After the hullabaloo has subsided, the hoarse and bleary-eyed delegates and onlookers return to their homes united in a common cause for the duration of the campaign.

Since the beginning of the convention system, the process for nominating a candidate has changed little. Only one device has been added—the presidential primary, introduced in the first decades of this century. A significant item in the reform program of the Progressive movement, it was urged as a means for democratizing government by taking the choice of a candidate away from the politicians and giving it to the people. Senator Robert La Follette, who had vainly attempted to have his Progressive delegation seated at the 1904 convention, was responsible for the enactment of a primary law in Wisconsin providing for the direct election of delegates to the national conventions. The following year, Pennsylvania went a bit further with a preferential primary in which delegates listed on the ballot were permitted to indicate their presidential choice alongside their names. Oregon pioneered in the first primary that made the voters' preference binding upon the delegates. By 1912, Theodore Roosevelt was able to challenge Taft in a dozen states which had adopted primary systems providing for the direct election of delegates, or the indication of a presidential preference, or both.

The popularity of the system has waxed and waned, but today it is used by fifteen states and the District of Columbia. Even though delegates chosen in the primaries represent no more than forty per cent of the total convention strength and more than half are unpledged, contenders for the presidential nomination increasingly have considered it important to participate in a number of primaries. The last four Presidents who received their nominations in open contests—Hoover, Roosevelt, Eisenhower, and Kennedy—all used the primaries as a tool in their efforts to obtain their nominations.

On occasion primaries have served to generate nation-wide support for candidates who have not been backed by party leaders. Voters have come to regard them as a measure of a candidate's ability to win an election. The refusal of Symington and Johnson in 1960 to enter the primaries made them appear potentially weaker than Kennedy as vote getters. That primaries have a psychological significance out of all proportion to the actual number of delegates chosen or pledged is apparent from the way a candidate's fortunes may be affected by the results in no more than one or two states. Wendell Willkie abandoned his efforts to secure the party nomination in 1944 after his poor showing in the Wisconsin primary. General Eisenhower's prospects for the nomination against Senator Robert Taft in 1952 were greatly enhanced when he received 100,000 write-in votes in the Minnesota primary. Kennedy's triumph over Humphrey in West Virginia in 1960 virtually assured him of the nomination.

Primaries have opened up a new dimension in the struggle for the Presidency. In the nineteenth century, presidential hopefuls, carefully observing the tradition that the office should seek the man, rarely announced their candidacy prior to the party convention. They were even expected to disavow that they were seeking the office up to the very eve of the party gathering. All this has become obsolete.

Active and open involvement throughout a long preconvention period now seems to be essential. The aspirant seeking the nomination must carefully consider timing in announcing his candidacy, and primaries have become an aspect of his political strategy. He has to decide whether to enter the primaries and, if so, which ones are likely to improve his prospects and which might set him back. In those states where the political organization is strong he must attempt to win its cooperation, and, where he confronts rival factions, he must gamble on the one which might yield the greatest political capital.

The candidate who enters the primaries undertakes as vigorous a campaign as if he were a presidential nominee. In the process he is involved in a public display of rhetoric, persuasion, strategy, and political combat. He must employ all his skill in coping with local political situations and address himself to the attitudes on national and international issues that prevail in the state which he has entered. At the same time he must deftly contrive to maintain a position which will cause him the least harm in areas of the nation where views on public policy are different. To project an image of statesmanship, he is required to express himself on a wide range of issues, but he must be highly adroit to minimize his vulnerability to attack. He always has to keep in mind that a position which may be advantageous in gaining the nomination may injure his prospects for winning the election.

Many who have gone through the grueling experience of a primary campaign are highly critical of the device. Adlai Stevenson called it "almost a useless institution." He deplored the excessive burdens it places on public officials, who are required to spend valuable weeks and months away from pressing duties to travel the primary trail. Furthermore, it was, he said, terribly expensive, physically exhausting, and "a very, very questionable method of selecting presidential candidates."

However it may be regarded, the primary is no more likely to be abandoned than the convention itself as an element in the nominating process. Increasingly the convention is likely to be a ratifying body approving the voters' decision in pivotal primary states, and increasingly an aspirant may be obliged to strengthen his claim to the nomination by an effective showing in the primaries. In essence, the dual system of primaries and conventions provides the advantage of an element of "grass roots" democracy and the highly developed process of selection by the political brokers.

The nominating process has also been affected by the rising importance of the President. As the acknowledged party leader, he has to a considerable extent pre-empted the influential place of the party bosses. If he exercises this role effectively, he can probably dictate the choice of the candidate he wishes to succeed him.

Calvin Coolidge and Harry Truman present interesting contrasts between the old and the new in presidential influence at nominating conventions. The former, with his "Whiggish" approach to office and disinclination to use party leadership, was indifferent to the nomination of his successor. He did nothing to advance or retard the prospects for Herbert Hoover, who received the nomination only because he was supported by the same groups which had backed the incumbent. Truman, on the other hand, was completely involved with the choice of a successor. After an unsuccessful attempt to recruit Chief Justice Vinson, the President turned to Adlai E. Stevenson. "I felt that in Stevenson I had found the man to whom I could safely turn over the responsibilities of party leadership," Truman recorded.

The presidential candidate in the nineteenth century, with but few exceptions, left the active campaigning to the party workers, nurturing the illusion of disinterested patriotism. He rarely made campaign tours, remaining quietly at home where he conferred with his managers, assisted in soliciting funds, and engaged in other behind-the-scenes planning. Generally his only public statement was the formal response to the committee appointed by the convention to notify him of his nomination, and it was made orally if the committee called in person.

When Stephen A. Douglas engaged in extensive campaign travels in 1860, his activities were criticized as "a regrettable innovation below the dignity of a candidate for the Presidency." In 1876, the Republican presidential candidate, Rutherford B. Hayes, questioned the propriety of attending Ohio Day at the Philadelphia fair, although he was governor of the state and the occasion was nonpolitical.

Officials of a railroad company were responsible for a scheme which permitted James A. Garfield to address the public during the campaign of 1880 without being censured for bad taste. They discovered that his farm was only eight miles from a station on the main line of the Northern Ohio. Struck by the commercial possibilities, they advertised special excursion rates from Cleveland and nearby cities to the home of the distinguished candidate, omitting to mention, however, that from the station to the farm was an eight-mile trip by horse and buggy. Nevertheless, thousands of citizens beat a path to the farmhouse, obliging Garfield to appear on his front porch and address them with some brief prepared remarks. After the turn of the century, however, it became the practice for candidates to engage in active electioneering throughout the country.

If the extent of participation by presidential candidates has changed, the heat generated by campaigns has been constant. The excitement and emotionalism which charge the atmosphere, the unrestrained rhetoric which flows freely, have always been characteristic and, to a greater or lesser degree, so have the charges, the slander, abuse, and innuendo which have been hurled at candidates in public addresses, at meetings, in newspapers and magazine articles. As Lord Bryce observed in his celebrated commentary on the American system, "Imagine all the accusations brought against all the candidates for the 670 seats in the English Parliament concentrated on one man, and read . . . daily for three months, and you will still fail to realize what is the tempest of invective and calumny which hurtles round the head of a presidential candidate."

Some campaigns have been especially scurrilous as when in 1836 it was bruited about that Van Buren was the illegitimate son of Aaron Burr and that his running mate had

a Negro ancestor, or in the 1868 campaign, when a rumor
was started that Ulysses S. Grant was an alcoholic and that
his opponent, Horatio Seymour, was of illegitimate birth.

Morality was presumably the issue in the campaign of
1884, but the manner in which both candidates were attacked descended to ignominious depths. The Republicans
exploited a youthful indiscretion by Grover Cleveland,
which had resulted in an illegitimate child, to smear the
candidate. In torchlight parades they bawled in a chant:

> Ma, Ma, where's my pa?
> Gone to the White House,
> *Ha! Ha! Ha!*

Then Democrats discovered a chink in the armor of "the
plumed knight." James G. Blaine, it seemed, had accepted a
bribe of railroad securities for favors rendered while he was
Speaker of the House. A letter to a railroad official had been
unearthed containing Blaine's instructions on how to cover
up the gifts. It ended with the admonition, "Burn this letter." Now Democrats also had a ditty to chant as they
paraded through the streets:

> Blaine, Blaine, James G. Blaine,
> The continental liar from the State of Maine,
> *Burn this letter!*

Clergymen on one side or the other joined the chorus. The
Reverend George Bull of Buffalo declaimed against Cleveland, "The issue is evidently not between the two parties
but between the brothel and the home, between lust and
law." The Reverend Henry Ward Beecher replied that he
would support Cleveland and that, if every New Yorker
who had violated the Seventh Commandment also voted for
the candidate, the state would be carried by 200,000 votes.
A prominent Republican newspaper promptly interpreted
this as an appeal to all adulterers to rally around their
leader.

When Theodore Roosevelt ran for office in 1912, he was
slandered as being an alcoholic who even frequently ap-

peared in public "under the influence," a drug addict, and partially insane. One editor exceeded the limits of permissible vituperation in print when he wrote that Roosevelt "lies and curses in a most disgusting way; he gets drunk, too, and that not infrequently, and all his intimates know about it." Roosevelt sued for libel and won.

Warren G. Harding, whose private life had not been unblemished, was a wide-open target for such ribald pot shots as premarital relations with his wife. It was also said that he had Negro ancestry.

Few candidates have escaped being spattered with some kind of muck, but on the other side are the efforts made to create an image that will accord with the national myth of a presidential personality. The President has come to embody the hopes and dreams of the American people, to be the living symbol of their virtues and ideals, the incarnation of their real or fancied rectitude. Campaign orators and biographers, accordingly, have dwelt on the candidate's honorable ancestry; on the abiding and beneficent influence of his parents, especially his mother; on his exemplary childhood, youth, and manhood; on (whenever possible) his simple, rural background; on his devotion to wife and children. He has been portrayed as a peerless leader, pure and unsullied, endowed with uncommon virtues, and, above all, as a disinterested statesman. Each phase of his career is embellished as a portent of future greatness, of preparation for the role to which destiny has assigned him.

If the candidate's background was largely political, the campaign biographer has often glossed over this fact, since from about 1840 on Americans have tended to mistrust the professional politician. (Politics is dirty business.) Before that time, campaign biographers of Adams, Jackson, Clay, and Van Buren used the word "politician" in a complimentary sense when describing their subject; later, the candidate was never referred to as "a mere politician" or "an active politician." James Buchanan was a student of the science of political economy; Rutherford B. Hayes was said to have mastered the study of politics, "which is but another name for contemporary history;" Cleveland, the reader was told, "knows little of the machinery of conducting close campaigns."

The ideal candidate, it seemed, was an amateur in politics whose activities were far removed from the sordid world of the professional politician. While allegiance to the party was expected of him, he was also expected to place loyalty to his principles above party whenever the two conflicted. Over the years, this theme has been woven into a system of major and minor premises which run like this: The candidate did not seek the office; it sought him. Accordingly, he owes no debt to party leaders or organizations; his only obligation is to the people. He will make his appointments and construct his policies as a free agent, guided only by what is best for the nation. Moreover, his stainless character makes him highly principled in his approach to men and policies. Thus William Jennings Bryan's adherence to principle "made his own party friends and managers shudder" at the way he was risking his political future.

In recent years, politics has been partially restored to the respectable status it once occupied. A presidential candidate is now considered to be more qualified if he is a seasoned politician, but the myth to some extent still lingers on.

An election campaign brings to the fore the discontents and grievances, the hopes and desires, of the electorate. It may precipitate a historic decision, as in the election of 1860, or mobilize sentiment for a new and bold program of economic rehabilitation, as in 1932, or induce a substantial shift in popular allegiance from one party to the other. Most presidential elections, however, do not engender any change in the established political pattern. Voting behavior is determined mainly by party loyalty. Only an extraordinary situation or a charismatic candidate can influence a sufficient number of voters to abandon their party and thereby make the minority party victorious. After such a temporary reversal, however, the former pattern is generally re-established. Woodrow Wilson's triumph in 1912 and 1916 represented this kind of transient deviation, for the Republicans remained the majority party. They were dislodged from the White House only because of a party split on the first occasion and because of the war situation on the second. Similarly, General Dwight D. Eisenhower's victories in 1952 and 1956 left party allegiance basically unaltered. His popularity, the confidence he inspired, the Korean War stalemate, and "cold war" frustrations combined to produce a margin of victory far beyond that achieved by his party in Congress.

One-party ascendency generally persists for long periods. A coalition of midwestern farmers, eastern industrial elements, and the middle class was responsible for Republican domination for more than three decades since the 1890's. Following the crash of 1929, a new coalition with its power bases in the South, the city machines, and the trade unions shifted the balance to the Democrats. The continued increase in urban population, coupled with the continuing decline of the farm vote, has made it difficult for the Republicans to recapture their lost position. If the past is any guide, some combination of circumstances, including the inevitable changes in political demography, as, for example, the movement of population to the suburbs, will again produce new party realignments.

The strategy for a presidential campaign is shaped by the structure and politics of the electoral college. Under the so-called unit rule, the man who receives a majority within a state is awarded all the electoral votes. For example, two million votes cast for John W. Davis in 1924 gave him 136 electoral votes, but six million from states where he failed to achieve a popular majority yielded him none. In 1960, Nixon received 3,732,312 popular votes in Illinois and New Jersey but—since he lacked a majority in either state—not a single electoral vote, all of which went to Kennedy, who carried the states by the minuscule amounts of 9,000 and 22,000, respectively.

To win the election a candidate must capture those states

which have a substantial number of electoral votes. The
man who receives a plurality in only twelve key states will
be victorious regardless of the number of popular votes his
opponent may amass in the other thirty-eight. Candidates
will therefore concentrate on the large and doubtful states,
saturating them with campaign dollars and campaign oratory, while those like Nevada and South Dakota are relatively ignored. The Kennedy organization, for instance, expended virtually all its efforts on the large industrial states.

Recommendations are constantly being made to correct
flaws and inequities in the electoral college system. Among
the major proposals are abolition of electors, determination
by popular vote only, election by districts rather than by
general ticket within each state, and sharing electoral votes
in each state between candidates in proportion to their
popular vote. The last proposal, embodied in the Lodge-
Gosset plan, if carried out, probably could have the effect
of strengthening minority parties in one-party states, encouraging campaigning in all states rather than in just the
pivotal ones, reducing the strategic leverage of organized
minorities in states with metropolitan areas, and ending the
abuse of "winner take all." As one authority says, "If the
President is to be the man of the people, if all the people
are to stand on the same footing, equal masses of people
must be given equal votes, equal bargaining power. Their
weight in the electoral college must be proportional to their
numbers."

Objections to reform come from a variety of interests,
each with its own stake in the maintenance of the status
quo. But unless changes are made—and there is little likeli-
hood of this—the presidential candidate will be compelled
to take electoral realities into account and direct the thrust
of his campaign accordingly.

There is one salutary aspect. To be victorious in the
urbanized, industrialized states with their large blocs of
electoral votes, the candidate must address himself to such
major concerns as civil and human rights, the effects of
automation, education, housing, transportation, and nu-

committee chairmen, the President has become the *de facto* legislative leader. Not only are major measures initiated in the White House and the agenda for legislative action formulated there but the President assumes responsibility for every stage in the progress of a bill until its final enactment. In seeking to obtain his objective he uses various devices—placating, cajoling, or coercing congressmen—always aware that the nation looks to him for leadership in shaping public policies.

As an elected official chosen by all the people, the President must be concerned with problems of national scope. Whereas the power of Congress is decentralized and diffused, the White House represents unity of command and singleness of purpose. Thus if the President fails to provide legislative direction, the Congress finds itself rudderless. Andrew Jackson and Grover Cleveland won reputations for courage because of the congressional measures they vetoed; today the Chief Executive is rated on his success in pushing his program through Congress.

Another striking illustration of the growth of the office is the contemporary role of the President as world leader. Under authorization of the Constitution the President has always been the nation's chief foreign policy maker and a chief diplomat. In the past he exercised these functions to keep the United States as much as possible out of foreign entanglements since the nation's objective was to concentrate on internal development and continental expansion.

By the end of the nineteenth century, however, American industrial eminence and power status cracked the cocoon of isolationism. Inevitably, the office of the President was affected. Theodore Roosevelt also foreshadowed the Chief Executive's new dimension as world leader. Aware of the country's stake in the preservation of the European and Asian balance of power, he never hesitated to use his influence in an effort to maintain or restore the equilibrium. Woodrow Wilson took the nation to the center of the world stage by his war leadership and his participation at the Peace Conference. Although he was unable to effect United

States' entry into the League of Nations, the country's withdrawal from international affairs was temporary. Under Franklin D. Roosevelt, the American Presidency assumed unprecedented responsibilities of world leadership, which it never again abdicated.

The modern President's constituency is global. He speaks not only for his own nation but addresses himself to a coalition of nations bound by a series of mutual assistance pacts, to the nonaligned countries, and to the United Nations. He must continually reconcile conflicting and competing interests with the security requirements of his own country. To assist him in formulating and implementing policies affecting America's position throughout the world is a huge network of advisors, agencies, departments, and bureaus—the Department of State and its Secretary, the National Security Council, the Central Intelligence Agency, the Department of Defense, and the White House staff, to name the outstanding ones. The final decision on any crucial matter and the sole responsibility for it, however, belongs, as it always has, solely to the President.

In this era, when one crisis treads upon the heels of another, the President is not only more burdened than ever before but must proceed with greater caution. He alone has the awesome responsibility of determining the use of nuclear weapons and must pilot carefully amid the potential hazards of miscalculation, irrational actions, or escalation of a "limited" conflict.

Over the years, the extraordinary flexibility of the Presidency has been clearly demonstrated. It has grown with the growing needs of the nation. Presidents who have acted boldly and imaginatively have enlarged and strengthened it. Such institutional forces as political parties have shaped it. Historical circumstances have molded it. In short, so extensive has been the development of the office of the President, and so steadily has its formal and informal power been aggrandized, that it would be almost unrecognizable to the men who created it.

2. The Philosopher-Statesman
as Politician

SHORTLY after the founding of the Republic, two groups with conflicting economic philosophies, political creeds, and social doctrines, one led by Alexander Hamilton, the other by Thomas Jefferson, clashed over the direction the new nation should take. This conflict led not to a trial by arms but to debate on the public platform and in the press, initiating what was to become a fixed American tradition—the peaceful transition of power.

Both Hamilton, Secretary of the Treasury, and Jefferson, Secretary of State in the Washington administration, approved of the basic governmental structure that had been adopted. Each, however, had a different vision of the nation's future which reflected his own character and philosophy. Hamilton, slim, elegant, with his finely chiseled features and commanding presence, though of plebian origin was the epitome of the aristocrat. With a snobbish mistrust of the people, he based his political creed on the British model of a ruling aristocracy of birth and wealth. The tall, slender Jefferson, with a face of "sunny aspect," connected with one of the "first families of Virginia" and one of the most brilliantly versatile men of all time, was an egalitarian. He believed that the people, if properly educated, could be trusted to rule themselves. Democracy, he felt, would thrive in a nation of independent yeoman farmers, whereas it would be trammeled in an industrialized society with its densely packed cities and propertyless workers. In Hamilton's hierarchy of values, property rights held the highest place; in Jefferson's, human rights.

To lay the foundations for economic stability and growth, Hamilton concluded that a partnership between government and the financial community was essential. Toward that end he proposed a legislative program which included creation of a Bank of the United States, funding the national debt at par by issuing new bonds, assumption of the states' debts, and excise taxes and customs duties to protect infant industries from foreign competition. Both Jefferson and James Madison, then a member of Congress, opposed these measures as discriminating in favor of the wealthy and the large bondholders of New England. They were also concerned that this legislation would lead to an excessively powerful central government.

The growing disunion over domestic policies became inflamed by developments abroad—the direction the French Revolution had taken and France's declaration of war against England. Conservatives were horrified by the violence of the Terror and fearful that trade with Britain, so vital to commercial New England, would be jeopardized. To liberals, an old friend was fighting an old enemy, with the issue the liberty of all humanity. Neither Jefferson nor Hamilton wanted war, however, and both supported Washington's proclamation of neutrality, though the former did so with reluctance.

As early as May 1793, Jefferson commented on the emerging political alignments:

> The line is now drawn so clearly as to show on one side: 1. The fashionable circles of Philadelphia, New York, Boston, and Charleston; natural aristocrats. 2. Merchants trading on British capital. 3. Paper [money] men. All the old Tories are found in some one of these three descriptions. On the other side are: 1. Merchants trading on their own capital. 2. Irish merchants. 3. Tradesmen, mechanics, farmers, and every other possible description of our citizens.

Though his aim and that of his followers was to oppose and block the Federalist measures of which they disapproved, Jefferson as yet had no thought of party in the formal sense.

Many citizens were disturbed at the growing factionalism. "The situation of the public good in the hands of two parties nearly poised as to numbers, must be extremely perilous," observed a Virginian. In the opinion of a New Yorker, "Party is a monster who devours the common good, whose destructive jaws are dangerous to the felicity of nations." From press and pulpit came warnings of the baneful effects of party division on the nation's welfare. When he left office, Washington declared that the party spirit has "its roots in the strongest passions of the human mind. . . . It serves always to distract the public councils and enfeeble the public administration." Furthermore, it set one segment of society against another.

To all of which Hamilton, who feared a coordinated and cohesive opposition, agreed. While the undisputed leader of the Federalists, he was not consciously organizing a party. His purpose was to set the nation on what he considered the right path and prevent those opposed to his ideas from thwarting him. But in the process, acting with the driving urgency of his intense nature, he succeeded in creating the first modern political party in the western world. Action produced reaction as opposition to Federalist domestic and foreign policies, expressed in private correspondence, in widely distributed pamphlets, and in the press haltingly but steadily solidified the Republican movement into a party. Congressional leaders and those on state, county, and town levels coordinated their activities. Candidates were now nominated for public office on the basis of their stand on national issues.

Jefferson was completely at odds with the administration. Serene, philosophical, abhorring combat, he resigned his office in December 1793. Retirement at his beloved Monticello was not, however, to last long. With party lines already clearly drawn by 1796, he was, as the natural leader of the Republicans, their unanimous choice for President. Aaron Burr was selected for the second office.

The Federalists, however, had a problem. Hamilton, who had resigned in 1795, should have been the logical choice, but they were afraid that his outspoken views and his controversial record would cost the party votes. Some of the other leaders were ruled out for one reason or another. John Adams and Thomas Pinckney were finally settled on, although numerous Federalists, including Hamilton, detested the former, and New Englanders were decidedly cool to the latter. The absence of united support behind the candidates was to have a strange outcome in the election. Republican lines held firm, but Federalists scattered their votes, with the result that Adams received 71, Jefferson 68, Pinckney 59, and Burr 30. The nation had a President of one party and a Vice-President of the other!*

From the beginning, the Adams administration was torn by problems of world politics. French interference with American shipping led to a virtual if undeclared war. The Directoire refused to accredit the new American minister, Charles C. Pinckney. Some months later, passions were further aroused by relevations of the XYZ affair, a brazen demand for a bribe by the French as a condition for settling differences between the two nations. The "hawks" among the Federalists, who had been clamoring for a declaration of war against France, became even more vociferous. They defied Adams, when he refused to recommend enlargement of the army, by voting for a build-up in the military forces. When he continued to resist their demands for a declaration of war, they were beside themselves with rage. Some accused him of having sold out to the Republicans. One Federalist was so infuriated that he "prayed to God" the President's horses would run away with him and "break his neck."

The Republicans, who were firmly opposed to military involvement, especially as it would align the nation with the British, were accused of favoring a foreign country over their own and even suspected of conspiracy to overthrow

---

* To avoid a repetition of this untenable situation, the Twelfth Amendment to the Constitution was adopted in 1804. It provided that separate ballots be cast for the two offices.

the government. In the capital, party animosity ran high. Jefferson commented in June 1798 that he saw "men who have been intimate all their lives, cross the street to avoid meeting, and turn their heads another way, lest they should be obliged to touch their hats." The congressional elections that year were conducted in an atmosphere of intense partisan rancor. A Maryland observer noted that wherever he went the election "seemed to take up the entire thoughts of the People, and party spirit rages every where with great violence . . . parties are beyond anything ever before known." Voting results showed a widespread and unmistakable cleavage.

Almost as soon as Jefferson arrived in Philadelphia, he had plunged into politics, assuming the leadership of his party. His opposition to administration policies was intensified with the passage of the alien and sedition laws by a Congress clearly controlled by the Federalists. He considered the legislation "so palpably in the teeth of the Constitution as to shew they mean to pay no respect to it," and the object of the anti-sedition measure to be "the suppression of the whig presses." Jefferson's response, the Kentucky and Virginia Resolutions that he and Madison drafted, initiated in effect his campaign for the Presidency.

In anticipation of the 1800 elections, Jefferson increased his political activities, carrying on a voluminous correspondence. Regarding the contest between the two parties as a battle of principles, he used every opportunity to expound his own philosophy. Early in 1799, he recorded his views on public policy. The Constitution, he said, must remain inviolable "according to the true sense in which it was adopted by the States," and he believed in "preserving to the States the powers not yielded by them to the Union." The government should be "rigorously frugal and simple, applying all the possible savings of the public revenue to the discharge of the national debt." He opposed a standing army in peacetime and instead advocated reliance on the militia for internal defense. "I am for free commerce with all nations; political connection with none," to keep the country out of European quarrels. He stood for freedom of religion and against any effort to make one sect ascendant over another, for freedom of the press, "and against all violations of the Constitution to silence by force and not by reason the complaints or criticisms, just or unjust, of our citizens against the conduct of their agents." These declarations were echoed repeatedly by his followers throughout the campaign.

Too experienced in politics to rely on mere affirmation of principles to win an election, Jefferson employed the methods of the practical politician working within a party. He personally wrote or directed the writing of innumerable tracts and acted as a private clearing house for their distribution. The number of pamphlets which he alone circulated throughout the country ran into the hundreds. In view of his position, he could not write letters to the press but urged his friends "to set apart a certain portion of every post day to write what may be proper for the public."

Exceedingly discreet in his public statements, Jefferson warned his correspondents not to permit anything he wrote to leak out: "A single sentence got hold of by the Porcupines [Federalist pamphleteers] will suffice to abuse and persecute me in their papers for months." Generally he avoided reference to political subjects even during the peak of the campaign, unless transmittal of the letter was made by private courier. He would "trust the post offices with nothing confidential, persuaded . . . they will lend their inquisitorial aid to furnish matter for newspapers."

The establishment of formal party organizations throughout the country was pushed, especially by the Republicans. A considerable degree of coordination, through a network of corresponding committees, already existed in New York and Pennsylvania. The party controlled the nomination of candidates there and endeavored to get them elected. In most other states party organization was thin. Republicans concentrated especially on Virginia, where Federalist organizational strength was growing, and New Jersey, where it was already effective.

On January 21, 1800, "a meeting of ninety-three members

of the Legislature and a number of other respectable persons" was held at the Capitol in Richmond "for the purpose of selecting in the different districts of this State proper persons to be supported by the Republican Interest as Electors of a President and Vice President of the United States." A "Republican Ticket" of electors was agreed upon, and a committee appointed to prepare a plan for conducting the campaign. Later, in accordance with the recommendations of this group, a "General Standing Committee" of five members was established at Richmond to head the campaign and act as a central committee of correspondence. Committees organized in eighty-nine counties included nearly every prominent Republican in the state. They were to receive communications from the general committee and in turn supply it with any information which would "promote the Republican Ticket." This extensive organization was "to communicate useful information to the people relative to the election; and to repel every effort which may be made to injure the ticket in general or to remove any prejudice which may be attempted to be raised against any person on the ticket."

In New Jersey, committees of three appointed in each township and county were to act in concert to nominate candidates for the state legislature and for Congress. Occasionally the Republicans captured control of the annual town meetings and appointed committees there; for the most part, however, the committees were selected by party meetings often held at an inn or tavern. The county committees generally assumed responsibility for directing the campaign in their counties, publishing political addresses, circulating handbills and pamphlets, and sponsoring party meetings. This plan of party organization was, for the most part, followed in other states and was also used by the Federalists.

Both parties, regarding the press as an important instrument for influencing the electorate, made strenuous efforts to establish new papers to support their cause. In the past, it had been customary for editors to profess nonpartisan-

ship, but many of the papers which began publication at
this time frankly proclaimed their attachment to one or the
other party. After the elections, the Federalist Fisher Ames
was to conclude that "the newspapers are an overmatch for
any Government . . . the Jacobins owe their triumph to the
unceasing use of this engine; not so much to skill in use of it
as by repetitions."

In a letter to Madison, Jefferson assessed the prospects of
victory. His figures showed that he would carry most of the
South while the Federalists, as in 1796, would carry New
England. He would need 2 more votes than he had received
that year for the necessary majority of 70. Pennsylvania,
New Jersey, and New York would be significant in determining the outcome. He could not count on Pennsylvania's
14 votes, as the state might not cast any vote at all (the
sharp political cleavage between the upper and lower
houses of its legislature had prevented enactment of a bill
to provide for the selection of presidential electors). New
Jersey looked more promising. Although a former supporter
of Adams, it now appeared to be deserting the Federalists.
"The Republican members here from New Jersey are entirely confident that their two houses joined together have a
majority of Republicans."

The key state in his opinion was New York. All 12 of its
electoral votes had gone to Adams, and Federalists still
dominated the legislature, but a new legislature was to be
elected in April. The Federalists were expecting to retain a
slight edge upstate; all depended, therefore, on the Republican showing in New York City. "If the city election of New
York is in favor of the Republican ticket, the issue will be
Republican; if the Federal ticket for the city of New York
prevails, the probabilities will be in favor of a Federal issue,
because it would then require a Republican vote from both
New Jersey and Pennsylvania to preponderate against New
York, on which we could not count with any confidence."

And victory in New York depended on Aaron Burr, the
smooth, scheming politician who had few peers in the arts
of intrigue and manipulation. A former United States sena-

tor and onetime state assemblyman, he had tumbled to the bottom of the political ladder. Now he intended to leap to the top via the vice-presidency, but only a victory in the strategically important city elections in April could assure him a place on the national ticket. A visit to Philadelphia won him Jefferson's reluctant support. Publicly, Jefferson maintained a statesmanlike aloofness from the political maelstrom, conveying the impression that he had consented to be a candidate only to "see this government brought back to its Republican principles." Realistically, he knew that he must depend on the politicians in the states, and, while he felt uneasy about his association with Burr, the crafty little New Yorker was probably the only man who could assure his victory.

Jefferson had made no mistake in judging Burr's talents. Audaciously, Burr plunged into the tangled factional Republican politics of New York, assumed the leadership of the party, and came out with a strong, solid slate of candidates in which all rival factions were represented. Hamilton, feverishly working to save the state for the Federalists, was able to turn up only a nondescript list of candidates which included a shoemaker, a bookseller, two grocers, three lawyers, and a bankrupt. He also had to fight a consummate politician who card-indexed every voter in the city, noting such items as his past political interests, his current interest, his general habits. To arouse apathetic citizens and get them to the polls, Burr indefatigably organized precinct and ward meetings, arranged for speakers, and frequently spoke himself. Equally important, he was able to attract devoted aides.

During the three days of the balloting from April 29 through May 1, Hamilton rode on a white horse from one polling place to the next, trumpeting the Federalist ticket. Burr was more than a match for him in energy and zeal. One of his aides reported to Congressman Albert Gallatin, a member of the party's high command, that Burr "has remained at the polls of the Seventh ward ten hours without intermission. Pardon this hasty scrawl. I have not ate for fifteen hours."

When the votes were counted, the entire Republican slate had been elected. Burr's supporters immediately began to boost him for the vice-presidency among party leaders in Philadelphia. Early in May, Gallatin wrote to his wife, "We had last night a very large meeting of Republicans in which it was unanimously agreed to support Burr for Vice-President." While party members in Virginia and North Carolina who had refused to endorse Burr in 1796 still had reservations about him, they were finally reconciled.

Aware that the New York election virtually doomed Federalist prospects for the Presidency, Hamilton endeavored to nullify its results by a desperate effort to have the electoral procedures in the state changed in order to prevent an "atheist in religion and a fanatic in politics, from getting possession of the helm of state." He wrote to Governor John Jay requesting that he call a special session of the legislature to provide for direct popular vote by districts in selecting the presidential electors instead of by the legislative body. This, he felt, would give the Federalists at least a few electors from the safe districts. "In times like these in which we live, it will not do to be overscrupulous . . . ," Hamilton wrote candidly. "It is easy to sacrifice the substantial interests of society by a strict adherence to ordinary rule." The governor did not reply. He had concluded that it would not "become him to propose a measure which would serve purely party purposes."

A group of dejected Federalist congressmen caucused at Philadelphia on May 3 to try to find some means of winning the election while at the same time "dumping" the hated Adams. Hamilton's loathing of the President had become so great that he wrote to a Federalist leader in Massachusetts, "I will never more be responsible for him by my direct support even though the consequence should be the election of Jefferson. If we must have an enemy at the head of the government let it be one whom we can oppose and for whom we are not responsible, who will not involve our party in the disgrace of his foolish and bad measures." Despairingly he concluded, "Under *Adams*, as under *Jefferson*, the government will sink. The party in the hands of whose chief it shall sink, will sink with it, and the advantage will be on the side of his adversaries."

But how could the Federalist leaders repudiate their own incumbent President without at the same time implying a vote of no confidence in the policies of the administration? They finally decided to repeat the maneuver which they had attempted in 1796 to keep Adams from the Presidency but which had failed only because some New England electors had defected. It was arranged to distribute the electors' ballots in such a way as to give the majority of the Federalist votes to Charles Pinckney of South Carolina rather than to Adams.

To influence those still reluctant to abandon the President, Hamilton circulated in pamphlet form a vitriolic attack on his private and public life. Invective was heaped upon venom on every page. Adams, he wrote, did not "possess the talents adapted to the *administration* of government," and "great and intrinsic defects in his character unfit him for the office of chief magistrate." Vain and jealous, he was incapable of judging issues impartially and on their intrinsic merit. Moreover, he had "an imagination sublimated and eccentric . . . neither to the regular display of sound judgment nor to steady perseverence in a systematic plan of conduct."

To the glee of the Republicans, Aaron Burr managed to obtain a copy of the pamphlet and had it printed and widely circulated. Many Federalists rose to the defense of the maligned Adams, but the damage was done. Hamilton, whom a majority of the party regarded as their spokesman, had disavowed the President. Inevitably, the division among the leading Federalists, displayed in so spectacular a manner, infected the rank and file.

Justifiably incensed, Adams countered with an equally savage attack on his assailant. "His exuberant vanity and

insatiable egotism," he wrote, "prompt him to be ever rest-
less and busy meddling with things far above his capacity,
and inflame him with an absolute rage to arrogate to himself the honor of suggesting every measure of government.
He is no more fit for a prompter than Phaeton to drive the
chariot of the sun. If his projects had been followed they
would absolutely have burnt up the world."

Intra-party feuding continued throughout the campaign.
Even men so highly placed in the administration as the
Secretaries of War and State were more loyal to Hamilton
than to the Chief Executive and carried on intrigues against
Adams until he was finally compelled to dismiss them. The
Secretary of the Treasury bombarded party members with
letters urging them to oppose Adams. "However dangerous
the election of Mr. Jefferson may prove to the community, I
do not perceive that any portion of the mischief would be
avoided by the election of Mr. Adams," he wrote. "We
know the temper of his mind to be revolutionary, violent,
and vindictive; he would be sensible that another official
term would bring him to the close of life. His passions and
selfishness would continually gain strength; his pride and
interest would concur in rendering his administration favorable to the views of democrats and Jacobins." The President, he charged, had unnecessarily antagonized the
British, had shown a lack of awareness about the financial
requirements of the country, and had displayed little sympathy for its commercial interests.

Calumniated by members of his own party, Adams also
received no mercy from the opposition. One widely circulated rumor was that Adams had planned a marriage between one of his sons and the daughter of the British
monarch, George III, so that he could found an American
dynasty that would reunite the country with Great Britain.
Only the efforts of George Washington, according to the
fanciful story, had saved the nation. When the Father of his
Country learned of the diabolical scheme, he purportedly
went to Adams and pleaded with him to abandon the plan,
but to no avail. Washington went a second time to renew

his plea, but again met with defiance. Not until Washington in desperation went a third time attired in his war uniform and threatened to slay Adams with his sword if he did not renounce the project did he abandon his cherished ambition to be king.

Another fabrication was so preposterous that it amused even the puritanical Adams. The story went that Adams had dispatched General Pinckney to England to procure four attractive damsels as mistresses—two for the General and two for the President! "I do declare upon my honor," Adams wrote with wry humor, "if this be true General Pinckney has kept them all for himself and cheated me out of my two."

The Federalists were equally intemperate in their attacks on Jefferson. Hamilton had provided a weapon by characterizing Jefferson as "that atheist"; now the candidate's comments in his *Notes on Virginia* and his views on the French Revolution were distorted and used against him.

The charge of atheism and all that it represented to the religious mind of the age was employed in a variety of ways. New England clergymen appealed from the pulpit to the fears and prejudices of the citizenry. Many divines took to pamphleteering. In "The Voice of Warning, to Christians on the ensuing Election of a President of the United States," one clergyman pleaded, "Christians . . . as you value eternity, vote against this infidel! By voting *for* him, you will do more to destroy a regard for the gospel of Jesus, than the whole fraternity of infidels with all their arts, their industry and their intrigues." Others assailed him for doubting that the Bible was divinely inspired, or for questioning the historical accuracy of the deluge story, or for opposing Bible instruction in the public schools. One Massachusetts newspaper warned its readers, "Should the infidel Jefferson be elected to the Presidency, the *seal of death* is that moment set on our holy religion, our churches will be prostrated, and some infamous prostitute, under the title of the Goddess of Reason, will preside in the Sanctuaries now devoted to the worship of the Most High."

If he was not attacked as an atheist, he was denounced as a deist, an equally serious opprobrium since it implied rejection of revealed religion. The Federalist-sponsored newspaper, *Gazette of the United States,* kept hammering away at the religious issue, reprinting day after day, "The Grand Question stated. At the present solemn and momentous epoch, the only question to be asked by every American, laying his hand on his heart, is 'shall I continue in allegiance to GOD AND A RELIGIOUS PRESIDENT; or impiously declare for JEFFERSON—AND NO GOD!!!' "

A formal party platform had not yet come into use—the term itself was still unknown—but voters were presented with a definite and compact statement of principles by the Republicans. In the preface to a pamphlet containing a number of his speeches, Charles Pinckney's statement was very much like Jefferson's declarations. The Republican interest, Pinckney wrote, desired "Never to have such acts as the alien and sedition laws . . . or too intimate a connexion with any foreign power," reduction of public expense, no direct tax "on the landed and agricultural interests only." Similar statements were made by Republican leaders throughout the country. This "platform" was printed on election day by the Philadelphia *Aurora* in parallel form, contrasting Republican promises with their opponent's record.

State and local committees of both parties compiled numerous statements in the form of resolutions or polemical disquisitions. Leaflets and broadsides were distributed under private and often anonymous auspices, either praising extravagantly or castigating intemperately. One pro-Federalist broadside declared, "Can serious and reflecting men look about them and doubt that if Jefferson is elected, and the Jacobins get to authority, that these morals which protect our lives from the knife of the assassin—which guard the chastity of our wives and daughters from seduction and violence—defend our property from plunder and devastation, and shield our religion from contempt and profanation, will not be trampled upon and exploded."

The official party literature was less lurid. Federalists emphasized the sound foundations laid by George Washington and continued by his successor, which they claimed were responsible for the nation's prosperity. Not only had the government prevented war with the two most powerful countries in Europe, but it had kept the peace without sacrificing either the national interest or the national honor. This plausible and rational argument was advanced in the hope that the status quo would be endorsed, but, foreshadowing a pattern in American politics, the appeal competed unsuccessfully with a more potent one, that it was time for a change.

A widely circulated Republican pamphlet succinctly outlined the need for a new administration. Republicans, it stated, regarded as urgent the repeal of the repressive Alien and Sedition Acts. The Anglophile orientation which tied the nation too closely to one foreign power was highly dangerous. They favored just and impartial relations with all powers so that peace could be maintained. The size of the standing army should be reduced and the revenue thus saved applied toward discharging the public debt. Abolition of direct taxation on land and agriculture would end discrimination against the farmer.

Electioneering by members of both parties was carried on strenuously. Impromptu meetings were held wherever people could be found to furnish an audience—at a horse race, a cock fight, a Methodist quarterly gathering. Candidates for the state legislature, for Congress, or for the electoral college would "mount the rostrum, made out of an empty barrel or hog's head" and harangue the assemblage. Opposing candidates often used the same platform to address the same audiences, offering a choice "then and there."

In the battle of the printed and spoken word, Republicans possessed a distinct advantage. They were supported by more newspapers, issued more pamphlets, and had more enthusiastic campaign workers. The issues they raised were also more effective. Adams felt, however, that the Federalists would be defeated not so much because of the issues or the Republicans' enthusiasm but because of the split in Federalist ranks and, more particularly, the underhanded activities of the Hamiltonian faction. "They must take the consequence," he wrote to a friend. "They will attempt to throw the blame upon me, but they will not succeed. They have recorded their own intemperance and indiscretion in characters too legible and too public. For myself," he concluded bitterly, "age, infirmities, family misfortunes have conspired with the unreasonable conduct of Jacobins and insolent Federalists to make me too indifferent to whatever can happen."

On December 4, the members of the electoral college met in their respective states. Four days later the returns from Pennsylvania, Maryland, and New Jersey were received in the capital. The tally was 19 for Adams and Pinckney, 3 for Jefferson and Burr. Delaware and Connecticut next added 12 to the Federalist side and New York 12 to the Republican. The next fortnight was a period of anxious waiting for both parties as the results dribbled in by letter and messenger.

South Carolina decided the issue. A Federalist victory there which had seemed a certainty was thwarted by the astute organizational activities of Charles Pinckney. In a stunning upset, eight Republican electors were chosen, pledged to Jefferson and Burr. Without these votes, the Republicans could not have won the Presidency. Federalist candidates had carried all of New England, New Jersey, and Delaware; Republicans won in Virginia, South Carolina, Kentucky, Tennessee, Georgia, and New York. In North Carolina and Pennsylvania the vote was split, with Republicans having the edge; and in Maryland, the vote was divided equally between the two parties.

The election of 1800 revealed the striking progress that had been made in achieving party organization and unity. In the previous election, votes were scattered among thirteen candidates; in this one, all but one elector from Rhode Island voted for either Jefferson and Burr or Adams and

Pinckney. This solid and unexpected party regularity was to create a major problem for the Republicans, for the final tally showed Jefferson and Burr tied with 73 votes each.

Jefferson assumed that arrangements had been made to avert such a contingency. As he had written to Thomas M. Randolph, "It was intended that one vote should be thrown away [in South Carolina] from Col. Burr. It is believed Georgia will withhold from him one or two. The votes will stand probably T.J. 73, Burr about 70, Mr. Adams 65." But something unaccountably went wrong in South Carolina. The vote which was to have been given to George Clinton went to Burr, and, with the party line holding in all the other states, the two Republican candidates tied.

President Adams, who received news of the Republican tie victory with anger and incredulity, was filled with foreboding for the future. "In the case of Mr. Jefferson there is nothing wonderful; but Mr. Burr's good fortune surpasses all ordinary rules and exceeds that of Bonaparte," he wrote to Elbridge Gerry. "All the old patriots, all the splendid talents, the long experience both of Federalists and Anti-Federalists must be subjected to the humiliation of seeing this dexterous gentleman rise like a balloon filled with inflammable air over their heads. . . . What course is it we steer, and to what harbor are we bound?"

Resolution of the issue now rested with the House of Representatives, not the newly elected House, which had a Republican majority, but the lame-duck legislature that the Federalists still controlled. The Constitution required balloting by state, with each voting as a unit. Although the Federalists, with their base in populous New England, had a majority of the entire House, Republicans dominated eight state delegations, the Federalists six, and two were equally divided. Nine states were required for victory, which made possible a deadlock that would leave the nation without a Chief Executive on Inaugural Day.

Opportunity for intrigue by the Federalists was ready made. "The Feds in the legislature have expressed disposition to make all they can of the embarrassment," wrote

Jefferson, "so that after the most energetic effort crowned with success we remain in the hands of our enemies by want of foresight in the original arrangements."*

Unlike Adams, most Federalist congressmen preferred Burr to Jefferson as the lesser of two evils but lacked sufficient numbers to have him elected. They hoped either to persuade enough Republicans to switch from Jefferson, or to create a deadlock that would compel Congress to select a temporary executive, or, alternatively, to have their majority in the Senate elect a President pro tempore until a new election. Their attitude made it plain that this first attempt to effect a peaceful transition of power from one party to another would face a critical challenge.

Washington, the new capital city where the Congress would meet to make its fateful decision, was less a city than a straggling village. The streets were narrow and unpaved, more like primitive dirt trails. Scattered clapboard dwellings surrounded the unfinished Capitol building. Two boardinghouses to accommodate congressmen stood on opposite sides; Republicans lived in one, Federalists in the other. The Speaker of the House enjoyed the luxury of a private room, but his colleagues slept in pairs. Gouverneur Morris, senator from New York and onetime minister to France, where he had become accustomed to sophisticated Parisian society, commented acidly on his new environment, "Building stone is plentiful. Excellent bricks are baked here; we are not wanting in sites for magnificent mansions. We only need here houses, cellars, kitchens, scholarly men, amiable women, and a few other trifles, to possess a perfect city. In a word, this is the best city in the world to live in—in the future."

The roads to the capital were equally crude. It took five days to travel from New York to Washington, with the carriages careening through pitch-black nights across gutted roads and crossing rivers on shaky bridges. One congressman, it was reported, was so fearful of being killed in a road

---

* Jefferson was referring to the constitutional flaw, later corrected, which made such a situation possible.

accident on the hazardous journey that he always carried his "death clothes" in his baggage so that he might be properly attired for his funeral. Bad as the roads were normally, rain or snow made them almost impassable, and the weather delayed the opening of the second session of the Sixth Congress from November 17 to 22, when a quorum was finally obtained.

Republican leaders met to discuss strategy. If the Federalists contrived a stalemate and then tried to enact a measure which would hand the Presidency over to a member of their party, perhaps Adams could be prevailed upon to perform one final service for his country by vetoing it, since "Mr. A. can gain nothing by it." Jefferson called on the President to persuade him that such a measure "would probably produce resistance by force" and even possible civil war. Adams was not convinced. Later he told Elbridge Gerry, "I know of no more danger of a political convulsion if a President pro tempore or a Secretary of State, or Speaker of the House, should be made President by Congress, than if Mr. Jefferson or Mr. Burr is declared such. The President would be as legal in one case as either of the others, in my opinion, and the people as well satisfied."

With this hope gone, the Republicans marshalled their forces in anticipation of a Federalist "seizure" of executive authority. Gallatin declared that "under no possible circumstances" should they consent to a new election. Governors McKean of Pennsylvania and Monroe of Virginia were notified to have militia ready to march on Washington "for the purpose, not of promoting, but of preventing revolution and the shedding of a single drop of blood." Gallatin advised the Republican states to refuse to obey a "usurper President" and to ignore any call for militia to support him. Jefferson told Governor Monroe, "We thought it best to declare openly and firmly, one & all, that the day such an act passed, the Middle States would arm, & that no such usurpation, even for a single day, should be submitted to."

A chain of express riders raced back and forth between Washington and the capitals of the states where Republicans were threatening to arm. Governor Monroe, advised "to be prepared to meet any emergency," held the Virginia legislature in constant session. "Pennsy. has her courier here & the report is that she has 22 thousand prepared to take up arms in the event of extremities," he was informed. Here and there angry mutterings could be heard that any man appointed President by the Federalists would be assassinated.

Aaron Burr, who could have prevented all the fuss and fury by simply making a public declaration that he did not want the place which was rightfully Jefferson's, remained silent. He realized that a House vote would give him a fair chance. As things stood, Jefferson was sure of eight states and Burr of six with the other two state delegations tied. It should have been easier for Jefferson to pick up one additional state than for Burr to add three, but Jefferson held New York and New Jersey by only one vote in each case. If opposition to him persisted, with deadlock the prospect, enough support might be switched to Burr to give him the two states. Moreover, Maryland, which was evenly divided, was also expected to go to Burr, thus giving him the necessary nine states and the Presidency.

Assessing the relative merits of the two Republicans, George Cabot contended that while Burr was moved by ordinary ambition, Jefferson, though ambitious, was also prompted by his Jacobin philosophy. Burr would be satisfied with power and wealth; Jefferson with nothing less than a fundamental alteration of society. Gouverneur Morris recorded in his diary, "It seems to be the general opinion that Colonel Burr will be chosen President by the House of Representatives. Many of them think it highly dangerous that Mr. Jefferson should, in the present crisis, be placed in that office. They consider him as a theoretic man, who would bring the National Government back to something like the old confederation."

Among the small minority of Federalists opposed to Burr was Alexander Hamilton. His deep mistrust of the New Yorker, based on his contacts with him, turned him into a supporter of his former enemy, Jefferson. If there was any man he ought to hate, Hamilton said, it was Jefferson, while with Burr he had always been on good terms. "But the public good must be paramount to every private considera- tion." Without doubt, he wrote to a leading member of his wing of the party, "upon every virtuous and prudent calcu- lation, Jefferson is to be preferred. He is by far not so dan- gerous a man; and he has pretensions to character. As to *Burr,* there is nothing in his favor. His private character is not defended by his most partial friends."

Passionately concerned about the welfare of his country, Hamilton bombarded the Federalists with letters warning and pleading that they not commit the tragic blunder of handing over the supreme position to Burr. He was, Hamil- ton declared, a conscienceless schemer with "no principle, public or private," and a lust for power that would drag their beloved country into the mire. "No mortal can tell what his political principles are. He has talked all around the compass. If he has any theory, 'tis that of a simple despotism."

But Hamilton had lost control of the leadership of his party since its defeat in the April elections in New York, and his embarrassing pamphlet attacking Adams also caused a number of Federalists to shy away from him. Moreover, some felt that his attitude toward Burr was motivated by personal hostility, which should not influence them.

His entreaties ignored, Hamilton turned in desperation to Federalist Congressman James Bayard of Delaware. Though the sole representative from his state, his vote would carry as much weight as the nine from Virginia. With eight states committed to Jefferson, Bayard's vote could be the decisive one. Bayard detested Jefferson and had no reason to oppose Burr, but he greatly respected Hamilton. A majority of the Federalists were disposed to vote for Burr, he informed Hamilton, and should a caucus be committed to him, he would hesitate to oppose it. How- ever, he concluded on a note that gave Hamilton some hope. "Their determination will not bind me, for though it might cost me a painful struggle to disappoint the views and wishes of many gentlemen with whom I have been accustomed to act, yet the magnitude of the subject forbids the sacrifice of a strong conviction."

When the Federalists caucused, the decision was to hold out for Burr. Even if they could not obtain the two states needed to defeat Jefferson, they felt they could still keep him out of the White House and appoint a President from their own party to serve until the next election. Three states could break the deadlock—Vermont and Maryland, whose delegations were tied, and Delaware. The first two decided to stand together and to accept Bayard as their leader. Thus, the well-kept hands of the thirty-three-year-old aristocrat held the trump card that would make the next President of the United States. And Bayard kept his own counsel, refusing all pressures to reveal for whom he would cast his vote.

Speculation and maneuvering continued. On Wednesday, February 11, 1801, the congressmen plowed their way to the Capitol through a deep blanket of snow which covered Washington for the electoral balloting. Representative Joseph H. Nicholson of Maryland had risen from a sickbed to vote for Jefferson. Burning with fever, he lay in a small room off the House chamber, attended by his wife, who gave him medicine and water. By 3:30 in the afternoon, after eight ballots, the deadlock was unbroken. As dusk fell and it appeared that the members would be there for the rest of the night, blankets and pillows were carried into the chamber. A motion to adjourn after the eighteenth ballot at eleven o'clock was voted down. There was another ballot at midnight, at one o'clock, at two o'clock, and on into the early morning hours with the same unvarying result: Jefferson eight, Burr six, and two states tied. After the twenty-seventh ballot at 8 A.M., the exhausted representatives agreed to adjourn and resume voting at noon. The ballots on Thursday, Friday, and Saturday remained unchanged. Wearily, the electors postponed action until Monday.

By now Bayard was worried. If the election of the Chief Executive remained unresolved, and should the Federalists attempt to install a temporary President, civil war might erupt. His little, sparsely populated state would then be caught in a vise between its powerful neighbors, Virginia and Pennsylvania, whose governors were threatening to send their militias to march on Washington. Delaware's very existence depended on the preservation of constitutional practice. Furthermore, Bayard and some of the other Federalists were becoming disenchanted with Burr, who refused to make any promise to promote the Federalist program as a price for their support. "He was determined not to shackle himself with Federalist principles," Bayard said, "and it became evident that if he go in without being absolutely committed," then Hamilton was right—Burr was another "Catiline." Bayard decided to let Jefferson win, but he would demand a price.

Through an intermediary, Baltimore Congressman Samuel Smith, Jefferson was approached to give assurances on four points, which were the same as those Hamilton had been pressing the Federalists to get from him: continuation of the fiscal system; adherence to a policy of neutrality between England and France; an increase in the size of the naval establishment; and retention of a number of Federalists in office. According to Bayard, Smith informed him the following day that he had been authorized by Jefferson to say that these items corresponded with his own intentions. Yet on that same day Jefferson wrote to Monroe, "Many attempts have been made to obtain terms and promises from me. I have declared unequivocally that I would not receive the government on capitulation, that I would not go into it with my hands tied."

On Monday when the thirty-fourth ballot was taken, the result was still the same. Bayard called the Federalists into caucus and informed the group that he would take no step to break the deadlock pending another effort to obtain a written commitment from Burr. He would wait a reasonable length of time, but since he held the vote of a state, "he could not consent that the 4th of March should arrive without a chief magistrate." Bayard apparently was aware that no such statement could be elicited from Burr, that in fact the wily New Yorker had been trying to ingratiate himself with the Republican leaders by a stream of correspondence to Jefferson, Gallatin, Livingston, and Smith, confident that he would not be deserted by the Federalists who were supporting him.

Although there appeared to be no prospect of electing Burr, the die-hard Federalists were determined to keep right on voting for him until inauguration day if necessary in the hope of wearing down the Republicans or having a Federalist appointed an interim President. The moderates reached the point of preferring a solution that would provide stability even if it meant turning to the hated Jefferson. After a long and stormy discussion, the caucus agreed that Burr could not be elected. At that point Bayard rose to declare his intention to vote for Jefferson. Pandemonium broke loose. "Deserter! Deserter!" rang out, but it was apparent that the long struggle was over.

The following day, with less than a month before inauguration, an exhausted band of men trailed into the House chamber to cast their thirty-sixth ballot. With a majority for Jefferson now inevitable, the Federalists from the two divided states, Vermont and Maryland, agreed to abstain, thus allowing the Republicans to cast the states' votes for Jefferson. Since Jefferson now had one vote more than he needed, Bayard turned in a blank ballot as did the representatives from South Carolina, and the other Federalists felt no compunction to change their votes. The final tally was Jefferson 10, Burr 4, 2 blank.

When the news of Jefferson's election reached Philadelphia, the city went wild with joy. The price of gin and whisky, the *Gazette of the United States* reported, rose "50 per cent since nine o'clock this morning. The bells have been ringing, guns firing, dogs barking, cats mewling, children crying, and Jacobins getting drunk."

As the boom of artillery awoke the inhabitants of Wash-

ington to the momentous event of the presidential inauguration, a solitary carriage some miles from the city was
pressing northward. In it was the defeated President. In the
small hours of the morning, he had crept out of the executive mansion bound for his home in Massachusetts, resolved
never to set foot in Washington again. Humiliated and
deeply embittered at having been rejected by the people he
believed he had served well, Adams could not bear to
watch the triumph of his hated rival.

The inaugural ceremonies were very simple, with none of
the elaborate pageantry of later years. At ten o'clock one
company of riflemen and one company of artillerymen
marched past the boardinghouse where the President-elect
had been living. At noon Jefferson left his quarters attended
by a number of congressmen and with a miscellaneous as-
sortment of people streaming in their wake. He walked the
two blocks to the Capitol and inside the Senate chamber
took the oath of office. Several minutes later he began to
read his address. One part was a superb plea for tolerance
and moderation:

> We are all Republicans, we are all Federalists. If there be
> any among us who would wish to dissolve this Union or to
> change its republican form, let them stand undisturbed as
> monuments to the safety with which error of opinion may be
> tolerated where reason is left free to combat it. . . . And let
> us reflect that, having banished from our land that religious
> intolerance under which mankind so long bled and suffered,
> we have gained little if we countenance a political intoler-
> ance as despotic, as wicked, and capable of as bitter and
> bloody persecution. . . . Every difference of opinion is not a
> difference of principle.

Jefferson's conciliatory message after a campaign marked
by acrimonious debate over passionately held ideological
convictions was to set the pattern for the aftermath of all
presidential contests. Once the sound and the fury sub-
sides, the new President must salve the wounds inflicted by
the verbal assaults. The opposition must be conciliated so

that through compromise the new administration can function effectively.

Interpreting electoral results, Jefferson had suggested that he was not merely the choice of one party, that an analysis of the ballots revealed that "former Federalists have found themselves aggregated with us and that they are in a state of mind to be aggregated with us." Up to a point this was true. The extremist views of the "high Federalists" led by Hamilton alienated many of the moderates, and the repressive Alien and Sedition Laws undoubtedly drew many Federalists into the Jeffersonian camp.

Nevertheless, the administration that came to power had its base of support among elements of the population different from those on which the outgoing one had relied. The Federalists had been defeated partly because of their programs, which favored the mercantile and investing classes. Northern commercial interests prospered from the Treasury Department's policy of high interest on new government loans, while the major tax burden fell on the farmers and planters. Resentment of taxes levied to finance naval and military preparations cost the Federalists many votes, especially in the interior where a rebellion by the farmers of eastern Pennsylvania over a direct tax on land and houses had been put down by troops. In the South, the sharp decline in tobacco prices which resulted when trade with France was cut off caused deep resentment. Another contributing factor, of course, was the internecine feud among the Federalists.

In later years, Jefferson was to call the election of 1800 "as real a revolution in the principles of our government as that of 1776 was in form." The facts, however, do not bear him out. For one thing, despite all the circumstances operating against John Adams, he came strikingly close to victory. A difference of a few hundred votes in the New York elections would have made the legislature of that state Federalist, and its electors would have turned the tide for Adams in the electoral college. Moreover, the election resulted in no fundamental alteration of the social and economic pattern of American life. The Hamiltonian system, in operation for a dozen years, had become an integral part of the economy. To abandon or repeal the existing funding, banking, or revenue systems might have plunged the nation into a depression and would have precipitated a bitter struggle among economic interests. An assault upon the Hamiltonian program might have pleased the Republican ideologues, but the necessity for dealing with the commercial interests would still have remained. Some Federalists, either naïve or alarmist, had imagined catastrophic consequences if the Republicans came to power. They could not see that Jefferson was neither able nor inclined to tear down an edifice constructed on a solid foundation; at most he could undertake some minor remodeling.

The campaign of 1800 marked the debut of the political party as an intrinsic factor in the election of a President. It had been waged by two distinct and organized parties which had made nominations, electioneered, and mobilized prospective voters. This development was an outgrowth of an alignment in Congress five years before of two opposing groups, each with its own leaders, and, among Republicans, a caucus for directing party affairs. Prompting similar alignments in the states, it was responsible for a partisan cleavage in the presidential contest of 1796 that extended beyond the congressional district to encompass the entire state.

Parties, however, had not yet become national organizations. Although in 1800 the two parties competed with each other in the election of congressmen, presidential electors, governors, members of state legislatures, and other officials, their activities varied with the prevailing constitutional and legal regulations in each state. Moreover, they lacked uniformity in machinery and structure—governors and presidential electors were chosen either by the legislatures or by popular voting; congressmen were elected either from districts or the state at large, and the county was the major electoral unit in some states while in others it was the cities or subdivisions thereof.

A significant aspect of the contest was the inroads made by Republicans into New England, which previously had been solid Federalist territory. By extending their appeal and base of power beyond any one section or social and economic group, they displayed the characteristics that were to become a permanent feature of the American party system. With two political parties competing, for the first time a vigorous appeal was directed to the electorate to judge between alternative leaderships and governmental programs. While property qualifications limited the number of legally qualified voters, a precedent was created for later campaigns when the franchise would be extended and a permanent party system established.

3. The Folk Hero in Politics

THE parties created by the Federalists and the Jeffersonian Republicans did not long endure in their original form. Drained by dissensions in the election of 1800, Hamilton's party continued to disintegrate as the New England commercial and financial enclaves from which it drew its strength steadily lost their dominant position in the nation to the South and West. Opposition to the War of 1812 provided the *coup de grâce*. Federalists celebrated British victories, attempted to defeat measures for conscription and financing the war, and even plotted secession and a separate peace. They were completely discredited when Andrew Jackson won a spectacular victory at New Orleans and a peace treaty was signed. A year later the Federalists chose their last presidential candidate.

In the campaign of 1816, James Monroe swept the electoral college with 183 votes, his opponent receiving only 34. During his administration, all but the last-ditch Federalists moved into the Republican camp, with the result that the two-party system practically ceased to exist. The flush of nationalism which followed the war, and the decline of Federalism, dissolved party alignments and party doctrine. The nation appeared happily united; an "Era of Good Feelings," as one Boston paper observed, had arrived.

Monroe was re-elected in 1820 with an almost unanimous vote, only one elector dissenting. The felicitous state of affairs did not last long. A crisis in foreign affairs, a financial panic which plunged the nation into a depression, and the controversy over admission of Missouri as a slave state produced the first rumblings of disaster. Other divisive problems arose or were intensified. There was the growing spirit of sectionalism over the tariff, internal improvements, and public lands policy. The manufacturing North supported a protective tariff, which was opposed by the agricultural South. The Old West parted company from the South on the tariff and internal improvements. Bills for improving roads and waterways advocated by the former were blocked by the latter.

Sectional antagonisms posed serious problems for any presidential aspirant for the election of 1824. To secure the nomination, he must retain the support of his own section and win that of other areas. The Republicans, a party more in name than in substance, represented an aggregation of heterogeneous viewpoints and sectional spokesmen. Jeffersonian at one extreme and Hamiltonian at the other, its members, who could not agree on any governmental policy, found it equally impossible to settle on a presidential candidate for the election of 1824.

A group of outstanding candidates vied for the office: Secretary of the Treasury William H. Crawford of Georgia, who was the leading contender, Secretary of State John Quincy Adams of Massachusetts, Congressman Henry Clay of Kentucky, Senators Andrew Jackson of Tennessee and John C. Calhoun of South Carolina. Despite popular opposition to "King Caucus," Crawford's friends convened a congressional caucus to make him their official nominee. Of the 216 Republican congressmen, only 66 troubled to attend what was to be the last such gathering in the nation's history. The other candidates were nominated by state legislatures, except for Calhoun, who dropped out in return for the vice-presidential nomination.

The returns in the electoral college gave Jackson 99 votes, Adams 84, Crawford 41, and Clay 37. Since none had a majority, the decision under the Constitution would have to be made by the House of Representatives. With Crawford virtually ruled out by a serious illness which had left him debilitated, Clay appeared in a strategic position to influence the outcome. Clay preferred Adams, who, he said, would not "inflict any wound upon the character of our institutions." He regarded Jackson as a hot-tempered, dictatorial man with no governmental experience, completely unfit for the office. Moreover, to promote his own political future the allegiance of the West was essential, which made Jackson his most formidable rival.

As it turned out, although Clay's vote was important, neither he nor his delegation cast the decisive ballot. Adams already had twelve states committed to him and needed only one more for the required majority. The New York delegation was so divided that one member, Stephen Van Rensselaer, could tip the scales. Clay and Webster pleaded and cajoled, trying to persuade him that a Jackson victory would jeopardize the property interests. Devoutly religious, the New York patrician went down on his knees to ask for divine guidance. When he opened his eyes after he finished praying, he noticed a slip of paper on the floor near his seat. It was a ballot with Adams's name. Interpreting this as a sign from the Almighty, he cast his vote for Adams, thereby making the New Englander President.

Jackson accepted his defeat with good grace until Adams announced his intention to appoint Clay his Secretary of State. Immediately there was an outcry from the Tennessean and his followers that a "corrupt bargain" had been concluded between the two men. Jackson wrote one of his friends that "the *Judas* of the West has closed the contract and will receive the thirty pieces of silver."

Rumors had been flying around for weeks that Clay had pledged his support to Adams in return for the number one Cabinet post. Several of Clay's followers repeatedly intimated to Adams that they would support him if Clay was accorded "a prominent share in the Administration." Adams finally assured one of them that if the West helped him in his election he would naturally take its needs into account in any program he would advocate.

While Adams was undoubtedly aware that rumors not only have a tenacious life but can sometimes spark political disasters, he would not refrain from making the appointment because, as he said flatly, "I consider it due to his [Clay's] talents and services, and to the Western section of the Union." As for Clay, the Cabinet post was the most likely step to the White House. He also felt, as he later stated, that he could hardly refuse to serve under Adams after having supported him in the House election; furthermore, he would have an opportunity to help plan the policies of the new administration. In any event, the appointment was a tactical blunder for which both men would pay dearly.

Jackson resigned his Senate seat, to which he had been elected only two years before, and left for home. At every stop on the journey he repeated his story of betrayal. *"The people [have] been cheated,"* he cried. *"Corruptions and intrigues at Washington . . . defeated the will of the people."* Adams and Clay had handed their opponents a perfect issue for kindling popular emotions.

Throughout his entire administration, Adams was plagued by the charge that he was propelled into office by an unholy deal, and he lacked the political skill either to dispel or overcome it. From the outset, his administration was a political disaster. A cultured man with intellectual tastes that were both wide and deep, he sought to enlist government in "the cultivation of the mechanic and of the elegant arts, the advancement of literature, and the progress of the sciences, ornamental and profound." His proposals included government sponsorship of scientific expeditions, astronomical observatories, and a national university, at a time when most Americans felt that such educational enrichment was a luxury they could little afford. Indeed, many considered his views not only unconstitutional but dangerous. Adams failed in his efforts to implement Clay's "American System," designed, through broad construction of national power, to advance the economic interests of all the sections. The tariff bill of 1828 which he signed was cursed as the "tariff of abominations." He also suffered defeats in diplomacy.

The campaign of 1828 began almost immediately after Adams's inauguration. Andrew Jackson, promptly renominated for the Presidency by the Tennessee legislature, began a quiet but carefully organized effort to wrest the office from Adams. He would prevail only if the factions opposed to the Adams philosophy and program, which were rooted in New England Federalism, were united into a cohesive, structured political party.

If anyone could help him succeed in this effort it was the "Little Magician," Martin Van Buren, senator from New York and one of the most consummate politicians of his day. Always impeccably dressed, fair-skinned, with light reddish hair and small brilliant eyes, the little man with his gracious manners and unshakable equanimity even in the heat of debate was an incomparable manipulator of men. He had created a state-wide machine in New York, the Albany Regency, in effect a governing council composed of the best political talent in the state. The Regency had forged an alliance with the southern states, but the concord had been steadily eroding as a result of the controversies engendered by the conflict over Missouri and other issues. This coalition would have to be recemented and the West brought in as a prerequisite for the creation of an enduring political party. Above all, as Van Buren saw it, the party would need a candidate behind which to unite. Andrew Jackson was the logical choice. He had received the largest popular vote in the last election and, as his views on public questions were unknown, he would not alienate any section.

Late in December of 1826, Van Buren arranged a conference with Vice-President Calhoun at which he outlined his strategy for victory. He was confident, he said, that he could command a substantial percentage of New York's electoral votes and influence those of Virginia and Georgia, an aggregate of almost 70 ballots. With the Jackson-Calhoun strength in Tennessee, Pennsylvania, the Carolinas, Alabama, and Mississippi, they could count on between 134 and 142 votes, slightly more than the necessary majority. Furthermore, he would persuade the influential southern editor and member of the "Richmond Junto," Thomas Ritchie, to join them.

The discussion ended on a note of mutual satisfaction. Several weeks later, Van Buren wrote to Ritchie, "If Gen Jackson & his friends will put his election on old party grounds, preserve the old systems, avoid if not condemn the practices of the last campaign we can by adding his personal popularity to the yet remaining force of old party feeling, not only succeed in electing him but our success when achieved will be worth something." He urged Ritchie and his group to join him, not simply to defeat Adams, but for "what is of still greater importance, the substantial reorganization of the old Republican party."

Through the unremitting efforts of Van Buren, Calhoun, Ritchie, and a number of other talented politicians, a party to support Jackson took shape. Reflecting a realignment of political forces, it included strict constructionist groups of the South as well as those which were pro-tariff but regarded Jackson as the lesser of two evils, the rising West, and Eastern labor. In the Adams camp were Federalists, some Westerners who favored internal improvements, a portion of protectionists in New England and the Middle states, and a small group of Clay's followers in the West and Southwest. As distinctive party labels did not appear for several years, both groups during the campaign of 1828 called themselves "National Republicans;" eventually, the Jacksonians identified themselves as "Democrats."

The problem for the Democrats was to create a voting majority out of an array of conflicting interests, groups, and factions—artisans and mechanics, bankers and farmers, planters and industrialists. From state to state and even within the states, the movement was divided on public policy. The new party would have been stillborn had the Jacksonians in and out of Congress insisted that agreement on national issues be a requirement for unity. Accordingly, no statement of purpose or policy was issued. The emphasis was to be on elevating a popular hero to the Presidency.

Another consideration, a relatively new one, was the need to win widespread popular approval. Tremendous political, economic, and social changes were transforming the nation. The industrial revolution had leaped the Atlantic, churning up a frenzy of development. Foreign and domestic commerce was expanding, the frontiers steadily retreating toward the western ocean, immigration enlarging the population. Everywhere roads were being cut through the dense forests, canals excavated, factories built. Democracy, which had been a ripple, was rapidly becoming a wave.

State after state was removing restrictive requirements for voting, so that by 1825, except in Rhode Island and Virginia, universal white manhood suffrage prevailed. In 1828, county or state conventions, which for some time had nominated state and local candidates, were employed by both parties to select presidential candidates. Delegates were generally appointed by ward or county committees and in a few cases were pledged to vote for a specific candidate. Some state legislatures served as nominating bodies, but this practice was soon to become obsolete. Presidential electors were now chosen by the legislatures in only two states. Everywhere else they were selected directly by the people, as a consequence of which the number involved in the electoral process by this change alone was increased by several hundred thousand.

This new fact of American political life was well understood by the Jacksonians. "Our true object," one declared, "is to . . . induce all aspirants for office to look to the people . . . for support." The Democrats proceeded methodically to launch an unprecedentedly massive campaign. They blanketed the country with print—newspapers, books, pamphlets, addresses, biographies, leaflets. New journals sprouted in virtually every state. By the summer of 1827, for example, nine new Jackson papers were started in North Carolina and eighteen in Ohio. By the following year, about 600 newspapers—50 of them dailies, 150 semiweeklies, and 400 weeklies—were being published at an estimated cost of a half million dollars a year. An army of devoted Jacksonians, laboring diligently to fill the columns of this colossal

press, created a network of correspondence from state to
state. One Massachusetts politician sent material to New
York with a note. "You have the same authority with this as
with the others—change, expunge, add or withhold entirely
at your discretion. I need not repeat that as to political
writings I have none of the vanity of an author, and consult
only the good of the cause and the party."

Fund raising was given the same exacting attention. In
addition to soliciting the usual large contributions, winning
support from local state organizations, and utilizing public
dinners and banquets, new and untried sources were
tapped. As the party's greatest single expense was mailing
literature, a way was neatly devised to shift most of this expense to the United States government by using the frank-
ing privilege not only for printing matter but for buttons,
banners, and insignia. It was estimated that taxpayers thus
contributed about a million dollars to the campaign. Money
was also obtained from the federal and state governments
in the form of congressional contracts for printing the nation's laws, and by awarding the position of state printer to
editors of official Jackson organs.

To reach every possible voter, local organizations were
essential. "Contending as we are against wealth & power,"
wrote one Jacksonian, "we look for success in numbers." So
systematically did the Democrats operate that by the end of
1827 nearly every county, city, and town of importance had
a "Jackson Committee" to sponsor meetings, raise money,
write propaganda, and correspond with other committees.
Local committees established in the election districts under
the supervision of state leaders arranged town meetings,
barbecues, parades, rallies, and other forms of entertainment to attract the populace. The county organization coordinated local and state functions and sent representatives to
the state convention, which selected the presidential ticket
and nominated candidates for state offices.

Behind all this frenetic activity, holding all the wires in
his powerful hands, was the acknowledged head of the
movement, General Andrew Jackson. It may have been

Albert Gallatin's description of Jackson as "a tall, lank, uncouth-looking personage, with long locks of hair hanging over his face, and a cue down his back tied in an eel-skin; his dress singular, his manners and deportment that of a rough backwoodsman" that helped to popularize the frontiersman stereotype. Actually, the pose of a backwoodsman was a deliberate effort to project a "democratic" image of a man of the people. Daniel Webster, who was not one of his partisans, commented in 1824, "General Jackson's manners are more presidential than those of any of the candidates. . . . My wife is for him decidedly." Others noted that he could be gentlemanly, distinguished, even elegant, and Josiah Quincy said that he "wrought a mysterious charm upon old and young."

While Jackson's formal education was limited, he had studied law and was appointed public prosecutor for the western district of North Carolina when he was twenty-one. He was so successful that he soon found himself with a large private practice and substantial land holdings. Later, he served briefly in both houses of Congress, followed by a six-year tenure as judge of the state supreme court. He lived like a gentleman on a fine and spacious plantation, racing his horses and entertaining lavishly. When war broke out in 1812, he promptly offered his services. The Battle of New Orleans made him a national hero and eventually a presidential possibility.

The General was sixty years old with a long record of public service when he made his second bid for the Presidency, but nothing in his background gave any clue to a political astuteness that was partly natural and partly derived from his army experience. His henchmen soon discovered that he was a superb politician. He was the first to break the tradition that presidential aspirants must remain silent and "above the battle." Beginning in 1824, he carried on a voluminous correspondence, met with delegations of politicians, and in general kept himself in the public eye, never letting anyone forget the "corrupt bargain."

Long letters which he wrote himself or had written for

him explaining, or clarifying, or refuting appeared regularly in the press. He drew the line only at traveling into other states or attending public dinners. "I have not gone into the highways and market places to proclaim my opinions," he declared proudly. He worked directly with correspondence committees that had been established by local organizations, with newspaper editors, congressional leaders, and his own Central Committee in Nashville. The Central Committee had been set up ostensibly to check "falsehoods and calumny, by the publication of truth, and by furnishing either to the public or to individuals . . . full and correct information upon any matter or subject within their knowledge or power, properly connected with the fitness or qualification of Andrew Jackson to fill the office of the President of the United States." While it may have served that avowed function, its main purpose was to unite the various Jackson committees throughout the country by means of correspondence.

Jackson's incessant activities worried many of his supporters. His quick temper might cause him to say something damaging, or he might express some views which would antagonize some sections or groups since, for example, they were portraying him as a protectionist in Pennsylvania while in Virginia as favoring a tariff for revenue only. At one point a member of his inner circle wrote him to plead that he should "forebear to write a word—that is all your friends desire of you until Congress is over. It is, I repeat, a matter of *most special* favor, that you be silent." Others were concerned that his conduct might appear unseemly. As one put it, "Candidates for the Presidency . . . ought not to say one word on the subject of the election. Washington, Jefferson, & Madison were as silent as the grave when they were before the American people for this office."

The candidate, however, had mastered the art of double talk and evasion. When the Indiana legislature asked him for a clear statement of policy, the General replied, "Not, sir, that I would wish to conceal my opinions from the people upon any political, or national subject, but as they were in various ways promulgated in 1824, I am apprehensive that my appearance before the public, at this time, may be attributed, as has been the case, to improper motives." At other times he was so ambiguous that he could be interpreted in several ways. His voting record in the Senate gave only faint clues as to his attitude on public policy. He had displayed a mild sympathy for Clay's "American System" and he favored a tariff because he thought it would end American dependence upon other countries for war materials. On the other hand, he opposed other tenets of Federalism, such as the creation of a national debt for national purposes. Generally he had aligned himself with the landholding aristocracy against the financial interests of the commercial East.

No such equivocation marked the attitude of President John Quincy Adams and the "Coalitionists," as his supporters came to be called. The spokesmen for New England's mercantile and commercial interests, they declared plainly their advocacy of federally sponsored programs not only for internal improvements but to advance the nation's intellectual and cultural life, higher tariffs to protect and stimulate industry, better banking facilities, and distribution to the states of federal surpluses to implement the national program.

Adams, also sixty years old, was the complete antithesis of his opponent in personality, background, interests, and style. That he reached the Presidency is more a testimony to the political traditions of the era than to his skill as a politician. He was a statesman with a brilliant record in diplomacy and had been an exceedingly successful Secretary of State, but he lacked one vital ingredient—personal appeal. "I am a man of reserved, cold, austere and forbidding manners," he described himself in his diary. "My political adversaries say a gloomy misanthrope, my personal enemies an unsocial savage. With the knowledge of the actual defects of my character, I have not had the pliability to reform it." He was balding, watery-eyed, generally unprepossessing, and he was stubborn and tactless.

The President unequivocally refused to involve himself in any aspect of the campaign. He gave no encouragement to those who wanted him to serve a second term and would make no public statement that he sought re-election. Despite provocations from the opposition, he remained silent, using the futile method of slaughtering those "vile calumniators" in the pages of his secret diary. Sometimes he almost appeared to be seeking defeat. Typical was his behavior when he was finally persuaded, after considerable resistance, to stop off at Philadelphia on his way home to Quincy as a simple courtesy to his supporters in that city. When he met the state leaders, he barely managed to conceal his irascibility and icily refused to attend rallies which had been arranged in his honor.

Against this clogging negativism, Henry Clay and several congressmen, especially Daniel Webster and John W. Taylor of New York, struggled to create a national party. Like the Jacksonians, they realized that it was vital to win the allegiance of the mass electorate. Large contributions were obtained by Webster, the unofficial party treasurer, and the coalition also used the public printers to enrich the campaign chest. Clay's position as a Cabinet member was a considerable advantage. Whenever possible, he removed Jackson printers and replaced them with Adams supporters.

A substantial amount of the money raised was spent on the press, since, as Clay put it, "The course adopted by the Opposition, in the dissemination of Newspapers and publications against the Administration and supporting presses leaves its friends no other alternative than that of following their example so far at least as to circulate information among the people." They established a considerable number of papers but did not have as many as those working for the Jacksonians, and they were not as skillful in linking them to their state or local organizations. Moreover, many of the editors were politically inept. True, the dour Adams was scant material for interesting copy. At the same time, they inadvertently aided his opponent. By frequent attacks on Jackson for his supposed vices, they succeeded only in advertising a colorful figure.

The Coalition, or National Republicans, also flooded the country with pamphlets, handbills, and broadsides, organized central committees and committees of correspondence, held local rallies, county meetings, and state conventions. In all this activity they lagged behind their opponents. Part of the problem, perhaps, was an excessive propriety in some cases and political naïveté in others. One state leader replied to Clay's suggestion for the organization of a committee that it would "excite the animadversions of our adversaries," and others informed him that it was impossible "in a country like ours where freedom of opinion and of action are secured . . . to organize a disciplined corps who will submit to the drill of some half dozen interested demogogues."

Political ineptitude cost the National Republicans the support of a new party, the Anti-Masons, which for a while they had in their grasp. This party was organized as a result of a bizarre incident in the western part of New York in 1826. William Morgan, a member of the Masonic Order, after a falling-out with his brethren, wrote a book revealing the secrets of Masonry, for which he found a publisher in his home town. When he refused to respond to the pleas of his friends that he keep his vows of secrecy, the page proofs were destroyed and Morgan mysteriously disappeared. Soon the entire area resounded with charges that Morgan had been kidnaped and drowned in the Niagara River. As the months went by and Morgan, alive, or dead, had not turned up, excitement continued to mount. Numerous meetings were held at which resolutions were adopted demanding the immediate apprehension of those responsible for putting him out of the way. Political reprisals were threatened against any officerholder or aspirant discovered to be a Freemason.

The Anti-Masons, now organized into a political force, began to turn toward the Republicans when the Jackson-dominated New York legislature refused to appoint a special committee to investigate the Morgan affair. With a little skill the Republicans might have won New York, but in the gubernatorial contest they failed to effect a coalition with the Anti-Masons, who put up their own candidate.

Tradition, which forbade presidential candidates to campaign, also made it unseemly for men holding public office to do so. When Secretary of State Clay and other members of the Cabinet, Senator Webster, and several of his colleagues attended public dinners, meetings, or rallies, they were denounced for "perambulating the country for electioneering purposes" and accused of wasting public time and money. In the fall of 1827, one paper complained that the entire administration was on the move, the President in Boston, Clay in Virginia, "the Secretary of the Navy in New York buying Tammany Hall," and the Secretary of War in Fredericksburg. Even if Cabinet members left Washington for private business, they were suspect. An opponent dubbed them "the travelling Cabinet," a catchy epithet which clung for the duration of the campaign.

Democratic leaders were less peripatetic, Van Buren being the only one who traveled extensively. Touring the southern states in 1827 ostensibly to visit friends, he was wined and dined at public and private banquets, hailed everywhere as the champion of southern rights. By the time he left the region, his natural charm and uncanny political skill had revitalized the North-South alliance.

Long before "mass psychology" became a studied tactic, the Jacksonians introduced methods for mass persuasion which have since become commonplace. "Our true object," wrote Duff Green, their leading newspaper editor, "is to . . . induce all aspirants for office to look to the people . . . for support." For the first time in a campaign, ballyhoo was employed to whip up enthusiasm: public rallies, barbecues, tree plantings, dinners, every form of involvement that could be dreamed up. One clever device was the adoption of a symbol with which Jackson could be identified. Since he had long been known as "Old Hickory," the country was inundated with hickory brooms, hickory canes, hickory sticks. Hickory poles were erected in countless towns and hamlets and adorned the corners of city streets. Local groups even organized to plant hickory trees in the village or town square.

Public rallies or street demonstrations were carefully organized and staged. Men on horseback with identifying party labels on their hats were frequently sent out in advance of a scheduled meeting. They used various methods to attract a crowd. One popular device was to toss small coins among the people as they rode by, while urging them to "huzza for Jackson." In Baltimore, a "Grand Barbecue" was arranged ostensibly to commemorate the defeat of the British in the War of 1812. "I am told by a gentleman who is employed to erect the fixtures that three Bullocks are to be roasted, and each man is to wear a Hickory Leaf in his hat by way of designation," Jackson was informed. The ceremonies opened with the firing of a cannon followed by a parade of 700 marshals. The crowd then drank to the health of the Hero of New Orleans while they listened to a dramatic oration on his thrilling exploits against the British and the Indians. When the speeches were over, the spectators were led in a new song called "Hickory Wood," after which they could gorge on the sumptuous feast provided for them.

The National Republicans turned up their noses at these affairs. An editor of one administration newspaper wrote, "If we go into one of these meetings, of whom do we find them composed? Do we see there the solid, substantial, moral and reflecting yeomanry of the country? No. . . . They comprise a large portion of the dissolute, the noisy, the discontented, and designing of society." One correspondent lamented to Henry Clay, "The ignorant and degraded class of our population are all against us—and the number of that description of people who push forward to the polls are really formidable." Not surprisingly, Jackson became identified as the candidate of the people and Adams as the spokesman for the privileged class who believed that "the few should govern the many [and] that the will of the Representatives should not be palsied by the will of his constituents."

Adams was not only indicted as an aristocrat but charged with trying to emulate royalty. "We disapprove the kingly pomp and splendour that is displayed by the present incumbent," declared resolutions passed by Jackson conventions. The accusation of "royal extravagances" was based on a report submitted to the Congressional Committee on Retrenchment that public funds have been used to purchase gambling furniture for the East Room, in particular a billiard table, cues and balls, and a set of expensive ivory chessmen. Adams's disclaimer that he himself had paid for this equipment and the certification by the Treasury Department that no government appropriation had been made for these items were, of course, ignored by the Jacksonians. Ritchie's *Enquirer* published an anonymous letter headed "The East Room" in which the President was censured for spending $25,000 of public money on gambling equipment, including dice, a billiard table, balls, cues, a backgammon board, and "soda water."

At public rallies and meetings, the Jacksonians kept blasting away that the Administration was undemocratic and contemptuous of the will of the people, that it used patronage, and that it recklessly squandered public funds. Their major emphasis, however, was on the "corrupt bargain." None of the efforts by administration spokesmen to deny the story could gainsay the fact that Henry Clay *had* been appointed Secretary of State by President Adams. In commenting on one of Clay's pamphlets dealing with the episode, the Albany *Argus* summed up the matter when it wrote ". . . nor do we pretend to allege that he does not prove now . . . the falsity of the charge . . ." but "the proof must be of no ordinary weight to dissipate the belief in the existence of such arrangements in the minds of the people."

For the first time in a presidential campaign, appeals were made to ethnic and religious prejudice. In the key states of New York and Pennsylvania, both parties deliber-

ately bid for the large foreign vote. They flooded the
German-populated areas of Pennsylvania with all kinds of
printed material in German and sent in speakers who
could address the people in their native tongue. While the
Republicans discussed administration policy and attacked
the Jacksonian program, the Democrats characteristically—
and shrewdly—plunged in with charges against the President of extravagance, corruption, and support of higher
taxes. The Pennsylvania "Dutch" were informed that the
Administration had sneered at them as " 'the *Black Dutch*,'
'*the Stupid Dutch*,' '*the Ignorant Dutch*' and other names
equally decorous and civil," while Jackson, on the other
hand, fervently admired them for their patriotism and their
innumerable virtues.

Jacksonians took full advantage of opposition blunders
with regard to the Irish. The Adams press in New York City
was strongly nativist, and one paper virtually guaranteed
the victory of the Democrats by writing that the population
of some districts was "mixt up with the dregs of all nations;
when we are told that we have among us half a million of
Irishmen"; that "our liberties and government [are] threatened by a further accumulation of such materials, without
education . . . and without attachment to the country . . . ,"
that "one man born among us . . . is worth . . . a regiment of
Europeans." Duff Green, on the other hand, wrote that
General Jackson "is the son of honest Irish parents. . . . That
natural interest which all true hearted Irishmen feel in the
fame of one who has so much genuine Irish blood in his
veins, has drawn down upon the heads of that devoted people, the denunciations of the partisans of Messrs. Adams &
Clay."

Adams was denounced in one place as being pro-Catholic
and in another as anti-Catholic. In Maryland, which had a
large Catholic population, he was accused of currying favor
with that religious group by attending Catholic churches
and seeking to obtain the nomination of Catholic candidates for public office in the state. Elsewhere the Jacksonians published excerpts from letters that Adams had writ-

ten while abroad which contained flippant remarks on Catholic doctrine or practice. His references in a Fourth of July oration in 1821 to the Church as "that portentous system of despotism and superstition," in which "neither the body nor the soul of the individual was his own," were widely distributed.

Voters were asked to consider the religious convictions of the candidates as relevant factors in judging their fitness for office. As Unitarianism in some areas was synonymous with atheism, the President, a Unitarian, was censured for his disbelief in the Trinity and the Incarnation. At a meeting in New England, he was denounced by one outraged citizen for having "intentionally and without the least necessity violated the laws of God and man by traveling and receiving public honors on the Sabbath." Jackson, however, was "a sincere believer in the Christian religion," performing "his devotions regularly with his family in his own House, and in a Presbyterian Church in his neighborhood," according to the party literature. One newspaper reported that he said prayers "every morning and night, also table prayers." In another much publicized story, after Jackson had issued an order against any unusual noise in his camp, an officer complained to him that a group of soldiers had assembled to pray. "Go, then, and join them," replied the General. "God forbid that praying should be an uncommon noise in my camp."

Each party tried to persuade clergymen to sermonize on the merits of its candidate. Newspapers, with no very scrupulous regard for facts, carried announcements of support by one denomination or another. An Administration organ in Pennsylvania stated that, of 197 ministers of the General Conference of the Methodist Episcopal Church, only 7 were favorable to Jackson, and these were from Tennessee. Ignored, of course, was the denial of the truth of this claim in the denomination paper, which further declared that only 167 members attended the conference and no inquiries had been made as to their political preferences.

Both sides operated on the premise that if enough mud is flung a little of it will always stick, or that it takes a long time for the truth to catch up with a lie. And as there were no statutes at the time against libel, the field was wide open for the crudest and most vicious kind of character assassination. Where no facts existed, "facts" were invented or twisted. Completely lacking in elementary decency was the purported story of Jackson's marriage, published in the Cincinnati *Gazette* and written by its editor, Charles Hammond, who apparently was motivated by a bitter personal hatred of the General. According to the tale, Jackson had persuaded Rachel Robards to desert her lawfully wedded husband and live with him in adultery. What had actually happened was that, after years of abuse and mistreatment, Mrs. Robards left her husband to go to Natchez with Jackson, chaperoned by a friend, Colonel John Stark. Later, having been informed that Robards had divorced her, she married Jackson, only to discover after several tranquil years that Robards had obtained legislative authorization to bring divorce proceedings in a court of law but had never taken any further steps. Technically, therefore, Rachel was a bigamist. Two years later, at Robards's request, his marriage was dissolved, and shortly thereafter the Jacksons had a second wedding ceremony performed.

For the two people involved, and especially for Mrs. Jackson, a public rehashing of their sad misadventure was bad enough, but Hammond's embellishments and distortions turned Jackson into an unprincipled home wrecker and seducer. "Ought a convicted adultress [sic] and her paramour husband to be placed in the highest offices of this free and christian land?" he thundered. Hammond republished his story in a booklet entitled *A View of General Jackson's Domestic Relations*, which was widely distributed by the Republicans.

Slanders against himself Jackson could shrug off, but this one, which struck at his beloved wife, who had never ceased to suffer because of an innocent mistake, cut him to the bone. He was also infuriated with Adams and Clay who, he believed, were responsible for the story in the first place, as Hammond, he was informed, had communicated with the Secretary of State when he was collecting material for his vicious article. Immediately he had a refutation prepared containing sworn testimony, letters, and affidavits, which was published in the Jackson press.

Not content with one juicy scandal, Hammond created another. "General Jackson's mother was a COMMON PROSTITUTE," he began a piece in his paper, "brought to this country by the British soldiers! She afterwards married a MULATTO MAN, with whom she had several children, of which number GENERAL JACKSON IS ONE!!!" In another article in the same issue he wrote that Jackson's eldest brother had been sold as a slave in Carolina.

Retaliating, the Jacksonians used the sexual theme against the President. They made the preposterous charge that when John Quincy Adams was Ambassador to Russia he had acted as a procurer for Czar Alexander I, providing him with an American girl. The gossamer thread out of which the tale was spun was a chance meeting of the Czar and an exemplary young woman, nursemaid to Adams's son, while she was taking the child to visit the monarch's sister. The fabrication was widely circulated and, astonishingly, given credence. In the West, the Democrats labeled the President "The Pimp of the Coalition," smirking that it was now apparent why he had been so successful as a diplomat.

Jackson's background was microscopically examined for anything that could possibly be used against him. One incident was blown up to make the General appear a monster who delighted in ordering military executions. During the Creek war, a group of militiamen mutinied, stole supplies, and deserted. When the six ringleaders were caught they were legally tried and sentenced. Among them was an itinerant preacher. This "innocent" father of nine helpless children, according to the Adams press, was shot by Jackson's orders. A widely distributed handbill bordered in black was headed "Some Account of some of the Bloody Deeds of

GENERAL JACKSON," with the six names across the top, under each of which was a macabre black coffin, followed by a description of the "murderers" and a maudlin verse entitled "Mournful Tragedy."

The most scurrilous accusation was complicity with Aaron Burr in his conspiratorial activities. The story had many ramifications. It was alleged that Jackson had persuaded a fellow Tennessean to join Burr's army; that he had supplied Burr with troops obtained from the governors of several states; that he was one of Burr's major officers; that he was slated to command all of Burr's troops in Kentucky and Tennessee after the conspiracy was under way; that he was the confidant of the woman whose husband's island on the Ohio River was to be the launching place for the operations; that he was privy to all of Burr's treacherous plans.

Poisonous as these barbs were, the Jacksonians rendered them harmless. By almost completely ignoring the major issues and incessantly proclaiming their candidate's so-called attributes, they had clothed him in the impenetrable armor of a folk hero. As one New York paper put it in bold type, it was proud to present the General as the "Soldier Boy of the First War of Independence. The Veteran Hero of the Second. He Saved the Country. Let the cry be Jackson, Van Buren & liberty." Jackson, the item declared, had fought Indians, defended his country when it was in peril, and vindicated the honor of womanhood by killing the man who had tried to besmirch his wife's good name.* Obviously, he was a different breed from the members of the elitist "dynasty" of the Virginia Succession and the Massachusetts Adamses.

Republicans sneered at the effort to portray Jackson as a farmer, "intended, no doubt, to operate upon the feelings of our northern farmers by holding up the General . . . as one of themselves, engaged in the same employment and actuated by the same feelings. The comparison . . . of our hearty yeomanry to . . . a man whose plantation is worked by

---

* This last was a fanciful creation by the editor.

slaves and superintended by an overseer . . . is almost too
ridiculous to be seriously noticed." However, the image of
Jackson which his supporters so skillfully drew and promoted remained indelibly impressed on the voters, and
their reaction reflected the power and persistence of the
agrarian ethos in American politics during the frontier
phase of the nation's development.

The administration forces tried to convince the voters
that the intricacies of government required skill and knowledge in public administration. "General Jackson is not qualified," one leaflet declared, ". . . he has had little experience
. . . if elected, could he possibly, even with the best intentions, discharge the complicated and arduous duties of
President?" Other pieces in a less kindly vein called him a
man of violent temper and a duelist, and even maligned him
as illiterate.

Weeks before the voting date, party leaders expressed
concern about fraudulent ballots. In October, the *National
Journal* warned that the Jackson party intended to carry the
election by an illegal vote and urged that care be taken to
prevent unqualified voters from exercising the franchise. At
local and state elections the previous year, numerous incidents reportedly had occurred. The challenger of a Jackson
vote in Virginia was manhandled by a mob near the polls.
Both parties had been accused of practising bribery on a
large scale in New York. Voters from Tennessee were said
to have crossed the border in hordes to vote in the Kentucky elections.

As the polls were open for three days, it was not unusual
for "floaters," who were paid fifty cents by party workers for
each time they went to the polls, to vote three or four times.
One method of recruiting "voters" was to round up sailors
in the port towns and escort them to the polls; another was
to enlist youths under the legal age. Clay was informed by
one correspondent that if the Jacksonians in Tennessee sent
in a thousand voters to Kentucky, the administration would
lose the state, but, he added, "We shall have two or three
thousand illegal ones of our own."

Party managers tried to outmaneuver each other in manipulating the vote. In many localities a voice vote was still the prevailing practice, and none of the states had a secret ballot. Moreover, as ballots were printed and distributed by each party, persuasive ward heelers could accost voters at the polls to pressure them into accepting their ticket. Intimidation or even physical assault were not uncommon when a voter refused the proffered ballot.

Where party organization was strong and where the vote was expected to be marginal, strenuous efforts were made to "get out the vote." Committees were appointed to bring in party supporters from their homes or from the local taverns. Election-day parades were organized, complete with flags and bunting, so that, like children following the Pied Piper, a whole aggregation of voters could be drawn to the polls.

On election eve, Duff Green published a clarion call. "TO THE POLLS!" he exorted. "To the Polls! The faithful sentinel must not sleep—Let no one stay home—Let every man go to the Polls—Let not a vote be lost—Let each Freeman do his duty; and all will triumph in the success of JACKSON, CALHOUN AND LIBERTY."

And to the polls Americans swarmed from September through November, as no single date had yet been nationally specified, 800,000 more than in the previous presidential election. When the final count was in, Jackson had won by 178 electoral votes to Adams's 83. If all the states had used the general ticket—Maine, Maryland, New York, and Illinois split their electoral ballot—his total would have been larger by 31 votes. His popular majority, however, was only 139,212 out of a total vote of 1,155,340, but still a smashing 56 per cent.

Sectionalism was an important factor in the outcome. Jackson carried the entire West with the exception of some counties in Indiana, Ohio, and Illinois where the influence of New England migrations was still strong, or where expectations of internal improvements fostered loyalty to the National Republicans. He won almost all of the tidewater

counties of the Old South except those with extensive
swampland, where the federal government had undertaken
large-scale improvements, and the ones influenced by the
urban populations of their major cities. In the East, Jackson
lost the western counties of New York State and districts in
Pennsylvania and Ohio where anti-Masonic feeling was
strong. Adams won New England, Delaware, New Jersey,
and—by one vote—Maryland. The candidates shared New
York, with the major portion going to Jackson.

The Adams followers were stunned. Incredible that the
American people should have rejected a man with a distinguished record of achievement in public life at home and
abroad, an experienced diplomat and statesman, an incumbent President. One observer, however, declared that the
campaign for Adams was "not of a sort to arouse popular
enthusiasm." His comment was valid, and the Republicans
failed to stir the people because they did not comprehend
the social and economic changes that had taken place in
the nation.

Americans had begun to realize that an intimate relationship existed between politics and their personal welfare.
The panic of 1819, which had brought a depression in its
wake, contributed to this awareness. All parts of the country were affected by the economic ravages resulting from
overspeculation in wildcat banking and from overexpan-
sion, but the South and West were particularly hard hit.
Banks that had overextended credit to men who bought
land with reckless disregard for future consequences began
to press for payment. Numerous foreclosures made the national bank an absentee owner of property in the West and
South, so the people, as Thomas Hart Benton graphically
put it, "may be devoured by it at any moment. They are in
the jaws of a monster."

Serious financial distress and the rude awakening from
dreams of becoming rich impelled many to seek a leader
who would guide them out of the wilderness of despair.
Debtors rushed into politics to obtain relief laws from state
legislatures. State governments were pressured to wage

bank wars against the national bank. Demands were made
for a change in the laws which permitted imprisonment for
debt, for the enactment of a national bankruptcy law, and
for other measures to relieve the victims of the depression.

With the rise in popular suffrage, the "technician" of
mass politics, who had existed only in embryonic form during the Jeffersonian era, now was almost fully developed.
He encouraged the increasingly extensive belief that the
people should control the choice of public leaders. Careers
in government should no longer be the exclusive preserve of
the social elite, or the bureaucratic specialist, but considered the legitimate aspiration of anyone who was qualified.

Jackson's first message to Congress reinforced this attitude. "The duties of all public officers are, or at least admit
of being made, so plain and simple that men of intelligence
may readily qualify themselves for their performance. . . .
In a country where offices are created solely for the benefit
of people, no one man has any more intrinsic right to official
station than another."

The immense throngs that poured into Washington on
inauguration day symbolized the new approach toward
government. Some fifteen or twenty thousand, according to
one estimate, came to share in the day of glory. These and
other thousands who could not make the journey to the
nation's capital had accepted literally the view that Andrew
Jackson was "one of them," that the election marked the
"triumph of the great principle of self-government over the
intrigues of the aristocracy." Daniel Webster commented,
"I never saw such a crowd here before. Persons have come
five hundred miles to see General Jackson, *and they really
seem to think that the country is rescued from some dreadful danger!*"

In keeping with democratic principles, the inaugural
ceremony, for the first time in the nation's history, took
place outdoors so that it could be witnessed by the people.
When the President finished his brief address, the crowd
surged forward to shake his hand, and it took strenuous
efforts to keep him from being crushed by his well-wishers.

Later the White House was turned into a shambles by the men, women, and children who pressed in to greet the President and partake of the promised refreshments. Thousand of dollars' worth of china and cut glass were shattered and furniture and rugs ruined in the struggle to get to the ice cream and spiked punch. "The President, after having been *literally* nearly pressed to death & almost suffocated & torn to pieces by the people in their eagerness to shake hands with Old Hickory," wrote one observer, "had retreated through the back way or south front & had escaped to his lodgings at Gadsby's."

The election of 1828 brought to power a new party that had succeeded in forging a coalition among the strategically important political elements—the laborers of the East, the small planters of the South, and the farmers of the West. Moreover, it reflected the upsurge of the democratic spirit and a growing political consciousness on the part of the "common man." The average citizen had an opportunity to express his will through clearly defined political parties and was able thereby in some degree to control public policy; his interest in the political process kept the government out of the hands of a narrow elite. The nationwide focus on the dramatic contest also served to stimulate the rise of a party system. In this sense, the Presidency could be said to have contributed to the creation of permanent party organizations.

4. The Invincible Log Cabin

BY the time Andrew Jackson had completed his first term in office, he had become for the mass of voters the "tribune of the people," and they returned him to office in 1832 with an even larger popular and electoral majority than before. However noncommittal on specific issues he may have been during his first election campaign, Jackson was completely sincere about the democratic character of government, maintaining that it should offer equal protection and equal opportunities to all the people. Not only should government posts be made available to the intelligent of any class in society, but officeholders should be rotated periodically to prevent an entrenched bureaucracy. He was also convinced that, when monopolies and other special government privileges to the rich were abolished, poverty and social inequality would disappear.

To the aristocratic and the affluent, his ideas were anathema. Those who had originally opposed him became increasingly hostile, denounced him violently, and continuously challenged his leadership. As time went on, they were joined by others who opposed his methods and policies.

In the South, the great planters were bitterly antagonistic to the President over the tariff and his position on states' rights. Enraged at the high duties of the "Tariff of Abominations" of 1828, South Carolina flirted dangerously with the idea of secession. A legal basis for a doctrine of nullification was formulated by John C. Calhoun, and, when the Tariff of 1832 offered no relief, the state issued a Nullification Ordinance. Jackson promptly denounced this measure as traitorous, requesting Congress to authorize the use of force should any attempt be made to carry it out. A critical showdown was averted when a compromise tariff was passed, after which the ordinance was repealed.

Business groups in the North and conservatives in the South turned against Jackson for vetoing the bill to recharter the Bank of the United States, which he called undemocratic, unconstitutional, and un-American. His vigorous exercise of executive authority brought down on him the imprecations of these and other elements, who dubbed him "King Andrew the First." In a widely circulated cartoon he was portrayed in royal robes and crown, with a scepter in one hand and a veto in the other, trampling on the Constitution, the judiciary, internal improvements, and the Bank.

This intense opposition finally coalesced into a new party to oppose the Democrats in the election of 1836. A congeries of diverse elements united, calling themselves "Whigs," a name taken from the middle-class English party which sought to limit the king's power. The label seems to have appeared first on a New York City ballot in 1834 and soon won general acceptance. Basically conservative, the party included the banking and business interests of the Northeast, the West, and the South, the large planters of the South, and some western farmers. It contained high protectionists and low protectionists, states' rights enthusiasts and ardent nationalists, and advocates of another national bank. Westerners were drawn to the party because it endorsed internal improvements, hoping it would press for a public land policy. In general, the Whigs were alarmed at social and economic reforms which might be disadvantageous to "property," and they feared the influence upon government by "the mob."

Lacking cohesion and even unable to agree on a candidate, the new party decided that it would be wise not to hold a national nominating convention as the Democrats had done four years earlier. The strategy was to run several candidates, each of whom would have sectional strength, so that enough votes might be drawn from the Democratic nominee to throw the election into the House of Representatives, where conceivably they might elect their own man. For the Midwest and the West, the nominee was William, Henry Harrison, an Indian fighter and a hero of the War of 1812; for the East, the brilliant Daniel Webster; and for the South, Senator Hugh Lawson White of Tennessee.

As for the Democrats, Jackson's choice of his Secretary of State, "the Little Magician" Martin Van Buren, as his successor was unopposed by the party convention.

When the election returns were in, Van Buren had 170 electoral votes to 124 for all his opponents. Continued prosperity, patronage, a superior party organization, and the reflected popularity of the retiring President had carried the country. Nevertheless, the Whigs had cause for satisfaction. They had received a large popular vote, won in the two Jacksonian strongholds of Georgia and Tennessee, and carried three border and slave states. Harrison's fine showing in the Ohio Valley marked him as a prospect for 1840, since states like Pennsylvania, Ohio, and Indiana were vital for victory.

Almost immediately the Whigs began to plan for the next campaign. Their problem was to select a candidate who would appeal to the mixed bag that composed their party. As a correspondent asked one of their leaders, "Into what crucible can we throw this heterogeneous mass of old national republicans, and revolting Jackson men; Masons and anti-Masons; Abolitionists and pro-slavery men; Bank men & anti-Bank men with all the lesser fragments that have been, from time to time, thrown off from the great political wheel in its violent revolutions, so as to melt them down into one mass of pure Whigs of undoubted good mettle?"

The strongest Whig organizations were those of Thaddeus Stevens in Pennsylvania and the New York combine led by "Boss" Thurlow Weed, editor of the Albany *Evening*

Journal, and Governor William H. Seward, and assisted by the capable journalist, Horace Greeley. At the outset, the New Yorkers favored William Henry Harrison, but soon a new warrior attracted the politicians, General Winfield Scott, acclaimed as "the Hero of Bridgewater" after some border incidents in western New York. Early in 1839, one politician reported considerable enthusiasm for the hero in the area, while another wrote, "Scott's name will bring out the hurra boys. The Whig party were broken down by the popularity . . . of old Jackson, and it is but . . . fair to prostrate our opponents, with . . . the weapons, with which they beat us. We shall recruit them from their ranks in mass." Thurlow Weed, after sounding out popular sentiment, decided to back Scott's candidacy.

The old Federalist faction in the party favored Daniel Webster, but he lacked strength in the West. Moreover, the politicians who wished to avoid the issue of the now defunct Bank of the United States considered him undesirable, since he had been clearly identified with that institution. When Webster was repudiated by a leading newspaper in his home state, he withdrew his candidacy.

Most deserving of the nomination and the outstanding contender was the magnetic Senator Henry Clay. The tall, black-haired Kentuckian had a national reputation for his brilliant leadership in Congress and over the years of his political life had won a devoted following. A former Secretary of State, he had also once been a presidential candidate. Militating against his selection, however, was his identification with the southern Whigs. While he could count on support in the South—he was heartily endorsed by the conventions in Virginia, Mississippi, Louisiana, Alabama, and North Carolina—and could possibly win Illinois, Connecticut, and Rhode Island, the key states essential to victory were New York and Pennsylvania. In the summer of 1839, Clay toured New York State, where he was warmly received, but at Saratoga Weed quietly informed him that as a Mason and a slaveholder he could not carry New York, suggesting that he withdraw gracefully while there was still time.

On December 4, 1839, at Harrisburg, Pennsylvania, the "Democratic Whig National Convention" began its sessions with twenty-two of the twenty-six states represented. The delegates for each state, equal to the number of representatives in Congress, were chosen either by the Whig members of the legislatures or by conventions called for that purpose. After the roll call and the selection of officers, two skillfully executed maneuvers put Clay at a disadvantage.

The first was an "amicable adjustment" which permitted the seating of two rival Pennsylvania delegations, thereby giving control to the Stevens faction, which had a majority in the combined delegation. The second was the adoption of the unit rule, which provided that "the vote of a majority of each delegation shall be reported as the vote of that State, and each State represented . . . shall vote its full electoral vote in committee." This immediately cut the ground from under Clay in New York, Pennsylvania, and Ohio, where his considerable minority strength would be wiped out. Moreover, the secret ballot would serve those who were adept at behind-the-scenes stratagems.

Before the balloting began, Thurlow Weed, assisted by Horace Greeley, neither of whom was a delegate, electioneered strenuously for General Scott. They buttonholed delegates on the floor, in the corridors, in their rooms, telling them solemnly that Clay had no chance of winning and emphasizing the "availability" of their man. At the same time, Thaddeus Stevens was working for his candidate, Harrison. Webster's withdrawal had given this General the support of New England, but it was not enough for victory. If the Scott delegates could be won over, the necessary majority would be assured.

On the first ballot Clay received 103 votes, Harrison 91, and Scott 57. With each new ballot, however, Clay's plurality dropped, Scott's position improved, and Harrison's strength remained stationary. Efforts were now made to promote Scott as a compromise candidate against both Clay and Harrison. Stevens, fearing that "defeat might be snatched from the jaws of victory," proceeded to engineer an astute stratagem. Somehow he had obtained a letter

which Scott had written to a fellow Whig in a transparent
attempt to win Abolitionist support. With studied casual-
ness, Stevens made its contents known to the Virginia
delegation, which had been considering Scott as a second
choice in the event Clay was put out of the running. As he
hoped, the Virginians promptly switched to Harrison, and
the Scott band wagon collapsed. It was all over despite
desperate attempts by Clay supporters to block a Harrison
victory. Late in the evening of the third day, Harrison received 148 votes, Clay 90, and Scott 16. In what was becoming a political ritual, a motion was introduced to make
the nomination unanimous.

One important item remained, nominating a Vice-
President, and here the Weed-Stevens forces were primarily
concerned with appeasing Clay's outraged supporters. Tumultuous midnight sessions marked by involved "horse-
trading" finally produced John Tyler, a dignified gentleman
of the Virginia Tidewater aristocracy. One observer writing
later about the convention lamented the addition of "Tyler
too" on the ticket. "There was rhyme," he sighed, "but no
reason in it." Expediency was reason enough, for Tyler, a
states'-rights advocate and a Southerner, provided balance
to the ticket.

Before the convention adjourned, one political innocent
reminded the chairman of what he regarded as an important oversight by moving that an "Address to the Country,"
a statement of the party's principles, be issued. He was
promptly cried down for making a ridiculous suggestion. "If
the voice of the West rolling down from the mountains and
along the valleys of the Atlantic, be not better than all the
addresses that ever were issued," one orator declaimed,
"then indeed a miracle has been wrought." Omission of a
party platform was deliberate. It would be safer and more
prudent to attack the administration while remaining noncommittal on Whig policy, thereby offending no one who
might otherwise be driven away from the party.

Henry Clay, who had been confident of the nomination
until the balloting, was overcome with bitterness when he
learned of his defeat. A friend who was with him in his

Washington boardinghouse reported that Clay shouted, "It is a diabolical intrigue, I know now, which has betrayed me. I am the most unfortunate man in the history of parties: always run by my friends when sure to be defeated, and now betrayed for a nomination when I, or any one, would be sure of an election." Nevertheless, several days later at a testimonial dinner given him by his friends and attended by distinguished Whigs, Clay calmly announced his support of the ticket. In a stirring and forceful speech, he declared, "We have not been contending for Henry Clay, for Daniel Webster, or for Winfield Scott. No! We have been contending for principles. Not men, but principles, are our rules of action." Astute politician that he was, Clay realized, as had many others before and since in a similar position, that his political future could be jeopardized by failing to rally behind his party's candidate.

Initial reaction among Whigs in the South was deep disgust that a "statesman and patriot" had been turned down for a Harrison. "Just think of a man such as Mr. Clay . . . without whom the Whig party would not this day exist, cast aside for a driveller," one of them snorted. These gentlemen apparently had not yet become aware of the new political realities created by a mass electorate. No longer could a select few caucusing quietly in private dining rooms arrange affairs to suit their interests and desires. In this new age, the only way for a candidate to reach the White House was on the shoulders of the masses.

While the affluent community could be counted upon to support the Whig ticket, the working people and the farmers would have to be enticed. To avoid the disastrous error of the Federalists, who had publicly professed their views, they would divert attention from Whig doctrine by making the campaign a carnival.

Ironically, the party whose roots were deep in the aristocracy of New England, whose progenitors were Alexander Hamilton, John Quincy Adams, and Daniel Webster, created an image of their candidate as a folk hero, the "Cincinnatus from North Bend," the "simple ploughman" born in a log cabin, the people's candidate. By accident they had stumbled upon an ingredient for success. A Democratic politician had sneered, "Give him [Harrison] a barrel of hard cider and settle a pension of two thousand a year upon him, and our word for it, he will sit the remainder of his days content in a log cabin." To the consternation of the Democrats, the lampoon, which had been published by one of their papers, was snatched up by the Whigs and converted into a badge of honor. What could be more appealing to the ordinary, decent, hard-working American than a simple man of the frontier, possessing, presumably, all the homely virtues of a tiller of the soil? The political myth of the humble origin of the presidential candidate was born. Men accustomed to follow the lead of genteel patricians would shout themselves hoarse with such plebian phrases as "log cabin" and "hard cider."

To start the campaign off in the right spirit, huge ratification meetings were held in dozens of major cities, climaxed on May 4, 1840, by the major event at Baltimore. From twenty-one states the faithful converged, the Whigs boasting an attendance of 100,000. The city was turned into a carnival, with banners flying everywhere and hard cider flowing as freely as water.

A spectacular three-mile parade through the city to the Canton Race Track where the oratorical festivities were to be held began, with a discharge of cannon, at 9:30 in the morning. Nothing was omitted—bands, costumes, horse-drawn cannon, trumpeters—from the trappings of pageantry more suitable for a circus show than a presidential ratifying assembly. Eight log-cabin floats symbolized the humble birth of the Whig candidate.

At the race course grounds, a steady parade of orators whipped to a frenzy the already enthusiastic cider-logged listeners. The chairman proclaimed the Whigs a "Log-Cabin Party," and Senator Clay affirmed that "we are all Harrison men. We are *united*. We must triumph." The spellbinding Daniel Webster shouted above the commotion, "The time has come when the cry is change, Every breeze says change—Every interest of the country demands it. . . .

We have fallen, gentlemen, upon *hard times,* and the remedy seems to be HARD CIDER." And so on and on until night fell and the assembled multitude returned to the city for food, revelry, and more speeches delivered from stands erected in the square. The festivities were continued all through the next day until almost midnight when the "convention" adjourned to "the fourth of March, 1841, at Washington, then and there to witness the inauguration of the People's President."

While the uproarious Whig celebration was making Baltimore ring, a group of 248 Democrats, to their dismay, found themselves in the same city for their nominating convention. They had assembled at the call of the Central Committee of the New Hampshire Democratic party, which had set the time and place some weeks before. Five states had not troubled to send delegates, and six were represented by less than half their prescribed quota.

Since the departure of "Old Hickory" from the White House, the party had lost considerable strength as a result of defections for personal, ideological, and economic reasons. To some, Van Buren, though a resourceful and smooth politician, appeared pallid and nondescript after the colorful, magnetic Jackson. Others, who blamed the depression which struck the country in 1837 on Jackson's banking policies, transferred their hostility to his successor. Northerners were alienated by the party's states' rights and proslavery orientations.

The atmosphere in the convention hall had all the excitement of a wake. Apathetically, the delegates went through the formality of accepting the recommendation of the nominating committee that Van Buren run for a second term. With equal lassitude they approved a stodgy, prosaic address which endorsed the program of the administration, approved the principle of states' rights, opposed federally sponsored internal improvements, a national bank, a protective tariff, and declared that the federal government should not interfere with slavery in the states.

Sparks began to fly, however, over the renomination of

the Vice-President, Colonel Richard M. Johnson of Kentucky, who had been Jackson's choice in 1836. An Indian fighter, a military hero, and a former senator, he was now opposed by the southern Democrats because reportedly he "openly and shamefully lives in adultery with a buxom young negro." After prolonged argument, the convention, unable to agree upon any one candidate from among the many favorite sons proposed, was compelled to accept Johnson.

So it was that the presidential contest of 1840 would be between the "Cincinnatus" from the West and the "red fox" or the "Little Magician" from the East. Martin Van Buren at fifty-eight was still at the height of physical and mental power. In background, experience, and intellect, he was undoubtedly superior to his opponent. With little formal education, he was admitted to the bar after six grueling years of apprenticeship in a law office and became a highly successful lawyer. His political activities won him a seat in the New York Senate, where he became head of the powerful political machine, the Albany Regency. Election to the United States Senate followed, then Governor of New York, Secretary of State, Vice-President, and finally President.

The career of William Henry Harrison, sixty-seven, was of a different caliber, and when nominated he was worn by years of frustration and adversity. Son of a governor of Virginia who had been a signer of the Declaration of Independence, he was a product of the southern aristocracy. After attending Hampden-Sydney College, where he was a student of the classics, he complied with his father's desire and went to Philadelphia to study medicine. But the profession had little appeal for him, and when his parent died he asked for and received a military commission from George Washington. He served on the Ohio frontier, then was appointed Secretary of the Northwest Territory, from which post he resigned on his election to Congress. After Indiana Territory was organized in 1800, he was appointed its governor, a post he held for twelve years. Heading the American forces, he won his heralded fame as the hero of

"Tippecanoe" in a battle fought against the Indians on November 7, 1811.

Returning to civilian life, Harrison represented his district in Congress for one session, then served in the Ohio State Senate for one term. Numerous efforts to obtain the governorship or return to Congress failed until in 1824 he was elected to the Senate. Four years later he resigned to accept the post of minister to Colombia, but his diplomatic service was of short duration. Within a year he was recalled because of complicity in a local insurrection. He was then fifty-six years old. An aging office seeker with a large family, he was compelled to accept the obscure job of Clerk of the Court of Common Pleas in Hamilton County, where he remained until the Whigs made him their standard-bearer.

In competing with Harrison, Van Buren's greatest handicap was opposing not a man but a legend. Men can be defeated, but to battle a myth is like tilting against a windmill. The Whigs sneered at Van Buren as a suave, aristocratic politician professing to lead a people's party. Unlike "King Mat," caricatured in a scurrilous "biography" as a fop "laced up in corsets, such as women in town wear," beruffled and perfumed, Old Tip dressed in the plain garb of the frontier:

> No ruffled shirt, no silken hose,
>   No airs does Tip display,
> But like the "pith of worth," he goes
>   In homespun "hodding gray."

The Whigs took a page from the Jacksonians and expanded it into a book. Parade banners were emblazoned with lifelike pictures of Harrison with his plow and team halted midway in the furrow. Cities and towns were plastered with picture posters of Harrison, plow in hand, standing in front of a log cabin. In one cartoon entitled, "The North Bend Farmer and His Visitors," Harrison is portrayed with one hand on his plow, the other extended in greeting to Van Buren and other members of the administration, saying, "Gentlemen you seem fatigued. If you will accept the fare of a log cabin, with a Western farmer's cheer, you are welcome. I have no champagne but can give you a mug of good cider, with some ham and eggs, and good clean beds. I am a plain backwoodsman. I have cleared some land, killed some Indians, and made the Red Coats fly in my time."

Voters were informed that George Washington had been a farmer and, as though they were being offered a new kind of soap, were urged to "try a Farmer this time," they would "never repent the change." Americans, one Whig editor wrote, were not "so enervated by luxury, as to forget their LOG CABIN origin," and Thurlow Weed solemnly declared, "The Log Cabin is a symbol of nothing that Van Burenism knows, feels, or can appreciate."

A meeting in Harrisburg, Pennsylvania, on January 20, choreographed by two clever strategists, Thomas Elder, a banker, and Richard Elliot, a newspaper editor, set the campaign pattern, which was to be duplicated in the remotest hamlet. On the stage they placed a transparency of a log cabin, nailed a coonskin to the wall, and set a woodpile and cider barrel nearby. When the audience saw this homely montage, they made the rafters ring with their delight and approval. Elder's contention that "passion and prejudice properly aroused would do about as well as principle and reason in a party contest" was to be confirmed.

The log cabin became ubiquitous. Campaign headquarters bore "log cabin" fronts; "log cabin cider" was generously dispensed at party rallies; "log cabin" song books were published and widely distributed; "log cabin" lithographs were used on the mastheads of Whig papers. The first campaign newspaper, edited by Horace Greeley, carried on its masthead the spellbinding words, *Log Cabin.*

The country was inundated with Whig souvenirs in every shape, manner, and form. There was the Harrison *Almanac* crammed with all sorts of "useful" advice and information, Harrison letter paper, the *Tippecanoe Textbook*, Tippecanoe Tobacco, Tippecanoe Shaving Soap, Log-Cabin Emollient, Harrison and Tyler neckties, handkerchiefs stamped with the face of General Harrison, Harrison badges, log-cabin buttons, a Harrison cane "surmounted by an oaken barrel, on one end of which were engraved the words 'Hard Cider,' and on the other 'Tippecanoe.'" Probably the most popular item was a whisky flask shaped like a miniature log cabin containing "Old Cabin Whisky." The liquor was made by the E. C. Booz Distillery, and so familiar did the containers become that the word "booze" reappeared as a popular substitute for whisky and eventually entered the American vocabulary.

Huge balls, intended to symbolize the gathering majority, were rolled from village to village and state to state by men and boys who sang as they went:

> What has caused this great commotion, motion, motion
> Our country through?
> It is the ball a-rolling on, for
>
> (Chorus)
> Tippecanoe and Tyler too—
> Tippecanoe and Tyler too.
>
> And with them we'll beat little Van, Van, Van,
> Oh! Van is a used-up man!

The Whig organization was superb. An executive committee composed of congressmen from various sections of the country served as the human nerve center of a massive structure, coordinating activities in the various states. A compilation was made of all the names on the mailing lists of Whig congressmen, and to each individual was sent such propaganda as "On the Regal Splendor of the President's Palace," a document giving the voters a choice of "Harrison and Prosperity or Van Buren and Ruin."

Equally efficient and hard-working were the organizations within each state. Presidential electors generally directed the campaign, issuing instructions to local leaders for establishing precinct committees, compiling polling lists, and preparing monthly reports from party workers concerning prospects in their local bailiwicks. Local Tippecanoe clubs mushroomed. In New York and Baltimore every ward had a club, as did many townships in rural areas. Louisiana claimed that there was a club in each parish in the state and that politics had "all but excluded the more prosaic pursuits of existence."

Special-interest groups such as immigrants and religious sects were not overlooked. While the Whig membership on the whole tended to be nativist, party leaders tried to win over the various nationalities, particularly the Germans. In New York, Philadelphia, Cincinnati, and Baltimore, German-language campaign papers were published and German-speaking Tippecanoe clubs established. The Mormons in Illinois were assiduously wooed. To appeal to Protestants, some Democratic leaders were attacked as heretics, while in areas where there were few Catholics rumors were spread that Van Buren was a Papist.

Emulating the Jacksonians, the Whigs made good use of the press. Inexpensive campaign sheets were published by state and county committees. Ohio had at least seventeen special campaign publications in addition to the regular pro-Whig newspapers, the latter packing their issues with partisan reports of political events. New papers were started everywhere. The most popular was Horace Greeley's *Log Cabin*, which was publishing 80,000 copies by the end of the campaign.

Stump oratory, which henceforth would become an indispensable adjunct of election contests, was ubiquitous. According to one partisan enthusiast, there were "five thousand or more speakers . . . 'on the stump' . . . from one end of the country to the other, their services everywhere and all the time in demand." Leaders of the party like Daniel Webster and Henry Clay traveled up and down the land. Aristocratic gentlemen from the South with courtly manners ventured North attired in linsey-woolsey and tried to adapt their speech to the idiom of the people. From the West came frontier politicians.

Never before had campaign funds been raised so systematically or spent so lavishly. The Whigs, with their core in commercial and industrial New England and conducting a campaign unprecedented in its popular appeal, had the best of both worlds in their solicitations. Wealthy entrepreneurs contributed generously while local organizations raised large sums from the general voters. No party activist was permitted to dodge his share of the financial burden. Each delegate to the Baltimore ratifying convention, for example, was assessed for the support of Whig journals. Methods varied according to local conditions. Thaddeus Stevens, who was in the iron manufacturing business, arranged for rebates from canal contractors to help subsidize the cost of campaign operations in Pennsylvania. Steamship and rail lines often gave reduced rates to passengers traveling to the various ratifying conventions. Many speakers paid their own way on the campaign trail, and even high-level leaders of the party dug deeply into their own pockets. Boss Thurlow Weed of New York saw to it that workers employed on public projects were assessed for party expenses—it was, after all, a people's crusade!

A perfect stick with which to beat the administration had been handed the Whigs in the form of a severe depression. Scarcely had Van Buren taken office when the economy came crashing down. Hundreds of business firms and banks failed, credit dried up, commodity prices declined, factories shut down, and unemployment soared. In New York City more than fifty thousand workers walked the streets vainly searching for jobs. Wages fell drastically but not the cost of living. Rioters in a number of cities demonstrated against flour speculators whose machinations kept up the price of bread.

While the Whigs, like most Americans, favored a laissez-faire approach by government, they did not hesitate to quote Van Buren's special message to Congress scolding those who were "prone to expect too much help from the Government" as an indication of his indifference to the people's woes. "Down with Martin Van Ruin!" became one of their battle cries, at the same time promising "two dollars a day and roast beef." They offered no program to carry out their pledge, relying on the usually effective device of blaming the party in power for any and all disasters.

The Democrats were denounced both as a vicious combination of "the wild aristocracy of the South" and "the equally wild mobocracy of the North." Younger Whigs preferred to call their opponents "Locofocos,"* which had a radical connotation as they represented the left wing of the Democratic party. The Locofoco elements came from the defunct Equal Rights Party—an outgrowth of the Workingman's Party of the late twenties—which had agitated for better conditions for the laborer, hard money, and the absolute separation of government funds from banking.

The campaign was fought not only in the press and on the stump but on the floor of Congress. No sooner had the twenty-sixth session opened than the House was involved in a fierce controversy over the seating of a contested delegation from New Jersey, each party claiming its members as the duly elected representatives. It took more than three weeks of disputation before a Speaker could be selected. Although the economy was still struggling to pull out of the mire of depression, and such vital issues as the banking system, internal improvements, public land policy, and the tariff required prompt consideration, not a statement was made or a move taken without calculating its effect on the prospects of Van Buren or Harrison.

All kinds of incidents became grist for the political mill. The President was blamed for failing to end the Seminole War and berated for permitting bloodhounds to be used against the Indians. The recommendation by the Secretary of War for a military draft of men between twenty and forty-five to strengthen defenses in the Southeast and on the Canadian border led to a denunciation of Van Buren for attempting to unite "the power of purse and sword." One congressman declared that it would enable the President to "take the crown and sceptre and announce to the world the

---

* The name originated at a New York party caucus in 1835 when the meeting was continued by the light of "locofoco matches" after the gas lights had been turned off by one faction in an effort to disrupt the meeting.

high sounding title of MARTIN *the 1st,* KING OF NORTH AMERICA."

Party spokesmen pressed for or opposed debt assumption and internal improvements and other public issues, but soon all policy questions were abandoned as they increasingly concentrated on slander and personal abuse of the two presidential candidates. Day after day the legislative chambers resounded with fanciful and extravagant charges that found a ready echo throughout the land. One such oratorical event was occasioned by an appropriation bill for the Cumberland Road. During discussions on the measure, Representative Isaac Crary of Michigan digressed to harangue for several hours on the dubious fighting qualities of General Harrison, sneering that he was only a synthetic hero.

The following day Tom Corwin, Whig Representative from Ohio, rose to reply. A clever speaker with a gift for satire, he had the House helpless with laughter as he mocked Crary in an imaginary adventure as a peacetime militia officer. "We can see the troops in motion; umbrellas, hoe and axe handles and other like deadly implements of war. . . . The general . . . mounted and equipped is in the field, and ready for action," Corwin related. Then a crisis occurs, a retreat is ordered, and "troops and general in a twinkling, are found safely bivouacked in a neighboring grocery!" The general whips out his "trenchant blade" and with "remorseless fury he slices the watermelons that lie in heaps around him. . . ." Published in Whig papers, reprinted and circulated in the thousands of copies, the address became one of the most important single pieces of propaganda. The derision of Crary was so effective that "the watermelon general," as he came to be called, was rejected in his bid for renomination.

For the next two months Congress and country wrangled over Tip's military reputation, the Democrats claiming that not he but Colonel George Groghan had been honored by citizens of Chillicothe as their defender against the Indians. "While a sword was in preparation for the victorious

Groghan," a senator declared, "a petticoat was contemplated . . . [for] Harrison." The "watermelon general" now had company in the "petticoat general."

After both sides exhausted the possibilities of this comic opera, they were ready for a new diversion. Representative Charles Ogle of Pennsylvania came to the rescue with a three-day discourse on "The Regal Splendor of the Presidential Palace." Reluctant as he was to talk about personal considerations, Ogle began, it was his duty to inform his fellow countrymen about the oriental splendor of the President's palace and the "pompous ceremonials" that took place at his "republican court." Thousands of the peoples' dollars had been wasted on effete landscaping "to gratify the taste of an exquisite." A number of hills were constructed "every pair of which . . . was designed to resemble . . . AN AMAZON'S BOSOM, with a miniature knoll or hillock on its apex, to denote the n--ple." For the house more than $20,000 had been spent for furniture. "What," Ogle demanded, "would the frugal and honest 'Hoosiers' think were they to behold a *democratic peacock*, in full court costume, strutting by the hour before golden-framed mirrors, NINE FEET HIGH and FOUR FEET and a HALF WIDE?" The President, he went on, ate from "*massive gold plate*" using "*French sterling silver services*," and the food was not those "old and unfashionable dishes" of fried meat and gravy, for these were regarded by "*gourmands, French cooks*, and *locofoco Presidents*" as exceedingly vulgar. Ogle rose to a climax with a declaration that he opposed an appropriation of some $3,000 for repairs of the White House because the money might be used to erect a throne and purchase, "a *crown, diadem, sceptre,* and *royal jewels*, with as little impropriety as former appropriations . . . have been expended," so that although the President did not have a royal title he would be invested "not only with its *prerogatives*, but with its *trappings*, also."

Ogle's venomous nonsense became another celebrated campaign text for the Whigs, who published it on the front pages of their papers. The contest for the highest office in the land had been reduced to the paltry dimensions of "log cabin" versus "palace," "hard cider" versus "champagne," the man of the people versus the aristocratic dandy. Soon a new ditty was added to those already current:

> Let Van from his coolers of silver drink wine
> And lounge on his cushioned settee,
> Our man on a buckeye bench can recline,
> Content with hard cider is he.

About a century before the era of the singing commercial, Whig strategists used rhymes set to music to help sell their product. For the first time, said one observer, "the power of song was invoked to aid a Presidential candidate." Harrison, said another, was "sung into the Presidency." Public meetings combined speechmaking with "music." "After a song or two," Greeley wrote to Weed, "[people] are more ready to listen to the orators." Aware also of the effect of repetition, the Whigs saturated the country with a plethora of songs having Tippecanoe in the title: "The Soldier of Tippecanoe," "The Flag of Tippecanoe," "Tippecanoe and Jackets of Blue," "A Tip-Top Song about Tippecanoe." The most popular of these masterpieces were collected by Greeley and published in the *Log Cabin Song Book*, which became the psalter of the campaign.

Democrats struggled to make themselves heard above this pervasive chorus. To counter "Tippecanoe" clubs they organized "Hickory" clubs and raised "Hickory" poles to compete with "Liberty" poles. Early in the campaign they decided to ignore the blasts against Van Buren and use the technique of attack. One paper charged Whiggery with being nothing better than disguised Federalism or "Federalism and abolition united," the mouthpiece for Daniel Webster despite the new "peoples' garb" and the popular accents affected. Their "stock in trade" was "false money, false doctrines, false speeches, false biographies, false rumors, and last not least, false heroes." A bid was made for the temperance vote by calling the Whigs' log cabins groggeries and claiming that their hard cider was frequently "diluted with whiskey." The methods and speeches of the Whigs indicated, their opponents contended, that they considered the voters ignorant, mindless barbarians willing "to sell their dear bought liberties for a holiday show or a mug of hard cider." Emulating the opposition, they tried their hand at rhymes:

> Hush-a-bye-baby;
> Daddy's a Whig,
> Before he comes home
> Hard cider he'll swig;
> Then he'll be Tipsy
> And over he'll fall;
> Down will come Daddy,
> Tip, Tyler and all.

To retaliate against the vituperation of Van Buren, the Democrats rumored that Harrison was a lecherous old man with a fondness for Indian squaws, that during his frontier days he had sired halfbreed Winnebagos, that he was given to profane language. They jeered that his much advertised "log cabin" was in reality a mansion, and that with his annual income of $6,000 he was "as rich as 'any man in this country.'" The story of the "petticoat general" was extensively circulated. One paper wrote that the General resigned his commission fully a year before the end of the War of 1812, thus abandoning his country "in the time of her utmost need." Another paper published in parallel columns Harrison's account of the battle at Fort Meigs as described in a campaign speech and the "official" version, which, of course, bore no resemblance to the other. So completely unfit for office was Harrison, alleged the Democrats, that he was not even permitted to answer his own letters; he "had passed into the hands" of a guardian without the formality of "a writ *de lunatico inquirendo*."

The charge of incompetency was made after Harrison decided to refer all his correspondence to a committee because his replies to questions, worded to suit the area and ideology of the correspondent, often fell into the wrong hands and were made public by his opponents. To a northern congressman, for example, he had written that the suggestion that he favored slavery was a vile slander, while to a Southerner he declared that he had "done and suffered more to support southern rights than any other person north of Mason & Dixon's line." He urged each correspondent to keep the opinions he expressed "confidential," heavily underscoring that word. Reprints of both letters were broadcast by Democratic papers with the comment that Harrison was an "abolitionist of the first water" in "all the New England states" and "a whole-hog slaveite" in the South.

Embarrassed and chagrined, Harrison thought it wise to follow the advice given him by Nicholas Biddle during his previous candidacy that he should "say not a single word about his principles, or his creed" and promise nothing, that not a single word should be extracted from him "about what he thinks now. . . . Let the use of pen and ink be wholly forbidden as if he were a mad poet in Bedlam." Accordingly, when a New York organization asked Harrison for his opinion on several issues, his correspondence committee replied that the General planned to "make no further declaration of his principles for the public eye," and as his views on all public questions had already been "fully and explicitly" presented, further elaboration was redundant.

But as the slander about his mental state seemed to be spreading, Harrison felt he could not remain silent. He broke with tradition and became the first presidential candidate to take off on the campaign trail. At the same time, he was so cautious that he might just as well have remained quietly in his "log cabin" as far as issues were concerned. In the twenty-three speeches he delivered, which ranged from one to three hours in length, Harrison related stories about his youth, about his experiences in fighting Indians, about his concern for his men when engaged in battle. In short, he performed like an after-dinner speaker at some convivial gathering. When on a few occasions he accidentally strayed onto an issue, he left his listeners more baffled than enlightened, straddling both sides of the fence in the same talk.

The Whig politicians continued to rely on drawing the voters into the chorus of "Van, Van, he's a used-up man," or

> Make way for Old Tip, turn out, turn out!
> Make way for Old Tip, turn out, turn out!
> 'Tis the peoples' decree,
> Their choice he shall be,
>   So Martin van Buren turn out, turn out!
>   So Martin van Buren turn out, turn out!

Democrats accused the Whigs of adding intimidation to their circuses of cider and log cabins in an effort to "persuade" the voter should entertainment fail. A paper in Albany wrote, "We understand that a Whig committee has been sent prowling around our city inquiring the politics of every workingman with the intention of throwing every Democrat out of employment." Workers in that city testified that they did lose their jobs for refusing to join in the singing of "Tippecanoe testimonials." Senator Thomas Hart Benton asserted that powerful businessmen in a position to "fix the market price" were attempting to coerce Democratic members of the business community. He cited newspaper advertisements which stated that merchandise would command higher prices if Harrison was elected.

While Democratic leaders were less frenetic than their opponents and at least made a gesture toward reasoned arguments in their addresses, the rank and file were as emotionally wrought up as were the Whig masses. Campaign rallies of both parties were frequently disrupted by groups hurling tomatoes, potatoes, or even rocks at the speaker, sometimes also shooting off pistols in the air. Newspaper editors were beaten, and one was caned to death. Whig speakers made wild threats to employ force should their party lose the election. Weed was told emphatically by a Michigan Whig leader that if Harrison were defeated the election would be "the last peaceable contest. . . . We must in that event either submit to the tyrant contemptible and vile as he is, or resort to a mode of redress in which implements of a very different character from the ballot box will be wanted." Even the sober John Quincy Adams feared civil war, and a council of Catholic bishops was moved to issue a call against the use of violence. As one commentator observed, "Men's minds are wrought up to a pitch of frenzy, and like tinder a spark of opposition sets them on fire. Riot and violence stalk unchecked through the streets, and lying is no longer considered a crime."

With the nation as tense as a bowstring, and mechanics of voting which encouraged bribery, intimidation, and other varieties of fraud,* a turbulent election day was anticipated. The Whigs left little to chance. As balloting time approached, the executive committee communicated with the central committee in each county to give last-minute instructions. Party workers were asked to secure polling lists for each district and check off each voter as "good, bad, or doubtful." Doubtful voters should be visited and the virtues of Whiggery impressed upon them. The need to make every effort to get out the vote was stressed. Transportation should be provided to take old people and invalids to the polling places—a familiar feature today but novel at the time.

Predictions that the vote would be unprecedentedly large turned out to be accurate—nearly eighty per cent of the eligible voters cast ballots, far exceeding the earlier high in 1828 of fifty-six per cent. In part the increase was due to the extension of the suffrage. Only in four states was a voter still required to give evidence that he owned property. In only one, South Carolina, which had abolished both the tax and property qualifications for suffrage, did the legislature rather than the people choose the presidential electors.

Of the 2,400,000 votes cast, Harrison received 1,269,763. The victor had a popular majority of less than 150,000

* The ballot was still open, and, as each party now printed its own in different colors, counterfeits in the color of one but containing the names of rival candidates were not uncommon.

votes, though he won nineteen of the twenty-six states in the electoral college, or 234 to 60 electoral votes. Democrats wailed that a shift of no more than 9,000 votes in the right states would have altered the verdict in their favor. In Maine, for example, Harrison won by only 211 votes and in Pennsylvania by only 349 out of a total of almost 300,000.

Nevertheless, the Whig candidate did score a decisive victory. While mathematical juggling might offer some consolation for the defeated party and a subject for parlor conversation, the fact remained that the Whigs had garnered fifty-three per cent of the total vote. The Whigs won popular majorities and carried most of the counties in five of the seven geographical areas in the country. They cut sharply into areas which had been Democratic territory four years earlier and elsewhere greatly increased their strength. In Connecticut, Delaware, Rhode Island, and Vermont, they made a clean sweep of every county, winning 173 counties that had voted Democratic in 1836. The Democrats lost New York and Pennsylvania for the first time since popular voting had been introduced there. Their victories were mostly in the South, but even there they won only in Alabama, Arkansas, Virginia, and North and South Carolina, and in the first three states their margin was reduced almost to the vanishing point, a sharp contrast with earlier elections.

A scathing comment on the campaign and a summation of the popular stake in the result of the election was made by the Philadelphia *Ledger*. "For the two years past the most ordinary operations of business have been neglected and President-making has become every citizen's chief concern." Since the result was unpredictable, many were afraid to start new enterprises, others retired from business, and still others did not carry on with the old vigor. "Millions of dollars will now change hands on election bets. . . . Millions of days have been taken from useful labor to listen to stump orators, and millions more to build log cabins, erect hickory poles and march in ridiculous, degrading, mob-creating processions." Whatever high hopes were inspired by the election of Harrison, the newspaper went on, they will prove delusive. "A national bank cannot be created; a sub-treasury cannot be repealed; the monetary expansion and speculation which the hope of these measures will create will be quickly followed by contraction, by ruin and the prostration of the speculators."

The triumphant Whigs naturally sang a different tune. "The people are free again," one paper caroled. "Our republican institutions are redeemed from the grasp of tyrants. Let the people . . . rejoice." To which the official organ of the Democratic party replied bitterly that the vast increase in votes had been accomplished by "a new species of voters —mercenaries—hired, bribed and purchased wretches which the corruption fund has secured for the Whig ticket. . . . It is the first instance in our Republic of the triumph of the power of money over the intelligence of the country." With considerable accuracy another journal commented, "We've been sung down, lied down, drunk down," while still another hoped that the "buffoonery of 1840" would never again be repeated, that this would be the last time when "coons, cabins, and cider" would "usurp the place of principles, nor doggerel verse elicit a shout, while argument, principle and reason are passed by with a derisive sneer."

The liberal use of symbolic themes and of slogans as a substitute for a discussion of the issues, a consequence of universal suffrage, became characteristics of later campaigns. In its appeal to the emotions of the electorate, in its emphasis on the personality of the candidates, in the employment of gimmickry and ballyhoo, the election of 1840 was a prototype of all future presidential contests.

5. "The Taste Is in My Mouth . . ."

THE manner in which the Whigs had conducted their campaign gave no indication that a virulently divisive sectionalism had begun to penetrate the very marrow of the nation's body politic. Conflicts of sectional interest were not a new phenomenon—they could be found as far back as the colonial era—but the one which was now burgeoning would eventually sunder the nation. As the breach steadily widened, the existing parties were to prove fatally inadequate to cope with the transcendent issue of slavery.

The Mason-Dixon line marked a division of two ways of life, two economic systems, two views of the nature of the federal Union. For many years the North and the South had supported opposing positions on the tariff, internal improvements, and extension of the central government's powers. Their rivalry became serious during the nullification crisis of 1832, but it was the institution of slavery that ultimately created an unbridgeable gulf.

In 1846, lines were drawn in Congress over the status of slavery in the territory expected to be acquired as a result of the war with Mexico. For the next four years, government was virtually paralyzed as the "free-soilers," both Whig and Democrat, insisted that slavery be excluded, while southern Whigs and Democrats demanded that it be permitted. The latter contended that, since the territories were owned by all the states, citizens had the right to take their slaves there.

Senator Lewis Cass of Michigan proposed a compromise: let the people within the territory decide by majority vote whether they would have slavery. Northern free-soilers rejected this "popular" or "squatter" sovereignty doctrine, as it came to be called, and for the first time Southerners began to talk ominously about secession. When Congress met in December 1849, the charged atmosphere made a compromise solution imperative. Early the following year, Henry Clay proposed an elaborate formula: California was to be admitted as a free state; the remainder of the Mexican cession was to be organized into two territories, New Mexico and Utah, where the principle of popular sovereignty was to apply; the slave trade was to be abolished in the District of Columbia; and a new and much stronger fugitive slave law enacted.

Clay's proposal occasioned one of the great Senate debates of the era. After some dazzling oratory and deft maneuvering, the omnibus measure was enacted into law, providing an uneasy and temporary truce. The Georgia legislature immediately adopted a resolution that if the Fugitive Slave Law were not strictly enforced the state would withdraw from the Union, while in the North the measure was greeted by a tremendous uproar among abolitionists and other humanitarians.

Nevertheless, the attitude that the preservation of the Union was more important than all other considerations still predominated. That the majority of the country supported the compromise settlement seems evident from the results of the election of 1852. The Whigs, mildly supporting the compromise, nominated General Winfield Scott, whose views were unknown but whose support by Northerners made him suspect in the South. The Democrats pledged unequivocal support of the compromise and firmly declared their opposition to renewed discussion of the slavery question. Their candidate, Franklin Pierce of New Hampshire, a "dark horse," had served without particular distinction in both Houses of Congress. As he retired before the sectional conflict had become critical, his views were unknown. Pierce won with the largest electoral vote in three decades—only four states went to his opponent—and his popular vote was equally impressive.

The defeat was all but fatal to the Whigs, who already had been badly split between the "cotton Whigs" and the "conscience Whigs," and they never nominated another candidate. During the next few years the party disintegrated. Among the Democrats, northern and southern politicians attempted to smooth out their differences, but Pierce's administration was a prelude to disaster.

The smoldering embers began to glow, fanned by the Kansas-Nebraska Act. Introduced and pushed through the 1854 session of Congress by Senator Stephen A. Douglas of Illinois, the measure provided that the region west of the bend of the Missouri be divided into two territories, Kansas and Nebraska, in both of which the inhabitants could accept or reject slavery. Since this area was situated above the 36° 30' latitude where, according to the Missouri Compromise, slavery was barred, the Kansas-Nebraska Act in effect repealed that compromise enforced since 1820. A bitter controversy ensued, with Northerners denouncing the act as a "gross violation of a sacred pledge" and a "monstrous plot" to benefit the southern slaveholders.

That fall, Douglas came to Illinois to justify his bill. Abraham Lincoln, who was practising law at the time, spoke out strongly in opposition. His speech, afterwards known as the Peoria Address, was his first major denunciation of slavery. He opposed the Kansas-Nebraska Act, he said, because it would permit the spread of slavery, which intrinsically was a "monstrous injustice." He wished to distinguish between the constitutional right of Southerners to own slaves and the extension of slavery into new territories. The question revolved around whether or not the Negro was to be regarded as a man in considering the principle of self-government. "If he is *not* a man, why in that case he who *is* a man may, as a matter of self-government, do just as he pleases with him." But if he is a man, is not self-government destroyed if he is not permitted to govern himself? When the white man rules himself and also another man,

Lincoln declared, it is despotism. His ancient faith taught him that all men were created equal and there could be "no moral right in connection with one man's making a slave of another."

As soon as the disputed territory was opened for settlement, immigrants began to pour into Kansas from North and South, many as legitimate settlers but some simply to press their particular ideology. Two separate governments were created, one proslavery and one antislavery, each claiming to be duly constituted. The upshot was violent clashes that left about two hundred dead. "Bleeding Kansas" became a symbol of the sectional conflict and another portent of the debacle to come.

The violence in the territory infected the legislative chambers. Language became rude and intemperate. Members came to Congress armed with pistols which were sometimes drawn in the heat of argument, or they turned the session into a fist-swinging brawl. One incident ended in a personal catastrophe. Senator Charles Sumner of Massachusetts, in an address he called "The Crime Against Kansas," made some sneering and abusive remarks about southern leaders, especially Senator Andrew Butler of South Carolina. Two days later, while Sumner was seated at his desk in the Senate, Butler's enraged nephew, Congressman Preston Brooks, attacked him with a cane, beating him into unconsciousness and inflicting such severe injuries that he was an invalid for years.

A competent President exercising firm leadership might have stablized the situation in Kansas. Pierce tried feebly to check the turbulence, but his own outlook made his efforts futile. Swayed by southern influence, he not only denounced the free territorial government as unlawful and treasonable but supported the proslavery government established by fraud—over 6,000 votes were counted, and there were less than a third that number of legal voters in the territory.

With the North hostile to Pierce, the Democrats considered it foolhardy to renominate him in 1856. They turned to

James Buchanan, who had been out of the country as Minister to Great Britain and was therefore uninvolved in the
slavery controversy. The "conscience" Whigs of the North,
to oppose the further extension of slavery, organized the
Republican party, selecting as their candidate the nationally famous "Pathfinder," John C. Frémont. The remaining
Whigs merged with the American or "Know-Nothing"
party, organized about ten years earlier to combat what
they regarded as the "alien menace." This party's candidate
was Millard Fillmore, who had served two years in the
White House after President Zachary Taylor's sudden death
in 1850.

Despite a frenzied campaign for "Free Soil, Free Speech
and Frémont" and charges that the Democratic candidate
was a tool of the South, Buchanan was victorious, with 174
electoral votes to 114 for Frémont and 8 for Fillmore. While
the Democrats had considerable strength throughout the
country, they would have been defeated without the almost
solid block of southern states, making the party in effect a
captive of the South.

By this time it is doubtful whether even the most brilliant
President—which Buchanan was not—could have brought
the slavery controversy under control. As it was, the President was pitifully inadequate at the most critical period in
the nation's history. He recommended the admission of
Kansas to statehood under the proslavery Lecompton
Constitution, further widening the rift in the Democratic
party.

The Dred Scott decision by the Supreme Court in 1857
added another inflammatory faggot. Negro plaintiffs were
denied the right to sue in a federal court because as slaves
they were not citizens. Moreover, they were declared to be
property and as such could be taken by their masters into
any of the territories. By thus making the Missouri Compromise unconstitutional, the Court not only gave judicial
sanction to what had already been accomplished by the
Kansas-Nebraska Act but went further. Henceforth, it
would be impossible for residents of the territory to ban

slavery even if they wished to do so. Most serious of all, the Court's ruling virtually precluded an attempt by Congress to compromise the issue.

The following year in the senatorial contest in Illinois, the subject was hotly debated, with repercussions that were to extend far beyond the state. Contending for the seat were Abraham Lincoln, the Republican nominee, and the incumbent, Stephen A. Douglas. At his party's state convention, Lincoln had delivered a carefully prepared speech in which his position on slavery was the most radical he had ever expressed. After four years of the Kansas-Nebraska Act, which, he said, had been intended to end the antislavery agitation, the situation had only deteriorated. " 'A house divided against itself cannot stand.' I believe this government cannot endure permanently half *slave* and half *free.*"

For the first time Lincoln joined the more extreme northern antislavery elements in supporting their so-called conspiracy theory that Supreme Court justices, congressmen, and the President himself were plotting to extend slavery. He now also questioned the means by which slavery had become entrenched in the South. The role of Douglas in the repeal of the Missouri Compromise, the requests by Presidents Pierce and Buchanan that the nation accept the Supreme Court decision curbing Congress's power over slavery in the territories, the Supreme Court decision itself —all, he said, were manifestations of a calculated plan. It only remained for the Court to declare that slavery could not be excluded from any state, an inevitable next step unless the political forces now in power in Washington were removed.

Senator Douglas saw Lincoln's candidacy as a formidable hurdle in his battle for political survival. He had to contend against the Buchanan administration, which was so antagonistic to him that it backed its own men against Douglas supporters in nearly every legislative district in the state. "I shall have my hands full," Douglas commented when told of Lincoln's nomination. "He is the strong man of his party—full of wit, facts, dates—and the best stump speaker, with his droll ways and dry jokes, in the West."

At the same time, Lincoln was pitted against a powerful opponent. Stephen Douglas was a seasoned campaigner whose speeches, delivered with clarity and force, were usually masterpieces of logic. He was not only immensely popular with the voters of his state but had a national reputation. Speaking at an outdoor rally in Springfield, where he launched his campaign, he drew thousands of people, who remained through a torrential downpour, their enthusiasm "impossible to describe," as one partisan paper reported. He was frequently interrupted by mammoth cheers and thunderous applause as he refuted Lincoln and explained his own position. "If Mr. Lincoln deems me a conspirator . . . all I have to say is that I do not think so badly of the President of the United States and the Supreme Court . . . as to believe that they are capable . . . of entering into political intrigues for partisan purposes." He insisted, as often before, that slavery could not exist in any territory unless it was supported by local laws and opinion, regardless of the Dred Scott decision. Popular sovereignty, he maintained, favored both North and South equally.

Republican strategists had planned for Lincoln to follow on the heels of Douglas, speaking in the same town on the same day. But when the Democratic press scoffed that Lincoln could obtain crowds only in this way, his managers suggested that he challenge his adversary to a series of debates. Douglas, approached by Lincoln's campaign manager, hesitated. "Between you and me, I do not feel that I want to go into this debate," Douglas confessed to his party managers. "The whole country knows me and has me measured. Lincoln, as regards myself, is comparatively unknown, and if he gets the best of this debate . . . I shall lose everything. Should I win, I shall gain but little." Nevertheless, he felt that he had no choice, and arrangements were made for seven debates.

The direct confrontation between the two candidates highlighted the contrast between them. The "Little Giant"

was short, handsome, wealthy, sophisticated, world-re-
nowned. His clothes were impeccable, and the white wide-
brimmed felt hat he wore was spotless. Lincoln, craggy-fea-
tured, unusually tall, lank and ungainly, with his neck
emerging "long and sinewy from a white collar turned
down over a thick, black necktie," wore "a somewhat battered stovepipe hat . . . a rusty black dress coat that should
have been longer," from whose sleeves his long arms extended several inches beyond the cuffs. "On his left arm he
carried a gray woolen shawl, which evidently served him
for an overcoat in chilly weather"; in his left hand he held a
cotton umbrella and a well-worn black satchel. Carl Schurz,
a Republican leader who thus described him, remarked that
he had seen in Washington "several public men of rough
appearance, but none whose looks seemed quite so un-
couth, not to say grotesque, as Lincoln's."

Similarly a study in contrast was the mode of travel of
the two men. Douglas had a private railroad car richly car-
peted in red, where he was served the finest food. On arrival at his destination, he was escorted to the meeting
place in a fine carriage drawn by six horses, sometimes accompanied by a military escort. Lincoln rode a dusty day
coach, sometimes on the same train as Douglas; when he
arrived, he generally walked alone to his hotel.

The Lincoln-Douglas debates were the high point of the
campaign. Special excursion rates for the entire series offered by the railroads drew people from great distances. For
the first one, scheduled on August 21 at Ottawa, the Democrats kept their arrangements secret. Douglas traveled by
river steamer to La Salle on Thursday night, remained privately closeted in Peru all day Friday, and made a triumphal entry into Ottawa on Saturday by special train. He
rode into town in a resplendent carriage driven by four
superb horses, to be greeted by a boisterous throng
headed by a band. A short while later the Republican train
carrying seventeen cars and its band arrived, whereupon
the opposing musicians began blasting away defiantly at
each other. For a whole day prior to the debate the sur-

rounding countryside was in a festive mood. Normal activities were virtually suspended. A pine wood platform was erected in the public square, into which about twelve thousand people crowded, sitting or sprawling on the grass.

It was impossible to learn from the press who was victorious in the first round, for newspaper reports were colored by partisan prejudices. Douglas papers declared that their hero's strong and unanswerable arguments had left Lincoln so weak that he had to be carried off the platform; Lincoln papers wrote that Douglas was left utterly crushed and his followers gloomy.

The second debate, at Freeport, drew a crowd estimated at 15,000 despite inclement weather. Lincoln put four questions to his rival, one of which, and the reply, was to assume historic significance: If slavery could not legally be barred from the territories, then how could it be excluded by the people of a territory under popular sovereignty? Douglas had stated his position before, but Lincoln's intent was to pin him down in a public statement that the South could not ignore. His response, which became known as the Freeport Doctrine, was that "the people of a Territory can by lawful means . . . prior to the formation of . . . a State Constitution . . ." exclude slavery. "It matters not what the Supreme Court may hereafter decide as to the abstract question" since "slavery cannot exist a day or an hour anywhere unless it is supported by local police regulations." While the reply satisfied the free-soilers, it further antagonized Buchanan and the southern Democrats. Douglas was in the untenable position of trying to drive a team of horses in two directions at the same time.

Throughout the debates Douglas repeatedly charged that Lincoln and his party were "Black Republicans" who favored racial equality. Pressed hard on one occasion, Lincoln stated that he had never favored allowing Negroes to vote, hold office, serve on juries, or intermarry; that "a physical difference" between the races would always prevent them from being social and political equals. While they lived side by side, he concluded, "there must be the position of superior and inferior, and I as much as any other man am in favor of having the superior position assigned to the white race."

Actually, as the debates revealed, Lincoln and Douglas were not far apart in their positions. Both deplored the explosive fury of sectionalism and wished to douse the fires of slavery agitation; neither desired an extension of slavery, and both fervently wished to preserve the Union. The basic difference was in their philosophical approach toward slavery. Lincoln abhorred the vicious system and believed that men of good will must inevitably oppose it, while Douglas was indifferent to its moral aspects, merely hoping that the agitation could be checked. "The real issue in this controversy," Lincoln asserted in the final debate of the series, "is the sentiment on the part of one class that looks upon the institution of slavery *as a wrong,* and of another class that *does not* look upon it as a wrong."

The Illinois system of apportionment, unduly weighted in favor of the Democrats, defeated Lincoln.* Although the Republicans received a majority of the total vote, they obtained only forty-six legislative seats as compared to fifty-four for their opponents. Douglas, however, won a pyrrhic victory, for his "Freeport Heresy," as the South called his Doctrine, cost him the support of his party in the South and thereby the White House two years later. As he had feared, his adversary profited from the publicity. Lincoln was boosted to national prominence. With considerable skill he had presented a moderate position and yet one which satisfied the Republican abolitionists. Moreover, by showing that he could better than hold his own with the famed Douglas, he demonstrated his qualifications for political leadership.

As soon as the senatorial contest was over, small-town Republican papers in Illinois and other western cities carried the masthead, "LINCOLN FOR PRESIDENT, 1860!!!" Although Lincoln was pleased, he did not as yet see himself

---

* At this time, senators were chosen by the state legislatures.

competing against the distinguished would-be contenders
for the White House. The outstanding aspirant was William
Seward, acknowledged party leader. Also highly regarded
were Salmon P. Chase of Ohio, twice governor and once a
United States senator, Edward Bates of Missouri, Simon
Cameron of Pennsylvania, and Justice of the Supreme
Court John McLean. Lincoln's primary interest now was to
build up the Republican party in Illinois and try again for
Douglas's seat in 1864.

During the following months Lincoln carried on a voluminous correspondence with political leaders throughout
the country, urging a policy of moderation. If the party was
to win in 1860, he maintained, it must avoid radical and
unpopular doctrines. "The point of danger is the temptation
in different localities to 'platform' for something which will
be popular just there," he wrote to Schuyler Colfax, a power
in Indiana politics, "but which nevertheless will be a fire-
brand elsewhere and especially in a national convention."
He cited as examples an antialien approach in Massachusetts, making obedience to the fugitive slave law in New
Hampshire punishable as a crime, repeal of the fugitive
slave law in Ohio, and squatter sovereignty in Kansas. "In
these things there is explosive enough to blow up half a
dozen national conventions. . . . In a word, in every locality,
we should . . . say nothing on points where it is probable we
shall disagree."

The crucial states in the forthcoming election were Indiana, Illinois, Pennsylvania, and New Jersey. Had the Republicans carried them in the previous presidential contest,
they would have won. The states were split on the slavery
issue, however, and Frémont, as an antislavery candidate,
had carried the northern counties of the first three but lost
the southern to Buchanan. Seward and Chase were on
record as firmly opposed to slavery. Lincoln, more moderate
than either, with the added advantage of being "sound" on
the tariff, an important issue in Pennsylvania and New Jersey, and a forceful speaker with a national reputation,
seemed a strong presidential possibility to the veteran Illi-

nois Republican State Chairman, Norman B. Judd. The shrewd politician became Lincoln's major promoter. As part of his initial strategy, he went East when the national Republican leaders met to decide on a convention site, and succeeded in having Chicago designated instead of St. Louis, which the majority favored.

Gradually, Lincoln permitted himself to accept the thought that he might possibly reach for the nomination. Twice in 1859 he mentioned that he was not qualified for the highest office, but early the following year he wrote Senator Lyman Trumbull, "As you request, I will be entirely frank. The taste *is* in my mouth a little." Still, foremost in his mind was the senatorial contest, for in February he appealed to Judd, "I am not in a position where it would hurt much for me not to be nominated on the national ticket, but I am where it would hurt some for me not to get the Illinois delegates."

Invitations to speak poured in from the East as well as his own Northwest. Lincoln traveled 4,000 miles to deliver twenty-three political addresses. The speech he gave at Cooper Union in New York on February 27, 1860, proved to be a milestone in his career, introducing him as a presidential possibility to the East. Lincoln had been asked by the Young Men's Republican Union ostensibly to give one in a series of popular political lectures, but those responsible for the invitation had another motive. On the advisory board of the organization were a number of former free-soil supporters such as William Cullen Bryant, the New York *Evening Post* editor, and Horace Greeley of the New York *Tribune*, who were determined to thwart William Seward's aspirations.

Despite a heavy snowstorm, an overflow crowd of 1,500 people jammed the hall, the largest gathering "of the intellect and culture of our city" since the time of Webster and Clay, according to Greeley. To this elite audience, Lincoln delivered a talk which was a masterpiece of moderation. He began by pointing out that the Founding Fathers understood that "no proper division of local from federal authority, nor any part of the Constitution, forbade the Federal Government to control slavery in the federal territories." The South, he said, had rejected constitutional policies, while the Republicans insisted upon adhering to them, but the party was not sectional or revolutionary. He condemned the insurrection of John Brown at Harper's Ferry and emphasized that not a single Republican had been involved. The whole controversy turned, he said, on the South's thinking slavery right and the North thinking it wrong, and "thinking it wrong, as we do, can we yield to them . . . in view of our moral, social, and political responsibilities?" Still, he declared, "wrong as we think slavery is, we can yet afford to leave it alone where it is. . . ." His concluding sentences brought the audience to its feet in a long, resounding ovation. "Neither let us be slandered from our duty by false accusations against us, nor frightened from it by menaces of destruction to the Government nor of dudgeons to ourselves. *Let us have faith that right makes might, and in that faith let us, to the end, dare to do our duty as we understand it.*" Men rushed up to shake the speaker's hand and congratulate him.

The following day, four leading New York papers printed the full text of the speech, accompanied by glowing editorial praise. The Chicago *Tribune* issued it in pamphlet form. Illinois politicians were jubilant at the response. They were also pleased that Lincoln had abandoned his "house divided" approach for "live and let live" as long as the South agreed not to extend slavery.

During the following weeks, Judd intensified his activities to insure solid backing for Lincoln by the Illinois delegation. Increasingly he was convinced that the other three doubtful states could be won over if Lincoln had his delegation behind him. In April he wrote confidentially to Senator Lyman Trumbull inquiring whether a "quiet combination" could not be brought about between the delegates from New Jersey, Indiana, Illinois, and Pennsylvania. United action, he said, would probably control the convention. "Nothing but a positive position will prevent Seward's nomination."

At the Illinois convention which met at Decatur on May 9, the "Rail Splitter" legend was born. While Lincoln was delivering a speech, he was interrupted by an elderly cousin who marched in carrying two timeworn fence rails, between which, bedecked with flags and streamers, was a banner reading, "ABRAHAM LINCOLN FOR PRESIDENT: The Rail Candidate for President in 1860," and that these were two rails from a lot of 3,000 which Lincoln and a relative had cut thirty years before. The audience, almost entirely composed of Lincoln supporters, went wild, whooping and cheering until part of the roof literally came down.

Lincoln was endorsed as the Illinois Republicans' first choice for the Presidency and their "favorite son." To insure against any defections, the committee appointed to select delegates to the national convention together with "other friends of Lincoln . . . retired . . . and, in a grove near by lay down upon the grass and revised the list of delegates, which they reported to, and which were appointed by, the convention."

A small group of Lincoln's supporters began to lay careful plans for the national convention. Four days before the opening session they set up headquarters in Tremont House, finest of all the city's hotels. In seeking to put Lincoln into the White House they were not pursuing a chimerical goal. While he would have to pit himself against a gaggle of candidates, he had the advantage of not being labeled either as a conservative or a radical in his party. The Republicans were a conglomeration of former "conscience" Whigs and Whigs indifferent to the slavery question, former free-soil Democrats and Democrats who had left their party for other reasons, nativists, abolitionists, advocates of a protective tariff, internal improvements and free land, champions of a Pacific railroad, and all others who for one reason or another were bound by a mutual hostility to the party of Pierce, Buchanan, and Douglas. And the widening rift among the Democrats immeasurably enhanced Republican prospects.

In mid-May, 466 delegates, thousands of observers, and

an impressive number of newspaper correspondents converged on Chicago. Those who had planned the Wigwam,
the large frame structure specially erected for the convention and designed to hold 10,000, had underestimated the
size of the crowd which would attend. In the city's forty-
two hotels perspiring managers were squeezing cots into
any available space. Liquor flowed freely, contributing to
the festive atmosphere, but behind the scenes, candidates
were being promoted with cool deliberation.

One of the most powerful of the king-makers was the
veteran New York politician, Thurlow Weed, who was
backing Seward. An observer reported that he had brought
with him a whole crew of New York politicians who
"marched in street parades with brass bands and Seward
banners to produce the impression that the whole country
was ablaze with enthusiasm for Seward." They lavished
champagne and cigars on the other delegates, spending
money freely, and "let everybody understand that there
was a great deal more to spend." Weed moved about "with
ceaseless activity . . . receiving . . . reports and giving new
instructions . . . now and then taking one into a corner of
the room for a secret talk, or disappearing with another
through a side door for transactions still more secret."

Seward unquestionably was the strongest contender. His
state had the largest delegation and the largest vote in the
electoral college. He was noted as a fearless opponent of the
slave power, he had championed a protective tariff and free
homesteads for western settlers, and his campaign was
managed by the nation's most efficient political tacticians.
Moreover, he projected an image of statesmanship.

The strategy of Lincoln and his managers was to mobilize
a "stop Seward" movement by winning over the delegations
of the doubtful states. Assured only of 22 votes from Illinois, Lincoln as a favorite son might well be eliminated
after the first ballot unless he increased his support. Pennsylvania, New Jersey, and Indiana must be persuaded that
nominating Seward would be futile since he could not carry
those states in the election. The argument was that, as the

symbol of the radical antislavery cause, the expositor of the
"higher law" concept, and the originator of the phrase "ir-
repressible conflict," Seward had alienated many moderates
whose support was essential.

On the eve of the convention, Lincoln arranged for his
manager, Judge David Davis, to meet with the Indiana delegation. Davis found it about equally divided for Edward
Bates of Missouri and Justice John McLean. He promised
that if Lincoln received the nomination and won the Presidency, the posts of Secretary of Interior and Commissioner
of Indian Affairs would go to two of their men, one of
whom was Caleb Smith, leader of an important faction.
Through Smith's efforts, Indiana's 26 votes were secured for
Lincoln.

A similar deal was concluded with Pennsylvania, which
had 54 delegates. Simon Cameron, the state's favorite son,
was making little headway in winning support. Davis,
learning that his backers would switch their votes if he
were promised the post of Secretary of the Treasury, wired
Lincoln. The reply came back quickly: "I authorize no bargains and will be bound by none." Davis knew, however,
that Lincoln was too shrewd a politician to shackle his
aides; more likely, he was responding merely for the record.
Davis ignored the wire. Lincoln, who knew that without
serious horse trading he could not possibly win, undoubtedly felt that he could rely on his manager to interpret his
message correctly. He could also depend on the sound judgment of Stephen Logan, another worker at the convention,
whom he had authorized to remove his name from the lists
should retreat be considered necessary. With two such directives, he astutely safeguarded himself against any potential charge of corrupt bargains. If his managers disregarded
his instructions, he would have a betting chance for the
nomination; if they obeyed his orders, he would at least
receive 22 votes from Illinois on the first ballot and be the
State's choice for senator in 1864.

The Pennsylvania delegation agreed to support Cameron
on the first ballot, McLean on the second, and Lincoln on

the third. As the first two represented only courteous gestures, a virtual commitment had been made to Lincoln. The New Jersey delegation, at a midnight caucus, was also persuaded to vote for Lincoln after a complimentary vote for its favorite son. Thus four pivotal states had been nailed down.

Mulling about how to keep the Seward claque out of the Wigwam, one member suggested having a large supply of extra tickets printed and distributed among Lincoln supporters with instructions to arrive early at the hall. The next day numerous Sewardites with legitimate tickets found themselves barred from entering, for, while they had been happily parading, their adversaries made good use of their bogus pasteboards.

Consideration of a party platform preceded the nominations. Sniffing the scent of victory, most delegates opposed either an endorsement of popular sovereignty or a commitment to the free-soil doctrine as expressed in the 1856 platform. They finally decided to straddle the positions. Freedom was declared to be the normal condition in the territories and legislation was advocated to deal with specific violations. Deliberately ignored were such impelling issues as the Fugitive Slave Law, abolition of slavery in the District of Columbia, and admission of additional slave states. Other planks endorsed federally supported internal improvements, a transcontinental railroad, a free-homestead law for western settlers, and a moderate protective tariff. Practically no important group interest in the sections outside the South was overlooked. The entire document was carefully worded to avoid having the Republicans labeled as a crusading party and to dispel the possible impression that they were committed to a single issue or group.

The nominating speeches which followed, unlike the long-winded addresses of a later day, were brief: twenty-six words placed the name of Seward before the convention, twenty-seven did the same for Lincoln, and, in rapid-fire succession, the other aspirants were named. But the re-

sponse sounds familiar. An observer reports that "no
language" can describe the "wild yell" of the Lincoln supporters when he was nominated. "A thousand steam whistles, ten acres of hotel gongs, a tribe of Comanches, headed
by a choice vanguard from pandemonium, might have mingled in the scene unnoticed." After he was seconded, to an
"absolutely terrific" ovation, reported a contemporary journalist, "It now became the Seward men to make another
effort. . . . The effect was startling. Hundreds of persons
stopped their ears in pain . . . no panthers ever struck a
higher note, or gave screams with more infernal intensity."
Looking out at the audience from the stage, he could see
nothing but "thousands of hats—a black, mighty swarm of
hats—flying with the velocity of hornets over a mass of
human heads." Once more it was the turn of the Lincoln
men. Columbus Delano of Ohio added another second to
Lincoln's nomination, provoking an uproar that "was beyond description. Imagine all the hogs ever slaughtered in
Cincinnati giving their death squeals together. . . . I
thought the Seward yell could not be surpassed; but the
Lincoln boys were clearly ahead."

As the balloting began, Seward was far in the lead, having arrived in Chicago with pledges of more than 150 votes
as against 22 for Lincoln. On the first roll call he led with
173½. Lincoln polled 102, Cameron 50½, Chase 49, Bates
48, and the remaining 42 were scattered. The second ballot
dashed Seward's hopes for a quick victory when he picked
up only 11 votes and Lincoln 79, putting the latter only 3½
votes behind the man who for years had been the acknowledged leader of his party. Pennsylvania had dropped
Cameron and gave 2½ of its votes to Seward, 2½ to
McLean, and 48 to Lincoln.

To obtain the required majority of 233, both contenders
had to draw on the votes dispersed among the minor candidates, of which 53 represented, on the whole, the sentiments of conservatives or practical Republicans who
considered Seward too radical or controversial on slavery.
Chase's 42½ votes were drawn largely from abolitionists,

but many of these would not go to Seward, principally because of Chase's personal antipathy to him.

As the third roll call began, the huge, packed hall was electric with tension. At the end, Lincoln was still shy 1½ votes for the nomination, but the outcome was now plain. Then the chairman of the Ohio delegation rose to announce a switch of four votes from Mr. Chase to Mr. Lincoln. It was all over. Delegation leaders immediately called for a unanimous nomination. "There was a noise in the Wigwam like the rush of a great wind, in the van of a storm—and in another breath, the storm was there. There were thousands cheering with the energy of insanity." A man on the roof who was reporting the results of the balloting to the mass of people waiting outside "now demanded by gestures at the sky-light over the stage, to know what had happened. One of the Secretaries, with a tally sheet in his hands, shouted— 'Fire the Salute! Abe Lincoln is nominated!' "

Selection of the vice-presidential candidate was an anticlimax. Still, serious consideration must be given to balancing the ticket. Of the two major contenders, Senator Hannibal Hamlin of Maine, an ex-Democrat, was favored over Cassius M. Clay, a Whig from Kentucky. He would provide a better geographical balance and might dispel charges that the Republicans were only a rejuvenated Whig party.

It had taken only two hours to make Lincoln a candidate for the Presidency—the balloting which began on Friday morning at ten o'clock was over by noon. No other presidential nomination was as fateful for the history of the nation, and few were as unexpected. No one was more astounded than William Seward. On the day the convention opened, practically all of Cayuga County turned up at the home of Auburn's most illustrious citizen to acclaim his triumph at Chicago. A cannon was drawn up outside ready to be discharged as soon as his nomination was confirmed. When a messenger arrived with a report of the first ballot, the crowd cheered uproariously. When Seward was handed the results of the second tally, he said confidently, "I shall be nominated on the next ballot." Cheers again. Still outwardly assured, he opened the third telegram and turned "pale as ashes" when he read the terse message: "Lincoln nominated—T[hurlow]. W[eed]."

Not only Seward was stunned. In Washington, sophisticated politicians and congressmen were shaking their heads in bewilderment. The next morning one paper commented, "The Presidential nomination occasioned much surprise and was not at once credited." Yet the result was politically logical. Lincoln was completely "available." All the other candidates were flawed in one way or another—too radical on slavery to please the conservatives or too conservative to please the radicals; too closely linked with the big-city corrupt machines for the reformers; too much identified with free trade to please the protectionists; too disposed toward immigration for the nativists or too "American" for the foreign elements. With his party a heterogeneous mixture, Lincoln had conducted himself shrewdly, studiously refraining from commenting on such controversial issues as nativism, temperance, the Fugitive Slave Law. He was moderate on slavery, opposing its extension but in a reasonable and conciliatory manner.

Moreover, while few outside Lincoln's own state made him their first choice, many thought of him as a second choice. He was the only favorite-son candidate at the convention with the solid backing of his delegation. His supporters, by assiduously portraying Seward as a radical, persuaded numerous delegates, particularly in the doubtful states, that he could not win the election. Their bargaining with federal positions—"heavily mortgaging the Presidential plum tree"—persuaded waverers to change their allegiance. The wildly enthusiastic claques which they supplied, used for the first time at a convention, who outnumbered and outshouted the Sewardites, no doubt psychologically influenced many delegates to shift their loyalty.

Lincoln, fifty-one years old when he received the nomination, had been a politician and a student of politics for almost three decades. From the daily newspapers, which were his favorite reading, he learned to sense the mood of the nation. His experiences on the frontier where he constantly met strangers made him perceptive about people and taught him to accommodate himself to diverse ideas without yielding his independence. Four terms in the Illinois state legislature, a term in Congress, his practice as a lawyer on the circuit, and extensive stump speaking in election campaigns all honed his political skill.

The turning point in his political life was the Kansas-Nebraska Act, which stirred him, he said, "as he had never been before." While as early as 1836 he already regarded slavery as a moral evil, protesting slavery resolutions passed in the Illinois legislature, his passionate involvement after the bill was passed lifted him from an insignificant politician to national prominence. In 1856 he joined the newly formed Republican party and delivered more than fifty speeches for Frémont all over Illinois. At the national convention that year he was promoted for the vice-presidency, receiving 110 votes on the first ballot.

Prospects for Republican victory in 1860 were enhanced by the open split in the Democratic party at its convention in April. A breach had been steadily widening not only between the Douglas and Buchanan factions, over the distribution of patronage, but also over the issue of popular sovereignty. Douglas Democrats regarded the Dred Scott decision as inimical to popular sovereignty, while to "southern rights" Democrats popular sovereignty was as dangerous as congressional prohibition of slavery in the territories.

A potent force in the South was William L. Yancey of Alabama, one of the region's extremists, who was convinced that the South's vital slave interests were being jeopardized by loyalty to the Democratic party and its northern champions. "If this foul smell of party which binds and divides and distracts the South can be broken," he declared, "hail to him who shall break it." Although his "Alabama Platform" calling for a guarantee that Congress protect slavery in the territories had been rejected at the party convention a decade earlier, he continued his agitation.

In anticipation of the 1860 convention, the Buchanan faction, led by Jefferson Davis and John Slidell, sought to destroy Douglas's southern support by demanding that the Democratic party formally repudiate his Freeport Doctrine and endorse congressional responsibility for protection of slavery in the territories. In July 1859, Yancey proposed that unless the platform included a specific plank endorsing free entry and federal guarantee of slavery in all the territories by legislation, the states'-rights supporters should walk out and organize their own convention. If the Republicans should win the election, he declared, the southern states should secede from the Union before inauguration.

A rupture was inevitable if the Buchananites remained firm, for Douglas said unequivocally that he would refuse the nomination if the party adopted "such new issues as the revival of the African slave trade, or a congressional slave code for the territories." He would respect the authority of the Supreme Court and comply with its decisions—an implicit endorsement of the Dred Scott ruling—but he would go no further.

When the convention assembled in Charleston, the platform was the first item on the agenda. Yancey promptly introduced his Alabama Platform and then turned to Douglas. "If you had taken the position directly that slavery was right, and therefore ought to be . . . you would have triumphed and antislavery would now have been dead in your midst." Instead, he went on, Democrats in the North joined the great abolitionist heresy which included Black Republicans, free-soilers, and advocates of squatter sovereignty, all of whom were opposed to slavery; "your admission that slavery is wrong has been the cause of all this discord."

When Yancey concluded, Ohio's Senator Pugh, a friend of Douglas, leaped to his feet. He was grateful, he said, that a Southerner had spoken with the frankness that revealed the full measure of the South's demands, but it was his section which was responsible for the ruination of the party in the North. He would remind Southerners that their cause had been championed by northern Democrats who were now being rewarded with scorn and threats to bolt. When they came to the convention, "the northern Democracy were thrust back and told in effect that they must put their hands on their mouths and their mouths in the dust." They would not be silenced, he warned solemnly, and the South was mistaken if it thought they would yield.

A prolonged wrangle on the platform ensued, which was finally resolved by a rejection of the southern radical position. Yancey and his delegation promptly rose and stalked out, followed by the entire delegations of Mississippi, Louisiana, South Carolina, Florida, Texas, and a scattering from Arkansas, Missouri, Georgia, Virginia, and Delaware. With the rules requiring a two-thirds majority of all the delegates for the presidential nomination, no candidate could be named. A motion was carried to adjourn and reassemble at Baltimore on June 18.

The interval gave Douglas an opportunity to reassess the situation. Was it possible or desirable to modify the platform, thereby allaying the apprehensions of many Southerners, without at the same time weakening the party in the North? He considered withdrawing his candidacy as a move that might prevent an irreparable breach within the party, but party members throughout the country insisted he was the only Democrat who could beat Lincoln.

In addition to the sectional cleavage over slavery, the Democratic party was being rent by an internal power struggle between Buchanan and Douglas which went back to 1856, when the two men were rivals for the presidential nomination. Administration policy of ignoring Douglas with respect to patronage in his own bailiwick intensified the hostility. The President turned over the task of dispensing patronage to Senator John Slidell of Louisiana and Congressman Jesse Bright of Indiana, two of his close friends, who distributed all the federal jobs in the area. Then when he urged Congress to admit Kansas to statehood under the Lecompton Constitution, the break became permanent. Douglas informed the President that he would publicly and absolutely oppose that policy. "Mr. Douglas, I desire you to remember that no Democrat ever yet differed from an administration of his own choice without being crushed," the incensed Buchanan warned. Unmoved, Douglas arose in the Senate in December 1857 and for three hours denounced the Lecompton Constitution.

The President made good his threat. Douglas reported to a friend, "The administration is more anxious for my destruction than they are for the harmony & unity of the Democratic party. You have doubtless seen that they are removing all my friends from office." Furthermore, they were "endeavoring to form an alliance with the Republicans of Ill. to beat me [for re-election to the Senate] with a Republican." The Buchananites failed and, as Douglas prophesied, the party was split, not only in Illinois but in every state in the Union, between administration and Douglas supporters.

When the Democratic party convention reassembled in Baltimore, three new delegations presented themselves, a conservative group loyal to the Union from Louisiana, a similar one from Alabama, and a group of moderates from Georgia, each claiming to represent the party in their states. The delegates who had walked out at Charleston demanded admission but refused to state whether they would abide by majority decisions. They were challenged by Congressman Montgomery of Pennsylvania. "It is because I love the country and the Union that I am determined that any man who arrays himself in hostility to it shall not, by my consent, take a seat in this convention," he said firmly. "I am opposed to disunion and I am opposed to the advocates of it. And I am opposed to secession either from this union or from the Democratic convention." He insisted that unless the dissenting delegations agreed to adhere to the principles and candidates approved by the party, they should under no circumstances be admitted.

Once more the "ultras" rose and marched out. They promptly held a rump convention. Composed largely of Buchanan officeholders from the North and extremists from the South, the group adopted the platform that had been turned down at Charleston. Senator John C. Breckinridge of Kentucky was nominated for President and Senator Joseph Lane of Oregon as his running mate. Later, at Richmond, the action was officially ratified, and the bolters claimed to be the only legal Democratic party in the country.

At the regular convention, with the dissidents gone, only 192½ votes remained, but the chairman ruled that a two-thirds majority of those present could nominate a candidate. Douglas became the party choice on the second ballot. Once again Lincoln and Douglas would be pitted against each other, but this time the stakes were the future of the country.

Douglas began the campaign with the handicap of a split party, and his stand on slavery would grind him between the sectional millstones. His voting strength would also be drained by a new group formed at Baltimore, the Constitutional Union Party. Composed of old-line Whigs, other pro-Union elements, and former "Know-Nothings" who felt unable morally to support any of the other parties, it impartially condemned northern and southern sectionalism. A vague platform declared for "The Constitution of the Country, the Union of the States, and the Enforcement of the Laws." Their candidates were John Bell of Tennessee and Edward Everett of Massachusetts.

The odds were in favor of Lincoln. He was regarded as a moderate, and the Republican platform had been designed to appeal to diverse groups. His party was united, with all of the disappointed presidential aspirants giving him their support. Job-hungry politicians north of the Mason-Dixon line, concluding that Lincoln was a better bet than either John Bell or Stephen Douglas, so thoroughly organized the electorate, especially in the doubtful states, that the party apparatus reached individual voters in all the precincts. Thurlow Weed pledged the wholehearted support of his New York machine.

Throughout the campaign, Lincoln remained at Springfield in an office at the Statehouse, where he saw callers each day and wrote voluminously on strategy to party workers across the land. After his formal letter of acceptance on May 26 in which he endorsed the party platform and pledged to adhere to it, he made no public statements. He and his managers agreed that silence would avoid possible misinterpretation of his views by his opponents. He resisted all pressure to speak or write, explaining to one correspondent, "What is it I could say which would quiet alarm? Is it that no interference by the government, with the slaves and slavery within the states, is intended? I have said this so often already, that a repetition of it is but mockery."

There was, however, no dearth of men to speak for Lincoln. A national committee established for the express purpose of directing the campaign sent speakers throughout the North. The peculiar circumstances within each state were carefully noted so that the appropriate men and propaganda could be chosen. William Seward toured New England and the Northwest, where he had a strong following among the "radicals" on the slavery question. Senator Henry Wilson of Massachusetts, a former cobbler, was sent to address working-class audiences, while the urbane and intellectual Senator Charles Sumner talked to the more sophisticated audiences of the large cities. Salmon P. Chase directed his appeal to former free-soil Democrats. Conservative William Dayton concentrated on the moderate Whigs of the East, Edward Bates on the nativists. Carl Schurz, who had fled Germany after the Revolution of 1848, toured the German-American communities. No locality, however obscure, was overlooked if it was a potential source of votes.

Printed material publicizing the Republican candidate was also in plentiful supply. The Chicago *Tribune* ran a 4,000-word biographical sketch of Lincoln at the beginning of the campaign, and others were soon distributed over the country. All emphasized the candidate's pioneer origin, that he had been born in a log cabin and worked at rail splitting. During an interview, Lincoln, replying to a question put to him by the reporter, held out a piece of wood. "Yes, sir, here

is a stick I received a day or two since from Josiah Crawford, of Gentryville, Indiana. He writes me that it is one of
the rails that I cut for him in 1825." One of the most popular and effective campaign papers was *The Rail Splitter*,
launched in Chicago at the beginning of the contest.

Campaign rallies were held everywhere. As Carl Schurz
remarked, "It looked as though . . . people had little else to
do than to attend meetings, listen to speeches, march in
processions, and carry torches after nightfall." A novel feature was the Republican "Wide-Awakes," a semimilitary
organization which was formed in Hartford, Connecticut,
during the spring gubernatorial campaign. Some fervent
young Republicans escorting a visiting dignitary to the lec-
ture hall wore caps and capes of glazed cloth to protect
their clothes from the dripping oil of the lamps they carried. Returning home, one of the men, attacked by a
brawny Democrat, knocked out his assailant with a blow
from his torch. To prevent harassment at future meetings,
the Hartford group organized a Wide-Awake Club. The
idea spread rapidly and similar groups were formed everywhere. Members wore uniforms which enterprising mer-
chants advertised: *"Wide Awake Uniforms: Prices Reduced:* Cap, Cape, and torch with flags will be furnished at
the cost price of $1.15." At their peak, there were several
hundred "Wide-Awake" chapters, each using as an emblem
a torch made of a rail on which was mounted a tin swing
lamp, and to which was attached a small flag inscribed with
the names of Lincoln and Hamlin. Each group had its officers and privates, the former distinguished by the colored
lanterns they were privileged to carry. Variations on the
theme appeared in the West, where the groups designated
themselves "Rail Splitters" and in some localities "Rail
Maulers."

Supporters of Bell and Everett thought the idea so effective that they organized groups of "Bell Ringers" who also
wore uniforms, carried torches, and in addition a wide as-
sortment of bells. They called themselves "Bell-Everetters,"
"Union Sentinels," and "Minute Men." Not to be outdone,

Douglas Democrats organized "Little Giants," or in some localities "Little Dougs," whose members were carefully drilled. One group in New York named itself "The Chloroformers," whose object was to "put the Wide-Awakes to sleep." These organizations performed valuable functions for their parties. They maintained order at rallies, sang, paraded, and kept the emotional pitch high.

As was customary, none of the candidates, with the exception of Douglas, appeared at rallies to make campaign addresses. Bell left Nashville only once during the entire campaign, and his journey was strictly nonpolitical. Breckinridge was prevailed upon to make a single appearance at a barbecue after the Democrats lost the Kentucky state elections in August.

The Republican appeal to the voters varied with the conditions prevailing in each state. In the industrial Northeast, the tariff was a bread-and-butter issue, far more important than a congressional slave code or popular sovereignty. When a group of Pennsylvanians asked Lincoln for his views, the candidate referred them to both the party plank on the subject and newspaper reports in 1844 which dealt with his support of Clay's protectionist program. In advocating an upward revision of tariff rates in Pennsylvania, Republicans were riding a popular crest, since that state produced half of the nation's iron output. They pointed out how under Republican leadership, the House in 1860 had approved an increase in tariff schedules only to be blocked by the Democratic-controlled Senate, which voted to postpone consideration of the measure. Breckinridge Democrats were assailed as free traders, and while they could not denounce John Bell, an old Whig protectionist on that issue, they suggested that since he was counting on southern support he would have to conform to southern free-trade policies.

The most strenuous effort was directed against Douglas. In one widely distributed pamphlet, he was depicted with deliberate exaggeration as an out-and-out free trader. One of his supporters urged him to favor higher import duties when he visited Pennsylvania since "The Republicans, in their speeches, say nothing of the nigger question, but all is made to turn on the Tariff." When Douglas followed this advice in a speech at Harrisburg, he was attacked both by the Republicans and southern Democrats as indulging in "the most unblushing effrontery" and transparent political deceit.

In Minnesota, Iowa, and Wisconsin, where the land question was paramount, Republicans concentrated on the need for a homestead law and a more liberal public land policy. When Carl Schurz returned to Wisconsin from the national convention, he told the German population that the party platform fully recognized their desire for free land and protection of the rights of naturalized citizens. To Californians, primarily concerned about a transcontinental railroad, Republican speakers informed their audiences that, while the Democrats had prevented construction of a Pacific railroad, their platform pledged government funds to build one.

Illinois required delicate handling. The state had two distinct political entities; the upper part was composed of migrants from northern states who were mostly German and Irish and antislavery, while the inhabitants of the southern counties came largely from the slave states. One Republican strategist suggested that "the most effective Document for all the region North of Rock River will be Lovejoy's last speech [Lovejoy was an abolitionist martyr], than for the whole state [to] prepare a Document composed of choice selections from Lincoln's. . . . I think Jeff Davis' last speeches would be good to distribute down in Egypt—vs Douglas Democracy." In the areas more or less indifferent to slavery, economic issues were stressed. At a rally in Springfield, slavery was mentioned on only two of the twenty-seven banners carried in the parade; the other slogans dealt with river and harbor improvements, a Pacific railroad, protection to American labor and home industry, free homes for the homeless.

In Indiana, conservative on slavery, great care was taken to show that Lincoln was a moderate. The slavery issue in general was soft-pedaled, with the Republicans campaigning for free land through a federal homestead law, advocating a Pacific railroad, denouncing corruption in Washington, and opposing polygamy (the Mormons were unpopular).

As about one fifth of the Northwest's population was foreign-born German and Irish, the Republicans concentrated on winning support of the former, who were in the majority —the latter were solidly and consistently Democratic. Lists of German voters were compiled and German translations of the proposed homestead bill were circulated. These efforts paid off, for the German vote helped Lincoln carry the region.

While a united Republican party could methodically plan strategy in the traditional manner, Stephen A. Douglas and Herschel V. Johnson, his running mate, had to create organizations in every border and slave state, in some of the northern states, and in California and Oregon. Weeks were spent in calling new conventions, organizing state committees, and overcoming legal obstacles. To add to their problems, the defected Democrats organized a "National Democratic Committee" which included such proslavery leaders as Senator Jefferson Davis of Mississippi, political allies in the North like Senator Jesse Bright of Indiana, close friends of President Buchanan, and key officeholders. Buchanan cordially received the committee and later endorsed the Breckinridge-Lane ticket.

Nevertheless, for some weeks after the convention Douglas was optimistic about victory, particularly when party workers returning from New England, the South, and the Northwest brought back cheering reports. To one supporter he wrote early in July that "we must make war boldly against the Northern Abolitionists and the Southern disunionists and give no quarter to either," for "the chances in our favor are immense in the East." As the election, he thought, might possibly go to the House of Representatives, with the decision turning upon Lincoln, Bell, and himself, friendly relations should be cultivated with Bell's supporters, but whatever happened "we can have no partnership with the bolters."

The task of fund raising for the Douglas campaign was directed by the prominent banker, August Belmont, who began the drive with a personal contribution of a thousand dollars. Although he drew important individuals into his finance committee, Belmont soon found to his dismay that after a month of solicitation not a single dollar had come in. The moneyed men, normally heavy donors, he wrote Douglas, were either completely apathetic or flatly declined to contribute because they were "afraid to lose their Southern customers by siding with us." Each congressional district organization was appealed to for a hundred-dollar contribution, but by mid-September hardly anything had been received. Belmont's pleas to several wealthy southern conservatives met with some response, but it could not begin to cover the requirements for an effective campaign.

Handicapped by lack of funds and by a paucity of organizations, Douglas decided to campaign on his own behalf. While the Presidency was undoubtedly an incomparable prize, he was motivated by a more urgent consideration. Lincoln and his party discounted the threats of secession by southern hotheads, but Douglas knew the southern temper better than his opponents. He was convinced that Lincoln's election would be followed by disaster, that only he could keep the nation from dissolution. With Lincoln safely at home, Republicans could look down their noses at his opponent's effort. "Douglas is going about peddling his opinions as a tin man peddles his ware," an Illinois paper sneered in an editorial. "The only excuse for him is that he is a small man, he has a right to be engaged in small business; and small business it is for a candidate for the Presidency to be strolling around the country begging for votes like a town constable."

To maintain at least the pretense of noninvolvement, Democrats announced that, as Douglas had not seen his mother, who lived in Clifton Springs, New York, for a long time, he would pay her a visit. During the month he took to reach his destination, the Republicans issued almost daily handbills, signed "S. D.'s Mother," which appealed for information about her wandering son. One of them read:

A boy Lost! Left Washington, D.C., some time in July, to go home to his mother. He has not yet reached his mother who is very anxious about him. He has been seen in Philadelphia, New York City, Hartford, Conn., at a clambake in Rhode Island. He has been heard from at Boston, Portland, Augusta, and Bangor, Me. . . . He is about five feet nothing in height and about the same in diameter the other way. He has a red face, short legs, and a large belly. Answers to the name of Little Giant, talks a great deal, very loud, always about himself. Has an idea that he is a candidate for President.

A New Hampshire paper gibed that, to visit his mother, he "naturally came to New Haven, Guilford, and Hartford . . . and at the latter place, he was 'betrayed' into a speech . . . at Worcester, some Judas 'betrayed' him into a speech. At Boston, betrayed again."

Driven by his fear of calamity, Douglas ignored the sniping and continued his grueling tour up and down the country. Even his sturdy physique began to rebel against the punishment to which it was subjected. When he arrived in Cincinnati in September, he was so hoarse and exhausted that he was unable to address the audience gathered to hear him.

Twice he traveled through the South to urge that it was "the duty of all to submit to the verdict of the people and to maintain the Union." At Norfolk he told his audience that he wanted no man to vote for him "unless he hopes and desires the Union maintained and preserved intact." He had not come South, he said, to purchase votes by making any promises that were contrary to his beliefs, but to try to unite all those who loved the Union around some "common principle" in order to preserve it. Questioned as to what his position would be if he were elected and the southern states seceded, he replied unequivocally that as it was the duty of the President and all in authority under him to enforce the laws, he would be bound by his oath to uphold the Constitution, and, accordingly, "would do all in my power to aid the Government of the United States in maintaining the supremacy of the laws against all resistance to them, come from whatever quarter it might."

In October, Douglas received word that the Republicans had won state elections in Pennsylvania and Indiana. Turning to his secretary, he said quietly, "Mr. Lincoln is the next President. We must try to save the Union." He went back to the South to reiterate passionately that there was no evil for which the Constitution did not have a remedy. "The mere inauguration of a President of the United States . . . without an overt act on his part . . . is not such a grievance as would justify revolution or secession." But his position was distorted on both sides of the Mason-Dixon line. The North stigmatized him as a proslavery advocate while the South branded him as an antislavery supporter, shutting its ears to his warning that "you cannot sever this Union unless you cut the heartstrings that bind father to son, daughter to mother and brother to sister in all our new States and Territories." At Montgomery, Alabama, he was pelted with rotten tomatoes and eggs, and in Tennessee attempts were made to wreck the train on which he was riding.

Fear of what might happen if Lincoln were elected spread through the South like a poisonous miasma. Though the Republican candidate had affirmed that he would not free the slaves, he was suspected of secretly being an abolitionist. In any case, his party's policy of containment not only spelled ultimate extinction of slavery but would permanently relegate southern representation in Congress to a minority status. Seward accurately assessed the situation when he said, "The controversy is not with the negro at all, but with two classes of white men, one who have a monopoly of negroes, and the other who have no negroes. One is an aristocratic class, that wants to extend itself over the new territories and so retain the power it already exercises; and the other . . . mean[s] that the aristocratic system shall not be extended."

Yet it was only a partial truth, for the desperate effort to maintain slavery went deeper. The institution had contaminated the atmosphere of the entire South. It dehumanized the black man but it also perverted the mind of his white master, investing it with conscious and unconscious fears. Emancipation conjured up for the slaveowner and middle-class whites nightmare visions of uncontrolled and uncontrollable hordes of blacks prowling over the country, of Negroes demanding social and economic equality, forcing their way into white churches, outvoting whites at the polls. To the poor whites it meant competition for jobs and the loss of whatever status they now claimed by virtue of having another group lower on the social ladder.

Among some Northerners, a Republican victory was viewed with apprehension for economic reasons. Involved in commerce with the South, they were concerned about the loss of a lucrative trade. Southerners were applying pressure by closing accounts, canceling orders, and discriminating between firms having Republican sympathies and those which were "sound" on slavery. One Georgia newspaper published a list of Northern firms under two headings, a "blacklist" of "abolitionist" establishments and a white list of "constitutional" firms. With this foretaste of things to come, Philadelphia businessmen refused to contribute funds to the Republican campaign, and the great New York City mercantile interests were solidly for the Breckinridge-Lane ticket.

Conflicts between Republicans and the rival Democratic factions shook Congress. Jefferson Davis thundered against Douglas in the Senate, and Republican spokesmen delivered biting harangues against the Buchanan administration. The Republicans made effective use of the Covode Committee report, prepared by a select committee of the House, which revealed the use of money and patronage in influencing the vote on the proslavery constitution in Kansas. An abridged version of the massive document exposing corruption in several government departments was circulated, one leader of the Republican campaign committee reporting that he was being supplied with 40,000 copies every day.

Legislative inaction also provided political ammunition. One Republican newspaper gleefully reported, "Congress has adjourned. The following popular measures were defeated by the action of the Democratic party: 1. The bill for the admission of Kansas. 2. The Free Homestead Bill. 3. The Pacific Railroad Bill. 4. The River and Harbor Improvement Bill. 5. The Tariff Bill." Before adjournment, a homestead act, though in emasculated form, had been approved by the Senate, which was controlled by the Democrats, and the House, which was controlled by the Republicans, but Buchanan played directly into the hands of the opposition by vetoing the measure. As nothing was more popular in the West than free land for the settlers, Horace Greeley could crow in the New York *Tribune*, "Does anybody suppose that Abraham Lincoln would ever veto such a bill?"

While the slavery issue was dividing churches, national parties, even families and, like a thorny, venomous weed, pricking men into near paranoia, the Republicans in the election campaign of 1860 virtually ignored it. Only the abolitionists were preoccupied with the subject. In protest against the position taken by the major parties at their conventions, they held their own convention in August, nominating the New Yorker, Gerrit Smith, as their presidential candidate. They excoriated the Republicans for their failure to denounce "slave hunting, slave holding, slave breeding" in their platform and assailed Lincoln as a hypocrite who in fact supported the Fugitive Slave Law, admission of additional slave states, and keeping the Negro in a position of inequality. Their continuous and violent diatribes helped rather than hurt the Republicans, confirming for many that Lincoln's party was indeed moderate and worthy of support.

As the campaign drew to a close, the parties opposed to Lincoln tried desperately to prevent him from obtaining a majority in the electoral college. If the election were to go to the House, one of the anti-Lincoln candidates might win, since voting would be by states, and each state had one vote. The rival Democratic parties made strenuous efforts to bring about a united front. Negotiations had to be conducted on the local level, as neither party had a real central organization. But local rivalries made fusion virtually impossible in all but a handful of states, where electors were apportioned for Douglas, Breckinridge, and Bell with the understanding that they would so cast their votes as to bring about Lincoln's defeat.

New York, a pivotal state for Lincoln, who needed its thirty-five electoral votes for victory, was one in which his opponents succeeded in achieving fusion. Thurlow Weed was not disturbed, but he left nothing to chance. On the eve of the election he dispatched last-minute instructions to his loyal campaign workers. *"Close Up the Work of Preparation To-Night:* Leave nothing for tomorrow but direct work. Pick out and station your men. . . . Let there be an assigned place for every man, and, at sunrise, let every man be in his assigned place. Don't wait until the last hour to bring up delinquents. Consider every man a 'delinquent' who doesn't vote before 10 o'clock. *At That Hour Begin To Hunt Up Voters."* New York produced a plurality of more than 50,000 votes for Lincoln.

In the final tabulations, Lincoln had 1,866,452 votes, Douglas 1,375,957, Bell 588,879, and Breckinridge 849,781. Douglas and Bell together had polled 100,000 more votes than Lincoln and, with Breckinridge, exceeded Lincoln's vote by more than a million. But having carried all the northern states except New Jersey, whose electoral vote he split with Douglas, Lincoln won in those states that were decisive in the electoral college. He would have been the victor even if the opposition had not been split three ways. If all non-Republican votes had been cast for one man, he still would have received an electoral majority of 169 to 134. That he could be elected with only 39.8 per cent of the popular vote indicated the increasing weight of the northern states both in the electoral college and in Congress.

A breakdown of the electoral votes revealed a political system that had virtually collapsed. As Herbert Agar put it,

"The map of 1860 is indeed the picture of a nation breaking in two." The Republicans polled all but 26,388 of their total popular vote in the free states, receiving not a single vote in ten of the southern states. In all the fifteen slaveholding states, Lincoln carried only two of the 1,109 counties, both of which were in the border state of Missouri. Of Douglas's total vote, less than ten per cent came from the South. He carried only 68 counties in the slave states, of which nearly two thirds were in Missouri. Breckinridge carried all the cotton states but elsewhere received few votes except in areas dependent upon trade with the South. Out of 749 counties in the free states east of the Rocky Mountains, he carried only 1 in his own right and 12 in Pennsylvania where fusion had been achieved. John Bell failed to win a plurality in any county outside of those in the fifteen slaveholding states. It was two contests in one—between Lincoln and Douglas in the North and between Breckinridge and Bell in the South—with practically no overlap.

Before the nation had gone to the polls, six southern governors and almost every senator and congressman from the seven states of the Deep South went on record as recommending secession if Lincoln were elected. On December 20, South Carolina seceded from the Union, and within six months most of the other slaveholding states followed. When the new President entered the White House, he would be at the head of a nation which had been split in half.

6. Silver-Tongued Crusader

FIVE weeks after Abraham Lincoln took the oath of office, the nation plunged into that most tragic of all conflicts, a fratricidal struggle which literally tore families apart. At the end, the Union survived but at a terrible price. The North sustained huge losses in dead, wounded, and permanently disabled. The South was bled of its youth and left prostrate, its economy shattered, its people emotionally ravaged.

The postwar years brought profound changes to the nation. In the South, economic, political, and social patterns were fundamentally altered. Burdened with the monumental task of reordering society, chafing under the domination of the hated conquerors during the years of Reconstruction, the South for generations became attached to one political party, with white supremacy the first article of its faith.

In the North the economy burst into frenetic activity. Investment capital found an outlet in rapidly expanding industrial enterprises, in exploiting natural resources required for manufacturing, constructing railroads to span the continent, creating corporate giants, promoting an economy based on mass production, and in financial manipulation and speculation.

As industry and technology advanced, the urban working class and the farmers were crushed under the steam roller of progress. The former had not as yet begun to play an influential role in politics, but the latter in the West and South were instrumental in forcing the issue on which the historic campaign of 1896 was fought.

Farming had long been a precarious occupation. Drought, declining prices, excessive and discriminatory freight rates, and high taxes had sucked the farmer into a whirlpool of debt in which he flailed helplessly. The agricultural revolution in the last decades of the century made farming in the West steadily more specialized and commercialized, more and more dependent on the complex processes of a cash economy. Mechanization had reduced the harvesting time for a one-acre crop from sixty hours of hand labor to less than three hours. Able to till more land, farmers mortgaged themselves to buy more acreage and more implements, only to be trapped by the old problems and a new one—the decline in purchasing power.

In the three decades since 1865, the value of money had trebled; this meant that a debt which previously could be paid off with one thousand bushels of wheat now cost the farmer the equivalent of three thousand. While commodity prices soared, increased crop yield and cultivation of additional farming areas created surpluses which forced farm prices steadily down. Victimized by an economic system he could not comprehend, the farmer concluded that two factors were responsible: the financiers of New York and London, who manipulated prices, and the scarcity of money in circulation.

Both of the major parties, the farmer was convinced, had become spokesmen for the moneyed interests and were totally unconcerned with his plight. "The parties lie to us and political speakers mislead us," Mary E. Lease, a farm leader, said bitterly. Formation of a new party was the only solution. The People's or Populist party, organized at Cincinnati in May 1891, was an outgrowth of several postwar agrarian movements of protest. Realizing that to become a national political force it would have to include more than just one economic group, its founders adopted a platform directed to labor as well.

The Populist program advocated wide-ranging social, economic, and political reforms: free coinage of silver at a ratio of sixteen to one and an increase in the amount of money in circulation, a graduated income tax, government operation of transportation and communication, control of monopolies, legislation to protect labor against the injunction, postal savings banks, direct election of senators, the initiative, and the referendum. In the presidential election of 1892, the Populist candidate General James B. Weaver polled over a million popular votes and received twenty-two votes in the electoral college; equally impressive, a number of Populists were elected to state and national offices.

The following year the disastrous drop in the nation's gold reserves precipitated a panic, which was followed by a depression that racked the country for four years. Desperate western farmers tossed overboard their demands for extensive reforms and concentrated on what they regarded as the only cure for their untenable situation—a monetary expansion through the free and unlimited coinage of silver. The silver issue swept the western plains. Angry men gathered at thousands of little country stores to denounce the gold standard, which, they were convinced, caused the havoc and was being maintained by an international conspiracy.

The clamor about silver seriously threatened the political influence of the Democratic administration. In Congress, the party divided between the silverites of the West and South and the eastern conservatives, led by President Cleveland, who were completely opposed to monetary inflation through increased governmental coinage of silver. Cleveland not only antagonized the free silverites by his initiative in having the Sherman Silver Purchase Act repealed but incurred their fierce resentment by denying them patronage support.

Southern Democrats, alarmed by the surprisingly large vote which the Populists had received in the elections of 1892, hoped the administration would undertake tariff and currency reform to ameliorate the section's difficulties.

When it failed to act and a substantial shift away from the party occurred during the depression, they felt betrayed. In the House, Champ Clark of Missouri lumped Cleveland with Benedict Arnold and Aaron Burr as one of the three greatest traitors the nation had ever had. Benjamin Tillman of South Carolina, campaigning for the Senate, asked to be sent to Washington so that he could "stick my pitchfork into his old ribs!" Later, on the floor of Congress, he thundered that "Wall Street and his connections with wealthy men have debauched his conscience and destroyed all sympathy with the masses." Throughout the South and West, animosity toward Cleveland became so intense that when the President planned a fishing trip to Colorado in the summer of 1894 he was warned that the people there were "in a desperate and frenzied state of excitement" and "the mutterings against the president . . . heard on every hand" were so violent that his life would be in danger.

Labor, too, became enraged at Cleveland when he dispatched federal troops to Chicago to crush the Pullman strike. With no relief from the depression, the cities became cauldrons of radical agitation. Workers who had been fired for striking against drastic wage cuts assailed the domination of the "plutocrats."

Political control by the administration kept slipping as Democrats in southern and western states, among them South Carolina, Virginia, Missouri, and Nebraska, rejected its authority. Silverites worked fiercely to capture state organizations. The breach in the party continued to widen with the passage of the Wilson-Gorman tariff bill and the sale of government bonds for gold to a banking syndicate created by the House of Morgan, a transaction highly profitable to the bankers. Late in 1894, a Morgan lawyer who heard of plans by insurgent Democrats to force a free-silver bill through the next session of Congress wrote the President, "They expect your veto, but do not care for it as they are making a plan for 1896 when the silver party should have swallowed the Populists as the Republican party did the Free Soilers. We are on the eve of a very dark night," he said prophetically, "unless the return of commercial prosperity relieves popular discontent."

To the Republicans, the "dark night" of their opponents meant a blaze of sunshine for them. Hopefuls for the presidential nomination sprouted in the warmth of the possibility that the White House was within reach. The prominent contenders were Governor Levi P. Morton of New York, Senators Shelby Cullom of Illinois and William B. Allison of Iowa, Governor William McKinley of Ohio, and Congressman Thomas B. Reed of Maine. The last three were especially strong as 1896 opened, with McKinley the front runner.

A number of factors sent William McKinley to the head of the race. In politics for twenty-five years, he occupied a pre-eminent position in the party. As a congressman, he had sponsored the Tariff Act of 1890, which associated him with protectionism and prosperity and endeared him to the industrialists. The victim of a gerrymander, he was defeated for another term that year, but his election as governor of Ohio in 1891 at a time of widespread Republican defeats, and re-election two years later by an unprecedented majority, enhanced a growing reputation. Years of party regularity and adherence to orthodox doctrine, refusal to engage in controversy, a disarming personality, a reputation as an honest politician, no real enemies, the simplicity of his life and thought, and the strategic importance of the state from which he came—all these made him highly "available." But of all his assets, probably the most important was his campaign manager, the shrewd industrial titan, Marcus Alonzo Hanna.

Hanna's original attraction to McKinley for his probity and high moral standards soon developed into a devoted friendship. As he wrote in 1892, McKinley was "true as steel. Nothing short of a miracle or death will prevent his being the nominee . . . in '96, and to that end I have enlisted, to accomplish which I am prepared to be politic and patient, but if to secure it sharper weapons are required I shall not hesitate to fight." And fight Hanna did, with huge sums of his own money and lavish amounts that he persuaded businessmen to contribute.

During the campaign of 1896, Hanna's influence and role were so pervasive that it was he rather than the candidate who was the major target of Democratic journalists, cartoonists, and politicians. He was castigated as a plutocrat who had decided to move from economic to political power, using a docile, subservient McKinley as his tool. In the famous Homer Davenport cartoons, Hanna, actually an enlightened industrialist and one of the first to engage in collective bargaining, was cruelly lampooned as a bloated capitalist cracking a bull whip over a skeleton marked "labor," with a dwarfed McKinley tucked under his belt or stuffed in his vest pocket. The facts were completely otherwise. Far from being a marionette dancing on Hanna's strings, McKinley planned or approved the entire strategy of the campaign, with Hanna his willing servant.

According to William Allen White, Hanna was "just a shade obsequious in McKinley's presence," and other observers noted that he treated the candidate with respect and deference in private as well as in public. White went so far as to say that for Hanna "the affection was deep to the point of abasement. McKinley . . . was just, even generous, but never infatuated; pleased, perhaps flattered at times, deeply, if gently moved, but never as passionate as Hanna was in their relations." McKinley was sincerely grateful to Hanna, completely loyal to him and a devoted friend, but his deepest emotions were not engaged.

Basically, McKinley was a simple man who remained a provincial Midwesterner, never read books, and had little inclination to probe theoretical questions. "I would rather have my political economy founded upon the everyday experience of the puddler or the potter than the learning of the professor," he once wrote. His obsession with the protective tariff as the magic talisman that would guarantee prosperity stemmed from his personal experiences as an ironmonger's son to whom the duty on foreign iron was not an abstract idea. The bromides about Americanism with which he peppered his speeches were genuine expressions of his beliefs.

At the same time, McKinley thoroughly understood the practical side of American politics. The friendship between McKinley and Hanna represented a perfect union of business and politics, of complementary characteristics and goals. Hanna believed that prosperity could be achieved for everyone through the policies and principles of the Republican party; McKinley regarded the great industrialists as leaders who would advance the nation to yet higher achievement. Both shared the view that whatever served the welfare of business promoted the welfare of the nation. The businessman was imaginative; the politician, stolid. While McKinley was the soul of affability, with a compassion and kindliness that charmed everyone, he lacked the intuitive understanding of men which made Hanna a superb organizer.

McKinley was a presidential prospect at the Republican national convention of 1892. President Harrison had alienated many party leaders, but according to traditional practice he was entitled to renomination. If an upset occurred, however, Hanna was prepared to act in behalf of his friend, but he hoped that this would not happen as it obviously was not a Republican year. Shrewdly assessing the situation, McKinley gave the President repeated assurances of his loyalty. He was appointed chairman of the convention, and when Ohio voted he had the delegation polled to make his support public, for the only vote Harrison received of the state's forty-five was McKinley's, made by proxy at his request. Harrison was renominated on the first ballot with 535 votes. Blaine received 182½, and McKinley 182 votes. Later at the hotel, Hanna exclaimed with relief, "My God, William, that was a damned close squeak!"

Two years later, during the congressional campaign of 1894, McKinley as the apostle of protectionism was the most sought-after Republican speaker, with more requests pouring in than he could possibly fill. His energetic performance was unequaled among the politicians of his party.

He covered sixteen states, even going into the South, delivering 371 addresses. In Iowa he spoke twenty-three times in a single day. Everywhere he was cheered for his denunciation of the Democratic Wilson-Gorman tariff, which he called "a free trade" law, and for his appeal for "protectionism, patriotism and prosperity." With the depression showing no sign of abating, the McKinley tariff, enacted during a prosperous period, was associated with good times, and he could be heralded, in the words of an Ohio newspaper, as "the advance agent of Prosperity."

Clearly registering the national mood, the Democratic majority in the House was overwhelmingly reversed and Republican governors and legislatures were installed in nearly every northern state. With this happy omen for 1896, Mark Hanna retired from his coal and iron empire to make politics and the management of McKinley's fortunes his full-time business.

Hanna began by directing his attention first to the South. While Southerners could not give the Republicans any electoral votes, they sent many delegates to the party's national convention. With their support, McKinley would be in a leading position, for he needed 453½ votes to secure the nomination, and nearly half of this number came from below the Mason-Dixon line. Early in 1895, Hanna rented a house in Thomasville, Georgia, and in March the McKinleys arrived for a three-week visit, during which time prominent Republicans from all over the region were invited to meet the distinguished guest. In congenial surroundings, the political situation was discussed in generalities, and though no one was deceived as to the purpose of the hospitality, McKinley's charm and statesmanlike bearing won him new admirers. Later, when the political bosses opposed to McKinley's candidacy attempted to win control of the southern local and state conventions, they found to their dismay that McKinley and Hanna had been there first.

Carefully, methodically, enlisting a host of devoted workers, Hanna put an organization together with branches throughout the country. He had copies of McKinley's speeches distributed everywhere. Badges, posters, and buttons also loaded down the nation's mailbags so that one opponent commented, "McKinley has plastered the land with his literary bureau," while Senator William Chandler of New Hampshire remarked, "If Mr. Hanna has covered every district in the United States in the same manner that he did those in Alabama, McKinley will be nominated." A direct line was installed between Hanna's house, headquarters for strategy meetings, and McKinley's.

While all the weather vanes seemed to point to McKinley as the popular choice, he was no favorite of the political bosses. Some were dubious about his attitude on the money question, and the powerfully entrenched chieftains wanted to retain control of the levers of national power, which they could accomplish only by dictating the choice of a candidate. In later years, two of McKinley's friends, Myron Herrick and Herman H. Kohlsaat, recalled that early in 1895 Hanna met secretly with the eastern leaders and sought to enlist their support in return for promises of patronage. According to Kohlsaat, when McKinley was informed that he could have a deal, he flatly refused to accede, stating, "There are some things in this world that come too high. If I cannot be President without promising to make Tom Platt [New York political boss] Secretary of the Treasury, I will never be President." The incident may be apocryphal, or it may be that McKinley, shrewd politician that he was, refused to conclude a bargain that could boomerang if it ever leaked out.

In any event, the bosses set out to defeat McKinley. They agreed to promote the aspirations of "favorite sons" in an attempt to drain off his potential delegate strength. Thomas B. Reed was counted on to hold New England; Governor of New York Levi P. Morton was selected by Platt for their state; Boss Matthew S. Quay himself would be the nominee for Pennsylvania; Iowa could be relied upon to support Senator Allison; Indiana, it was hoped, would remain loyal to ex-President Harrison, Illinois to Senator Cullom, and

Minnesota to Senator Davis. If necessary, additional favorite sons could be tossed into the political pot to keep it boiling until the desired result was achieved.

When Hanna learned of the plan, he knew that everything hinged on promoting the impression that McKinley's candidacy was irresistible, appealing to all classes, sections, and viewpoints. If local politicians sniffed even the possibility of his defeat, they would be tempted to turn elsewhere; convinced of his success, they would not hesitate to make a definite commitment. Capitalizing on the growing disenchantment with machine rule, McKinley's candidacy was trumpeted as "The People Against the Bosses"—an unbeatable slogan Hanna reportedly originated.

Except for Iowa, McKinley's position was strong everywhere west of the Mississippi. Various methods were employed to win over the doubtful states. McKinley aides descended on Indiana for a round of private meetings with leaders as soon as former President Harrison announced that he was not a candidate. When they left, the state was secure. Even where the opposition was firmly in control, hard work brought results, as for example in New York and Pennsylvania, where Hanna obtained pledges of seventeen and eight votes, respectively.

At the state convention in Ohio, the powerful leader of a rival faction was won over and persuaded to place McKinley's name in nomination. The platform adopted there strongly advocated a return to protectionism for reviving prosperity, but, to avoid political difficulties for McKinley in the areas west of the Mississippi, the silver issue was evaded. Sound money was cautiously supported, with both silver and gold to be kept at a parity arranged by international agreement.

In Illinois, a key state, local politicians were supporting Senator Cullom. As the McKinley forces had no base of operations within the regular organization, an independent leader, Charles G. Dawes, was enlisted to mobilize whatever pro-McKinley sentiment he could find. Dawes, a superb organizer, influenced the district conventions to act favorably but during the state convention in April, a sharp dispute placed the outcome in doubt for several days. At the last moment Senator Cullom withdrew and the delegates were instructed for McKinley, virtually assuring him of the nomination. Six weeks before the national convention, a Democratic newspaper in New York wrote that McKinley "may die before the convention meets, or be incapacitated by paralysis, but hardly any other event can deprive him of his present advantage."

Nevertheless, the bosses continued to oppose McKinley until the very end. Platt circulated a private memorandum to his lieutenants in mid-May that the candidate was not as "well balanced" politically as Governor Morton, not as well educated and trained in public affairs as Senator Allison, or as astute a political leader as Senator Quay.

> He is simply a clever gentleman much too amiable and impressionable to be safely entrusted with great executive office, whose desire for honour happens to have the accidental advantage of the association of his name with the last Republican protective tariff. . . . On the money question nobody can look at McKinley's record and read the flabby things he has said without perceiving that he has no fixed opinion but has been turned and twisted by changing public opinion.

Any lingering hopes the political chieftains might have had must have been completely dashed when they arrived for the convention at St. Louis. McKinley signs seemingly fluttered from every pole and rafter; McKinley buttons and canes were ubiquitous; McKinley's name seemed to be on every tongue. A drink composed mainly of bourbon concocted by the South Carolina delegates was labeled "The McKinley." Worse still, McKinley was favored by a major portion of the delegates, and his forces, controlling the National Committee, were shaping all of its decisions in his interest. Thomas B. Reed's manager was so shaken that in a public interview he blurted out that McKinley would be nominated on the first ballot.

With his superlative business skill, Hanna had fashioned an organization that operated with consummate efficiency. About a week before the convention was to open, he and his associates established headquarters and immediately plunged into work. One adjutant handled public relations and communications facilities; another came prepared with material to defend the right of McKinley delegates to be seated if their credentials were challenged; while a third was to greet the delegates. All had met at McKinley's home for final instructions. Every detail had been settled, including the platform, the temporary and permanent chairmen, the vice-presidential candidate.

McKinley remained at home in Canton, but all the decisions and strategy were firmly in his hands throughout. A communication link of two telegraphic installations and a direct wire was set up between his bedroom and Hanna's office. The youthful Charles W. Fairbanks of Indiana, chosen by McKinley to deliver the keynote address, consulted with the candidate several hours before he left for St. Louis. Even the denomination of the clergyman to deliver the opening prayer had been thoughtfully considered. To avoid possible criticism from the anti-Catholic American Protective Association on the one hand or from the Catholics on the other, McKinley requested Rabbi Sale of St. Louis to deliver the invocation.

With McKinley's opposition hopelessly outmaneuvered and outflanked, the convention would have been a cut-and-dried affair but for the money issue. During the preconvention jousting, McKinley had remained silent, hoping that he could wage the campaign on the issue of protectionism. At one point, when mounting pressure had compelled him to make a statement, he responded evasively, authorizing an aide to say only, "No man's friends have a right to call upon him to foreshadow the party's platform. . . . Major McKinley will respond to the platform but he will not dictate what the platform shall be." While he favored a double monetary standard, he feared that whatever position he took would be costly. If he came out for bimetallism the eastern support would be undermined, while if he endorsed gold the western delegates might bolt in sufficient numbers to lose him the election.

Still, a decision had to be made, and the McKinley group decided they would have to risk alienating the West. Now the question was whether the platform pledge should endorse "the existing standard" or use the word "gold." Both meant the same thing, but "gold" would sharpen the statement. They finally settled on "gold." An unequivocal stand would force the Democrats to declare for silver, which would either split their party wide open or cause enough defections in the eastern states to make that area solidly Republican. The Midwest would then be the crucial area, which it was hoped could be carried by a combination of industrial workers and conservative farmers.

The anticipated opposition from the western silver Republicans came on the third day, after the party platform was presented. Senator Henry M. Teller, spokesman for the group, rose to present his minority report. He began by reminding his audience of his lifelong devotion to the party, which he would leave only with deep grief, "but I cannot, before my country and my God agree to the provision that shall put upon this country a gold standard, and I will not." He was convinced that the plank meant "ultimate disaster and distress to my fellowmen," and if adopted then he must, as an honest man, sever his connection with the political organization which made it one of the main articles of its faith. The silver plank which he submitted was defeated by 818½ to 105½.

Senator Joseph G. Cannon of Utah next delivered a lengthy statement on behalf of the western silver delegates who were going to leave the convention. He was constantly interrupted by shouts of "Goodbye," "Put him out," "Let him print it." When he finished the hall was in bedlam, with men shouting and swearing and tossing paper into the air. To the accompaniment of frenzied cries of "Go, Go," which were partially drowned out by the blare of the band, Teller and Cannon walked out of the hall followed by a group of thirty-four delegates and alternates from Montana, Utah, Colorado, Idaho, and South Dakota.

After the commotion subsided, the remainder of the proceedings was a mere formality. The delegates went through the motions of placing the candidates in nomination. Joseph Foraker, a political power in Ohio who was won over to McKinley by a pledge of support for a senatorial seat, did the honors for the candidate: "The darkest hour is just before the day. The twentieth century will have dawned bright and clear; God lives; the Republican party is coming back to power and William McKinley is to be President of the United States." The first ballot gave McKinley the nomination with 661½ votes as against 268½ for all the other candidates. With dispatch, the convention then proceeded to nominate Garret A. Hobart of New Jersey for the vice-presidency, the man previously singled out by the McKinley-Hanna organization. The meeting then adjourned.

Two myths developed about the nomination of McKinley. The first, subsequently swallowed up by the second, was that McKinley owed his victory to his tremendous grass-roots popularity. After his nomination, one of his opponent's supporters rose to declare, "The Republicans, the rank and file, have made the nomination this afternoon, and not Mark Hanna." The other was typified by the comment of one newspaper reporter that McKinley was a puppet in the new "Hannaverian dynasty" masterminded by that political and organization genius, Mark Hanna, and another press item that "Hanna owns McKinley" who had been left "bucked and gagged behind doors, barred against all visiting questions." Governor John Peter Altgeld of Illinois said of the convention that it was the "most mediocre . . . ever held by that great party . . . manipulated in such a way that it will be known in history as 'Mark Hanna's trust.'" As the years went on, this myth prevailed and McKinley's genuine political skill became almost completely obscured.

When the news was received of McKinley's nomination, Canton was overrun by throngs of worshipful admirers from cities and towns throughout the state. They converged on the McKinley house to the accompaniment of the deafening din of cannon, guns, firecrackers, gongs, bells, tin horns and whistles, and the blare of bands. More than 50,000 were in the crush between five o'clock and midnight, when the exhausted nominee, his right hand numb from the incessant handshaking, was at last permitted to retire.

McKinley's supporters anticipated an easy victory in November. Their optimism ballooned when the Democrats, gathering for their convention at Chicago early in June, revealed a schism reminiscent of 1860. The eastern wing of the party supported President Cleveland while the South, West, and Midwest regarded the administration's financial policies as disastrous and were determined not to permit any equivocation on the free-silver issue. By repudiating the "gold bugs" in the party, the latter hoped to shatter the alliance that had been forged in 1860 between the eastern industrialists and the western farmers, drawing away the disaffected agrarians.

Among the numerous aspirants for the nomination, none was in a dominant position or had an aggressively strong organization to back him. The most outstanding was Congressman Richard P. Bland, nationally known as "Silver Dick Bland" for his passionate championship of the free coinage of silver and his co-sponsorship of the Bland-Allison Silver Purchase Act of 1878. Another serious contender was the impressive-looking Horace Boies of Iowa, elected governor in 1889 in a traditionally Republican state, who became a potential national leader when two years later Iowa voted in the entire Democratic ticket. Several governors were also considered, and if the convention adopted a free-silver platform the field would be wide open for a prominent Democrat in the silver movement, which included such men as Senators Benjamin Tillman and John W. Daniel, and William Jennings Bryan. The question was whether any one could obtain the two-thirds majority required by the convention.

At preliminary conferences, the silverites made careful plans to secure the necessary majority by increasing the number of delegates from the territories and seating two contested delegations. They won their first victory and demonstrated their ability to beat back the opposition when the convention rejected the National Committee's recommendation of the conservative David B. Hill of New York for temporary chairman and by a majority elected their choice, Senator John W. Daniel of Virginia. After that it was apparent that the conservatives were outnumbered. A silverite was selected permanent chairman. The Committee on Credentials reversed the decision of the National Committee to seat the gold supporters in the contested delegations from Nebraska and South Dakota and succeeded the following day in accrediting the silver delegation from Michigan.

When the platform came up for debate, the tension in the hall was almost palpable. The major point was the declaration in the majority report, "We are unalterably opposed to monometallism, which has locked fast the prosperity of an industrial people in the paralysis of hard times. . . . We demand the free and unlimited coinage of both silver and gold at the present legal ratio of sixteen to one, without waiting for the aid or consent of any other nation."

Senator "Pitchfork" Ben Tillman, noted for his pyrotechnic oratory, led off with a slashing attack upon the administration. He was followed by Senator Hill of New York, who defended the President and opposed the silver plank. "Be not deceived," he pleaded. "Do not drive old Democrats out of the party . . . to make room for a lot of Republicans and Populists and political nondescripts who will not vote your ticket at the polls." Two more conservatives spoke, and then it was the turn of the youthful William Jennings Bryan, former congressman from Nebraska.

Bryan's opening sentences immediately captured his audience. Speaking with the evangelical fervor of a medieval crusader defending his faith, he proclaimed, "I come to speak to you in defense of a cause as holy as the cause of liberty—the cause of humanity." Principles were eternal, he asserted, and silver was a principle for which he had come to do battle. He went on to describe the two philosophies of government which were competing with each other. "There are those who believe that, if you will only legislate to make the well-to-do prosperous, their prosperity will leak through on those below. The Democratic idea, however, has been that if you legislate to make the masses prosperous, their prosperity will find its way up through every class which rests upon them." If the urban centers favored gold, he would reply that "the great cities rest upon our broad and fertile prairies. Burn down your cities and leave your farms, and your cities will spring up again as if by magic; but destroy our farms and the grass will grow in the streets of every city in the country."

The convention sat spellbound. "We have petitioned, and our petitions have been scorned; we have entreated, and our entreaties have been disregarded; we have begged, and they have mocked when our calamity came," he concluded his peroration. "We beg no longer; we entreat no more. We defy them. . . . Having behind us the producing masses of this nation and the world, supported by the commercial interests, the laboring interests, and the toilers everywhere, we will answer their demand for a gold standard by saying to them: You shall not press down upon the brow of labor this crown of thorns, you shall not crucify mankind upon a cross of gold."

For the fraction of a moment there was silence. Then the hall exploded with a roar that shook the walls. Men shouted, cheered, leaped on chairs, waved hats, canes, handkerchiefs, papers, anything they could put their hands on. If it had been possible to ballot right then, Bryan would undoubtedly have been nominated by acclamation. By the following day, however, emotions had cooled, and for several ballots the convention deadlocked between Bland and Bryan. Not until the fifth ballot was "the boy orator of the Platte" awarded the prize.

A legend soon evolved that Bryan's oratory, especially his "cross of gold" peroration, had won him the nomination. The New York *Herald* wrote, "A phrase has nominated a

candidate for the presidency . . ." and the St. Louis *Post
Dispatch* stated, "With his eloquence Mr. Bryan cut his
way through and at one bound landed from a possibility
into a winner's seat." Possibly Bryan might not have been
nominated without so stirring an address, but it was not the
only factor.

Despite Bryan's youth—he was only thirty-six years
old—and his brief experience in political life as a congressman for two terms, he had already achieved a national
reputation as the most forceful speaker on the "silver circuit." His striking face with its high forehead, thick black
hair, and glowing eyes combined with an extraordinarily
beautiful voice and superb oratorical skill, which electrified
his listeners, made him an idol in large sections of the South
and West. His preconvention organization consisted of himself, his wife, and a small clerical staff, but he was a master
at publicity. Skillfully he kept his name before the public
with a vast correspondence, personal contacts, and public
addresses. During the preceding year he had spoken in
virtually every state in the country.

Astutely, he had realized that if he started his campaign
ball rolling too early it might prematurely lose momentum,
but he did not discourage speculation about his candidacy.
For several months before the convention he was mentioned in newspapers and public talks as a potential candidate. By the end of May he was openly soliciting support
and he came to the convention backed by many devoted
friends. In addition, almost every delegation from the western states, the southern states, and the territories had a few
members who were ready to spring to action on his behalf.
He was not overly optimistic about his chances, but he
hoped that events and his carefully prepared address would
make him "the logic of the situation." On the morning of
the platform debate, a front-page story in the Chicago
Tribune was headlined, "Bryan, Boy Orator of the Platte in
the Presidential Race."

That the silverites had captured control of the Democratic party and would make silver the dominant issue in

the campaign was patent when the convention named Arthur Sewall, a free-silver advocate, the vice-presidential candidate. At the same time, Sewall, an eastern railroad director, shipbuilder, and banker, would balance the ticket.

The Populists were now faced with a dilemma. Should they join forces with the Democrats? "If we fuse, we are sunk; if we don't fuse, all the silver men we have will leave us for the more powerful Democrats!" lamented one of the leading Populists. Another noted in his diary, "I like Bryan, but I do not feel that we can safely adopt the Dem. candidates. I fear it will be the end of our party."

Two days before their convention opened at St. Louis, Populist leaders gathered to discuss the problem. It was apparent that they were split along sectional lines, West versus South. The Southerners had succeeded in establishing the party in their region only after a bitter struggle against the Democrats, and now to join with the detested "Bourbons" would stick in their craw. To Westerners, for whom silver had a direct economic significance, Bryan and his platform offered an opportunity to realize their demands. Prolonged and heated discussions only exacerbated the differences. The day before the convention a Populist leader commented, "The Southern delegates . . . are still sore enough to walk out of the convention if they are not given their own way. On the other hand, the silver men from the West are generally determined to have Bryan or walk out. This is a question that cannot be compromised."

For three days the convention swayed back and forth from fusion to independent action. Only the determination to preserve the Populist party, the first reform party since the Civil War to attain national recognition, kept it from disintegrating. When it appeared that the pro-Bryan faction would win out, those opposed to fusion hoped at least to nominate their own candidate for Vice-President. Senator James K. Jones, Bryan's campaign manager, who had come to the convention to promote a common front, wired Bryan to ask whether he would accept the nomination without Sewall, at the same time suggesting that he refuse. Bryan took his advice, but through inadvertence or design his position was not made known to the convention. A number of contradictory versions of the telegraphic exchange spread among the delegates. One was that Bryan had never sent any message; another that he was willing to accept a Populist running mate.

The last hours of the convention were completely chaotic. Bryan was nominated, whereupon violence almost erupted as some triumphant paraders attempted to seize the state banner of the Texas delegation, which sat silent and stony-faced, and carry it into the procession. Finally, the vice-presidential nomination was awarded to Thomas E. Watson of Georgia, and the convention adjourned.

Henry Demarest Lloyd, who hoped the Populist party would develop as a broad social-reform movement, expressed the despondency of those opposed to fusion. "A party which hates [the] Democracy accepted the Democratic nominee and a party which has no faith in silver as a panacea accepted silver practically as the sole issue of the campaign." Moreover, he went on, "The Free Silver movement is a fake. Free Silver is the cow-bird of the Reform movement. It waited until the nest had been built by the sacrifices and labour of others and then it laid its eggs in it. . . . The People's party has been betrayed."

The politics of 1896 brought together some strange bedfellows and shattered long-standing party relationships. There was Marcus Daly, the multimillionaire owner of Anaconda Mines, whose tremendous stake in silver made him a devoted financial supporter of the "embattled farmers" in their crusade against the "Eastern despots" and "British tyrants." For several years he had donated generously to the American Bimetallic League to promote its educational efforts for the free and unlimited coinage of silver. Prior to the Democratic party convention, he and his associates spent almost $300,000 to secure delegates pledged to free silver.

On the other side was the eastern financial oligarchy— men like Whitney, Fairchild, Belmont, Villard, influential in banking and railroad circles—and conservative Democrats elsewhere who found both the candidate and the platform of their party unacceptable. For many of these men party loyalty was a strong tradition, but when the party was captured by the silverites, they were overcome with rage and disgust. "We want to see the defeat of the Democratic Ticket," one of these lifelong Democrats said venomously, "and we shall try to draw away as many voters as we can from it."

Gold Democrats from various states organized a convention to nominate their own candidates. They met at Indianapolis on September 2 and 3 where, under the banner of the National Democrats, they endorsed John M. Palmer of Illinois and Confederate General Simon Bolivar Buckner. Some hoped that the new group would regain control of their party if Bryan were defeated; most, however, were primarily concerned with bringing about a McKinley victory and maintaining "sound money."

After his nomination, Bryan told a group of admirers that this would be a "campaign of sentiment" to arouse the conscience and spirit of Americans in the battle for a righteous cause. Bryan's journey from Chicago to his home in Lincoln, Nebraska, took on the aspect of a triumphal procession. Huge throngs gathered at every railroad station en route, waving banners, tossing flowers, cheering wildly, some even climbing telegraph poles to catch a glimpse of him; "he seemed a sort of knight errant going about to redress the wrongs of a nation," wrote Woodrow Wilson.

The popular enthusiasm which Bryan evoked indicated that public apathy would not be a feature of this contest. Before his nomination, Hanna and the other McKinley managers had anticipated an easy campaign conducted in the usual manner with the "outs" trying to dislodge the "ins." Afterward, Hanna observed that it "will be hard work and hard work from the start." People in the throes of economic malaise might very well respond to the proffered solution of sixteen to one offered by that incomparable speechmaker.

Assessing the requirements for victory, Hanna concluded that Bryan probably would win the South and the Far West. The Northeast seemed safe for McKinley. That left the Midwest as the crucial area, the states of Ohio, Illinois, Michigan, Indiana, and Wisconsin, the loss of any one of which could be fatal.

Hanna established headquarters in Chicago, then went East to set up an auxiliary office in New York and to raise funds. He was introduced to the great Wall Street establishments by the railroad tycoon James J. Hill, a lifelong Democrat who had abandoned his party because of his devout belief in the gold standard. With businesslike efficiency Hanna devised a procedure for extracting cash. Banks and insurance companies were assessed a percentage of their assets and commercial houses assigned contribution quotas based on their volume of business. Campaign staff members were assigned to supervise the collections, to watch for any weak spots in the system. Money began to flow in. Standard Oil contributed $250,000, New York Life $50,000, railroad corporations $174,000. More than a fourth of the contributions sent to the Chicago office were in amounts of $1,000 or more. By the end of the campaign about $3.5 million had been raised. Expenditures were double the amount they had been in 1892, a certain indication of how seriously McKinley and his aides took the campaign.

A substantial amount of money was allocated for propaganda, or what Hanna called a campaign of education. "There is an intense feeling everywhere, and much interest in this money question," one of McKinley's aides, William S. Osborne, wrote the candidate in mid-August, "and we have got to furnish the literature that will enlighten the people." About 250 million pieces of printed matter, dealing at first with the currency question and later with protectionism after the silver issue had lost momentum, were distributed throughout the country. Some 275 different pamphlets and broadsides were printed in German, French, Spanish, Italian, Swedish, Norwegian, Danish, Dutch.

Country newspapers were supplied either with copy or
with plates. According to one reliable estimate, the amount
of material circulated in 1896 exceeded by fifty per cent the
total issued by the Republican National Committee in all its
previous campaigns. Theodore Roosevelt sneered at the
avalanche of propaganda smothering the country. Hanna,
he said, "has advertised McKinley as if he were a patent
medicine."

Chicago headquarters also established bureaus and departments to handle special-interest groups. There was a
"Colored Bureau," a traveling salesmen's bureau, a women's
department, an organization for bicyclists. The speaker's
bureau mobilized 1,400 speakers to travel up and down the
country. Nothing was overlooked. Even spies were installed
at Democratic party headquarters so that Hanna could
keep tabs on the opposition.

One of the master strategist's brilliant ideas was to en-
shrine McKinley as a patriotic symbol on a par with "Old
Glory." Hanna had begun at the convention by passing out
buttons with only the American flag printed on them. During the campaign millions of flags were distributed everywhere for demonstrations. Then Hanna dreamed up the
idea of having a flag day in honor of the candidate. The
Republican committee went to work, providing flags in all
sizes, dispensing posters, buttons, hats, and horns, and helping organize monster parades in the large cities. Prosperous,
dignified New Yorkers responded as though called to defend their country from imminent peril. More than 100,000
men solemnly marched while more than 750,000 lined the
streets to cheer. "The flag was everywhere," wrote the New
York *Tribune*. "It flaunted from every window . . . it flew
from every roof; . . . every man in the whole vast line carried a flag of his own which he held aloft. . . . Many of those
who marched yesterday have known what it is to march in
war under the same flag that covered the city in its folds
yesterday all the day long." In San Francisco a flag parade
lasted four hours.

By contrast with this massive effort, the activities of the

Democratic National Committee were amateurish. A speaker's bureau was established in Chicago from which some campaign literature was sent out and a handful of Bryan clubs and Silver clubs were organized in various parts of the country. The total effort was pitifully inadequate. From the outset the Committee was shackled by lack of coordination among the Populist, Silver, and Democratic parties but most of all by lack of funds.

A plea in sympathetic papers by Senator Jones, chairman of the National Committee, for small contributions to counteract the huge sums donated by wealthy Republicans brought only a scanty response from "the plain people." The most important single source of funds was William Randolph Hearst, who gave $15,000 and succeeded in raising an additional $25,000 through his paper, the New York *Journal*. A few other affluent Democrats made contributions, but none came within striking distance of the amounts furnished by their Republican counterparts. The total sum Bryan was estimated to have spent on his campaign was about $300,000, approximately one tenth the amount put out by the Republicans.

Press support was also meager. The only major Democratic newspaper in New York which championed Bryan was Hearst's *Journal*. In New England and the Midwest, the important dailies opposed him; in the South, some of the most influential papers refused to endorse the Democratic ticket. No previous campaign had occasioned such a tremendous shift in newspaper sentiment. Moreover, virtually the entire world of industry and finance displayed an attitude toward the Democrats that can only be described as paranoid fear. During the party convention the Philadelphia *Press* wrote, "The Jacobins are in full control at Chicago. No large political movement in America has ever before spawned such hideous and repulsive vipers. . . . The Altgelds and Tillmans who have . . . seized the reins of control incarnate a spirit of communism and anarchy which is new to American politics on any large scale. This riotous platform is the concrete creed of the mob. It is rank

populism intensified and edged with hate and venom. . . .
Such a noxious and nefarious profession of faith has never
before been made in this country even by an escaped band
of lunatics."

After Bryan's nomination, the New York *Times* published
a letter from a terrified reader who warned that "within six
months of Bryan's election mobs would be rushing up and
down our streets howling for bread" and the country would
descend to anarchy; "the Republican form of Government,"
he solemnly declared, "is on trial here." Depositors were
informed that the banks would fail; policyholders that insurance companies would be unable to fulfill their obligations; stock and bondholders that the value of their invest-
ments would plummet. In some instances, the execution of
contracts was made contingent on McKinley's election.
Farmers were advised that if Bryan was defeated they
would be able to renew their loans at low interest rates.
Never before had voters been so intimidated with the threat
of personal economic catastrophe.

Free silver was also denounced as a doctrine as heinous
as free love. Clergymen, especially in the large and influential urban churches, cried out against it with a passion
ordinarily reserved for the most infamous heresy. The
Democratic platform had been made in hell, shrilled one
man of the cloth, with Altgeld and his associates as the
devil's stenographers and prompters. Another declaimed,
"Once more is society rent with strife over not what belongs
to ordinary politics, but what belongs to national conscience and to civilization itself."

Bryan himself was viciously maligned as a "Popocrat," a
mountebank, an anarchist, a socialist, a revolutionary. The
depths to which the press sank is illustrated by an article
published in the New York *Times* on September 27, signed
"An Eminent Alienist." On the basis of Bryan's speeches,
the writer stated, he could only conclude that the candidate's mind "was not entirely sound," and if he won the
election there would be a "madman in the White House."
On the same page, the *Times* editorially concurred and

went on, "What, however, most of all entitles us to say that
Mr. Bryan is of unsound mind, whether we call this condition unsoundness in English or insanity in Latin, is that his
procedures are not adaptations of intelligent means to intelligent ends."

Against all this vituperation and the other handicaps
with which the Democratic party had to contend, there was
little more than the asset of Bryan himself. With the zealot's
unshakable belief in the righteousness of his cause, Bryan
was convinced that he could win the election merely by
taking his message to the people. All he asked was sufficient
funds to travel across the land.

Bryan began by going to New York. He had requested
that he be notified of his nomination there so that "our
cause might be presented first in the heart of what now
seems to be the enemy's country, but which we hope to be
our country before this campaign is over." It was not a very
auspicious start. August 11, the day of his address at Madison Square Garden, was breathlessly hot and humid. The
hall was suffocating. Governor Stone's notification speech
dragged on interminably. Bryan, fearing misquotation in
the papers, had decided to read his speech, and his delivery
lacked the captivating impact of his extemporaneous per-
formances. Many in the audience walked out before he finished, but not the great number a hostile press later reported. On the whole, it was a tribute to Bryan that anyone
remained in that insufferable heat for two hours to listen to
a talk he could read in the papers the next day. Newspaper
exaggeration about the "desertions," however, spread, and
Bryan's visit to New York became generally regarded as a
"failure."

With unflagging energy Bryan conducted a whirlwind
campaign, often making twenty or thirty addresses to as
many as 100,000 people in a single day. Two thirds of his
major stops were in the eight states of the crucial Midwest,
where he sought to capitalize on the prevailing agricultural
distress and years of Populist agitation. He improvised his
talks, gearing his remarks to the nature of his audience. To

farmers in Illinois he spoke about the evils of mortgage foreclosures, asserting that legislation was making their lives harder all the time because "the non-producing classes have been producing the laws." In Minnesota, he attacked the railroad wreckers and coal barons. He assured the flour merchant that with free coinage of silver he would receive twice as many dollars for his product. To an urban working-class audience he denounced "government by injunction," the dispatching of troops to break up strikes, and endorsed a direct income tax.

The theme which predominated, to which he returned again and again, was the free and unlimited coinage of silver. "Where there is more money in circulation there is a better chance for each man to get money than there is when money is scarce," he declared. The simplistic solution which he offered as a panacea reflected his simple, fundamental faith: "The great political questions are, in the last analysis, moral questions."

In all, Bryan traveled 18,000 miles, delivering more than 600 addresses which reached an estimated five million people in twenty-seven states. Most of the time he made his own arrangements, purchasing train tickets, sometimes even carrying his own luggage; not until October was he provided with a private railroad car. Speaking continuously and every day except Sunday, his voice sometimes gave out. Only his extraordinary physical stamina kept him from collapsing from total exhaustion. The youthful candidate's vigor and his superb oratory employed in passionate exhortation against the "masters of capital" and for his panacea of free silver enkindled hundreds of thousands of people. During one address a man in the audience was so carried away that he cried out, "Bryan, I'm not a Christian, but I am praying for you."

The large, enthusiastic audiences which the Democratic candidate was attracting began to worry McKinley's advisors. They met in Chicago to formulate some counter action. "We have got to get McKinley out on the road to meet this thing and I wish you would go out to him . . . and map

out a campaign for him," Hanna suggested to a member of
the inner circle. But McKinley firmly refused to campaign.
He had already gone on record, he said, that he would not
do so and now to reverse himself would be an acknowledg-
ment of weakness. "Moreover, I might just as well put up a
trapeze on my front lawn and compete with some professional athlete as go out speaking against Bryan." At the
same time, the politically astute McKinley realized that if
he remained in the background he would leave himself
open to the accusation that he was merely a front. He decided to emulate Benjamin Harrison, who had conducted a
very successful "front porch" campaign. His own would be
carefully planned and carried out on an extensive scale.

For weeks before the election, Canton became a Mecca
and McKinley's home a shrine to which hundreds of thousands of the faithful came to worship. Preparations and
stage management were flawless, often including even dress
rehearsals. When a delegation wrote McKinley for an appointment to visit him, a dossier was prepared on its com-
position so that the candidate could make some personal
remarks. The leader was requested either to come in advance with a copy of his own remarks, or send a copy, or
meet privately with McKinley before the official ceremony.
The candidate was taking no chances that an unfortunate
slip might be made by either man. One time after the delegation spokesman read his prepared statement, McKinley
said in his kindly way, "My friend, that is a splendid
speech, a magnificent speech . . . but is it quite suitable to
this peculiar occasion? . . . Now you go home and write a
speech along the lines I indicate and send me a copy of
it."

Delegations were greeted at the station by a uniformed,
mounted company called the "Canton Home Guards," organized by one of McKinley's neighbors. While they were
being marched with pomp and ceremony to the candidate's
home, one of the "guards" had already dashed off on horseback to give McKinley the names of the leader and the
delegation so that he could pull the proper greeting out of

his files. Visitors were dazzled by the city draped in red, blue, and white bunting and awed by a decorated arch surmounted by the candidate's portrait which had been erected over the street leading to his house. Gathered on the front lawn, the delegation was greeted by their smiling, genial host, who looked every inch the statesman in an impeccable starched shirt, long double-breasted coat, white vest, and carnation in his buttonhole. McKinley listened attentively to the leader's address, thanked his guests warmly for honoring him by coming to his home, and then read his prepared speech, which was stuffed with platitudes and clichés: "In this contest patriotism is above party," "National honor is dearer than party name," "this government is one of honor and of law, and . . . neither the seeds of repudiation nor lawlessness can find root in our soil or live beneath our flag." Later, after shaking hands with everyone, he held an informal reception. When it rained, the gathering assembled in the town's auditorium or a specially built tent.

Between June 19 and November 2, 750,000 people in more than 300 delegations from thirty states visited McKinley. Railroads assisted in drawing the hordes by offering special fares for the excursion. In one day alone, Canton shook with the tramp of sixteen delegations from a dozen states. Children accompanying their parents piped:

> Governor McKinley, he's our man;
> If we can't vote for him our papas can.

Visitors left in a glow from the attention they had been given by the great man. They carried away a picture of a dedicated patriot, who in addition was kindly, home-loving, and devoted to his wife and mother. They also carried away souvenirs—pieces of wood whittled from the porch, the house, the picket fence, even leaves of grass plucked from trees and shrubs and blades of grass from the lawn. By election time the fence was gone, the porch threatened to collapse, and the lawn was completely denuded, looking "as if a herd of buffalo had passed that way."

McKinley emphasized three themes: the currency question, the protective tariff, and the danger of setting class against class. He would have preferred to concentrate entirely on the tariff as the key to a prosperous America, but Bryan forced silver upon him. In his letter of acceptance, he had set to rest all doubts on the part of the "gold bugs" that he might equivocate, declaring that until a ratio between the two metals was fixed by international agreement, it was the "plain duty of the United States to maintain the gold standard." Money, he piously asserted, should be kept free of speculation and fluctuation and ought never be made an issue of partisan politics.

Aware of the middle-class fear of inflation, he declared that he was opposed to a currency whose value would change from day to day. Free silver would not mean more money for everyone, and debts honestly contracted should be paid as honestly. Since everyone owned property of some kind, free silver, he warned, threatened each individual. At the same time, McKinley realized that if he concentrated on the money question he would forfeit the support of the free-silver Republicans in the West who had not already deserted to the Democrats. Accordingly, he linked protectionism with sound money, while tarring the Democrats with free silver and free trade. He evoked cheers and applause from a group of Ohio wool producers when he asserted, "As free wool degraded your industry so free silver will degrade your money. You have already been fleeced by loss on your flocks and you don't propose to be fleeced further by loss on your money."

The industrial worker having supplanted the farmer as the base on which the nation's prosperity rested, a special appeal would have to be directed to him. At the outset of the campaign, McKinley pledged a tariff law which would "give preference to home manufactures and adequate protection to home labor and the home market." He also castigated the opposition for seeking to drive a wedge between capital and labor, between employers and employees, proclaiming, "We are all political equals here—equal in privilege and opportunity, dependent upon each other, and the prosperity of the one is the prosperity of the other." In a country whose mythology regarded a class system as alien, this struck a responsive chord.

To a visiting delegation of Pennsylvania steel workers he said that partial free trade was responsible for diminished employment and earnings. "We do not propose now to inaugurate a currency system that will cheat labor in its pay." For a full day's work a laboring man expected "to be paid in full dollars good everywhere in the world. . . . We want in this country good work, good wages, and good money."

National excitement mounted to fever pitch as election day drew near. Monster torchlight parades organized by the Republicans wound through city streets with financial and industrial leaders at their head. In the churches clergymen vehemently exhorted their congregations to defeat Bryan. One minister ranted that the nation was "on the eve of the greatest political battle this country has seen for years, if ever. . . . McKinley stands for . . . patriotism and honor . . . Bryan for anarchy, repudiation and national dishonor." Another urged that the country "grind its heel relentlessly and unpityingly into the viperous head that is lifting itself up in venomous antagonism to all government."

The Republican candidate wound up his campaign in Canton with a huge rally. About forty bands made the city resound with stirring marches, and in response to Hanna's request that flags be flown, "Old Glory" fluttered in the breeze for miles around. "Glorious old banner it is," McKinley sermonized. "So long as we carry it in our hands and have what it typifies in our hearts, the Republic and our splendid free institutions will be forever secure."

At Ottumwa, Iowa, Bryan too was delivering his final address. He had appealed, he told the crowd, "to the great producing masses" and to all others who believed that the nation's prosperity depended on "those who toil." Reaffirming his belief in silver, he declared, "My hand has been used until it is sore, but it can handle a pen to sign a free-coinage bill, if I am elected. I have been wearied with work, but I still have the physical strength to stand between the people, if they elect me, and the Wall Street syndicates which have been bleeding this country."

So Bryan ended as he had begun, calling for righteousness with the fervor of an ancient Hebrew prophet. Economic equity and social justice would be possible only when the silver issue was resolved. He offered the voters a genuine choice: they could either endorse eastern orthodoxy or align themselves with those waging a frontal attack against it. Seeking to mobilize the "producing masses" on the farms and in the factories into an effective force of protest, Bryan had rejected the traditional role of the presidential candidate in American politics—broker for the diverse and competing interests in the land.

That the campaign had aroused an unprecedented interest among the people was indicated by the number who turned out to the polls. The vote was the largest ever cast in any presidential contest. McKinley received 7,104,779 votes to Bryan's 6,502,925, and in the electoral college 271 to 176. It was the greatest victory scored by a Republican candidate since Grant's in 1872, but still not a landslide.

A breakdown of the balloting revealed that McKinley won most of New England, where he received two thirds of the votes. Bryan lost all three mid-Atlantic states, two of which, New York and New Jersey, Cleveland had carried four years earlier. He also lost by a substantial margin all five of the states of the old Northwest—Wisconsin, Michigan, Indiana, Ohio, and Illinois—which had given Cleveland almost 60 electoral votes in 1892 and which Hanna had considered vital for victory. McKinley won notable triumphs in Delaware, Maryland, West Virginia, North Dakota, Kentucky, Iowa, and Minnesota; all but the last two had been carried by the Democratic candidate four years earlier. He also captured Oregon and California.

By adopting a radical monetary policy, the Democrats had alienated the Atlantic seaboard, a doubtful region for both parties since 1872. Until this election, the plurality in a key state like Pennsylvania had never exceeded 80,000, but McKinley rolled up more than 300,000. The results were just as striking in states like New York, Connecticut, and New Jersey, which previously had been about evenly divided. Bryan scored major gains only in the sparsely settled western states, a dubious victory since they were of little consequence in terms of electoral votes.

Staking all on sixteen to one in the belief that this formula would solve the problems afflicting society, Bryan was the only candidate, in the words of one historian, who ever "ran for the Presidency on the strength of a monomania." Under Hanna's relentless barrage, the silver theme was pounded away into insignificance so that finally Bryan was left expending his energy on a shadow. The silver candidate had failed to persuade the urban laborers, without whose support victory in the new industrial age was virtually impossible, that his interests were allied with those of the farmer, that both would benefit from free silver. McKinley had maintained that farm prices were not dependent on silver but governed by supply and demand; hence the solution to farm distress was an expanded consumers' market which would develop when full tariff protection enabled factories to reopen. "I believe it is a good deal better to open the mills of the United States to the labor of Americans than to open the mints of the United States to the silver of the world," he had kept repeating to visiting delegations.

In short, Bryan could not prevail against the alluring siren song of protection and prosperity which was chanted endlessly by the massive chorus assembled by that masterly political director Hanna, or against the scandalous intimidation that was particularly effective with an unsophisticated electorate. Fundamentally, however, Bryan's defeat reflected the passing of a nineteenth-century agricultural society. The campaign was a confrontation between the past and the future, between the politics of nostalgia and the politics of realism.

Many of the silverites refused to acknowledge that their cause had been repudiated, contending that fraud and coercion had been so pervasive as to preclude an honest vote. Sewall and Altgeld believed that another assault on the citadel of plutocracy and corruption would rout the money power. Populist leaders, however, regarded the defeat as a severe blow to their movement. By hitching their wagon to the Bryan silver star and subordinating their reform goals, they had sacrificed much of their own identity and dissipated their élan. Ignatius Donnelly was left hopeless about the future and disillusioned with the masses. "It seems useless to contend against the money power," he wrote in his diary. "Every election marks another step downward into the abyss. . . . The people are too shallow and too corrupt to conduct a Republic." Despite a "splendid candidate," a "gigantic campaign," the unity of reform elements, and a depression, "the bankrupt millions voted to keep the yoke on their own necks!"

The conviction of Bryan's followers that currency was the "yoke" which was dragging the people deeper into the social and economic morass in which they were foundering produced the illusion of the silver talisman which would lift them out of it. Moreover, in their eyes money was "the dollar of the contract" and its value should remain stable—men should not receive less for the same amount of labor at one time than at another.

Because of this "silver monomania," the campaign of 1896 has sometimes been described as a "crackpot circus." On the contrary, it was conducted on a higher level than most campaigns by the silverites who, misdirected though they may have been, made an earnest effort to confront issues and problems as they saw them. Bryan focused on the dichotomy between poverty and privilege, and on the indifference to the tribulations of many Americans displayed by public men such as E. L. Godkin of the *Nation,* who wrote that every farmer who protested his lot was a worthless individual, or Secretary of Agriculture J. Sterling Morton, who declared in his annual report, "The intelligent, practical and successful farmer needs no aid from the government. The ignorant, impractical and indolent farmer deserves none. It is the beneficent arrangement of the order of things . . . that legislators are not permitted to repeal, amend or revise the laws of production and distribution."

The irrationality was in the hysterical response to the Bryan challenge. Those who had been frightened witless at the prospect of a Democratic victory reacted to the election results as though the nation had been rescued from impending doom. Indicative were the intemperate and nonsensical comments of the New York *Tribune* the morning after the election: "The thing was conceived in iniquity and was brought forth in sin"; it originated in "a malicious conspiracy against the honor and integrity of the nation. . . . It has been defeated . . . because right is right and God is God." Bryan, it continued, rivaled the arch traitors in American history "in deliberate wickedness and treason."

Defeat of the Democrats marked the end of a long period of evenly balanced parties in national politics. After the contest a significant change in the voting pattern was evident. The outlines of party realignment had been discernible two years earlier when Republicans won considerable majorities almost everywhere in the congressional elections. Now, having succeeded in forging an effective coalition of industrialists, white-collar workers, and laborers, as well as a substantial number of farmers, the Republicans had become the majority party.

7. Armageddon in Chicago

S HORTLY after his re-election to a second term, William
McKinley was struck down by the bullet of a self-
confessed anarchist and with him was interred an era which
he came to symbolize. The day of the sturdy yeoman farmer
and the independent artisan had long since passed, but the
myth of rugged individualism still clung, shaping the philosophy and practice of government. At the same time, ap-
palling evils spawned by industrialism flourished and grave
problems swelled to alarming proportions. One per cent of
the nation's families owned almost ninety per cent of its
wealth; the average worker toiled sixty hours a week, and
almost two million children spent their days in fields and
factories. An accelerating trend toward consolidation in
industry was destroying competition. The great corporations were dominating the basic industries, and their tremendous economic power made them highly influential in
politics.

Progressive reformers believed that the tie between business and politics must be severed before conditions could
be ameliorated, and that government must be made more
responsive to the will of the people. They campaigned for
the commission and city manager forms of municipal government, local home rule, the direct primary, the short ballot, the initiative and referendum. They sought to have existing child labor laws strengthened and boards established
to regulate utilities and railroad rates.

Reflecting and influencing progressive thought in the first decade of the century was the sensational literature of exposure which became known as "muckraking." In 1902, a group of journalists began to publish indictments of social, economic, and political malfeasance in a number of widely circulated middle-class periodicals. Their exposés ran the gamut from traffic in prostitution to the venal connection between crime and politics in city and state governments, fraudulent advertising, and poisoned foods and drugs. Shocked by this morass of corruption and public immorality, many voters for the first time realized the necessity of transforming government from a passive to a positive force in order to curb the abusive practices of utilities and corporations, halt the exploitation of men, women, and children, and eradicate urban evils. In the White House they now had a man who responded readily to this viewpoint.

After his equable predecessor, the youthful, electrifyingly dynamic Theodore Roosevelt seemed to shoot sparks in all directions. Though basically a conservative, he astutely recognized that change was inevitable and, if the nation was to be spared revolutionary upheavals, political leadership must institute reforms. The business community was infuriated when he directed the Attorney General to bring suit under the Sherman Antitrust Act, hitherto almost a dead letter, against the Northern Securities Company, a gigantic railroad-holding corporation. It was equally incensed when he used the weight of his office to achieve a settlement of the anthracite coal strike, compelling the mine owners for the first time to deal with the union.

A good executive, Roosevelt said, "must take a very active interest in getting the right kind of legislation." Among his notable achievements were a greatly strengthened railroad regulation act, the Pure Food and Drug Act, a meat inspection measure, and the movement for conservation of natural resources. Ignoring agonized cries of "executive usurpation" from private interests, Roosevelt appointed investigatory commissions to probe sectors of the economy hitherto considered immune to public scrutiny. In January

1908, he submitted to Congress the strongest message yet written by a President calling for a comprehensive program of business regulation. Favoring the principle of big unions as a countervailing force to big business, he rebuked the judiciary for abuse of the injunctive writ in labor disputes. His "trust busting," however, was more so in name than in fact, for having recognized the advantages of large corporate enterprise he advocated their regulation rather than dissolution.

Some of Roosevelt's progressive policies were not original with him. The Populists and Bryan had pressed for similar reforms but their support came largely from a rural constituency. Roosevelt was successful in winning over white-collar, middle-class Americans. Predominantly Protestant and urban, of old stock, this group represented a significant political force. The result was an urban-rural concensus that cut across party lines.

One of the most popular of Presidents, Roosevelt need only have said the word to be renominated in 1908, but he was opposed to third terms. His successor, William Howard Taft, whom he had personally selected, turned out to be a painful disappointment to him and a calamity to the Republican party. Taft, who yearned to be a Supreme Court Justice, accepted the presidential nomination with great reluctance, yielding to pressure from his wife and Roosevelt. At a time when dynamic leadership was essential, his inflexible, legalistic, and restrictive view of the presidential office was fatally anachronistic. Lacking any taste for politics, he had little political skill and committed one blunder after another. Unfortunately, too, the Republicans, on the verge of an open breach between conservative and progressive factions, required an adroit and subtle handling completely alien to him.

Conscientiously, Taft tried to carry on Roosevelt's programs and achieved a fair amount of success. On a number of crucial issues, however, he aligned himself with the unpopular "standpatters" or blundered in a way that made him seem to be one. He antagonized the progressives who sought a downward revision of the tariff by failing to veto the Payne-Aldrich bill, which revised most duties upward, and then in an address called it "the best tariff bill that the Republican party has ever passed." In a dispute over conservation, Taft dismissed Gifford Pinchot, head of the Forestry Service, a devoted conservationist greatly admired by Roosevelt, thereby convincing the progressives that the President was controlled by powerful private interests.

For his part, Taft found the progressive leaders, or "insurgents" as they were labeled, personally obnoxious, considering them either fanatics or demagogues who were out to destroy him and the party. As the reform movement pushed forward, Taft drew back, setting limits beyond which he would not go. He was opposed to insurgency, he wrote his brother, which demanded that "everybody should have the same amount of wealth and comfort and education, leading to discontent with everything."

In the spring of 1910, the schism between Taft and the progressives opened wide when he intervened in a number of state primaries seeking to "purge" his opponents. The President's efforts were a miserable fiasco. All the progressive Republican senators won and forty incumbent Stalwart congressmen were defeated. Then, in the November elections, the Republicans lost control of the House for the first time in sixteen years. In the Senate the nominal Republican majority was nullified by an alliance between Democrats and insurgent Republicans. Democratic candidates also won gubernatorial elections in more than half the states. It was obvious that the voters had rejected the Taft brand of conservatism.

Adding to Taft's tribulations was the rift with his good friend, Theodore Roosevelt. At the core was their divergent philosophies of government. Taft's view that "We have a government of limited power under the Constitution and we have got to work out our problem on the basis of law" was completely antithetical to Roosevelt's pragmatic approach and broad constructionism. Shortly before returning home in June 1910 from a ten-month sojourn in Africa and

Europe, Roosevelt had been convinced by Gifford Pinchot that the President not only had "twisted around" his policies but had joined with the reactionaries, alienating both Roosevelt's friends and a majority of the voters. Roosevelt coldly refused an invitation to the White House, signing his note formally, "Most sincerely yours."

Within days of his arrival at Oyster Bay, Roosevelt was besieged by progressives who pleaded with him to take the leadership of the party away from Taft as the only way to avert a Republican defeat in the forthcoming presidential election. For the next eighteeen months, however, Roosevelt refrained from publicly challenging the President. Re-entering the political arena, he hoped to be able to unite the party behind "a sound progressive" program which would also win public support, but he had gone too far to the left for the conservatives.

At Osawatomie, in September 1910, Roosevelt went even beyond his last message to Congress, offering a complete prospectus of national Progressive reform which became known as the "New Nationalism" and the "Square Deal." The federal government was obligated, he said, to promote human welfare and social justice, and the judiciary to defend human rather than property rights. He urged passage of graduated income and inheritance taxes, workmen's compensation laws, an act prohibiting child labor, more stringent laws to regulate corporations, and tariff revision. He denounced the federal courts as the strongest barrier to social justice and advocated recall of judicial decisions at the state level. Though his speeches were more moderate in the East, he failed to mollify the conservatives, who were almost hysterical in their criticism of his views. To Taft, these were "wild ideas," an unwarranted assault on the fundamental law.

Toward the end of January 1911, a group of insurgents organized the National Progressive Republican League to work against Taft's renomination by supporting the candidacy of Senator Robert La Follette of Wisconsin, a pioneer in the battle for progressive government. By mid-October, it had developed sufficient momentum to hold a national convention. Three hundred delegates representing thirty states assembled in Chicago. They unanimously approved a resolution that "the record of Senator La Follette in state and nation makes him the logical candidate for President of the United States" and urged that organizations be formed in all states to promote his nomination.

Many of the League members would much have preferred Roosevelt, but the Colonel refused to align himself with the group. Still a relatively young man, active, bursting with energy and thirsting for a return to power, Roosevelt would not have hesitated to enter the lists if he had felt that a Republican could win in 1912, but "I dare say I should be defeated," he wrote to a friend, "for poor Taft, with the assistance of Aldrich, Cannon and others has put a burden upon the Republican party under which any man who attempts to lead it will stagger." There were other considerations—opposition to his candidacy by the East and the extremist views of some progressives which he found unpalatable.

Still . . . still . . . the taste was in his mouth. His protestations rang hollow when shortly after the League conference an editorial in *The Outlook,* a journal with which Roosevelt was associated and for which he wrote regularly, stated that the endorsement of La Follette should be regarded as a recommendation rather than a pledge or commitment to any one man. A friend of La Follette's who visited Roosevelt reported to the former that Roosevelt wanted the Presidency but had held back because he thought that Taft could not be defeated. Now he had changed his opinion and also recognized that the progressive movement "is a whole lot bigger than he has ever believed it to be." Moreover, "you are developing such strength that being nominated in 1912 becomes a possibility. And even if you should fail of the nomination, your leadership of the Progressive movement would become so established that you would be in the way in 1916."

Just about that time, on October 26, 1911, the administration instituted an antitrust action against the United States Steel Corporation. A major part in the government case was the acquisition by the company of the Tennessee Coal and Iron Corporation in 1907, which Roosevelt at the time had tacitly, if not actually, approved. The implication was obvious: either Roosevelt had been guilty of collusion in the formation of a giant monopoly or he had been duped. According to Roosevelt, he had talked over the acquisition with Taft at the time and Taft had been "enthusiastic in praise" of the action.

Enraged at Taft's "playing small, mean and foolish politics," Roosevelt began to give serious consideration to his own candidacy. He intimated to Governor Hiram Johnson of California the day the suit was announced that he might be persuaded to run if he were assured that the people wanted him. Two months later, he informed one of his Progressive friends that he would consider accepting the nomination if it could be clearly demonstrated that no political intrigue was involved and that he had consented not to gratify his ambition but solely "because the bulk of the people wanted a given job done and for their own sakes, and not mine, wanted me to do that job." In January he wrote to Governor Osborn of Michigan bluntly suggesting a draft. Could Osborn and five other governors who were urging his candidacy either separately or in a joint letter say that the people of their states wished him to run for the Presidency and ask whether he would accept the nomination? "What do you think of the plan? . . . It seems to me that this offers the proper way to get at the situation."

Partly, Roosevelt was swayed by a number of Progressives who continuously importuned him to become a candidate. These men turned to the magnetic Colonel because they feared that La Follette, a regional figure, was too little known to win the election. Despite their public support of the senator, they privately assured Roosevelt that he could count on them at the propitious time. At a conference at the end of January, several founders of the League, including Amos and Gifford Pinchot, requested La Follette to withdraw in favor of Roosevelt. When he refused, they left the organization.

La Follette distrusted Roosevelt, regarding him as mercurial and opportunistic rather than a principled progressive. He suspected, and with some justification, that he had been used all along as a "stalking horse" to determine the strength of the Progressive movement. Moreover, Roosevelt appeared ready to move in when Taft's position seemed to have weakened, while he himself had entered the contest as a matter of principle to advance progressivism at a time when the President seemed unbeatable. He determined to wage an open fight, but he could only shadowbox against an adversary who refused to materialize as a presidential contender. Roosevelt would say neither yea nor nay, while he privately encouraged efforts on his behalf. In an editorial, the New York *World* commented:

> The plan is working well. Mr. Roosevelt is playing fast and loose. He will not deny that he will take the nomination. Roosevelt headquarters have been opened in Chicago. . . . Roosevelt clubs are being organized throughout the west. . . . With Taft out of the way, the road is clear for Roosevelt and a stampeded convention. That is the real work that La Follette is doing. Consciously or unconsciously he is the Roosevelt decoy duck.

Roosevelt met surreptitiously with every one of the political leaders eager for his candidacy and requested them to furnish him with reports of sentiment in their respective bailiwicks. Their detailed findings, state by state and city by city, which came in daily, were carefully analyzed. Most indicated that La Follette had no chance and that Taft, if nominated, would not be elected. Also encouraging for Roosevelt was that he could count on some valuable support. George Perkins, a Morgan partner, pledged funds, and Frank Munsey the backing of his publications.

Still, how should Roosevelt proceed? Was 1912 the year, or would 1916 hold out better promise? If he passed up 1912, a Democratic administration might be popular enough to win a second term. Or there was always the possibility that by 1916 another Republican leader would emerge to challenge his nomination. Yet if he ran now enough standpat Republicans might sabotage him and insure a Democratic victory.

The issue was more or less decided for Roosevelt by La Follette himself. On February 2, the senator administered a death blow to his chance for the party nomination when he addressed the Periodical Publishers Association in Philadelphia at a banquet attended by outstanding journalists, publishers, congressmen, and other public notables. He was exhausted from overwork, his youngest daughter was facing serious surgery, and the stampede to Roosevelt was like the taste of gall in his mouth. His prepared address was an admirable presentation of the best in progressive thought, a foreshadowing of the legislative enactments of the New Freedom and the New Deal. Then, overcome by bitterness, he launched into a rambling, two-hour tirade, some of which was incoherent, against the "moguls" of the publishing world. He charged them with creating press monopolies and declared that pooled advertising eventually would control the newspaper and magazine press of the nation. When he finished, the red-faced toastmaster jumped up and broke the shocked silence. "I want to apologize to the newspaper press of the country in general for the foolish, wicked and untruthful attack that has just been made upon it." What was left of the audience—many had already walked out—averted its eyes from La Follette slumped in his seat, white-lipped and ashen.

A week later, Roosevelt decided to come out openly against the man he had made President. By prearrangement, seven midwestern governors made public a letter requesting him to run. On his way to Columbus, Ohio, where he was to deliver a major address, Roosevelt paused at Cleveland on February 21 to announce, "My hat is in the ring." Several days later he replied officially to the governors' letter. "I will accept the nomination for President if it is tendered to me and I will adhere to this decision until the convention has expressed its preference."

Taft sagged in dejection when he heard the news. "It is almost a conviction with me," he told his secretary, that Roosevelt would beat him at the convention. "I shall continue to fight to the last moment, but when you see me claiming a victory or my friends claiming a victory for me, remember that I feel I am losing a battle and that I am not blind myself, no matter what my friends may put out."

Roosevelt's address at Columbus evoked fervent enthusiasm from the Progressives. Remedial legislation was imperative, the Colonel asserted, to redress the nation's social and economic imbalance and to put it on the path between the "sinister reactionaries" and the "furies of discontent." But no comprehensive program of reform was possible until the states' courts, citadels of reaction, were first curbed, and accordingly he advocated popular recall of judges. Conservatives for whom the courts were sacred reacted as though Roosevelt had touched a raw nerve. Taft, with his reverence for the judiciary and legal processes, charged that those who advocated such a proposition were extremists who would plunge the country into a condition without parallel except for the French Revolution or the anarchy of South American revolts. Such advocates of extremism were not progressives, he declared, but "political emotionalists" or "neurotics."

Headquarters for Roosevelt were established in New York City, a national executive committee selected, and a group organized in Chicago with its own captain to direct western operations. In addition, a press bureau was established, together with such subsidiary organizations as the United Progressive Federation, the National Progressive Italian-American League, the American Progressive German Alliance, and a number of other linguistic groups which even included minorities like the Lithuanians, Hungarians, and Syrians.

With Taft backed by the administration's patronage power, by its control of the party's organizational apparatus, and by a large bloc of delegates, Roosevelt concluded that his only chance for the nomination would be via the new presidential primaries. He was the first candidate to perceive their significance as a means for obtaining national voter support. If he won them all, it would demonstrate that he, not Taft, was the more popular Republican and entitled to be the party choice.

Only seven states thus far had adopted the presidential primary. As a stratagem, Roosevelt's manager challenged the opposition to participate in primaries in every state in the country so that the people could make their desire known. But since Taft was already in the favored position, his chairman parried by suggesting that it would not be fair to change the rules in the middle of the game. The Roosevelt forces, however, would not give up, and fierce quarrels ensued in northern state legislatures as to whether a primary should be instituted. In the end, five more states adopted the device. Roosevelt then embarked on a campaign so strenuous that at its conclusion even his bull-like strength was drained.

The contest was a brutal one. While the President would have liked nothing better than to retire, he was driven by a sense of honor, conscience, and stubborn pride. Taft was shaken to the core by Roosevelt's vitriolic personal attacks. Roosevelt accused him of being "disloyal to our past friendship . . . disloyal to every canon of ordinary decency." He called him feeble and incompetent. When Taft denied that he was subservient to political bosses, Roosevelt charged him with being guilty of "the grossest and most astounding hypocrisy."

Stung into defending himself, Taft departed from the tradition that a President does not engage in a political campaign, much less a preconvention struggle, but he was no verbal match for his opponent. He only sounded pathetic and abject when he told a New England audience, "I am here to reply to an old and true friend of mine, Theodore Roosevelt, who has made many charges against me. I deny these charges. I deny all of them." Or to another group, "I am a man of peace. I don't want to fight. But when I do fight, I want to hit hard. Even a rat in a corner will fight."

As the struggle proceeded in primaries and state conventions, Roosevelt decided that wherever he could charge the Taft organization with fraud in selecting delegates, he would attempt to organize contesting delegations. Since the Taft forces controlled the National Committee and thereby the Credentials Committee, the Roosevelt delegates would have little chance, without some kind of coercion, of being seated at the convention if rival delegations from the same state presented themselves. Accusations of dishonesty and fraud, he hoped, would so arouse popular indignation that the preliminary rulings of the temporary officers would be overturned, giving control to his side.

Scenes at some of the state conventions were reminiscent of the brawling, lawless "wild West." In Oklahoma, when two hundred contested Roosevelt delegates were ordered unseated by the state central committee, they shoved the doorkeepers aside and took over the convention. Three men were carried out of the hall after being mauled in fist fights. Throughout the proceedings the atmosphere was tense with the threat of gunplay. The Taft man who presided was warned that if he attempted any chicanery he would not walk out alive, and to underscore the point a Roosevelt supporter stood behind him all day with his hand on his gun. In Michigan, even the presence of state troops could not prevent a mass altercation on the platform. The convention, in hopeless disagreement, divided and elected two chairmen. Then, amid chaotic disorder, both "conventions," directed from the same platform, selected two sets of delegates.

The climax was the primary election in Ohio, important because of the large number of delegates involved and because it was Taft's home state. Each side arrived with its heaviest artillery. Roosevelt came with the top brass of his organization, Taft accompanied by Cabinet members and congressmen. Roosevelt covered some 1,800 miles delivering ninety addresses in one week. Taft traveled even more extensively and gave more speeches. By now the President was flayed raw by Roosevelt's cutting tongue, but the strongest language he could bring himself to use against his rival was "dangerous egotist," "demagogue," "flatterer of the people." Roosevelt, with a complete lack of decency, called Taft "a fathead who had an intellect a little short of a guinea pig." La Follette, entering the race in mid-May, hurled charges at both. Roosevelt captured every district delegate.

At the end, Roosevelt had won nine primaries, giving him 278 delegates, Taft only one and 48 delegates, La Follette two and 36 delegates. Obviously Roosevelt was the popular choice among the rank and file. Moreover, he and La Follette had received twice as many votes as had Taft, an indication that progressivism was on the rise.

Depressed by the preconvention battering he had suffered, Taft would have been happy to withdraw from the contest if a conservative like Senator Elihu Root or Chief Justice Charles Evans Hughes could have been substituted. He stayed in, he said privately, only "to defeat Mr. Roosevelt, whose nomination . . . would be a great danger and menace to the country. His constitutional views are of such character, and his mendacity, his unscrupulousness displayed in deceiving the public and arousing one class against the other . . . make him a man to be avoided if possible as a candidate." If he withdrew, a number of the delegates pledged to him might go over to Roosevelt, "and that I cannot permit. Personally, I have no desire to continue as a candidate. I had no desire to do so when I went on the stump, but the fear of Mr. Roosevelt's success made it necessary."

Although Roosevelt had not planned to attend the Chicago convention, he acceded to the pleas of his lieutenants who insisted that his presence was essential. On his arrival he was greeted by a throng of cheering admirers who had converged on the city. Twenty thousand flocked to hear him give an address on the eve of the convention, and the five thousand who were able to squeeze into the hall heard one of the most ringing speeches of his career. Taft, he charged, was a creature of the party bosses who were intent on stealing the nomination. He personally had examined the evidence, and there was not the shadow of a doubt that his and not Taft's were the legally constituted delegates. "What happens to me is not of the slightest consequence; I am to be used, as in a doubtful battle any man is used, to his hurt or not, so long as he is useful and is then cast aside or left to die. . . . It would be far better to fail honorably for the cause we champion than it would be to win by foul methods the foul victory for which our opponents hope. But the victory shall be ours. . . . We fight in honorable fashion for the good of mankind; unheeding of our individual fates; with unflinching hearts and undimmed eyes; we stand at Armageddon, and we battle for the Lord." Once again the battle for the Presidency was to be a holy crusade, with the hosts of righteousness arrayed against the forces of evil. Roosevelt and his followers were now doing the Lord's work.

There would be nothing spiritual, however, about the struggle for control of the convention. Taft claimed a total of 557 delegates, or 17 more than was needed for the nomination. About 250 of these had been disputed by Roosevelt, but the National Committee, composed mostly of Taft supporters had declared them legitimate. Roosevelt, lacking about 80 votes towards the nomination, then decided to formally challenge the credentials of 72 of the number contested.

As the delegates assembled, the atmosphere in the hall was heavy with sullen resentments which erupted into acrimonious exchanges. From the moment the gavel sounded, speakers could barely be heard above the tumult. Anticipating possible violence, the Committee had employed police squads to patrol the building, and, though few were aware of it, the decorations around the railings to the rostrum concealed barbed wire. Both the Taft and the Roosevelt forces had hired detectives to try to prevent bribery of delegates.

The first order of business, election of a temporary chairman, created pandemonium. Nominating and seconding speeches for Senator Root, the Taft candidate, were drowned out by shouts of "liar," "thief," "swindler." Taft supporters were equally unreserved in counterattacking the opposition's selection of Governor Francis E. McGovern of Wisconsin. Root was elected by the slender margin of twenty-nine votes, but the regulars were now in command. A motion by Governor Hadley of Missouri, floor leader for the Roosevelt men, to substitute Roosevelt's contested delegates for Taft's was ruled out of order.

On the second day the Credentials Committee, also stacked with Taft supporters, met to confirm the action of the National Committee with respect to the disrupted delegates. During its deliberations the hall rocked with the turmoil. With all his skill as a parliamentarian, Root was unable to control the inflamed delegates. Again Governor Hadley moved that the contested seats be awarded to the Roosevelt men, charging that the Taft delegates were "burglars and pirates elected by naked theft." He demanded that the seventy-two seated Taft men be forbidden to vote on their own qualifications. Root, quoting the rules of the House of Representatives, declared that while a delegate could not vote on his own right to a seat, he could on the validity of the others. Amid jeering and cat-calls from the gallery, Hadley's motion was defeated. The Credentials Committee awarded the Taft men permanent seats, and the chance for Roosevelt's nomination was gone.

Only a compromise candidate could now avert a disastrous party split. Senator William E. Borah of Idaho, a progressive, was approached by a prominent "organization man" to accept second place on a ticket headed by Justice Hughes. Roosevelt men, too, were huddled in conferences weighing the advantages of compromise. Roosevelt insisted, however, that he would agree to nothing unless his seventy-two contested delegates were first seated, after which he would abide by the choice of the convention. His condition was rejected by the Taft supporters. Most likely Roosevelt made his offer knowing that it would not be accepted, for he had no intention of withdrawing his own candidacy. He had even arranged before the convention to bolt if he did not receive the nomination.

With the chasm between the Taft wing of the party and the insurgents unbridgeable, nothing remained but to go through the hollow ritual of selecting Taft. On the last day, a small-town newspaper editor from Ohio, Warren G. Harding, placed Taft's name in nomination. President Taft, he said, was "the finest example of lofty principles since the immortal Lincoln bore the scourge of vengeful tongues without a murmur from his noble heart," and he described Taft as "measuring his capacity by the exactions of experience; testing his patriotism by every demand of honesty, courage, and justice." Only one ballot was required to give Taft 561 votes, Roosevelt 107, and La Follette 41. In protest, 344 delegates refused to vote.

Before leaving Chicago, Roosevelt held a mass meeting at which he announced the formation of the Progressive party. A committee was appointed to arrange for a convention to meet in the same city on August 5. Almost at once, influential, high-ranking supporters began to drop away. Practical politicians, they argued that a family quarrel was one thing, divorce quite another. Governor Hadley, who had been one of Roosevelt's staunchest backers, wrote that the triumph of progressivism in his state could be achieved only by working within the Republican party. Of the seven governors who officially had launched Roosevelt's bid for the nomination, only Hiram Johnson remained with him. A number of progressive senators, including La Follette, endorsed the Democratic party's candidate; others indicated that while they favored Roosevelt they were opposed to a new party. Of the entire progressive Republican phalanx in the Senate, only five endorsed the new party. Angry and disgusted, Roosevelt exploded, "What a miserable showing some of the so-called Progressive leaders have made. They represent nothing but mere sound and fury. A year or two ago when it was merely a question of loud words they were claiming to be much further advanced than I was, but they have not the heart for a fight, and the minute they were up against deeds instead of words they quit forthwith."

The rank and file, however, held fast. More than 2,000 delegates, including a score of women, representing every state except South Carolina, and about 13,000 spectators gathered for the convention of the Progressive party. More like an assemblage of crusaders than a political conclave, they fervently sang "Onward, Christian Soldiers" and the "Battle Hymn of the Republic." They listened to the solemn addresses with earnest concentration, undiverted by brass bands or noisemaking activities. On the second day, when the leader of the new party entered the hall to deliver his formal address, the assemblage cheered and shouted itself hoarse for a solid hour without prompting from artificial devices or claques.

Roosevelt began his "Confession of Faith," as he called it, with an attack on the two major parties as boss-ridden, controlled by the forces of privilege, and divided only by artificial lines. Repeating his earlier proposal for judicial recall, he demanded that the people and not the courts be the ultimate arbiters of their own destinies. Then he proposed the most sweeping changes in public policy ever made by a major candidate for the Presidency. Repeating the "New Nationalism" program of positive governmental action he had set forth as Osawatomie, he enlarged upon it to include direct election of senators, an effective corrupt practices act, nationwide presidential preference primaries, publication of campaign expenditures, the initiative, referendum, and recall, and woman suffrage. His purpose, he declared, was the achievement of democratic ends through the employment of Hamiltonian means. A deafening ovation acclaimed his charter of reform.

The proceedings were less harmonious when the convention settled down to business. Controversy developed over admission of southern delegations from which Negroes systematically had been excluded. Many northern progressives were unhappy with the deliberate policy of Roosevelt and other party leaders of encouraging "lily white" organizations in the South in order to win support. To avert a head-on clash on the floor, a formula was approved which gave the states in question authority to reject any delegation they deemed unlawfully constituted. In effect, this was a victory for the exclusion policy. Social justice apparently stopped short of the color line.

Another dispute arose over the platform. Most of the Progressives, especially those from west of the Appalachians, favored a vigorous antitrust plank and expected that one would be included. A resolution calling for a strengthened Sherman Act was, in fact, approved, but as a result of strong pressure from Roosevelt and George Perkins it was eliminated from the platform at the last minute. Some delegates were particularly disturbed, as this seemed to them an indication that Perkins, the party's financial angel, was exerting an undue and unwholesome influence.

The Progressive party was a political potpourri, containing many other seemingly unlikely advocates of reform in the business community such as the newspaper and magazine mogul, Frank Munsey, and the head of Crucible Steel, H. H. Wilkinson. Though they advocated change, their concept of government was paternalistic. As Munsey told Roosevelt, the government must "take on a more parental guardianship of the people." The masses "need encouragement, the sustaining and guiding hand of the state. . . . It is the work of the state to think for the people and plan for the people—to teach them how to do, what to do, and to sustain them in the doing." There were intellectuals like William Allen White, editor of the *Emporia Gazette*, the idealistic social worker Jane Addams, the scholarly university professor Albert Bushnell Hart. Probably the most curious member of the fraternity was the corrupt city boss William Flynn, one of the few who had real political experience. The movement was predominantly middle-class, and the party platform, which incorporated all of the proposals in Roosevelt's acceptance speech, was not socialistic, as opponents charged, but rather an antidote to socialism.

On the third and final day, the convention adopted the

platform and nominated as its candidates Roosevelt and Governor Hiram Johnson. Adjourning in the same evangelical spirit as when they began, the delegates sang the "Doxology."

At the time he decided to engage in the contest, Roosevelt had no clue as to who the Democrats would nominate. Later he remarked that had he known it would be Woodrow Wilson, whom he considered very able and potentially an "excellent" President, he would not have entered the race. In any event, he was now aware that his prospects for victory were considerably dimmed by the candidacy of the man who would challenge him on his own platform of progressive reform.

Woodrow Wilson, at long last, had the possibility of fulfilling a lifelong ambition. From early youth he had craved the role of statesman, to have his hands on the wheels of power. After years as a university professor, teaching American history and political institutions, writing and lecturing extensively in his field, he had his first opportunity to exercise leadership when he was appointed president of Princeton University in 1902. His involvement in controversies stemming from his effort to implement his concept of an institution of higher learning brought him to national attention. Colonel George Harvey, editor and publisher of *Harper's Weekly,* saw in Wilson a possible presidential candidate and mentioned this at a dinner given in Wilson's honor in 1906. Few took Harvey's proposal seriously, but he continued to promote Wilson, giving frequent publicity to his views and activities in the periodicals which he controlled. Four years later, however, when Harvey suggested to the New Jersey boss, James Smith, Jr., that Wilson would be a winning gubernatorial candidate, Smith and the other party leaders agreed. For some time they had had their eye on the irreproachable academician as a respectable front for their control of the state. Offered the opportunity, Wilson promptly consented, won the election by a sizable majority, and carried in with him a Democratic Assembly.

To the dismay of the bosses, Wilson turned out to be a

hard, independent force, uncannily adept at political leadership, instead of the pliant tool they had visualized. Even worse, they had not taken seriously Wilson's affirmation of progressive ideals. His political views had undergone a considerable transformation in a relatively short time. Only three years earlier he had defended the conservative principles and policies then under attack by the reform movement, but as governor he made New Jersey one of the leading reform states. A fine orator, skillful with words, clear and convincing, occasionally witty, he could fire his audiences.

With the support of a public which he aroused, by the skillful and judicious use of patronage, and through the help of three influential independent Republicans, he demolished the influence of the old-guard politicians. Under his merciless pressure, the legislature enacted a drastic election reform bill, measures to regulate public utilities, an employers' liability law, and educational improvements. In addition, he defeated the Smith machine when it tried to control the election of a United States senator.

By the spring of 1911, Wilson was regarded as a leading prospect for the presidential nomination despite opposition from machine bosses in some of the large states and from many prominent conservatives. Wilson-for-President clubs were spontaneously organized throughout the country, and progressive Democrats assured him of their support in the preconvention campaign. The editor of the Washington *News* wrote him that his position "on the pending government issues . . . will instantly constitute you the inevitable leader for 1912." At a banquet, the Hudson tunnel builder, William Gibbs McAdoo, toasted Wilson as a "future President of the United States."

Early in March, a group of enthusiasts raised funds to finance a tour for bringing Wilson to the attention of the West. The trip was highly successful. Attacking machine politics and corporate domination of the country's political life, calling for the direct primary, the initiative, referendum, and recall, Wilson endeared himself to the progressive

Democrats. The *Rocky Mountain News* of Denver wrote, "Why is [Wilson] the most frequently mentioned Democratic candidate for the Presidency? We think the answer is to be found in two words: progressiveness and courage." A newspaper in Pasadena, California, commented, "No citizen of the United States has ever been given a heartier or more sincere greeting than that accorded the great reformer of the east."

The reaction of conservative Democrats, however, was quite different. Wilson's insistence that government be made more responsive to the will of the people, through such devices as the initiative, referendum, and recall, labeled him as a radical on the Bryan order among the middle and upper class, for whom this reform was somehow linked with socialism and a general attack on property rights. The New York *Sun,* one of the original boosters of his candidacy, turned violently against him. In the South, especially in his own state of Virginia, he was accused of abandoning his convictions, those of "safe and sane" Democracy, in order to obtain radical support. Alarmed that he might lose the support of the state, Wilson sought to repair the damage by declaring that such reforms were not necessary in states where effective representative government existed, "as I believe there is in Virginia and in the South in general." In any event, he continued, his proposal should not be made a national issue but left to the discretion of the individual states.

Wilson's attack on the "money power" and "Wall Street" elicited outraged cries even from that part of the press which was not conservative. Was he "Bryanizing?" asked the New York *World.* "How like Mr. Bryan's language of sixteen years ago!" One of his supporters wrote him that in Cleveland's day "our hopes were wrecked by the free silver blunder, and we feel that the party's greatest weakness and danger is still its proneness to go wrong on questions of finance." Again retreating from a position that threatened to become a political liability, Wilson confessed that the demands of public life had prevented him from making a comprehensive investigation of the money question and promised to give the matter "sincere study."

Disturbed by the antagonism to their candidate, his advisors felt that Wilson must become identified with a "safe" reform issue. They decided that the tariff, which concerned many influential elements in the population, would be most suitable. To gain him a wide hearing, an interview was arranged with the New York *World*. Many Democrats were greatly relieved when Wilson asserted, "The tariff question is at the heart of every other economic question we have to deal with, and until we have dealt with that properly we can deal with nothing in a way that will be satisfactory and lasting." Some months later, in a New York address, he denounced Republican collusion with businessmen in writing tariff schedules and affirmed that big business and government must be separated in the matter of tariff legislation.

Energetically, Wilson traveled up, down, and across the country, covering 9,000 miles by the end of 1911. Devoted followers were working tirelessly for him, among them the invaluable Colonel Edward M. House. A former student and one of his earliest champions, William L. McCombs, became his campaign manager. In October, McCombs set up an office in New York from which he sent out hundreds of letters to newspaper editors and public officials soliciting help in promoting Wilson's candidacy.

For a while Wilson appeared certain of the nomination among a plethora of candidates. Oscar W. Underwood of Alabama, chairman of the House Ways and Means Committee, a "favorite son," could be pretty well discounted because he came from the deep South. Governor Judson Harmon of Ohio, a conservative, was opposed by Bryan and a group of liberals. Governors Thomas R. Marshall of Indiana and Simeon E. Baldwin of Connecticut were favorite sons who hoped for a deadlock but would be glad to accept second place on the ticket.

Wilson's chief rival was Speaker Champ Clark, congressman from Missouri, but few political observers felt that he would make an appreciable showing despite nu-

merous factors in his favor. Clark had a good record in the
House, he had served the party faithfully, and the state
machines seemed to favor him. Nevertheless, many felt that
he lacked sufficient distinction to commend him for the
highest office in the land. The New York *World* warned
that his nomination would be a disaster to the Democratic
party and, if he were elected, he would be a disaster to the
country.

Yet by the spring of 1912, Clark had made spectacular
progress. His numerous friends in Congress were directing
his campaign in almost every state. In February, Clark
headquarters had been established in Washington and
shortly thereafter in Chicago and Arkansas. Unlike Wilson,
Clark had a consistent progressive record during his long
public career which made him the natural inheritor of the
Bryan movement throughout most of the West. Moreover,
he was endorsed by the influential publisher and a power in
the Democratic party, William Randolph Hearst, who was
venomous toward Wilson for having coldly rebuffed his
offer of support.

Beginning in January, Hearst threw the entire weight of
his yellow journalism into his effort to defeat Wilson. Unfortunately, the candidate was vulnerable on an important
matter of which Hearst could take full advantage. In 1902,
Wilson had published a *History of the American People*
which had a decidedly conservative slant. One of Clark's
supporters quoted directly from the book to buttress his
own conclusion that Wilson "had a profound contempt for
the Farmers' Alliance, the Populists, greenbackers, bi-
metallists, trade unionists, small office seekers, Italians,
Poles, Hungarians, pensioners, strikers, armies of unemployed." Furthermore, Wilson had exhibited a marked preference for the contributions of the Anglo-Saxon races to
American civilization.

Day after day, on the front pages of his papers in every
major city of the country, Hearst lambasted Wilson for
being contemptuous of eastern and southern Europeans and
also printed anti-Wilson letters from various immigrant so-

cieties. In March, in a lengthy explanation to the press as to why he opposed Wilson, he called the candidate a Federalist who distrusted the people and a modern Judas "perched upon his little hillock of expediency . . . keenly alert to every scent or sound and ready to run and double in any direction."

Up until April, none of the Democratic aspirants was significantly ahead, the results of campaigns in six states which had thus far selected delegates showing no obvious advantage to any one. The turning point was the Illinois primary on the ninth of that month. Clark had powerful, well-organized backing in the state and the support of Hearst. Wilson, with no organization there of his own, could not possibly hope to defeat Clark. Nevertheless, he decided on a last-minute, last-ditch, intensive campaign tour of Illinois. It was a serious tactical blunder. By entering, he naturally gave the impression that he expected to win, and when Clark achieved a landslide victory, Wilson suffered a serious setback. The next morning a Missouri paper commented, "The Illinois verdict takes Champ Clark out of the favorite son class and places him at once in the lead," while an Eastern paper wrote jubilantly, "The back of the Wilson movement was broken yesterday in Illinois." When Clark came into the House chamber the day after the election, he was lustily cheered by his fellow Democrats as "the next President."

To machine politicians in the other states, Clark's victory in Illinois seemed to indicate which way the wind was blowing. The efforts of McCombs and his lieutenants to sell Wilson to the leading party bosses failed; without a power base of his own, Wilson had little to offer them. All through the primary campaign period in Nebraska, William Jennings Bryan, still an extremely potent force in the party, refused to indicate his preference for either Clark or Wilson, considering them both progressive. Clark captured the entire Nebraska delegation and went on to win in one state after another.

The Wilson movement, which was staggering to a halt,

seemed to revive somewhat with the candidate's decisive victory in the New Jersey primary at the end of May, but Wilson himself was not very hopeful about his chances. "Just between you and me," he wrote to a friend, "I have not the least idea of being nominated, because the makeup of the convention is such, the balance and confusion of forces, that the outcome is in the hands of the professional, case-hardened politicians who serve only their own interests and who know that I will not serve them except as I might serve the party in general."

Democratic party rules required a two-thirds majority for the nomination, but traditionally the aspirant strong enough to attain a simple majority almost always went on to victory. Not since 1844 when Van Buren was defeated had a candidate in this position failed to win the nomination. Prospects for Champ Clark on the eve of the Baltimore convention were bright. About 435 delegates were pledged to him and, while 545 were necessary for a majority, 224 were controlled by various bosses and organization leaders. In addition, he was fairly sure of the 90 votes controlled by Tammany, which would be more than enough to give him a commanding lead. Wilson, on the other hand, could definitely rely on only 248 delegates, or at most no more than one third of the total votes, assuming he captured various uninstructed delegates.

The convention opened on the afternoon of June 25. Bryan immediately made his presence felt by seeking to defeat Alton B. Parker, the choice of the conservatives, as temporary chairman. He failed. Then he proposed a resolution calling for opposition "to the nomination of any candidate for president who is the representative of or under obligation to J. Pierpont Morgan, Thomas F. Ryan, August Belmont, or any other member of the privilege-hunting and favor-seeking class" and, secondly, that any delegates representing the interests of those men withdraw from the convention. The hall exploded into an uproar so violent that the police were helpless. Never before had so astounding a demand been made at the gathering of a major party. Finally, Bryan was persuaded to withdraw the second part of his resolution, whereupon the first was endorsed.

Nominating and seconding speeches began late on Thursday evening, continuing tediously until seven o'clock the next morning, when the first ballot was at last taken. The tally gave Clark 440½ votes, Wilson 324, Harmon 148, Underwood 117½, Marshall 31, Baldwin 22, Sulzer 2, and Bryan 1. The next day, after nine ballots, the results were virtually unchanged. On the tenth, Wilson picked up 28 votes but received a devastating blow when Tammany Hall, shifting its 90 from Harmon to Clark, gave the latter well over a majority. Clark supporters became frenzied with delight, marching, singing, waving banners, shouting for an entire hour. Clark prepared a telegram of acceptance, expecting to obtain the nomination on that or the next ballot.

When Wilson received the news, he felt that it was all over and sent a message to McCombs instructing him to tell his delegates that "they were not to vote for him any longer if they thought they ought to vote for someone else." McCombs stubbornly refused to concede defeat. While the Clark demonstration was going on, he, Albert S. Burleson of Texas, and the other managers ran around to the Underwood delegates, with whom they had earlier worked out an agreement. Although the Underwood forces consisted of little more than a hundred delegates, they held the decisive balance. It had been agreed that if Wilson should drop out, his delegates would be delivered to Underwood, in return for which they would hold firm for Wilson. The Underwood forces had resisted considerable pressure from the Clark supporters, including an offer of the vice-presidency for their candidate. For one thing, Underwood refused to accept second place; for another, Wilson was the second choice of many of the Underwood delegates; and thirdly, they believed that a deadlock would ensue between Wilson and Clark which might conceivably make Underwood the compromise candidate. Accordingly, when the Wilson forces implored them to hold firm, they agreed. On the eleventh ballot, which was completed at four o'clock Saturday morning, it was apparent that the anticipated Clark landslide had been blocked.

Nothing significant happened after that until the fourteenth ballot. The Nebraska delegation was committed to Clark, but Bryan had become exceedingly disturbed when Boss Murphy of Tammany Hall gave New York's votes to Clark, seeming to confirm what he had been told by his brother, that a bargain had been struck between Clark and the New York machine. He had therefore persuaded a number of his delegates to switch to Wilson on the previous ballot, and now, when Nebraska was being polled, he caused an uproar when he rose to explain why he had changed his vote. The convention, he said, was pledged by the anti-Wall Street resolution not to support any candidate obligated to the financial tycoons, and Nebraska would not back any man who was "willing to violate the resolution . . . and to accept the high honor of the presidential nomination at the hands of Mr. Murphy."

Furiously, the Clark men berated Bryan, but their candidate's vote began to recede, and at adjournment that night Clark had 463½, Wilson 407½. Monotonously the balloting continued the next day and the next. By the end of the week, on the twenty-sixth ballot, Wilson managed to pick up some 83 votes. Tammany and the other conservative leaders desperately scurried from one delegation to another, vainly trying to persuade them to withdraw support from Wilson.

On Monday, the glimmer of a break in Wilson's favor appeared when first Indiana and then Iowa cast part of their votes for him, putting him in the lead but leaving him still short of a simple majority. To win he needed Illinois and Alabama. Roger Sullivan, who controlled the Illinois delegation, had promised McCombs that if Wilson's nomination appeared likely he would come to his aid. Although Sullivan was not particularly enchanted with Wilson, he was a mortal enemy of Hearst, and he knew that if Clark were elected he could expect few favors from the White

House. As a majority of his delegation favored Wilson, he kept his promise and delivered his 58 votes on the forty-third ballot.

Wilson now had a majority. The next switch was the two Virginias, giving him over 600 votes. But he still lacked the required two thirds, for which he required the votes of Underwood's supporters. Wilson's managers pleaded with John H. Bankhead of Alabama to release his delegation. Finally, before the forty-sixth ballot, Bankhead consented. At this point, with the end discernible, the convention was in a turmoil. All the other candidates withdrew. Only a scattered few of the delegates voted for Clark as a sentimental gesture. At 3:30 P.M. on the seventh day of the convention, Senator Stone of Missouri moved that the nomination be made unanimous.

The delegates, prostrated with fatigue, wanted nothing more than to go home, but a Vice-President still had to be nominated and a platform adopted. Both were quickly disposed of. Underwood, whom Wilson preferred, refused, and Thomas R. Marshall of Indiana was nominated. The platform, completed several days before, was in the best progressive tradition, with a definite aura of Bryanism. It called for a downward revision of the tariff, criminal as well as civil prosecution of trusts, additional legislation to implement the drive against private monopolies, effective regulation of railroads and communications systems, and extensive banking reforms. With organized labor in mind, it demanded jury trials in contempt cases resulting from the liberal use of the injunction and proposed that labor be exempted from the provisions of the Sherman Antitrust Act. Also endorsed was speedy ratification of the pending amendments for an income tax and for the direct election of senators.

When the campaign opened, Wilson regarded Theodore Roosevelt as his real rival. "I feel that Roosevelt's strength is altogether incalculable," he wrote. "The contest is between him and me, not between Taft and me. I think Taft will run third, at any rate in the popular if not in the electoral vote."

Roosevelt, he continued, "appeals to their [the people's] imagination; I do not. He is a real, vivid person, whom they have seen and shouted themselves hoarse over and voted for, millions strong; I am a vague, conjectural personality, more made up of opinions and academic prepossessions than of human traits and red corpuscles."

The hapless Taft, pinned with the conservative label and opposed by two champions of progressivism, was despondent about his prospects as early as July. As he wrote to his wife, "Sometimes I think I might as well give up so far as being a candidate is concerned. There are so many people in the country who don't like me." What he probably meant and what depressed him most were the cruel attacks of his erstwhile friend who four years earlier had cheered his entry into the White House. Now Roosevelt's animosity toward Taft was so intense that every now and then he could not refrain from injecting such cutting and childish sneers in his addresses as, "I have noticed several Taft badges in your town and they are the appropriate color of yellow." As the campaign progressed, Taft's misery spilled over. It was hard to realize, the President wrote to his wife, "that we are talking about the same man whom we knew . . . it is impossible to conceive of him as the fakir, the juggler, the green goods man, the gold-brick man that he has come to be."

To uphold what he considered the proper, dignified posture for a President, Taft would not campaign. He made almost no addresses after his acceptance speech on August 1, relying entirely on Root, Lodge, his Cabinet members, and other prominent Republicans. "I have been told that I ought to do this, ought to do that . . . that I do not keep myself in the headlines," he told a newspaper correspondent. "I know it, but I can't do it. I couldn't if I would, and I wouldn't if I could."

Roosevelt, on the other hand, characteristically made sure that he kept his name in the headlines. Tirelessly he traveled through New England, covered the Midwest, went on to the Pacific coast, returned to the corn belt, made a ten-day swing through the South, and then back again to the

Northwest. His ability to attract and stir the multitudes had not diminished with the years. If anything, the excitement and devotion he inspired was even greater than before. Ten thousand people jammed the railroad station in Providence to welcome him, and thousands had to be turned away from the hall. Those who were fortunate enough to get in paid a dollar for a seat. At Los Angeles, 200,000 people lined the streets as he rode from the station. Shops closed their doors for the day and the entire city was in a gala mood.

With his innate skill in obtaining publicity, Roosevelt could always be counted on for something sensational, as when he climbed into the locomotive of a transcontinental express and ran it for some miles. He dramatically displayed his legendary courage after being shot in the chest by a crazed, would-be assassin while in Milwaukee on his way to the hall to deliver a speech. Papers and a wallet which he carried in his breast pocket saved his life, but he was bleeding and badly shaken. Nevertheless, he insisted on giving his address, standing on the platform flanked by several aides ready to catch him if he should collapse. He earned the frenzied plaudits of the onlookers when, with apparent magnanimity, he protected his assailant from their fury. It was a cleverly calculated gesture, for, as he wrote to a friend, "I would not have objected to the man's being killed at the very instant, but I did not deem it wise or proper that he should be killed before my eyes if I was going to recover."

For the most part, Roosevelt ignored Taft, concentrating his fire on Wilson. The campaign developed into a debate between two divergent progressive views on how government should respond to the fundamental economic problems of the day—the "New Nationalism" of Roosevelt versus the "New Freedom" of Wilson. Roosevelt sought an equilibrium among the various components of American society—laborers, farmers, industrialists—to achieve the greatest good for the greatest number. The controlling force would be the federal government to prevent one group from gaining domination over the others. As he saw it, the problem was that both capital and labor, lacking a sense of national unity, indifferent to the country's welfare, were each selfishly seeking its own advantage. He scorned both the avaricious businessman and the fiery radical, warning that conservatism was as much to be feared as demagoguery, that the unscrupulous reactionary and the irresponsible agitator both stood "on the same plane of obnoxiousness."

Industrial concentrations, Roosevelt believed, were inevitable, and large trusts were not necessarily evil; in fact, they were generally highly efficient in production and distribution, but they must be kept under control. "We are face to face with new conceptions of the relations of property to human welfare," he asserted. "Property [is] subject to the general right of the community to regulate its use to whatever degree the public welfare may require it." Strongly influenced by Herbert Croly's *Promise of American Life*, Roosevelt had come to believe long before the campaign that regulation of large units of industrial enterprise rather than their fragmentation or dissolution provided the best direction for the nation's economic future.

Throughout his campaign, Roosevelt consistently emphasized the need to augment the power of the federal government, advocated control rather than destruction of the trusts, and supported reforms which later became objectives of the welfare state, such as federal intervention in labor disputes, an expanded federal health program, a federal child labor law, minimum wages for women, fair wages to industrial workers.

Wilson found his campaign theme one afternoon in mid-August when he met Louis D. Brandeis, an outstanding progressive lawyer and exponent of regulated competition and enterprise free of monopoly control. Tariff reform had become a shopworn issue, and while Wilson believed that the problem of monopolies would have public appeal, he did not know how to tackle it. After a three-hour conversation with Brandeis, he was persuaded to make it the paramount issue in his campaign. Since he had only a limited knowledge of the complicated subject, he happily accepted the brilliant Boston attorney as his mentor, allowing himself to be educated and guided. Brandeis shaped his campaign, keeping him steadily supplied with the results of his own research.

In one lengthy memorandum, Brandeis outlined for Wilson the basic difference between the Progressive party and the Democrats on the solution to the trust problem. For the former, the greatest good for the greatest number, he wrote, was to be achieved through regulating monopolies, while the latter stressed the regulation of competition. Government's role was to prevent the growth of monopolies, to see that competition was maintained in all branches of private industry and restored wherever it was stifled by the trusts. He objected to the Roosevelt formula because, as he said, "no methods of regulation ever have been or can be devised to remove the menace inherent in private monopoly and overweening commercial power." The difference between the two parties, he concluded, was "fundamental and irreconcilable. It is the difference between industrial liberty and industrial absolutism, tempered by governmental (that is, party) supervision."

Wilson, with his evangelical bent and his exceptional skill as a writer and orator, transmuted the information he was fed into vibrant, moving invocations to preserve fundamental liberties which would be hopelessly subverted were his rival to win. In his first important speech of the campaign before a huge audience of workers in Buffalo on Labor Day, he stigmatized Roosevelt's program as a paternalistic one which inevitably would end up by making the workingman a ward of the federal government. "My kind of leading will not be telling other people what they have got to do," he asserted. "By leading I mean finding out what the interests of the community are agreed to be, and then trying my level best to find the methods of solution by common counsel. That is the only feasible programme of social uplift that I can imagine."

Increasingly, Wilson emphasized that he was battling for the restoration of America's traditional way of life, for an

economic equality of opportunity without which political
democracy could not be fulfilled. The major cause for inequities in income, he told one audience, was the success of
the great monopolistic combination in acquiring a considerable part of the nation's wealth and resources by price
fixing, collusive agreements, control of the sources of raw
materials, and unbridled, cutthroat competition. It was the
duty of the federal government to end these evil practices;
when this had been done monopoly would no longer exist.

The trust question became "a second struggle for emancipation. . . . If America is not to have free enterprise, then
she can have freedom of no sort whatever." Pecuniary considerations like markets and profits were less important
than the eternal truths by which men lived, the perennial
struggle for liberty. Wilson utilized the power of his
rhetoric to evoke a dream of the future which industrial
capitalism was not likely to make a reality: "Are you not
eager for the time when the genius and initiative of all the
people shall be called into the service of business, when
newcomers with new ideas . . . independent men, shall be
welcomed, when your sons shall be able to look forward to
becoming, not employees, but heads of some small . . . business, where their best energies shall be inspired by the
knowledge that they are their own masters, with the paths
of the world open before them? Surely you must feel the
inspiration of such a new dawn of liberty."

At first Wilson had announced that he would not engage
in "swings around the circle," as he felt long stumping tours
were neither impressive nor dignified. Within weeks, however, he was on the campaign trail and between September
and election day had covered every section of the country.
He was ably assisted by a covey of southern spellbinders
who fanned out through the North and West under instructions from the speaker's bureau.

A carefully organized, smoothly running campaign committee directed all operations. Wilson clubs were established everywhere and supplied with literature, buttons,
and posters. Articles and editorials were distributed to hun-

dreds of newspapers and magazines, a *Democratic Text-book* published and widely circulated, and, of course, the necessary funds were raised. A total of $1,110,952 was contributed, of which about one fourth came from affluent men who donated $5,000 or more. Absent from the list of donors were those associated with the "money trust," Morgan, Belmont, and Ryan, who Wilson insisted should not be solicited, but whether substantial contributors like Cyrus McCormick, of the Harvester trust, or the nation's leading brewer, Jacob Ruppert, had cleaner hands is a moot point.

Roosevelt jeered at Wilson's fervent exhortations for a program to destroy monopoly and restore competition as nothing more than "rural toryism." His point was valid, for Wilson's approach, if not naïve, was anachronistic. American society was no longer rural but industrial. It was a fantasy that free competition could be restored without losing the advantages of modern mass production and distribution made possible by large corporate enterprise.*

In any event, Wilson had one important advantage possessed by neither of his opponents: his party was not split. The consequences for both Taft and Roosevelt of that cleavage was manifest in the defections which eroded the effectiveness of their party organizations. Many Roosevelt men nominated for state or local office or for Congress resigned from the Republican party to join the Progressives. In a few cases the regular Republican organizations supported Roosevelt. California and South Dakota electors were pledged to Roosevelt, putting the Taft people in the position of bolters. Where the Taft organization in a number of states compelled state and congressional candidates to pledge their loyalty, separate Progressive tickets appeared. Sometimes the two groups fused, with candidates for office remaining neutral as between Roosevelt and Taft in order to insure their own elections.

The Progressives, compelled to organize and cement a

---

* Ironically, when Wilson was in the White House, his program was more like Roosevelt's than the one he himself had proclaimed.

national party in about three months, concentrated on the
head of the ticket. They effected some arrangements with
the regular Republicans on the lesser offices, or in some
instances let them go by default, which accounted for the
small number of Progressive congressmen elected in proportion to the total vote cast for Roosevelt. While Wilson
had some organizational problems, too—a revolt against the
Tammany control of Boss Murphy or the threat in New
Jersey to split the party by a three-way contest for a senate
seat—they were minor annoyances compared with the situation of his opponents.

The impetuous Roosevelt was to find that some chickens
hatched in the days of his Presidency came home to roost.
His past flamboyant record of imperialism and militarism
made him suspect to peace organizations, and his record of
political opportunism worried many Progressive purists. "I
wish I could believe he intended to do a single honest
thing," wrote one reformer, "or that he would carry out a
single plank in the platform if he were to be elected. . . . I
cannot." Wilson, on the other hand, had an unblemished
record of independence and reform during his tenure as
governor. Moreover, he won the esteem not only of the progressives within his own party but also of many independents and Republicans for his moderate and elevated
approach. Among the more than 40,000 members of the
Wilson Progressive Republican League were such outstanding figures as Jacob Schiff, the banker-philanthropist, Dr.
Harvey W. Wiley, leading exponent of pure food legislation, Louis D. Brandeis, Raymond B. Fosdick, and Herman
J. Ridgway, publisher of Everybody's Magazine.

As all presidential candidates of a major party must,
Wilson sought to win over various minority groups in the
population. Often he walked a tightrope. He had to placate
the women's rights groups without offending those opposed
to female suffrage. He had to deal adroitly with temperance
advocates, foreign-born elements, and various religious
groups. Attacked for being both pro- and anti-Catholic,
Wilson replied, "I am a normal man, following my own

natural course of thought, playing no favorites, and trying to treat every creed and class with impartiality and re-spect."

More delicate and troublesome was the problem of the Negroes in the North. Although they were not yet an effec-tive political force in the large states, Democratic managers wished to neutralize the effect upon liberal opinion of the party's indifference or hostility to their situation. Only the previous year, Senator James K. Vardaman of Mississippi had made a campaign pledge to seek repeal of the Four-teenth and Fifteenth Amendments, and one of Wilson's managers, Josephus Daniels, had editorialized in his North Carolina paper, "We abhor a northern policy of catering to negroes politically just as we abhor a northern policy of social equality."

Wilson himself was not rabidly racist, but he was a Southerner and shared the prejudices of his region. He would have preferred to avoid the entire issue, but he was pressed to make some statement, especially by the progres-sives in the party. His campaign advisor on the race ques-tion was Oswald Garrison Villard, liberal editor of the New York *Evening Post* and one of the founders of the National Association for the Advancement of Colored People. Noth-ing could be accomplished among the Negroes, Villard wrote Wilson, "until we have an utterance from you which we can quote. . . . They know that besides yourself, both Mr. McAdoo and Mr. McCombs are of Southern birth, and they fear that the policy of injustice and disfranchisement which prevails not only in the Southern states, but in many of the Northern as well, will receive a great impetus by your presence in the White House."

Finally, Wilson sent a message to a meeting of the Na-tional Colored Democratic League in which he said that he favored "justice executed with liberality and cordial good feeling." If he became President, the Negro people "may count upon me for absolute fair dealing and for everything by which I could assist in advancing the interests of their race in the United States." A disappointingly pallid statement, it was nevertheless something, and, as many Negro leaders resented the Progressive party's lily-white, exclusionist policy in the South, they supported Wilson.

With considerable skill, the Democratic candidate managed to reassure big business, appeal to the workingman, and attract the middle class. At a talk in Hartford, he presented himself as the champion of conservatism. "We ought to go very slowly and very carefully about the task of altering the institutions we have been a long time in building up," he said. "I believe that the ancient traditions of a people are its ballast." The following day when he addressed factory workers at Fall River, Massachusetts, he declared that labor's rights were not recognized even by the laws of the United States. An employer could dismiss all his workmen for no other reason than union membership. "So the thing is absolutely one-sided. I believe we ought to hold a brief for the legal right of labor to organize." The American Federation of Labor supported Wilson as it had Bryan four years earlier.

A gathering in Philadelphia gave him a thundering ovation when he asserted that the middle class was being crushed "between the upper and the nether millstones" of capital and labor. The middle class, he said, no longer controlled the American economy, and he feared that socialism would triumph unless the strangle hold of a few monopolies was broken. "We have entered the lists in order to free the average man of enterprise in America, and make ourselves masters of our own fortunes once again."

This was the first presidential campaign in which two major candidates proposed bold programs of economic reforms by government to heal some of the cankers produced by an industrial age. Despite Wilson's contention that Roosevelt's solution would greatly aggrandize governmental power—he argued that the history of liberty was the history of the limitation of governmental power—both candidates charted the new course on which the nation henceforth would travel. In his last address of the campaign, Roosevelt expressed the pragmatic philosophy that would inspire future government policy: "We are for human rights and we intend to work for them. Where they can be best obtained by the application of the doctrine of states' rights, then we are for states' rights. Where in order to obtain them, it is necessary to invoke the power of the Nation, then we shall invoke to its uttermost limits that mighty power."

Remarkably little personal vituperation and slander was vented, except for Roosevelt's occasional pot shots at Taft and the blustering of die-hard conservatives who were alarmed that "sound doctrine" would be subverted, until it became apparent that Taft would be defeated. Then conservative journals, enraged at Roosevelt for his apostasy, which they felt was responsible for the coming debacle, denounced him with venom. The New York *Sun* predicted that if he ever reached the White House he would never leave, the New York *World* that victory would only whet Roosevelt's appetite for another term and yet another until tyranny was enthroned. One publisher warned that a Roosevelt triumph would be followed within ten years by a bloody revolution which would be succeeded by despotism. In an editorial entitled "Roosevelt or the Republic," George Harvey charged that Roosevelt was the first President "to glory in duplicity, the first braggart, the first bully, the first betrayer of a friend who ever occupied the White House." If he won the election, "civil strife . . . would almost inevitably ensue from patriotic resistance to usurpation by a half-mad genius at the head of the proletariat."

By the middle of October all the newspaper polls predicted a Wilson victory, and gamblers were offering six-to one odds in his favor. On election day, within a few hours after the balloting ended, the results were obvious. At ten o'clock that night Wilson was notified by telegram that he was President. He received 6,286,214 votes, Roosevelt 4,216,020, and Taft 3,483,922. In the electoral college, the returns were Wilson 435, Roosevelt 88, and Taft only 8 from Vermont and Utah, the worst showing of any major presidential candidate up to that time.

Taft was shattered. Although he had early abandoned hope of victory, he had not expected so overwhelming a defeat. It was all Roosevelt's fault, he was convinced. Hundreds of thousands of Republicans must have voted for Wilson to prevent that man from going to the White House. Roosevelt drew his votes from "the faddists, the radical progressives, the people with isms, the emotional clergymen and women in states where women voted, and all the factional sore-heads in the Republican party. . . . What I got was the irreducible minimum of the Republican party that was left after Roosevelt got through with it."

The former President's understandable bitterness clouded his judgment. In fact, no third party since the Civil War had performed as well as the Progressives, who carried Minnesota, Michigan, Pennsylvania, South Dakota, California, and Washington. Wilson's nomination, however, had precluded the possibility of victory, since they could not rely on defections of progressive Democrats. Moreover, even the progressive Republicans had split, many of them, especially in the West, following La Follette in support of Wilson. With a program more attractive to the urban than the agrarian sections, Roosevelt drew a substantially greater proportion of his support from the larger cities, though he failed to attract the labor vote to any appreciable degree, and he made no real inroads in the "solid South." While the "Bull Moose" party ran a full national ticket in most states, it elected only one governor and a dozen or so congressmen. On the state and local level, Progressive candidates with but few exceptions trailed their Republican and Democratic opponents.

That the nation had swung to the left was indicated by the Socialist party vote. Eugene V. Debs polled almost 900,-000 votes, an increase of over half a million from 1908. He probably would have done even better but for the liberalism of two of the major candidates.

The Progressive party was completely Roosevelt's show, a tribute to his tremendous personal appeal. He was the cement that held it together, and when he lost interest a few years later the party disintegrated. Roosevelt had used it primarily as a vehicle for defeating Taft and advancing his own political ambitions. He lacked the commitment to genuine progressivism that inspired many of his dedicated followers, who assumed that he was as passionately devoted to the cause as they were. While he used fighting slogans about social justice to cheering crowds, in his own circle he was sarcastic about some of the progressives, calling them "cranks," "parlor socialists," or "so-called reformers" who came dangerously near the mark of lunacy.

Despite its brief existence, the Progressive party served a useful function, as did many of the other short-lived third parties. Without their illumination of the dark corners of American society and their pressure to sweep out the malignities lurking there, the major parties would have moved much more slowly in the direction of reform. Many of their proposals which seemed wildly radical to some at the time were later considered essential for the welfare of the nation and adopted with little fuss.

For the country, the Republican debacle of 1912 was most propitious, as it put into the White House a man who emerged as one of its great leaders. During Wilson's eight-year tenure, he elevated the Presidency to new heights and enlarged its powers. After him there would be a brief hiatus in leadership, but the foundation he had put down was solid enough to build on.

8. "I Pledge You . . . a New Deal"

THE impetus toward reform all but flickered out with America's entry into World War I. When peace came at last, a self-indulgent nation, irritated by the derangements which inevitably follow a major conflict or perhaps merely exhausted by eight years of moral exhortation, turned gratefully to the pacifier of "normalcy" and "serenity" promised by Warren G. Harding, Republican candidate for the Presidency in 1920. Harding's chief qualification for the high office, which he never sought or even wanted, was that he looked like a President. Nevertheless, he scored the most sweeping triumph since the second election of James Monroe, carrying every state outside the solid South.

Overwhelmed by his responsibilities, President Harding was happy to delegate policy making to others. Amiable and guileless, he was easily duped by those whom he trusted. Shortly before the nation was rocked by the scandal of flagrant corruption at the highest levels of government, Harding died, apparently of a stroke.

In Calvin Coolidge, the successor to the White House, Americans had a man who exactly suited their desire to maintain the status quo. Stolid and unimaginative, the personification of the admired virtues of thrift and frugality, and a firm believer in leaving well enough alone, Coolidge could be relied on not to disturb them. During his administration, reform was a shadowy, almost imperceptible wraith. The appointment of conservative, business-oriented men to federal commissions for regulating industry resulted in a marked relaxation of governmental supervision. Tax legislation and other aspects of public policy were designed to favor the business community.

When Coolidge refused to run for a second full term, Herbert Hoover became the leading contender. Hoover's was the classic American success story of rags to riches. Born of poor parents, orphaned in childhood, working his way through school and college, he had become wealthy enough at the age of forty to retire from mining engineering. As director of Belgian War Relief and food administrator at home during the war, his name became almost as well known as Wilson's both in the United States and Europe.

With an outstanding reputation and no apparent partisan affiliation, he was regarded by Americans of both parties in 1920 as ideal presidential timber. Franklin D. Roosevelt commented, "He is certainly a wonder and I wish we could make him President of the United States." When some Democratic leaders went to persuade him to try for the candidacy, he announced that he was a Republican. At the Republican convention he attracted some support, but he had no organization behind him and the politicians preferred a solid party man.

For the next eight years, Hoover served as Secretary of Commerce, performing his duties with characteristic efficiency. Aspiring for the presidential nomination in 1928, he was unopposed by any strong contenders and was elected on the first ballot. The Republican platform pledged to continue the policies of the previous administration. Running against Governor Alfred E. Smith of New York, a Roman Catholic, and at a time when the country was in a feverish glow of prosperity, Hoover won over fifty-eight per cent of the popular vote. "We shall soon, with the help of God, be in the sight of the day when poverty shall be banished from this nation," he announced.

The twenties, a decade of governmental complacency
and public apathy, of large pockets of grinding poverty in
the midst of wealth, of national power and withdrawal from
international responsibility, of prohibition and the contempt for law which it produced, came to an inglorious end
with the stock market crash in October 1929. Prices of securities plummeted ruinously, some losing as much as
eighty per cent of their September value, and for the next
two-and-a-half years the market continued to slide downward. The Wall Street debacle was a prelude to prolonged
economic depression not only in the United States but in
Europe.

Within the next few years, between twelve and fifteen
million Americans were unemployed. Throughout the country there were people who were slowly starving to death. In
rural areas families evicted from their homes by mortgage
foreclosures huddled in flimsy tents in midwinter; in the
cities on street after street a depressingly familiar sight was
furniture piled up on the sidewalk belonging to families
evicted from apartments. Thousands of families unable to
pay their bills lived without heat or light; children were
kept out of school because they had nothing to wear. On
the outskirts of almost every town and city homeless men
lived in rickety shanties put together from crates or barrels,
subsisting on whatever scraps of food they could find, often
from garbage pails or the city dump.

This unprecedented crisis required a bold, imaginative
leader who would not be reluctant to experiment. Hoover
possessed exceptional administrative skills—few American
Presidents entered office with such high public expectations
of great achievement—but his views were obsolete. He
stubbornly clung to nineteenth-century tenets of "rugged
individualism," believing that the main function of government was "to investigate, call conferences, and make suggestions that would increase the efficiency of business and
agriculture" and that governmental assistance to the needy
would destroy the American system of free enterprise.

For two years Hoover kept issuing variations on the

bromide that all that was needed was a restoration of confidence, until even some Republicans began to gag. Senator Fess of Ohio declared that "every time an administration official gives out an optimistic statement about business conditions the market immediately drops." Finally, in 1931, the President took some steps to aid large-scale business institutions on the theory that if they revived the effects would percolate down. The Reconstruction Finance Corporation and the Federal Home Loan Bank Act were constructive measures, but they did nothing to alleviate the indescribable human misery.

Hoover remained adamantly opposed to direct federal relief and to a public works program to reduce unemployment, for which liberals in both parties pleaded. He vetoed several bills for such purposes, calling the projects "the most gigantic pork barrel ever proposed to the American Congress" and "an unexampled raid on the public treasury." With incredible disregard for the temper of the nation, he ordered the Army to dislodge an encampment of war veterans who had trudged to Washington in the heat of the summer of 1932, some with their wives and children, to petition Congress for advance payment of war service bonuses due them in 1945. Commanded by no less than the Chief of Staff General Douglas MacArthur, cavalry troops with drawn sabers, six tanks, and a column of steel-helmeted infantry with fixed bayonets drove the ragged, emaciated marchers out of their shacks with tear-gas bombs and then set fire to the makeshift structures.

With the President's unpopularity mounting to hatred, the Democrats took full advantage of their vulnerable target. Charles Michelson, an experienced newspaperman employed to handle publicity for the National Committee, performed an annihilating propaganda job. An endless stream of anti-Hoover material flowed from his bureau, including editorials for newspapers and speeches for the use of prominent Democrats. It swamped the desperate efforts of the Republicans to create a more attractive image of Hoover. They were also handicapped by the President himself. Hoover alienated people with an extreme reserve which made him appear cold and distant. "There was always a frown on . . . [his] face and a look of worry," a close White House observer commented, which gave the impression "of a fellow who was always afraid of losing his job."

Hoover's relations with the press were also unfortunate. Extremely sensitive to criticism, he was apt to become peevish. The lack of rapport with the reporters was reflected in their dispatches, and these, in turn, reinforced public feeling. Jokes about the President which circulated through the country were a measure of the attitude toward him. One had the President asking his Secretary of the Treasury to lend him a nickel to buy a soda for a friend, to which Mr. Mellon replied, "Here's a dime. Treat them all." In another, a Kansas farmer declared that Hoover was the greatest engineer in the world, since "he had drained, ditched, and damned the United States in three years."

As the presidential election year approached, even Republicans were secretly shaking their heads about Hoover's prospects and hoping it might be possible to "dump" him. Many party regulars were unhappy with him on a personal basis and disturbed by his political ineptitude resulting from lack of experience in politics. "There is not a single soul thus far I have met, stand-pat, Progressive or otherwise, who believes Hoover can be elected," Hiram Johnson wrote in February 1932.

The National Convention which met at Chicago on June 14, 1932, was a pallid, dispirited affair, with little of the hoop-la customary at such gatherings and with a marked absence of Hoover banners, buttons, and pictures. Proceedings were dull and routine. The platform opposed excessive government spending and direct federal relief, called for continuation of the tariff policy, and in all other matters endorsed the Hoover record. It was adopted without discussion except for the prohibition question, which precipitated a heated exchange. In the end a plank was approved which straddled the issue, pleasing neither the "drys" nor the "wets."

Among the Democrats, for whom the White House was in reach for the first time in sixteen years, the problem was the choice of a candidate. The party had been left bruised and fragmented after the 1928 election. Opposition to Alfred E. Smith, a Catholic, a "wet," and a symbol of urbanism, had permitted the Republicans for the first time since Reconstruction to make inroads into the South, winning support among those of the Populist and Progressive tradition, religious fundamentalists, prohibitionists, and the rural elements who distrusted big business and city people. In addition, the Democrats continued to be wracked by internal dissensions between the conservatives who controlled the party machinery and the liberals.

The attitude of the conservatives was expressed by the Chairman of the National Committee, the multimillionaire industrial executive John J. Raskob. The party, he said, should "do everything to take the government out of business and relieve trade from unnecessary and unreasonable government restriction." He would urge a protective tariff and suspension of the antitrust laws. To the Democrats of the West and the South such a stand was anathema, a betrayal of the party's most cherished traditions. It was also considered inimical by one prominent northeasterner, the governor of New York, Franklin D. Roosevelt.

The split between the rural and the urban party members could be mended, Roosevelt was convinced, but the mortar must be composed largely of liberalism, that is, by opposing the domination of the business interests, and not as Raskob suggested, by making a bid for their support. He feared, he wrote a senator in 1931, that the party would be misled "along conservative or reactionary paths by those who fatuously believe that we can successfully compete with our Republican friends for the support of certain interests." This group would hardly be likely "to accept an invitation from us when they already own the original article, and they certainly have owned the Republican organization for many years." To another friend he wrote that the Democrats must not surrender to those who would make them "a party of high tariff and a friend to those vested interests" who for years had dominated the Republicans. "If we win, we must win because we are progressive."

For some time Franklin Delano Roosevelt had been regarded as presidential timber. In terms of personality, background, and experience, he was certainly "available." Of an old and distinguished family, the only son of wealthy parents, Roosevelt had received an excellent education, practiced law for a while, and then entered politics. His magnetic qualities, which later captivated the nation, and his extraordinary political skill were apparent in 1910 when Republican Dutchess County sent him to the New York Senate, the first Democrat from that district in half a century. Later appointed Assistant Secretary of the Navy by Wilson, he filled that post with distinction for nearly eight years, resigning to run for the vice-presidency in 1920. The Republican victory returned him briefly to his law practice, for shortly thereafter he was stricken by poliomyelitis, which left him paralyzed from the waist down. He spent the next three years in a determined, grueling struggle to get back on his feet, finally succeeding with the aid of a cane and steel braces.

To put Roosevelt in the White House was the most passionate wish of his devoted friend, the frail, wizened Louis M. Howe. In 1911, Howe, then a reporter, came to interview Roosevelt. "Almost at that first meeting," he later said, "I made up my mind that . . . nothing but an accident could keep him from becoming President." Now, satisfied that Roosevelt had surmounted his physical handicap, he took up his plan. Howe decided that Roosevelt should make a bid for the governorship in 1932, then try for the White House in the next election. In 1928, however, Alfred E. Smith persuaded Roosevelt to run for governor in order to strengthen the ticket in New York. Smith lost the state but Roosevelt, at a time of a Republican avalanche, was elected by a majority of 25,000. Two years later, cutting deeply into traditional Republican territory, he was re-elected by a huge plurality, almost twice that of the matchless vote-getter Smith in his best year as gubernatorial candidate. The day after the election, Will Rogers commented, "The Democrats nominated their President yesterday, Franklin D. Roosevelt," and newspapers throughout the country predicted his probable nomination.

All the same, preconvention strategy had to be plotted carefully. If Roosevelt adhered to political tradition and remained quiet until election year, he might be forced out of the race even before he could announce his candidacy. On the other hand, an open campaign would make him the target of all his rivals. As only one third plus one of the delegates was required to defeat him, enough votes could be tied up behind "favorite sons."* Weighing the risks, Roosevelt decided on action, but sub rosa. He would not admit even to his close advisors, except for Howe, that he was seeking the candidacy. When he arrived in Albany after his re-election, he told reporters that he was "giving no consideration or thought or time to anything except the duties of the Governorship. I repeat that now, and to be clearly understood, you can add that this applies to any candidacy, national or otherwise, in 1932."

Meanwhile, Louis Howe, Roosevelt's chief of staff, began operations in January 1931. He rented several rooms in a building on Madison Avenue and rehired a few girls who had worked for him on the gubernatorial campaign. His purpose was to establish an organization, "Friends of Roosevelt," which would disseminate publicity and solicit funds but which ostensibly was independent of the candidate. It rapidly became a publicity factory of unparalleled size and scope.

The initial move was to reach leaders of all state organizations, members of Congress, and anyone who had expressed an interest in Roosevelt's nomination. A tabulation was mailed, prepared by James A. Farley, New York State Democratic Chairman who became one of Roosevelt's chief

* Until 1936 when the rules were changed to allow for a simple majority for nomination, the Democratic party convention had always required a two-thirds majority.

aides, comparing the governor's performance in the predominantly rural upstate counties with the votes of other
Democratic gubernatorial candidates as far back as 1916,
together with an "interpretative" pamphlet. Farley estimated that the letter-writing campaign was the largest ever
conducted in American politics. "We went on the theory
. . . that people love the personal touch; they delight in believing there is a close link between them and the folks
who run the show."

Various points were stressed in approaching potential
supporters. To some, Roosevelt's background and religious
affiliation were discreetly introduced as a contrast to that of
Alfred E. Smith. Southerners were informed that Roosevelt
was "reasonable" on prohibition—while he was a "wet," he
was not an extreme "wet." To Westerners, his progressive
record as governor was emphasized. And to those who were
opposed to machine politics, his opposition to the bosses
when he was a member of the New York Senate was
stressed.

Money to finance the campaign was obtained from
wealthy Democrats such as Frank Walker, a New York attorney; Henry Morgenthau, Sr., former Ambassador to
Turkey; William H. Woodin, the industrialist whom Roosevelt later appointed to his Cabinet; Edward J. Flynn, boss
of Bronx County; Jesse I. Straus, the New York merchant,
later Ambassador to France; and Joseph P. Kennedy, the
financier, later made head of the Securities and Exchange
Commission.

In the summer of 1931, the genial and engaging Farley
left on a carefully planned tour which took him into eighteen states in as many days. He traveled more than 30,000
miles, meeting over a thousand Democratic leaders. With
his incomparable gift for making friends and inspiring enthusiasm, Farley was a matchless choice for winning adherents. "All I did," he later recalled, "was to drop into a
town and meet the people I had written to . . . and then just
give them a plain heart-to-heart talk, the kind everybody
understands—no highfalutin stuff . . . telling them why I

thought Roosevelt was the best man to nominate and why he had the best chance to win." When he returned home, he sent each individual whom he had seen a personal letter signed with his distinctive signature in green ink.

One thing that disturbed Roosevelt was Farley's report that wherever he went he was questioned about the Governor's physical fitness for the Presidency; he had been aware for some time of a whispering campaign that he would be unable to bear the rigors of the office. "I find that there is a deliberate attempt to create the impression that my health is such as would make it impossible for me to fulfill the duties of a President," he wrote to a friend. "To those who know how strenuous have been the three years I have passed as Governor of this State, this is highly humorous, but it is taken with great seriousness in the southern states particularly."

To spike the rumors, Roosevelt arranged, presumably at the suggestion of Earle Looker, a Republican writer, to be examined by a group of eminent physicians selected by the Director of the New York Academy of Medicine. Looker was invited to come unannounced to observe, which he did on three occasions. The medical report and Looker's conclusions were reported in the July 25, 1931, issue of *Liberty* magazine. Roosevelt, wrote the journalist, "seemed able to take more punishment than many men ten years younger." Thousands of reprints of the article were sent out by Howe to every Democratic chairman and to anyone who had ever questioned Roosevelt's stamina. Additional thousands went off to prominent Democrats in the name of the "Friends of Roosevelt."

Until the end of January 1932, Roosevelt maintained the fiction that he was not a candidate for the nomination. The primary election in North Dakota provided the occasion for a formal statement that he would run for the nomination, as under the laws of that state a candidate was obliged to declare his availability before he could enter the primary. Roosevelt now added to his tight little organization Representative Homer S. Cummings of Connecticut, an old friend from the days when Roosevelt was Assistant Secretary of the Navy. Cummings had been variously a member and chairman of the Democratic National Committee for years and was highly influential on Capitol Hill. Using his considerable persuasive powers, and with the aid of two friends in the Upper House, he induced twenty-four senators and a number of congressmen who previously had not expressed any presidential preference to announce their support for Roosevelt. One of the senators wrote to a friend after attending a Roosevelt meeting, "I was surprised to learn how nearly unanimous the sentiment is in his behalf."

The swing toward Roosevelt had been gathering momentum since early the previous year, partly as a result of several polls which Jesse I. Straus had financed. In the first of these, taken among delegates and alternates to the 1928 convention, Roosevelt was favored by more than half of those who indicated their presidential preferences. The second, which surveyed 1,200 businessmen in every state but New York, gave him a margin of five to one over Smith and two to one over the industrialist Owen D. Young, regarded as a favorite of the business community. Three additional polls showed Roosevelt well in the lead.

Relatively new to American politics, these polls attracted considerable attention and led many newspapers and periodicals to undertake some on their own. One of the most important, conducted by the Scripps-Howard chain, substantially confirmed the earlier findings and also indicated that Roosevelt should go on to win the election in November. The surveys not only influenced the professional politician but had an impact on the public.

Nevertheless, Roosevelt would still have to fight hard for the nomination. The National Committee had encouraged local candidates wherever it could, and a gaggle of "favorite sons" had lined up: House Speaker John Nance Garner of Texas, Governor Albert Ritchie of Maryland, Newton D. Baker, Secretary of War in Wilson's Cabinet, Senator James Reed of Missouri, Governor George White of Ohio, Governor William Murray of Oklahoma. Most were relatively unknown outside their own states, but collectively they could block Roosevelt on the first ballot.

The most formidable threat was Alfred E. Smith. After his defeat in 1928, Smith vowed that he would never run for office again, but as election time approached the presidential virus flared up. Moreover, the friendship between the two men—Roosevelt had made the nominating speech for Smith in 1924 and again in 1928—had disintegrated, a casualty of the political wars. Smith had become increasingly rancorous as the governor first refused to take his recommendations on appointments and then rebuffed his efforts to be the power behind the throne. Perhaps also an unconscious jealousy of the younger man for his success contributed to the rift. In any case, twelve days after Roosevelt declared himself, Smith formally announced his availability.

Few felt that Smith really had a chance, but supported by Raskob and his group and his strength in the East, he could deadlock the convention, opening the way for a compromise candidate. Farley claimed that Roosevelt could count on 668 votes on the first ballot, only 102 short of the number required for the nomination. Yet even if the estimate was correct, it was still considerably shy of the essential two thirds.

The maneuvering would have to be intricate, a minuet of advance and retreat. When he discovered that the Smith-Raskob group was spreading rumors that he was secretly "dry," Roosevelt put his position on record. Late in February, he stated categorically to a Buffalo dinner audience of some thirteen hundred people that he favored repeal of the Prohibition Amendment and return of the liquor-control problem to the states. Having thus pleased the Eastern "wets," he went on to propose that states establish liquor-control plans which would bring in new revenue—a suggestion that would be likely to appeal to the "drys."

One of Roosevelt's most serious problems was the corrupt, Tammany-controlled New York City government headed by Mayor James J. Walker. The investigation by

Samuel Seabury that he had authorized uncovered a staggering amount of evidence of bribery, graft, and other unethical procedures. Roosevelt was being pressed hard to take action, but fearful of losing not only New York's 96 electoral votes but also those of Illinois, Indiana, and New Jersey, which were also run by political machines, he kept temporizing and endeavored to steer a middle course. His efforts were a fiasco, for he succeeded only in infuriating Tammany and alienating reform-minded intellectuals.*

On international issues Roosevelt had to be extremely cautious to avoid estranging not only the isolationists in the party hierarchy but the majority of the American public, which was fiercely against involvement in European affairs. Thus far he had been successful in adhering to his policy of not commenting on foreign relations, but early in 1932 William Randolph Hearst forced his hand on the extremely touchy subject of the League of Nations. The publisher, attacking Roosevelt in his papers as an internationalist, roiled up a considerable stir. Finally, he demanded on his front pages that the candidate state his views publicly.

Three days after Hearst's challenge, Roosevelt recanted his earlier allegiance to the League. Addressing the New York State Grange on February 2, he declared that he was not apologizing for having worked on behalf of an organization which sought to prevent war. During the intervening years, however, Wilson's idea, he said, had been transformed into a meeting place to discuss "strictly European political national difficulties" in which the United States should have no part. Moreover, the principal members of the League had shown no disposition "to divert the huge sums spent on armaments into the channels of legitimate trade . . . and payment of obligations." In view of these facts, "I do not favor American participation."

* After his nomination Roosevelt summoned Mayor Walker to appear before him in the executive chamber and for days relentlessly pounded him with questions. Some prominent Democrats, alarmed at possible Tammany vengeance, urged him not to remove Walker from office. Roosevelt was spared a decision when the Mayor resigned.

The speech achieved its purpose with the isolationists in the party. Even more important, with Hearst placated, the Eastern block of Garner votes which the publisher might be able to influence would not go to Newton D. Baker, an uncompromising internationalist, and certainly not to Smith, an uncompromising "wet." His Wilsonian followers, however, were badly shaken in their faith in him, and many of his liberal supporters, disgusted with his handling of the Tammany issue, became increasingly antagonistic.

Throughout the preconvention campaign Roosevelt was belabored both by the left and the right. The *New Republic* referred to him as "a liberal-minded man of excellent intentions" but "not a man of great intellectual force or supreme moral stamina." Oswald Garrison Villard of the *Nation* echoed this appraisal, adding that Roosevelt lacked intellectual capacity, boldness, and originality in finding solutions to vexing problems. Elmer Davis described him as a man who believes "the shortest distance between two points is not a straight line but a corkscrew." The Scripps-Howard press called him "irresolute," concluding a front-page editorial with the damning comment, "In Franklin Roosevelt we have another Hoover."

The most stinging criticism came from Walter Lippmann, who called Roosevelt "a highly impressionable person," warning against taking too seriously the progressivism of this "amiable man" who had many "philanthropic impulses" but who, being too eager to please, was "not the dangerous enemy of anything." During his three years as governor, Lippmann said, he had been so cautious that not a single act involved political risk. Lacking a firm grasp of public affairs, devoid of strong convictions, "Franklin D. Roosevelt," continued Lippmann, "is no crusader. He is no tribune of the people. He is no enemy of entrenched privilege. He is a pleasant man who, without any important qualifications for the office, would very much like to be President."

As it turned out, of course, these ordinarily astute observers had misread the candidate, whether because of the stratagems he felt compelled to perform in order to win the nomination or because, as Raymond Moley commented in a letter to his sister, the impression people get from his charming manner is that "he is soft or flabby in disposition or character." That was, however, "far from true," he went on. "When he wants something a lot he can be formidable— when crossed he is hard, stubborn, resourceful, relentless." He appeared naturally warm and friendly because he enjoyed being pleasant and engaging. "And being a born politician he measures such qualities in himself by the effect they produce on others."

Moley, a professor at Columbia University, was one of a group of academicians recruited as policy advisors to assist Roosevelt with his campaign. Each man, a specialist in some area of public policy, not only drafted speeches but served to fill in the gaps in Roosevelt's knowledge. A columnist on the New York *Times*, writing a piece about the group, dubbed it the "brain trust," and the phrase stuck. Roosevelt was an apt pupil, absorbing information like a sponge. With the aid of his assistants, he developed the theme that ran through all his speeches: responsibility of the government for the welfare of the nation; to vanquish the depression, help must start at the bottom, not the top, of the economic pyramid, with the "forgotten man," the millions of workers and small businessmen and farmers whose lives had been blighted by a calamity not of their own making.

Of all the Democratic aspirants, Roosevelt alone called for sweeping reforms in the economic system and was critical of the country's business leadership. While he talked in general terms, he advocated a resilient approach which would permit change, experimentation, and novel departures. Responding to a suggestion by Smith that a large public works program be undertaken by government to relieve unemployment, Roosevelt declared in a radio address that public works could be no more than a stopgap. "A real economic cure must go to the killing of the bacteria in the system, rather than to the treatment of external systems."

Purchasing power, he insisted, must be restored to the farmer, since on his dollar the livelihood of every city worker depended. Furthermore, government assistance in the form of loans should go not only to banks and corporations but to small homeowners to prevent evictions through mortgage foreclosures.

In another address, Roosevelt asserted that the country required "imaginative and purposeful planning" based on "the national community of interest—economic planning not for this period alone but for our needs for a long time to come." To the graduating class of Oglethorpe University on May 22, he emphasized the need for a pragmatic approach in realizing desired objectives. "I believe that we are at the threshold of a fundamental change in our popular economic thought," he said. "We need to correct by drastic means if necessary the faults in our economic system from which we now suffer."

To receive the nomination, Roosevelt would have to carry the South and West, since the East was largely Smith's territory. Even in New York, the results of the state convention revealed that he could count on probably less than half the delegates. Roosevelt won the primary in New Hampshire but, flushed with victory, committed a strategic blunder by entering the Massachusetts contest. He was maneuvered into working with a minority faction led by Boss James M. Curley, who, thinking that through the candidate he could regain control of the organization, encouraged him with excessively optimistic predictions. As Smith was still a favorite in the state and the regular machine was extremely powerful, Roosevelt was crushingly defeated. A pro-Smith tide swept over New England, carrying along all but Vermont.

Roosevelt's sojourns at Warm Springs, Georgia, had made him well known and popular in the South. Nevertheless, he took nothing for granted. He made increasingly frequent trips to the resort, where he swam and dined with politicians and worked with the regulars in the firmly entrenched, powerful state organizations. His efforts were re-

warded with the support of the delegations from twelve of
the southern and border states, only three withholding their
endorsement.

Elsewhere the Roosevelt organization met with frustra-
tion. In Ohio and Indiana, the obstacle was Newton D.
Baker, for whom Roy Howard of the powerful Scripps-
Howard newspaper chain was quietly working as a compromise candidate while purportedly supporting Smith.
Political prudence required that Roosevelt maintain cordial
relations with Baker and two other Ohio "favorite sons,"
Governor George White and former presidential candidate
James Cox, and not engage them in primary contests. The
Ohio delegation was instructed for White with an informal
arrangement that, if he did not pick up additional delegates
at the convention, it should switch to Baker. Farley hoped,
however, that at the convention he could persuade the delegation to support Roosevelt.

Indiana similarly remained elusive, selecting an uninstructed delegation despite Farley's blandishment that its
gubernatorial candidate, Paul V. McNutt, would be rewarded with the chairmanship of the Committee on Permanent Organization at the Convention. He later learned
that Roy Howard had made a deal with McNutt for at least
eight votes for Baker on the first three ballots in exchange
for his newspapers' support of the state ticket.

Illinois, with fifty-eight delegates, was backing a favorite
son, Senator J. Hamilton Lewis. Efforts by Farley to obtain
a second-choice commitment for Roosevelt were obstructed
by Mayor Anton Cermak of Chicago and the powerful
Cook County machine, which was friendly to Smith and
working for a deadlocked convention. After a meeting with
all the delegates, he finally succeeded in working out a
somewhat satisfactory compromise. The delegation would
not be bound by the unit rule after the first ballot, thereby
permitting each member to vote his own preference. But
this still left Illinois an unknown quantity.

Of the seven primaries in which the two major aspirants
competed, Roosevelt won four, Smith two—New York and

Massachusetts—and in the last, California, Roosevelt out-ran Smith but lost to John Nance Garner. When the struggle for delegates had ended, thirty-four states and six territories were pledged to Roosevelt, enough to give him a majority but not the requisite two thirds.

The convention opened at Chicago on June 27 with 1,154 delegates and thousands of onlookers in a mood of euphoria, which was somewhat dampened the following day over the choice of a permanent chairman. The National Committee had backed Jouett Shouse, a Smith supporter, against the Roosevelt man, Senator Thomas J. Walsh of Montana. Shouse lost by 98 votes, but the outcome indicated that, while the Farley contingent was in control, Roosevelt would still have a struggle.

About the platform there was little disagreement except over repeal of prohibition. "Here we are," wrote John Dewey, "in the midst of the greatest crisis since the Civil War and the only thing the two national parties seem to want to debate is booze." A "wet" plank was adopted by a substantial margin. There was the usual pledge to reduce expenditures and balance the budget. The farmers were promised in general terms better mortgage financing, control of crop surpluses, and whatever measures were necessary to raise prices. Other planks dealt with enforcement of antitrust laws and the regulation of public utilities, holding companies, and stock market trading. Republican policies, of course, were attacked vigorously, but most of the alternative proposals tended to be vague. Still, the platform did favor unemployment relief by the states, an expanded public works program, unemployment and old-age insurance, and reduction in hours of labor. A renascent liberalism was contesting the rugged individualism of Hoover.

To insure that delegates committed to Roosevelt did not stray, and to try to influence the waverers, Farley sent personal letters to all of them and Howe mailed an autographed picture of Roosevelt together with a small record "containing a message especially for you, from the Governor." The message was inconsequential but this was one means of utilizing the magnetic quality of Roosevelt's voice. Another device was an open telephone circuit from the candidate's study in Albany connected to a loudspeaker at the Chicago headquarters. When delegates arrived, they were ushered into a private suite where Roosevelt greeted them over the microphone with, "My friends from Oregon . . ." or whatever the state was, followed by some personal comment. He answered questions and expressed his views. In the main room, the delegates could study a huge map of the United States on which were blocked in red all the states in the Roosevelt column. This was most impressive, since it indicated that Roosevelt clearly had a majority.

The intensive drive and psychological offensive continued right down to the moment of balloting. Roosevelt's lieutenants, recalling the conventions of 1912 and 1924 when party division prolonged the voting interminably, aimed for a quick victory. Otherwise, it might be possible for the other candidates to unite in an effective "stop Roosevelt" movement and settle on a compromise candidate. In Farley's words, "the undercover" phase was carried on "by means of all the stratagems that human wit and ingenuity can contrive." The objective was to hold the lines intact while trying to persuade enough waverers so as to win a first-ballot nomination. "The nervous strain during this period of suspense," Farley recounts, "was very close to the limit of physical endurance. . . . I was working eighteen and nineteen hours a day, conversing with hundreds of people, constantly consulting with other leaders, receiving reports from every delegation, and meeting at least twice daily with several hundred newspapermen." Dozens of other "manipulators" and "maneuverers" kept up the same dizzying pace.

Nominating addresses began on the afternoon of June 30. Each was followed by seconding speeches, "a merciless and unholy flood of oratory," as Farley put it, which kept blasting away at the delegates, who became increasingly limp and bleary-eyed as the hours passed and the dawn approached. Many favored adjournment to provide some rest before the balloting began, but the Roosevelt men feared that their acquiescence might be construed as weakness. Farley consulted with Roosevelt, who advised an immediate ballot.

The roll call began at 4:28 A.M. At the end of the first ballot Roosevelt led with 666, more than a majority and far ahead of his nearest competitor, but still 104 short. On the second ballot he picked up 11½ votes, which was fortunate, for a decline might have had a fatal psychological effect. His floor leader moved for adjournment but this time the opposition refused, hoping to knock Roosevelt over on the third ballot. During the roll call, Roosevelt narrowly escaped a major setback. Under the impression that the convention would adjourn after the second ballot, Senator Pat Harrison of Mississippi returned to his hotel room. Voting for Roosevelt under the unit rule, the Mississippi delegation was being held by the slender margin of 10½ to 9½ votes. Harrison learned from a radio report that the third ballot was in progress. Partially dressed, he dashed to the convention hall to cast the decisive vote in his delegation. The third ballot ended at nine o'clock in the morning, with Roosevelt still lacking 87 votes. Adjourning until that evening, the stupefied delegates reeled to their hotel rooms for some sleep.

For the Roosevelt adjutants, however, there was no rest. The key to the nomination was Texas and California, whose votes were committed to Garner. On the eve of the convention, Farley, conferring with Representative Sam Rayburn, Garner's campaign manager, had held out the promise of the vice-presidential nomination, if Texas should support Roosevelt; he failed to obtain a pledge. Other Roosevelt leaders similarly had been unsuccessful with California. Not even Hearst, who after lengthy telephone conversations had agreed to exert pressure, could persuade the delegation to change its vote. Finally, Farley, after consulting with Howe, went to see Rayburn. At the conclusion of a brief conversation, the Texan promised, "We'll see what can be done."

In the meantime, Garner, in Washington, was disturbed at the way the balloting was proceeding. He phoned Rayburn to say that the time had come to force a decision. Roosevelt was obviously the choice of the convention. "We don't want to be responsible for tying up this convention and bringing on another Madison Square Garden that might defeat the party candidate in November." Later that afternoon when Rayburn indicated that Garner had released his delegation, McAdoo of California proceeded to obtain his delegation's consent to switch.

Since only the men behind the scenes were aware of what had happened, the convention expected more weary hours of balloting after it reassembled that evening. When California was called for the fourth ballot, McAdoo arose and rocked the hall with an announcement: "California came here to nominate a President. She did not come here to deadlock this convention or to engage in another disastrous contest like that of 1924." Amid a deafening outburst of cheers and boos from the galleries, he cast his state's 44 votes for Roosevelt. In rapid-fire succession most of the other states followed, only Smith refusing to release his delegates to make the vote unanimous. Afterwards, learning that Roosevelt intended to accept the nomination in person, Smith and his followers left Chicago before the scheduled arrival.

Anticipating his nomination, Roosevelt had decided weeks before to ignore the long-standing tradition that the candidate act as though the nomination came as a stunning surprise and deliver his acceptance weeks later after receiving formal notification. To save time he intended to fly to Chicago. He kept his plans secret and when queried by reporters, bantered, "Now I'll tell you what I'm going to do. I'm going to bicycle out to Chicago. I'm going to get one of those quintets, you know, five bicycles in a row. Father will ride in the first seat and manage the handle bars; Jim will ride second, then Elliott, then Franklin, Jr., and then John."

At a time when flying as a mode of transportation was

still uncommon, Roosevelt's dramatic announcement that
he would travel to the convention by air sent a surge of
hope through a torpid, despondent nation. Somehow the
flight became a symbol of action to come, a dimly felt
portent that the long, dark night of despair was finally coming to an end.

Due to arrive at 2 P.M., the plane was delayed for hours
by strong headwinds. At the convention hall, the vice-presidential nomination of Garner, a foregone conclusion in view
of Farley's arrangements, was dragged out to keep the rest-
less delegates in their seats. As the flight fell further behind
schedule and as radio reports reached Roosevelt of the
growing impatience of the audience, he began cutting more
and more paragraphs from his acceptance speech. When
the plane landed, Roosevelt stepped out, cheerful and smiling, refreshed by a nap on the way. A natural politician, he
was completely unperturbed when the crowd pressing
around him knocked off his hat and he almost lost his
glasses.

At the stadium, Roosevelt was greeted with a mammoth
ovation. "I regret that I am late," he apologized, "but I have
no control over the winds of heaven and could only be
thankful for my navy training." His decision to come to
Chicago, he said, might be considered unprecedented, but
these were unprecedented times. Some traditions were foolish and should be broken. "Let it be from now on the task of
our party to break foolish traditions," but one tradition
which he wished the Democrats to preserve was that of
liberalism, both in thought and in policy.

In his acceptance speech, Roosevelt addressed himself to
all major segments of society, assuring them that their problems would be dealt with: for the farmer a crop control
program to reduce ruinous surpluses and a plan to redis-
count mortgages; for the businessman a lower tariff to re-
juvenate foreign trade; for the unemployed, federal relief.
He advocated regulating the sale of securities, a self-sup-
porting public works program, reforestation programs, and
repeal of the prohibition amendment. He promised to work

for a more equitable distribution of the national wealth. Concluding, he declared that everywhere "millions of our citizens cherish the hope that their old standards of living and of thought have not gone forever. These millions cannot and shall not hope in vain. I pledge you, I pledge myself, to a new deal for the American people. Let us here assembled constitute ourselves prophets of a new order of competence and of courage. . . . Give me your help, not to win votes alone, but to win in this crusade to restore America to its own people."

The weary delegates were lifted to their feet in thunderous cheers and applause, and a benumbed nation, roused to hope, responded with equal fervor. On the following day a Rollin Kirby cartoon showed a farmer leaning on his hoe, symbolic of the nationwide misery, looking upward at the sky in mingled hope and confusion at a plane bearing on its wing the legend, "New Deal." The phrase, which was in common use, had not been deliberately inserted as a slogan, but Roosevelt's delivery had given it a special significance. At once it caught the popular imagination and became a slogan that summed up the promise of Roosevelt's Presidency.

Even as he was leaving the stadium, shaking hands with the well-wishers who crowded around him, Roosevelt's mind was already leaping ahead with plans for the campaign. Late that night he had a long conference with Raymond Moley, during which he instructed him to set the brain trust to work immediately preparing papers on major issues and proposals. The "idea factory," which in addition to Moley consisted of Rexford G. Tugwell, Adolph A. Berle, Jr., Samuel I. Rosenman, and Basil O'Connor, was reinforced by two valuable new recruits, General Hugh S. Johnson and Bernard M. Baruch. In the following months, numerous professors, business leaders, and political chieftains, representing the entire spectrum of economic philosophy from liberal to conservative, were asked to contribute suggestions.

The brain trust served not only as a policy-generating

group but also as a clearinghouse for ideas, with which it was deluged. As Moley described it, "We were at once working up the material for specific speeches, pushing ahead with the broad economic education of ourselves and Roosevelt, adopting or rejecting thousands of ideas that poured in on us, and trying to observe the elementary political maxim that no one who voluntarily offered suggestions or plans, however silly . . . must be sent away unhappy." The group operated successfully, Moley commented, because each member possessed tact, good humor, and a strong constitution. "Consider the difference of opinion and temperament that inevitably cropped up in such groups," he wrote, "the crucial decisions on policy and political strategy that had to be made, the endless meetings, telephonings, draftings, and checkings it all entailed, and you get a picture vaguely hinting at the swirling chaos, the dizzying turmoil of July and August."

Farley was assigned to direct the organizational activities for obtaining votes. Insofar as it was humanly possible, he and Roosevelt established personal contact with members of a vast network. As he had utilized the local party groups in the campaign of 1930, Roosevelt now made the state organizations responsible for getting out the vote. State chairmen, called to national headquarters for briefings and consultations with party leaders, returned home with renewed impetus to work for victory. Farley sent personally signed campaign pamphlets and letters totaling more than a million and a half copies to county and precinct workers in every state. News releases in the hundreds of thousands and millions of pieces of printed matter and buttons were distributed throughout the country.

To obtain reliable information on the changing political picture in each state, Roosevelt instituted a new procedure which he had found effective during the primary campaign. In the past it had been the custom to rely on reports of the national committeemen, state chairmen, and individual scouts but, as they tended to be influenced by those with whom they came in contact, their judgment, often either too optimistic or too pessimistic, was not reliable. Now clipping bureaus supplied daily newspaper editorials and pertinent political items from every paper in the country. These items, at times amounting to fifteen thousand a day, were carefully sifted and the relevant ones expertly condensed for transmission to Roosevelt and his personal advisors, national committeemen, aides at headquarters, and the campaign chairmen.

Overseeing the entire colossal apparatus was the candidate himself. Always ready to listen and to confer, to utilize all the available brains and skill, the final decisions were nonetheless his. From the outset, he held the reins of leadership firmly in his hands. Moley later commented that Roosevelt "so sharply delegated authority and so clearly maintained personal contact with each of us that there was never the semblance of conflict and never an overlapping of function." To which Louis Howe added, "Never in forty years' experience have I known a Presidential campaign being so completely controlled, dominated, and directed . . . by the candidate himself."

By contrast with the exuberant Roosevelt, glowing with vitality, with his infectious smile and buoyant manner, the sedate Hoover would have appeared a pale shadow under the best of circumstances; now, the target of widespread attack, he looked funereal. He had only one thing in common with his opponent—he, too, was in personal command, directing the strategy of an election campaign which soon became a merciless personal duel between the two men, one of whom, ironically, had lauded the other only a dozen years before as a man who would make an ideal President.

At first Hoover intended to limit his campaigning to about three or four addresses on major issues. Good form required a President to leave the campaign largely to subordinates and to the party professionals. Moreover, until the Democratic convention, Hoover regarded Roosevelt as probably "the easiest man to beat." After public reaction to the plane trip and the acceptance speech, he and many other Republicans as well were considerably less sanguine.

Genuinely fearful that his defeat would usher in an era of untried experiments dangerous to American freedoms and liberties, he began to view his campaign as a crusade for the preservation of traditional values. While his aides were devoted to him, he believed that they did not have sufficient national prestige and generally lacked the skills required to make an impact on the voters. If his case were to be presented properly, he would have to do it himself.

In September, when Maine went to the polls to elect state officials and delivered that traditionally Republican stronghold to the Democrats, Hoover was badly shaken, especially since his party had made much of the slogan, "As Maine goes so goes the nation." "It is a catastrophe for us," he said. "It seems that we have got to fight to the limit." By the end of the month he was even more depressed as news from his advisors kept coming in that the western states, so long loyal to the Republican party, were now in open revolt. To Stimson he confided that "the only possibility of winning the election, which is lost now, would be exciting a fear of what Roosevelt would do." But to his disheartened party workers he presented a façade of indomitable determination. "Talk right out," he told one of his purveyors of gloom. "Don't mince words at all. Say just what you think and mean. It is unnecessary to tell me that Kansas, Missouri, Iowa, Minnesota, and the Dakotas are lost today. I know it. I have been given that information forty times this week. But this fight isn't over yet. We have just started. I shall fight every inch of the way. We can pull out of this."

Hoover decided to open his campaign with a major address early in October in Iowa, the state where he was born. As he worked painstakingly on the speech, advance copies of a *Literary Digest* poll sent his spirits plunging once again. Then as the time for his appearance in Des Moines approached, it seemed that this was the last city he should have chosen. The first of a planned series of strike demonstrations was being staged, and rumors reached him that he would be subjected to a barrage from the hostile farmers. Apprehensive Iowa party leaders rushed to Washington to urge that he cancel his trip, but that was, of course, out of the question.

The whistle stops on the way west gave Hoover little cause for encouragement. If the small crowds were not actually unfriendly, they were decidedly cool. After one stop he remarked that the trip reminded him of traveling on the Harding funeral train. At Des Moines he was greeted by farmers carrying placards proclaiming their discontent. Doggedly he continued on into Michigan, Indiana, Ohio, West Virginia, and Maryland.

Compelled to defend his administration, Hoover's nine addresses, all of which he prepared himself, were omnibus in nature, unlike those of Roosevelt's, each of which dealt with a single theme. Since he could not reply to the many charges made against him by his rival, he delegated members of his Cabinet to follow up every one with a refutation. Some, like Ogden Mills and Patrick Hurley, worked tirelessly, but neither they nor the President could dispel the conviction of the American people that inadequate White House leadership was responsible for their misery, a point which Roosevelt hammered home incessantly.

Throughout the campaign, the unfortunate Hoover struggled to rip from himself the tag, "Hoover depression," fastened to him by the opposition. The calamity, the President maintained, had begun in Europe, whose economy had been crushed by the staggering cost of the war, and not, as the Democrats charged, in the United States as a result of frenzied and unregulated stock market speculation and the irresponsible floating of securities. Belatedly, Hoover had come to realize that the welfare of the United States was inextricably bound with that of Europe. Now the Democrats were throwing back into his teeth his optimistic declaration after the stock market crash that the business of the nation was "on a sound and prosperous basis," which ignored the situation overseas. They could mock him with "prosperity is just around the corner," a statement he never made but which was based on such assertions as "the country has turned the corner," delivered in January 1930, and "we have now passed the worst and with continued unity of effort we shall rapidly recover," which he said in May.

What probably most upset Hoover, a decent and humane man, was the charge that he was heartless and callously indifferent to the desperate plight of millions of Americans. In one address he expressed his pain and bewilderment. "I shall say now the only harsh word that I have uttered in public office," he told his audience. "I hope it will be the last I shall have to say. When you are told that the President of the United States, who by the most sacred trust of our nation is the President of all the people, a man of your own blood and upbringing, has sat in the White House for the last three years of your misfortune without troubling to know your burdens, without heartaches over your miseries and casualties, without summoning every avenue of skillful assistance irrespective of party or view, without using every ounce of his strength . . . to help, without using every possible agency of democracy that would bring aid . . . then I say to you that such statements are deliberate, intolerable falsehoods."

The fact remained, however, that Hoover was bound as with steel bands by a philosophy which prevented him from considering federal aid to ameliorate the dire situation. He believed that where private charity was inadequate it was the responsibility of state and local governments to provide relief. Appropriations from the federal treasury, he was convinced, would impair "something infinitely valuable" in American life and strike at the roots of self-government.

In his last address at Madison Square Garden, Hoover declared, "This campaign is more than a contest between two men. It is more than a contest between two parties. It is a contest between two philosophies of government." Roosevelt, he warned, was proposing solutions which would "destroy the very foundations of our American system." Obsessed with the question of the tariff, on which he had harped continuously in his speeches, he cried, "The grass will grow in the streets of a hundred cities, a thousand towns; the weeds will overrun the fields of millions of farms

if that protection be taken away." The election, he concluded, would decide "the direction our Nation will take
over a century to come."

This somber, negative, and defensive appeal was a striking antithesis to Roosevelt's broadcast on election eve. After
recounting his impressions of the millions of people he had
seen during the thousands of miles he had traveled, Roosevelt said he hoped that the unity which he had observed
would make it possible for him to lift the nation out of the
morass of depression. As to his own role, he went on, a
man knows that "when the light of favor shines upon him, it
comes not, of necessity, that he himself is important" but
because "for a brief moment in the great space of human
change and progress some general human purpose finds in
him a satisfactory embodiment. To be the means through
which the ideals and hopes of the American people may
find a greater realization calls for the best in any man; I
seek to be only the humble element of this restoration."

In this and in other talks during the final week of the
campaign, Roosevelt spoke as though he were the President
while the occupant of the White House gave the impression of being a desperate challenger. His tones and words
were those of a man confident of himself and of the outcome. For Hoover, the campaign had been an agonizing
ordeal, which left him exhausted and dispirited. For Roosevelt, it had provided excitement and heady stimulation,
leaving him refreshed and sanguine.

Few men in public life enjoyed campaigning as much as
Roosevelt, who regarded it as "unadulterated joy." As he
toured the country on his campaign special, his practice
was to say little of any consequence at the numerous whistle stops; he indulged in pleasantries and left policy statements to the formal, scheduled addresses. The procedure
varied little. When the train, filled with reporters, politi-
cans, speechwriters, and secretaries, came to a halt, Roosevelt stepped out on the platform on the arm of his eldest
son, James. To the waiting crowd he would smile and say
something like, "It's nice to be back in so-and-so. I am just

out here to look, learn, and listen." Then he would introduce his attractive daughter and daughter-in-law and, present his son, who was getting prematurely bald, with the joking comment that he had more hair than James did. As the crowd roared in appreciation, the train was already pulling out, Roosevelt waving cheerily. His grin and good humor were unfailing. One reporter observed that "Roosevelt smiles and smiles and smiles and it doesn't get tiresome. He can smile more than any man in American politics without being insipid." Regardless of how late into the night he worked, of how many appearances he was compelled to make or hands to shake, he always appeared fresh and vigorous the next morning.

It was one thing to captivate crowds at train stops with his charm, quite another to expound ideas that were significant and appealing to a ravaged, despondent people. In seeking the nomination, Roosevelt had been the champion of the party's liberal wing; as presidential candidate he had to take into account its conservative elements. The Democrats were united in their desire to return to power, but their leading spokesmen had not been talking with one voice. Garner maintained that if the federal government had not encroached on the rights reserved to the states, "we perhaps would not have the present spectacle of the people rushing to Washington to set right whatever goes wrong." Smith declared that "the Forgotten Man is a myth and the sooner he disappears from the campaign the better." Another prominent Democrat even saw Hoover as a radical, denouncing him for "following the road to socialism at a rate never before equalled in time of peace by any of his predecessors."

Bombarded with advice and suggestions from all quarters, Roosevelt listened, smiled, and nodded. He took a bit from here, a bit from there, and charted his own ideological course, navigating by improvisation and guided by pragmatic considerations. He was not always consistent. In his first address on July 30, he declared that greater government intervention in the economy was essential, while at the same time he clung to the hallowed doctrine of the balanced budget. "Any government, like any family, can for a year spend a little more than it earns. But you and I know that a continuation of that habit means the poorhouse." Moley commented that "the frightening aspect of his method" was his receptivity, his willingness at times to accept contradictory recommendations made by advisors in his zeal to advance programs politically acceptable in different parts of the country. This receptivity, however, was basic to his political skill, even his political genius. Out to win an election, he became a sounding board for the grievances of an afflicted nation and, drawing upon a variety of proposed remedies, attempted to weave them into a program containing political coherence, if lacking in consistency of economic theory.

The specific outlines of the New Deal, as they would later take shape during his Presidency, were only faintly foreshadowed in Roosevelt's campaign addresses. Each dealt with a specific theme, depending on the need of the area where it was given. At Salt Lake City, he talked about rehabilitating the sick railroad industry, and at Boston he stated that the federal government had a solemn duty to see to it that no person starved. He categorically rejected Hoover's contention that the depression originated abroad, insisting that it was a domestic phenomenon. He spoke eloquently about the need to restore purchasing power and end mass unemployment, help the farmer by raising agricultural prices, lower the tariff except for protection to agriculture.

Taken all together, his addresses represented no concrete program of liberal reform, but what somehow filtered through was a promise of dynamic, imaginative leadership that would not hestitate to venture on to new, untried paths to solve the nation's grievous problems. The promise was credible, rooted as it was in his philosophical commitment to the exercise of executive power and responsibility. As Roosevelt told a reporter in September, "The Presidency is not merely an administrative office. That's the least of it. It is more than an engineering job, efficient or inefficient. It is preeminently a place of moral leadership. All our great Presidents were leaders of thought at times when certain historic ideas in the life of the nation had to be clarified."

An intuitive politician, he wisely ignored the counsel of some of his closest advisors that he refrain from an extensive campaign tour. They tried to dissuade him by pointing to previous candidates who lost the election barnstorming while their rivals remained quietly at home. Their real concern, despite all outward signs of Roosevelt's extraordinary vitality and good health, was that he might not be able to hold up. Roosevelt, however, was revitalized by his contacts with crowds of people, drawing energy from each handshake. Moreover, public exposure, he felt, should dispel once and for all any doubts about his physical endurance.

Roosevelt planned a tour that would take him all the way to the West Coast. A major point of concentration was to be the farmers, overwhelmingly Republican for many years. The problem was how to formulate a program for farm relief that would be broad enough to appeal to the varied agricultural elements without at the same time alarming the eastern conservatives. The preparation of the address Roosevelt gave at Topeka, Kansas, a key agricultural city, illustrates how his speeches evolved.

After soliciting suggestions from Governor Harry H. Woodring of Kansas, Roosevelt turned to his brain trust. Moley asked a specialist on farm subjects, M. L. Wilson, to draw up a memorandum, and Wilson, after sketching one out, had Henry A. Wallace, another agricultural authority, go over it carefully with him. The memorandum was forwarded to Rexford Tugwell, who worked it over. Henry Morgenthau and an assistant contributed notes on the farm debt, farm taxation, and the planned use of land. Hugh Johnson prepared a draft speech. Roosevelt contributed the introduction and some additional material. In one place he inserted a paraphrase of Lincoln: "This Nation cannot endure if it is half 'boom' and half 'broke.'" Gathering all this together, Moley prepared a draft which went the rounds of the brain trust for revision. Then it was turned over to several farm editors and senators for suggestions or corrections, after which Moley then prepared a draft that Roosevelt, as he later wrote, "would pencil over with comments. The draft would shuttle back and forth, back and forth, between us until the language of the original memorandum prepared by someone or other was almost completely obliterated."

The final copy of the Topeka address fulfilled Roosevelt's purpose of a broad appeal. Its ambiguous nature was indicated by the comments of the president of the Illinois Agricultural Association: "To those of us who have been very closely associated with previous efforts to solve the farm problem, a number of things could be read into his speech. Within the last two days I have been told by men in position to know that John Simpson . . . says 'The Governor was referring specially to the Farmers Union solution to the question. . . .' To many others, they are equally sure he was referring to the allotment plan of Mr. Wilson. Still others of us believe . . . that his speech could refer to the principles of the Rainey bill." While the address was not completely satisfying to any of the farm leaders, at least it alienated none of them. At the same time, Roosevelt did introduce the new concept of social management into agricultural affairs, stating, "We must have, I assert with all possible emphasis, national planning in agriculture. . . . We need unity of planning, coherence in our Administration and emphasis upon cures rather than upon drugs."

On the West Coast Roosevelt directed his appeal to progressive Republicans. In Portland he advocated regulation of public utilities and the right of communities which were dissatisfied with private service to establish their own service owned and operated by the government. "Judge me by the enemies I have made," he concluded. "Judge me by the selfish purposes of those utility leaders who have talked of radicalism while they were selling watered stock to the people and using our schools to deceive the coming generation."

In his most important address of the campaign, delivered at the Commonwealth Club in San Francisco, Roosevelt set forth with broad strokes the New Deal's rationale. The essence of his speech was that it was essential for government, within the framework of the existing economic system, to act as a controlling force for the public welfare, since "Equality of opportunity as we have known it no longer exists." The last frontier had long since been reached, and more than half of the population lived in cities where they were unable to derive a livelihood by cultivating their own land. Now the task was one "of distributing wealth and products more equitably, of adapting existing economic organizations to the service of the people." Private economic power, he said, has become a public trust, and if businessmen failed to assume the responsibility which accompanied power, the government must act swiftly to protect the common good.

Back in the East, Roosevelt gave his views on social welfare, unemployment, and fiscal policies. Relatively orthodox in his economic philosophy, he was unable to reconcile economy in government with the obvious need for federal spending to relieve the widespread distress. In a radio address on October 13, he advocated federal aid where local and state resources were inadequate, public works including playgrounds and housing to alleviate unemployment, and compulsory state unemployment insurance. A program of this kind would cost money, he said, and while he favored governmental economy, he would not have it practised at the expense of starving people. He repeated this theme six days later in Pittsburgh in a coda to an address, but the main thrust of his talk was a slashing attack on the Hoover administration's "spendthrift" fiscal policies, the unbalanced budget, which, he asserted, had brought the nation to bankruptcy.

Roosevelt charged the administration with "the most reckless and extravagant past that I have been able to discover in the statistical record of any peacetime Government anywhere, any time." The depression in the United States had not been triggered off by events abroad. "No, we need not look abroad for scapegoats. We had ventured into the economic stratosphere—which is a long way up—on the wings of President Hoover's novel, radical and unorthodox economic theories of 1928, the complete collapse of which brought ab 'ut the real crash in 1931." To correct this, Roosevelt p.'omised that the cost of government operations would be reduced by twenty-five per cent, and he would see to it that the men appointed to his Cabinet effected economies in their own departments.*

Then he concluded with a qualification that virtually nullified everything he had said previously. "If starvation and dire need on the part of any of our citizens make necessary the appropriation of additional funds which would keep the budget out of balance, I shall not hesitate to tell the American people the full truth and ask them to authorize the expenditure of that additional amount." Perhaps it had not fully penetrated to Roosevelt, even in that year of famine, how much spending would be required, or perhaps he had succumbed to the garden variety of demagoguery. In any event, within eight months Roosevelt was to proclaim that the "true deficit" might exceed one and a half billion dollars—"a deficit so great that it makes us catch our breath."

On the eve of the election, Villard's *Nation* commented in disgust that "neither of the two great parties, in the midst of the worst depression in our history, has the intelligence or courage to propose a single fundamental measure that might conceivably put us on the road to recovery." This evaluation was politically naïve in its expectation that a presidential candidate should provide a specific programmatic blueprint when he has to win the support of an electorate divided in its demands and its approaches to the solutions of grave problems. Walter Lippmann wrote to

---

* The speech, after three years of deficit spending, rose to plague Roosevelt in 1936. To silence the criticisms, he asked Rosenman to draft an explanation which he would deliver in Pittsburgh. After Rosenman reread the address, he wryly told Roosevelt that there was only one explanation he could give—to deny categorically that he had ever made it.

Senator Borah that, while he had "the deepest reservations about Franklin Roosevelt," it would be a relief to be finished with the present administration, which was so discredited it was no longer useful as an instrument of government. "And even assuming that Roosevelt isn't any better than Hoover, a new man for a while will be better than a man who's worn out and used up." For an astute political commentator, Lippmann's judgment was surprisingly clouded. While Roosevelt's tacking on some issues and his evasiveness on others undoubtedly blurred his image, his disposition to experiment and his firm advocacy of social and economic planning for the general welfare were clearly apparent. Moreover, his speeches did foreshadow, if in vague terms, many aspects of what was later to be known as the New Deal program.

In the end, after months of oratory, an expenditure of almost three million dollars each by the Republican and the Democratic national committees, and reams of newsprint (which largely favored Hoover), the American electorate decisively repudiated the administration. Hoover had become the symbol of the nation's despair and the scapegoat for its distress. He was blamed for excessively high taxes and governmental expenditures, for retaining prohibition, for wasteful fact-finding commissions and for failing to take the recommendations of his own experts on these commissions. Appeal to "rugged individualism" was a travesty to despairing men who had lost the very bootstraps with which to pull themselves up.

Long before the nation went to the polls on November 8, betting in Wall Street ran five to one in Roosevelt's favor. When the final returns were in, Hoover had gone down to a crushing defeat with 59 electoral votes to his opponent's 472, carrying only Maine, New Hampshire, Vermont, Connecticut, Pennsylvania, and Delaware. Roosevelt received 22,821,857 popular votes to 15,761,841 for Hoover.

Franklin D. Roosevelt's victory reawakened hope in a people made torpid by adversity. No one in the entire land, however, not even the President-elect himself, had any inkling of its real portent. Under Roosevelt's leadership, the Democrats would be welded into an effective majority party which, for the next two decades, would retain its hold not only on the White House but, except for a brief interval, on Congress. More significant, the innovations he instituted, his approach to his office and to the role of government, were to set the nation on a course from which it would probably never again depart.

9. Military Hero vs. Reluctant Candidate

THE twelve years following the election of 1932 have been aptly termed "The Age of Roosevelt." Characterized during his first campaign as a man "without any important qualifications for the office who would very much like to be President," Roosevelt completely shattered tradition by being re-elected to that office for a third term and then a fourth. Under his dynamic leadership, a nation charred by economic disaster rose like a phoenix from its ashes. Those were turbulent years, of programs that succeeded and experiments that failed, but the net result was an enlargement of governmental responsibility in the spheres of economic and social welfare which not only influenced the lives of Americans at the time but would affect those of unborn generations.

It was also a time of tragedy as the United States was plunged into the savage ordeal of war, prodigally spending its blood and treasure for four grim years to resist and destroy a monstrous bestiality that would have poisoned the earth. A world power, which for years had insulated itself from involvement in world problems, the nation was drawn to the center of the international stage where it was pinned by its might and prestige. This new and challenging position and the nature of the global struggle demanded from the President the utmost in statesmanship both at home and abroad. Filling myriad roles—executive leader, director of the economy, party leader, director of foreign policy, public opinion mentor, head of the Grand Coalition—Roosevelt elevated the Presidency to a position of unsurpassed importance.

A measure of the indelible impression Franklin D. Roosevelt left on his countrymen—and even on their children—is the reaction his name can evoke so many years after his sudden death in April 1945. There are those who become suffused with adoration when he is recalled and, on the other side, those who execrate his memory with a fierce passion. When he was alive, not many could remain indifferent to the indisputably towering figure in the White House.

Few men abruptly thrust into Roosevelt's place would not have appeared dwarfed, and for a time Harry S. Truman suffered from the comparison. A solid, middle-class citizen, unsophisticated, lacking the dazzle and polish of his predecessor, Truman had to win over the American public on the basis of his integrity, his sound common sense, and his strength as an executive leader.

Truman came to power at one of the most critical periods in the nation's history with little preparation to guide him through a complex maze of domestic and world problems, and with no time for apprenticeship. Arrangements had to be made for the organizational meeting of the United Nations at San Francisco, for a conference with Churchill and Stalin to coordinate policy on defeated Germany, and to plan the final phase of the struggle against Japan, which was to include the momentous decision of using the atom bomb.

Hardly had the flames of combat been extinguished when the icy chill of the "cold war" descended. Conflicting national interests, opposing ideologies, and rivalry for the allegiance of countries had transformed erstwhile allies into intransigent antagonists. The fear that Greece and Turkey would succumb to Communist domination prompted President Truman in March 1947 to ask Congress for an appropriation of $400 million to assist those nations economically and militarily. In announcing America's determination to enlist its moral and material resources during peacetime to redress the balance of power in the Old World, he promulgated a bold new departure in foreign policy. The Truman Doctrine committed the United States to the principle of containment of communism and, specifically, tc protect free and independent governments on the European continent "who are resisting attempted subjugation by armed minorities or by outside pressures." Early in 1948, Congress approved the Marshall Plan, a program of massive conomic assistance to rehabilitate the moribund economies of Western Europe. Some months later, Truman neutralized the Russian blockade of West Berlin by authorizing an airlift of food and supplies to its beleaguered population.

Considerably less successful were Truman's efforts at home. His "Fair Deal" program, an extension of Roosevelt's New Deal, foundered on the rocks of legislative opposition in Congress, controlled for the first time in sixteen years by the Republicans, who had scored sizable gains in the midterm elections of 1946. Using the slogan "Had enough?" the Republicans had capitalized on industrial unrest, soaring prices, shortages of consumers' goods and housing, resentment by farmers and businessmen over remaining wartime controls.

As the presidential contest of 1948 approached, Truman's popularity was at rock bottom. To avert what they thought would be inevitable defeat, an astonishing number of Democratic party leaders, liberal and conservative, Northern and Southern, sought to "dump Truman" and prevail upon General Dwight D. Eisenhower to be the party candidate. Among them were James and Elliott Roosevelt, Mayors Frank Hague of Jersey City, Edward J. Kelley of Chicago, William O'Dwyer of New York and Hubert Humphrey of Minneapolis, Senators Richard Russell of Georgia and Lister Hill of Alabama, Walter Reuther of the CIO, and the officers of Americans for Democratic Action. The most cutting insult was a telegram to the President sent by one Democratic leader urging him to head the movement to "draft" Eisenhower!

When the General unequivocally refused to be a candidate, the Democrats were "stuck with Harry." Gloomily they endorsed him at the convention, almost certain that he would be trounced by the strong Republican combination of Governor Thomas E. Dewey, a known vote-getter, and his running mate, Earl Warren, the popular governor of California. They became even more despondent when the party was splintered by defections from both its right and its left wings. Adoption of a strong civil rights plank precipitated a bolt of several southern delegations, who formed the States' Rights or "Dixiecrat" party, with Senator J. Strom Thurmond of South Carolina as its presidential candidate. Liberal elements, charging that Truman's containment policy would intensify the cold war and ultimately lead to conflict with the Soviet Union, formed the Progressive party, which nominated as its candidate Henry A. Wallace, who had been Roosevelt's third-term Vice-President.

With prospects for Republican victory brighter than at any time since 1928, Dewey's strategy was to refrain from saying or doing anything that might antagonize anyone. Smooth and impeccably dressed, he carried on a campaign that was the epitome of caution and banality. In faultlessly phrased sentences, he intoned the need for unity and efficiency in government, his intention to promote social progress, and to work for peace through the United Nations. One observer characterized him as a machine with a cellophane cover. All commentators and publicists, friendly or hostile, were certain that he would win. Public opinion polls unanimously predicted his victory. As early as September 9, pollster Elmo Roper announced that Dewey was so far ahead that no amount of electioneering could change the picture. Reflecting the consensus, one paper editorialized, "The election must be held if for no other reason than to find out which national pollster comes the closest."

Truman, however, was unperturbed by the defeatism of the Democrats or the elation of the Republicans. While his opponent's campaign was run by professionals assisted by scores of energetic party workers on all levels, lavishly supplied by funds, and supported by nearly two thirds of the press, Truman cheerfully battled practically alone. Barnstorming and whistle-stopping across the country, he traveled more than 30,000 miles. To hundreds of gatherings in large and small communities he denounced the "do-nothing" Eightieth Congress for selling out the people's interests, and the Republicans as "old moss backs . . . gluttons of privilege . . . all set to do a hatchet job on the New Deal." Spurred on by enthusiastic members of the audience who yelled, "Give 'em hell, Harry," he willingly obliged. In his homely, unvarnished language, this average man who happened to be President talked to the average man about what the administration had tried to do for him and what it planned to do in the future.

Up to the very end Truman exuded an air of confidence, impervious to the knells of doom that constantly sounded around him. A day or so before the election, when Truman was to deliver an address at Madison Square Garden, a newspaper publisher who had just come down from the President's suite sent journalists in the bar into roars of laughter when he told them, "The old boy still thinks he's going to win. He's standing there under the shower telling everybody that he'll sweep the country." The early edition of the Chicago *Daily Tribune* carried a headline the morning after the election, "Dewey Defeats Truman," over a news story which reported a sweeping victory of the Republican ticket by "an overwhelming majority of electoral votes."

On election night, pollsters and political analysts watched the returns with growing incredulity as Truman maintained and then increased the lead of the first returns. The President went to bed early in the evening at a little spa about thirty miles from Independence and slept soundly, but an increasingly hollow-eyed Dewey kept an all-night vigil at his hotel in New York. At five o'clock in the morning he told reporters that he was "still confident"; not until almost noon did he concede defeat. When the final returns were in, Truman had carried the country by the

astonishing margin of two million votes. The electoral returns were 303 for Truman, 189 for Dewey, and 39 for
Thurmond.

Innumerable "explanations" were later offered by the
red-faced experts for the most stunning political upset in
the nation's history. Publicist Gerald W. Johnson's interpretation was that Truman won because "the common man
took matters into his own hands, regardless of the politicians, regardless of the great lords in business and journalism, regardless of the experts and wiseacres. He is con-
spicuously the common man's choice."

The personal appeal of the folksy Truman as against
that of the slick Dewey was one factor. More significant was
the Democratic campaign. Superficially summed up by a
New York *Times* reporter as "patched together with Scotch
tape, rubber checks and sheer bravado," it actually had
been devised very astutely. The strategy was to make the
Republicans appear solely responsible for the "do-nothing"
Eightieth Congress. Ignoring the fact that the conservative
Democrats had joined with the Republicans to oppose the
administration's Fair Deal program, Truman had summoned Congress into special session after the conventions,
knowing full well that it would not enact his legislative
program. Then Truman belabored the Congress for defeating his efforts to halt accelerating prices by refusing to pass
an anti-inflation law, for undermining various New Deal
farm programs, and for its opposition to labor by passing
the Taft-Hartley Act over his veto. Again and again he
warned that a Republican victory would jeopardize all the
gains made during the years of Democratic rule.

To those voters who had cast their ballots in support of
the Fair Deal, the triumph was a hollow one. While the
House shifted to Democratic control, Congress continued
to reject Truman's legislative proposals. The Democratic
southern bloc prevented passage of a civil rights program,
and a conservative Democratic-Republican coalition defeated all the liberal measures requested by the President.

Although blocked on the home front, President Truman continued to receive the bipartisan support on foreign policy initiated in his previous administration until two major events dissolved the unity. The first was the collapse of Nationalist China. Up to the time the country fell to the Communists late in 1949, Republicans in Congress had exhibited little concern, even effecting a cut of $167 million from the appropriation requested by the President to aid the Nationalist government. Nevertheless, with their eyes on the 1950 and 1952 elections, they found it a potent issue for exploitation, charging the administration with responsibility for the debacle. The second was the conflict in Korea. Liberated from Japanese occupation at the end of the war, Korea had been arbitrarily divided at the thirty-eighth parallel, with the northern half under Russian control and the southern under American. While the separation was intended to be temporary, the line hardened into a permanent one, a symbol of the chasm produced by the cold war.

Under United Nations auspices, elections held in the south led to the establishment of the Republic of Korea in August 1948 with Dr. Syngman Rhee as President. Immediately thereafter the United States withdrew its forces from the country. The Soviet Union refused to allow the United Nations commission into its zone, but after the Democratic People's Republic of Korea was proclaimed the following month at Pyongyang, it, too, withdrew its forces. With both Korean governments militantly claiming sovereignty over the entire land, border clashes occurred repeatedly during the next two years. On the night of June 25, 1950, the smoldering powder keg blew up when North Korea hurled its forces across the dividing line, demolishing the South Korean defenses within a matter of hours.

President Truman acted at once, calling for an emergency session of the United Nations Security Council. When the People's Republic ignored the Security Council's order to cease the aggression, the Council voted to aid South Korea, whereupon Truman committed American

forces to the defense of the country. General Douglas Mac-
Arthur was appointed to command the United Nations
forces, to which ultimately sixteen nations contributed some
degree of land, sea, or air support, though the major financial and military burden was carried by the United States.
Both Congress and the American public applauded Truman's action, Senator Arthur H. Vandenberg, the Republicans' major spokesman on foreign policy, calling it "cour-
ageous and indispensable." Before long, however, feelings
about American involvement would change considerably.

Well-equipped, seasoned fighters with the advantage of
surprise attack, the North Koreans swept south, capturing
almost the entire peninsula. During the following months of
sanguinary fighting, the battle lines seesawed back and
forth. Seoul, the capital, was freed from the Red forces and
then retaken in January 1951 after MacArthur's troops,
which had advanced to within fifty miles of the Chinese
frontier, were forced back by a massive concentration of
Chinese "volunteers." General MacArthur now declared
that the only way to win the war was to bomb the "privileged sanctuary of Manchuria," blockade China, and use
Nationalist troops stationed in Formosa to attack the mainland.

Truman and the Joint Chiefs of Staff, however, opposed
such action, fearing that it might bring Russia, bound by a
mutual assistance pact with China, into the conflict and set
off World War III. Moreover, a massive commitment of
United States forces in Asia would leave Europe exposed to
Soviet power. The United Nations concurred with this position, but MacArthur refused to accept the decision, criticizing it publicly despite an explicit presidential order to
refrain from doing so. To maintain the constitutional principle of civilian supremacy over the military, the President
was left with no alternative but to dismiss the popular General, evoking furious denunciation from the American public.

A long, exhaustive Senate investigation of the Truman-
MacArthur controversy concluded that, as General Omar

Bradley put it, MacArthur's proposed military strategy would have extended the war to the mainland of Asia, involving the United States "in the wrong war, at the wrong place, at the wrong time and with the wrong enemy." In the meantime, General Matthew B. Ridgway, who had been put in command of the forces in Korea, had succeeded in driving the Chinese Communists out of the south. Nevertheless, it was apparent that the peninsula could not be united under Syngman Rhee's leadership. Both sides, acknowledging a military stalemate, agreed to seek a truce. For the next two years negotiations dragged on interminably, caught on the apparently hopeless snag of repatriation of prisoners of war.

At home, frustrated Americans who could not comprehend the subtleties of the complex situation were asking how was it that a mighty power like the United States, with all its resources, was unable to conquer half of a tiny, primitive land? Typical was a letter sent by one woman to the White House: "Why don't we use the wonderful weapons which we have perfected . . . to bring them [the Communists] to their knees as we did the Japanese?" Even more perplexing was that after all the bloodshed the United States should seek a truce simply to restore the status quo ante. A scapegoat answer was readily available for what had become labeled "Truman's war"—obviously the administration was "soft on communism."

Opponents of the administration exploited the case of the State Department official, Alger Hiss, accused of being a Communist and convicted of perjury, to frighten a naïve and confused public into believing that the country was being undermined by traitors and spies in the government. Alarm was whipped into paranoia by a cunning demagogue, the junior Republican senator from Wisconsin, Joseph R. McCarthy, whose name has become a synonym for one of the most ignominious periods in the nation's history.

McCarthy first came to national attention in February 1950, when, addressing the Republican Women's Club of

Wheeling, West Virginia, he charged that the nation was in its present "position of impotency" because the State Department was "thoroughly infested with Communists" and waved a sheet of paper on which purportedly was listed the names of the vipers. During the next four years a considerable segment of a free, enlightened people allowed itself to be intimidated by a vulgar mountebank who viciously maligned not only ordinary men and women but some of its most distinguished citizens in the coarsest, most abusive language. Prominent Republican senators, men of intelligence and integrity, like Robert A. Taft and Eugene D. Millikin, either overtly or tacitly endorsed McCarthy. Although none of his reckless charges were ever substantiated either by himself or the Federal Bureau of Investigation, innumerable careers were wrecked and lives ruined as "guilt by association" replaced the traditional canons of law and ethics.

To the issues of communism and Korea, over which the Republicans were gleefully rubbing their hands in anticipation of the 1952 election, was added that of corruption in government. A Senate investigation subcommittee revealed that liaisons existed between crime syndicates and Democratic politicians and that administration officials on the federal level used their positions to line their pockets. Although President Truman was in no way involved and the scandals were by no means as extensive as those during the "Teapot Dome" era, they provided another stick with which to beat the administration.

Republicans began to see the gleam of victory ahead, but who should be the shining knight to storm the bastions? Over the years, the dynamic spirit that had once infused the party had shriveled, leaving it paralyzed by conservatism and blind to the necessity of shifting political strategy to accommodate to a predominantly industrial and urban society. In order to capture the White House, the support of the labor and urban vote was essential, but the alliance in Congress between the Old Guard and the intensely anti-labor Bourbon Democracy of the South had labeled the party antilabor, antifarmer, and anti almost everything necessary to secure the support of a winning combination.

Impervious to these facts, the dominant faction was convinced that Republicans had gone down to defeat in 1940, 1944, and 1948 because they had nominated "liberals" like Willkie and Dewey, "me too" candidates who had apologized for rather than defended the legislative record of the party. To this group the logical choice was Senator Robert A. Taft, an outstanding congressman and party leader, who had been returned to office in the midyear elections by a landslide despite the opposition of organized labor in his state. Taft's antipathy to the New Deal philosophy and programs and his denunciations of government spending were a matter of record. His major defects, which had militated against a successful bid for the nomination in the past, were his narrow isolationism and his lack of political sex appeal. Cold and austere, he conveyed the impression of an efficient calculating machine. When Taft announced his candidacy in September 1951, he was joyfully hailed by the Old Guard, the isolationists, the "Asia Firsters," and party machine politicians everywhere except in the East.

Equally convinced on the opposite side that "Mr. Republican's" brand of Republicanism would be a disaster were the moderates and the internationalists, who were strongly entrenched in the East. They recognized that, to win, the Republicans as a minority party would need the support of independents and Democrats who would never back an extreme conservative, a critic of organized labor, an isolationist, and a man who had been "soft on McCarthy." At the same time, only an outstanding personality could dislodge Taft. Accordingly, a group of distinguished Republicans, which included Governor Dewey and Senators Henry Cabot Lodge of Massachusetts, Frank Carlson of Kansas, and James H. Duff of Pennsylvania, turned to Eisenhower, the only man they felt could be successfully pitted against the senator from Ohio.

General Dwight David Eisenhower was the archetype of the American dream: a beloved national hero who had pulled himself to the top by his bootstraps. Born into a family in modest circumstances, he entered West Point, after which a combination of ambition, personal merit, and luck sent him steadily ahead in his military career. As Commander of the North African invasion during World War II, he served with distinction, and later, as Supreme Commander of the Allied Expeditionary Forces in the invasion of Western Europe, he demonstrated exceptional ability not only for military leadership but for diplomacy. After a term as Army Chief of Staff, he retired to civilian life, accepting an appointment as President of Columbia University in June 1948. Showered with accolades for his brilliant achievements, Eisenhower remained modest and unassuming.

In common with most career men in the armed forces, Eisenhower had never evinced any interest in politics and often expressed the characteristic impatience of the military with contentious pressure groups. He had little admiration for politicians, tending to regard their actions in pursuit of self and group interest—normal to the democratic process —as unpatriotic. No one knew whether he was a Democrat or a Republican. When the county clerk of Abilene, Kansas, was asked in December 1951 whether the General had ever registered for either political party, he replied in the negative, adding, "I don't think he has any politics."

To politicians of both parties in 1948 Eisenhower appeared to be a peerless candidate for the Presidency. No sooner had he settled into his office at Columbia University than he was besieged by Democratic and Republican leaders, but he could not be persuaded to run for office. He was convinced, he declared, that "the necessary and wise subordination of the military to civil power will be best sustained . . . when lifelong professional soldiers, in the absence of some obvious and overriding reason, abstain from seeking high public office." His decision to remove himself "completely from the political scene is definite and positive. . . . I could not accept nomination even under the remote circumstance that it were tendered me." Appointment as

Supreme Commander of the newly created NATO forces in Europe temporarily ended speculation about his future plans.

In September 1951, Senator Henry Cabot Lodge visited the General at his NATO headquarters in France to plead that he was desperately needed by the country. The continuing centralization of power in Washington, he told Eisenhower, would not be halted until a Republican was in the White House, but victory would elude the party unless he headed the ticket. Also, his candidacy would dispel the impression abroad that the Republican party was too isolationist to address itself to the problems of the contemporary world. Four months later Lodge announced that General Eisenhower would accept the Republican nomination if it were offered to him. The following day from Paris, Eisenhower issued a press statement that Lodge and his colleagues had a right to "attempt to place before me next July a duty that would transcend my present responsibilities." He himself would do nothing to seek the nomination and under no circumstances would he request to be relieved from his duties in Europe prior to the Republican convention.

The impressive Dewey organization promptly went into action to mobilize support behind Eisenhower's candidacy. In the first show of strength between the General and Taft, the former's backers were confirmed in their belief that they had a winner. Eisenhower defeated his opponent handily in the New Hampshire primary, and in Minnesota, where his name had not been entered, he rolled up an unprecedented 100,000 write-in votes. He also won several other major primary victories, but toward the end of spring Taft began to forge ahead. Campaigning hard while Eisenhower was still abroad, Taft reinforced his reputation as the party's chief spokesman and began to pile up a substantial number of delegate commitments. Disturbed by the trend, Eisenhower's supporters prevailed upon him to return to the states and make himself "available." On June 1, five weeks before the scheduled opening of the convention, the General arrived home, a civilian now in the role of political gladiator.

Eisenhower launched his campaign at an outdoor rally in his home town of Abilene. His speech, a patchwork of generalities and platitudes, urged constant alertness to the peril of world communism, deplored the secrecy at Yalta and regretted the loss of China, advocated cooperation among capital, management, and labor, and opposed excessive centralization of government. As one Taft supporter wryly observed, the address was a plea for home, heaven, and motherhood.

Fierce struggles for delegates were waged in a number of states. In three—Texas, Louisiana, and Georgia—the claims of the rival party factions remained unresolved, so that the convention would have to pass on the legitimacy of each of the delegations. Throughout the South, the Republican organizations were tightly knit groups which were nourished by the patronage that could be obtained when their party controlled the White House. In the past, selection of delegates to the national conventions had been cut-and-dried affairs. This time Republicans and Democrats who supported Eisenhower appeared in force at the local and county meetings and elected members to the state conventions, which in turn were to choose delegates to the national convention. However, when they appeared at the state conclaves, they were disqualified or ejected by the Taft forces. Eisenhower supporters naturally claimed that a "steal" was taking place. In Dallas, Eisenhower charged that, in disenfranchising the delegates elected to support him, "the rustlers stole the Texas birthright instead of Texas steers." It was, he said, "a betrayal of the whole Republican party and of its principles," and he warned that no party can clean up government corruption "unless that party— from top to bottom—is clean itself, and no party can tolerate a rigged convention and hope to win."

When the convention opened in Chicago on July 7, Robert Taft seemed to occupy as advantageous a position as had his father forty years earlier. He arrived with enough pledged delegates to make his prediction of nomination on the first ballot seem credible. Moreover, his organization controlled the National Committee, the vital Credentials Committee, and, in fact, all the convention machinery including selection of the temporary and permanent chairmen; and the keynote speaker, General Douglas MacArthur, was also an avowed Taft man. Eisenhower's position was not unlike the one Theodore Roosevelt had been in. He, too, was the undoubted choice of rank and file Republicans but lacked about a hundred delegates to win the nomination. Since the contested Taft delegates from the South would probably be seated, his hope lay in the three hundred or so delegates pledged to favorite sons or still uncommitted.

A major battle seemed inevitable. After the gavel sounded, the confidence of the Taft organization was shaken by a bombshell—a statement by twenty-three of the twenty-five Republican governors urging that none of the disputed delegates be permitted to vote on the disposition of their own cases. If this change in the rules was adopted, Taft would lose as many as sixty-eight delegates and his grip on the convention as well. To the dismay of the Old Guard, a "fair play" resolution sponsored by the Eisenhower forces was approved after acrimonious debate, and with it the balance of power perceptibly shifted.

The floor debate over the contested seats which followed degenerated almost into a brawl. At one point Senator Everett Dirksen of Illinois stabbed a finger at Governor Dewey as he shouted, "We followed you before and you took us down the path to defeat!" Finally, by a vote of 607 to 531, the convention approved the seating of the Eisenhower delegation from Georgia. Taft supporters, recognizing that further strife was futile, conceded on the Texas and Louisiana delegations, which accordingly went to Eisenhower.

On the first roll call, Eisenhower received 595 votes, Taft 500. The remainder were scattered among the minor contenders, Earl Warren, Harold Stassen, and Douglas Mac-

Arthur. With Eisenhower only 9 votes short of victory, state delegations now followed the familiar practice of seeking recognition from the chair to switch their votes. Some 280 Taft "bitter enders" held out. Not until later that day, after Taft conferred with his successful rival and pledged him his support, was a motion adopted to make the nomination unanimous.

While many delegates had deserted the acknowleged leader of their party for the man who appeared to be a sure winner, the determining factor in Eisenhower's nomination was political self-interest. In the end, what proved decisive was patronage, the state patronage which the governors controlled and the potential federal patronage if a Republican won the White House. Taft had hoped to receive about 20 votes from the New York City delegates, but Dewey openly admonished them that he would still be governor for the next two and a half years and that he had "a long memory." He is also said to have reminded them of the jobs allocated to each delegate's district and mentioned that there could be new appointees two days after he returned to Albany. Both factions bid for the support of Governor John S. Fine of Pennsylvania, offering him a Cabinet post, an ambassadorship, even the vice-presidency. Most astonishing was the alleged promise by the Eisenhower group of the federal patronage, which by long precedent is a senatorial courtesy. To obtain Fine's promise to deliver his delegates, Senator Duff of Pennsylvania, an Eisenhower supporter, was said to have relinquished his prerogative to this award. In any case, both on the "fair play" amendment and in the balloting, Pennsylvania supported Eisenhower.

For Vice-President, the convention approved Eisenhower's choice of Senator Richard M. Nixon of California. Only thirty-nine, Nixon, it was felt, would appeal to youth, and his major role in the Alger Hiss case as a member of the House Un-American Activities Committee would emphasize the issue of communism in government.

The party platform denounced the Democrats for "their goal of national socialism," for "appeasement of Communism at home and abroad," for the China debacle and the war in Korea. The Republicans promised a balanced budget, reduction in the national debt, and a cut in taxes. The "me tooism" scorned by the conservatives could not be entirely abandoned, as was indicated in the planks advocating full parity prices for farmers and extension of the social security system.

In his preconvention campaign, Eisenhower had been the beneficiary of careful planning, effective organization, the exertions of innumerable supporters, and a liberal use of money. The major campaign group, Citizens for Eisenhower, spent about $1.2 million, and large sums were raised by other groups throughout the country. A conservative estimate is that the total expenditure ran to about $2.5 million; if the free time and services contributed by corporation executives and ordinary party workers were measured in dollars and cents, additional hundreds of thousands would have to be added. Big business leaders were heavily involved, and there were indications that their pressure, more than that of political influences, accounted for the shift of some delegate support to Eisenhower. Taft's campaign cost even more, and in both cases the amount was larger than had ever been lavished on a preconvention battle.

By contrast with these elaborate machinations, the efforts of the Democratic party aspirants and their supporters were paltry. With Truman's announcement early in April that he would not run again, the field was wide open. The major contender was the liberal Senator Estes Kefauver of Tennessee, who had become a national celebrity when the proceedings of his special Senate committee investigating crime were televised. No favorite, however, of either Truman or the party bosses, Kefauver conducted a strenuous handshaking, street-corner campaign which won him a surprising number of primaries. Among favorite sons were Governor W. Averill Harriman of New York, Senators Richard B. Russell of Georgia and Robert S. Kerr of Oklahoma, and Vice-President Alben W. Barkley, none of whom exerted himself greatly to promote his own candidacy.

Truman's personal choice was Governor Adlai E. Stevenson of Illinois. Of all the candidates, Stevenson, a grandson and namesake of Cleveland's Vice-President, was the most "available." A Princeton graduate, he had studied law at Harvard and Northwestern Universities, practiced law in Chicago, and was one of the "bright young men" recruited by the New Deal, serving in a series of posts in Washington. After the war he was appointed Special Assistant to Secretaries of State Edward R. Stettinius, Jr., and James F. Byrnes, served as delegate to the United Nations organizational conference at San Francisco, and later was an alternate delegate to the U.N. In 1948 he was elected governor of Illinois by the largest majority ever received by a candidate in that state. His effective fight against corruption and his battle for progressive legislation against the inertia of the Republican-dominated legislature won him a national reputation. In many respects Stevenson appeared a midwestern version of Franklin D. Roosevelt, but more intellectual and introspective, lacking the former President's supreme self-confidence and ambition for the White House.

Beginning in 1952, Stevenson was continually pressured by people from all over the country to seek the Democratic nomination. Just as consistently he refused, insisting that he was interested only in being re-elected to the governorship. In January, newspaper reports that he had visited the White House at the President's invitation aroused nationwide speculation that Truman had asked him to become a candidate. Shortly thereafter, a group of admirers in Illinois, which included faculty members of the University of Chicago, announced in a full-page advertisement in the Chicago Sun-Times the formation of the "Illinois Committee Stevenson for President," urging the public to support its efforts. The committee followed this up with a four-page brochure about Stevenson to voters all over the country, to Democratic congressmen, senators, governors, state chairmen, National Committee members. At no time did the group have any contact with Stevenson or receive any encouragement from him.

In March, Truman sent for him again. Stevenson went

secretly to prevent increasing conjectures about his candidacy. An old friend whom he visited on his way commented that he seemed "reluctant and unwilling to admit that he could possibly be the only logical candidate for the Democratic nomination . . . [or] that he could be nearly so serious a figure in American public life as his admirers were insisting that he was."

Throughout the spring a spate of articles appeared in the nation's press and in leading magazines about "The Reluctant Candidate," as *Newsweek* put it in one issue which had Stevenson's picture on the cover. On April 16, in accepting renomination for governor, Stevenson issued a statement which, the New York *Times* commented, effectively removed him from the presidential race. He was a candidate, Stevenson said, for governor of Illinois, "and I cannot run for two offices at the same time. . . . In these somber years the hopes of mankind dwell with the President of the United States. From such dread responsibility one does not shrink in fear, self-interest or humility. But great political parties, like great nations, have no indispensable man." He had unfinished work to complete in Illinois and "could not accept nomination for any other office."

When he reiterated in a press release shortly before the Democratic convention that he wanted no other office but the governorship, that he "will ask the Illinois delegation to continue to respect his wishes and he hopes all of the delegates will do likewise," the party leaders abandoned hope. His Illinois supporters, however, who had renamed their organization the "National Committee Stevenson for President," proceeded with their plans, operating on a shoestring. They sent a lengthy letter to every delegate and alternate to the convention urging that Stevenson be drafted. "We have no doubt," it concluded, "Governor Stevenson, devoted as he is to public service, will respond to the call of higher duty and will accept the Democratic nomination for President." A thousand large "America Needs Stevenson for President" buttons were ordered, paper badges with Stevenson's name were printed, and kits containing lapel buttons and literature prepared. On July 16, headquarters were opened at the Hilton Hotel in Chicago.

The vigorous activities of this committee, and the fact that none of the acknowledged candidates sparked any great enthusiasm, revived interest in the draft. The Washington *Post* commented on July 18 that there were two curious facts about the convention: it was the first "free and open" one in twenty years, and "the more avowed candidates arrive in Chicago, the more talk there is about a fugitive from the nomination—Gov. Adlai Stevenson of Illinois." During the next two days journalistic speculation was rife, stimulated by press releases from the committee that Stevenson's name would be placed in nomination by several delegates who offered to do the honors.

On the opening day of the convention the draft movement was fired to additional impetus by the masterly welcoming address delivered by Stevenson in his official capacity as governor. As James Reston of the New York *Times* wrote, "The 'reluctant candidate,' who has been trying to talk himself out of the Democratic Presidential nomination for the last five months, talked himself right into the leading candidate's role this afternoon with a fifteen-minute address that impressed the convention from left to right." Syndicated columnists Joseph and Stewart Alsop commented that the grass-roots sentiment among the delegates was apparent in the completely unorganized demonstration accorded Stevenson when he made his speech of welcome.

At a meeting called by the committee that same day to plan strategy, attended by delegates from several states, Governor Henry F. Schricker of Indiana, an early partisan of the reluctant candidate, agreed to place Stevenson's name in nomination. Francis J. Myers, a former senator from Pennsylvania, was designated floor leader. Later Myers issued a press statement through the committee office that at a meeting of the Pennsylvania delegation "it was conclusively decided that Governor Stevenson is the choice of the convention," and that its members believed this reflected the attitude throughout the country. "Following that decision, a group of delegates representing 25 states asked us to assist in the Draft Stevenson movement." The next day newspapers all over the country carried headlines on the "Stevenson Boom."

Nominations began late Thursday afternoon. The names of Senators J. William Fulbright, Estes Kefauver, Robert S. Kerr, and Richard B. Russell, and of Governor W. Averell Harriman, were placed before the convention. (Opposed by labor, Barkley had withdrawn on the first day of the convention.) Then Stevenson was nominated by Schricker, who made a fervent twelve and a half minute address ending with "there are times when a man is not permitted to say no. I place before you the man we cannot permit to say no." The convention, reported the New York *Times,* "really went wild."

It took only three ballots to nominate Stevenson. On the first, Kefauver received 340, Stevenson 273, Russell 268, with the remainder scattered among the other candidates. Stevenson picked up 51½ on the second ballot while Kefauver gained only 22½. The trend was now apparent, and when balloting resumed, after the dinner recess, one state after another began to switch its votes. The final tally for the three leading contenders was Stevenson 617½, Kefauver 275½, and Russell 261.

Never before had the nomination been bestowed on a man who genuinely did not want to run for the office, who even insisted that delegates not vote for him. Moreover, it was brought about by an authentic grass-roots movement directed by a group of zealous amateurs. In addition to the qualities which had attracted such enthusiasm and devotion during his single term as governor was the advantage of a leader who could unite the party, since he was not attached to any one faction. That he was also an uncommon politician was immediately obvious from his acceptance speech. Delivered in the early hours of Saturday morning, Stevenson's address was memorable for its eloquence and genuine humility. "I accept your nomination—and the program," he began quietly. "I should have preferred to hear those words uttered by a stronger, a wiser, a better man than myself. . . . That my heart has been troubled, that I have not sought this nomination, that I could not seek it in good conscience, that I would not ask it in honest self-appraisal, is not to say that I value it the less. Rather it is that I revere the office of the Presidency of the United States."

Uncharacteristic of American political oratory, too, was Stevenson's unvarnished presentation of some of the hard facts of twentieth-century life and his plea for rational thought. He was concerned, he said, that the election be used "to debate issues sensibly and soberly," and that the Democrats should view the campaign "not as a crusade to exterminate the opposing party . . . but as a great opportunity to educate and elevate a people whose destiny is leadership . . . of a world in ferment." The American people should be told honestly that a long and costly struggle lay ahead to overcome the great enemies of man—war, poverty, and tyranny. It would be better, he concluded, for the Democrats to lose the election than that the people be misled.

The nomination of Stevenson, a moderate on civil rights, enabled the northern and southern Democrats to close ranks and unite. For the Republicans, Eisenhower's nomination underscored the division within the party. Taft, embittered by his defeat, was also dissatisfied with the platform. His supporters, who represented significant elements of the party's leadership, especially in the Midwest, were not even lukewarm toward the hero-candidate. To win in November, it would be necessary to mollify them.

On September 12, Eisenhower invited Taft for a "unity" meeting at his home. The defeated candidate presented his successful rival with a statement of principles to be endorsed as the price for support by the conservative wing of the party. Included in the "understanding" was a pledge that his supporters would not be discriminated against with respect to federal patronage. The statement was accepted, with only minor changes, and was made public. Taft announced that he approved of Eisenhower's domestic policies and that there were only some "differences of degree" in their views on foreign policy. Critics referred to the encounter as "the surrender at Morningside Heights," and Stevenson commented that "Taft lost the nomination but won the nominee."

The flimsy bond sealing the split could not permanently resist the tug of opposing points of view represented by the Tafts and McCarthys on one side and the Lodges and Deweys on the other, but it would serve for the campaign. There were enough issues, real or imaginary, which both factions could use in their own way, such as soaring prices, high taxes, corruption in government, the war in Korea.

In his acceptance speech, the General had pledged "a fighting compaign" and "a crusade . . . to sweep from office an administration [of] wastefulness, arrogance and corruption in high places." If he was temperamentally unsuited and lacked oratorical skill to carry on a crusade in the Bryan or Roosevelt manner, he had other attributes which might serve as well or better: sincerity, warmth, an engaging grin, and a hero's command of popular adulation. To the Republican strategists, the "marketability" of the Eisenhower personality was immediately apparent and plans were made to exploit it.

For the first time in a presidential campaign, the resources of an advertising agency were utilized to promote the candidate. Under the supervision of Robert Humphreys, head of the party's public relations division, Batten, Barton, Durstine & Osborn drew up and presented to Eisenhower and his associates an elaborate plan which outlined where the votes were, why the Democrats had won most of them in the past, and what the Republicans must now do. Assuming, it stated, that the party could count on its natural strength of about twenty million votes, the memorandum suggested concentrating on the forty-five million "stay-at-homes," the people who went to the polls only when aroused. To get them out, a campaign that used a "me too" approach or only promised to improve on the present administration would be futile; "the recommended strategy is: 'Attack! Attack! Attack!' " As to the "product," since both the presidential candidate and his running mate had "a high degree of salesmanship in their manner," the more often they appeared in public the better. Television was ideal "to make the most of the ticket's human assets." Reduced to its essentials, it was a matter of "merchandising Eisenhower's frankness, honesty and integrity, his sincere and wholesome approach."

Later, Sherman Adams, who had noticed that Eisenhower appeared perturbed during the briefing by the public relations men, asked him what had bothered him. "All they talked about was how they would win on my popularity," the General replied. "Nobody said I had a brain in my head."

Eisenhower undertook a whirlwind tour by train and motorcade through thirty-four states, covering more than 40,000 miles. Included in the itinerary was the deep South, rarely honored by a Republican candidate, where he visited every state but Mississippi. Wherever he went not a thing was left to chance. Before he arrived in a town, an advance man had already set up newspaper, radio, and television coverage. Hard on the advance man's heels came a task force of crowd builders which arranged a telephone campaign and recruited cheerleaders to throw tons of confetti and distribute campaign buttons and rally invitations.

For the major addresses the plans were even more detailed. A thirty-nine-page booklet was prepared just for Eisenhower's appearance in Philadelphia, specifying, among other things, "fresh cut roses (25,000) . . . noisemakers (3,000) . . . flags (5,000) . . . programs (25,000)." It included the specific instructions that at Independence Hall the General must stand in such a manner that he could be photographed with his right hand on the Liberty Bell.

Like his backers, Eisenhower was inclined toward a philosophy of moderation in government and throughout his campaign he stressed "the middle way." He assured his audiences, as Dewey and Willkie had before him, that he had no intention of repealing the New Deal, which was accepted by Americans of all persuasions, and that he would continue to support "what we call social gains." In one address he asserted, "Social security, housing, workmen's compensation, unemployment insurance, and the preservation of the value of savings—these are things that must be kept above and beyond politics in campaigns. They are *rights* not *issues*."

Dealing with the issue of corruption, he made the "scandal-a-day" administration and "the need for a new broom" familiar slogans. The "mess in Washington," Eisenhower asserted, was not confined to one bureau, one agency, or one department; it was a "top-to-bottom" mess of waste, extravagance, inefficiency, and incompetence, of "corruption such as makes us hang our head in shame, of bungling in our affairs at home, of fumbling in the life and death matter of war and peace."

He charged the administration with laxity in guarding against the dangers of internal communism. At first the General merely promised that he would make certain that government employees were loyal Americans, but by early October he became less restrained, indicting the men "who cheered the blithe dismissal of the Alger Hiss case as a 'red herring.'" Later he pledged that, if elected, the "pinks" and the Communists and the "disloyal" would be ruthlessly ferreted out.

Soaring prices and high taxes were naturally blamed on the Democratic administration, Eisenhower warning that, unless the tide of inflation was reversed, savings, insurance, pensions, and social security benefits would ultimately vanish. The party in power was also held responsible for the war in Korea, a consequence of the "real and terrible blunders" of failing to build up the defensive strength of the Asian country, and for the abandonment of China to the Communists. He criticized the Truman policy of "mere containment," asserting that a genuine peace program must have as its central objective "the restoration of the captive nations of Europe" and of Asia. But he gave no indication as to how the enslaved peoples could be liberated.

Eisenhower was at his best at the whistle stops, where he could talk informally instead of struggling with the rhetorical devices and flourishes required in the formal speeches prepared by his writers. A military man accustomed to a rapid reading of a straightforward presentation of facts, he was troubled by the repetitions characteristic of a politician's address. "This *sounds* very good, but isn't the idea pretty much the same as what we say way back at the beginning?" he would ask. It seemed, indeed, to matter little what he said at these brief stops. The wide grin and the warm handshake were immediately endearing, and his obvious sincerity when he spoke was captivating. "When he utters the most obvious platitude," observed one reporter, "they look at that serious face as if they had heard something that ought to be graven on stone and passed on to the third and fourth generations." According to a story circulating among the newsmen traveling with the candidates, one of the reporters was supposed to have asked, "Where are we now?" as he looked out of the window of the campaign train. "Crossing the thirty-eighth platitude," sighed another.

Criticizing individuals was distasteful to Eisenhower, and his sense of personal pride and integrity deterred him from engaging in wrangles with his partisan detractors. The people who came to hear him, he maintained, wanted to know what he had to say and not what he thought about someone else. If they believed him and placed their faith in what he would do, that was fine; if they didn't, there was nothing he could do about it. An Eisenhower aide later recalled that the General told him, "If they don't want me that doesn't matter very much to me. I've got a hell of a lot of fishing I'll be happy to do."

Yet this forthright candidate abjectly surrendered to political expediency as meekly as any politician avid for a job. Although he abominated Senators William E. Jenner and Joseph R. McCarthy for vilifying General George C. Marshall,* his wartime superior whom he greatly admired, he

---

* In 1951, McCarthy had charged Marshall with being involved "in a conspiracy so immense and infamy so black as to dwarf any previous venture in the history of man," and called him "a front to traitors." Jenner had denounced Marshall as "a living lie."

endorsed both men for re-election and even appeared on the same platform with them.

One incident in relation to McCarthy caused Eisenhower considerable embarrassment. For an address he was to deliver in Milwaukee, the senator's home city, he instructed his speech writer, Emmet John Hughes, to include a personal tribute to Marshall. Hughes complied with four paragraphs ending with, "I have been privileged for thirty-five years to know General Marshall personally. I know him, as a man and as a soldier, to be dedicated with singular selflessness and the profoundest patriotism to the service of America." The lines were never delivered. Before he reached his destination, Eisenhower was persuaded to delete them so as not to offend McCarthy and jeopardize the ticket in the state, but an advance text of the speech had already been given to the press.

Another occurrence shook the entire Republican hierarchy. On September 18, the New York *Post* featured a story under a front-page headline that Richard M. Nixon had been the beneficiary of a secret fund of some $18,000 contributed by wealthy Californians for his expenses during his tenure as senator. Nixon promptly confirmed the existence of the fund but declared that it was not secret, had been used for political expenses, and had not obligated him to the donors in any way. However, with Eisenhower's heavy stress on morality in government, Republicans panicked. Some, including several major newspapers, suggested that Nixon remove himself from the ticket. Finally, party leaders decided to have Nixon present his case on television. Eisenhower, who was in the East (Nixon was on the West Coast), decided to wait for the response before making any move.

The stakes in the performance were high both for Nixon and for his party. If the nominee were compelled to exit— something which had never occurred before—the party would be besmirched; on the other hand, if the Republicans lost in November, Nixon, whose rise in public life had been meteoric, would be the chief scapegoat and his political career finished.

A national hookup of 64 NBC television stations, 194 CBS radio stations, and virtually the entire 560-station Mutual Broadcasting radio network was engaged by Batten, Barton, Durstine & Osborn at a cost of $75,000. To reach a maximum audience, the half-hour slot following the popular Milton Berle show was arranged for.

The television program was to become historic in campaign folklore. It opened with a picture of the American flag promptly followed by Senator Nixon's calling card, apparently meant to symbolize the dignity of the senatorial office. Then the candidate appeared, sitting on a couch flanked by his wife and daughters. His face grave, his voice deep with sincerity, Nixon presented his case.

There was no secret about the fund, he declared, and not a cent had gone for his personal use. The money was spent to defray the "political expenses of getting my message to the American people . . . the speeches . . . for the most part concerned [with] exposing this administration, the communism in it, the corruption in it." Taxpayers, he declared, should not be expected to pay for such activities. He was proud to say that not one of his contributors had ever asked for a special favor.

What followed was the most maudlin soap opera, shrewdly designed to tug at the heartstrings of a sentimental public. Nixon related the Horatio Alger story of his life—helping his parents in the family grocery, working his way through college, practising law while Pat taught school during the early years of his marriage. After his return from the war they had to live modestly in a "modest" house for which he had to borrow money from his parents that they took from their savings. He gave an accounting of everything he owned, from his G.I. life insurance to a 1950 Oldsmobile to his wife's "respectable Republican cloth coat."

Then came the smashing climax. He hoped, Nixon said, that the politicians would not attack him for another gift he had accepted, a dog named Checkers. "The kids, all the kids love the dog . . . and regardless of what they say about it, we are going to keep it." Mrs. Eisenhower and several Republican dignitaries who were watching the show were reported to have "clutched their handkerchiefs and dabbed their eyes." When the strains of hearts and flowers faded out, Nixon concluded firmly and resonantly that regardless of the outcome he would continue the good fight, going up and down the land "until we drive the crooks and the communists and those that defend them out of Washington." The decision as to his fate, he said, rested with the Republican National Committee, and would his listeners express their opinion by wire whether or not he should withdraw from the campaign?

At the conclusion of the program a Hollywood producer phoned Nixon to congratulate him on the greatest performance he had ever seen. About one million individuals wired or wrote to demand that Nixon be kept on the ticket. The following day the candidate flew east to meet with Eisenhower. "Dick, you're my boy!" the General cried, warmly embracing him as the camera bulbs flashed, recording the touching scene for posterity. The ordeal was over, and the Republican campaign could proceed untarnished.

Also serving to "exonerate" Nixon was the disclosure in headlines, the day before the broadcast, of a fund for Stevenson. An official of a mimeograph company doing work for the State of Illinois charged that the governor personally had solicited contributions from businessmen. Stevenson confirmed this immediately, explaining that the money supplemented the salaries of members of his administration who had left better paying positions for employment in state government. Nothing went to him or to any other elected official. No impropriety had been committed, since there was no "connection between the contributors and the beneficiaries." Still, the Republicans could now smirk. Stevenson, however, ignored Nixon's public suggestion that he also bare his financial soul, and no one in his party pressed him to do so.

Television was used as a major publicity medium for the first time in a presidential campaign. A New York advertising agency, Ted Bates and Company, recommended "maximum penetration: use spots." After some research, the agency had concluded that the Republicans would win if forty-nine counties in twelve states could be won away from the Democrats; therefore an "all-out saturation blitz" of these counties should be launched by radio and television in the last three weeks of the campaign. "The spots themselves would be the height of simplicity." People from each of the areas would ask Eisenhower a question, to which his reply would indicate that he understood the problem and was determined to do something about it when elected. "Thus he inspires loyalty without prematurely committing himself to any straitjacketing answer." Before preparing the scripts, the agency submitted a number of items culled from Eisenhower's speeches to public opinion analyst Dr. George Gallup, who selected three for concentration: corruption in government, taxes, and the cost of living.

Purchasing prime commercial time on regularly sponsored shows, the Republicans invested an estimated $1.5 million for the spots. In some areas Eisenhower appeared several times in one hour; in New York alone, 130 spots were broadcast the day before election. At the end of a show, instead of the usual blurb, a voice announced, "Eisenhower answers the Nation!" The next voice was the Man in the Street: "Mr. Eisenhower, what about the high cost of living?" In sympathetic tones the candidate replied: "My wife, Mamie, worries about the same thing. I tell her it's our job to change that on November fourth." Or, an irate citizen: "It was extra tough paying my income tax when I read about the internal revenue tax collectors being fired for dishonesty." The reply, in a firm tone: "Well—how many taxpayers were shaken down, I don't know. How many crooks escaped, I don't know. But I'll find out after next January."

Before Eisenhower began to campaign, he remarked naïvely to his speech writer, "All I can hope to do in this or any other campaign is to say what *I* believe." While he undoubtedly agreed with much of what he was given to mouth, his sense of dignity was repelled by the cheap salesmanship of the spots. When the scripts were being prepared, he shook his head and muttered, "To think that an old soldier should come to this."

The Democrats, who sneered at the programs as a "huckster's blitz, a super-colossal, multi-million dollar production designed to sell an inadequate ticket to the American people in precisely the way they sell soap, ammoniated toothpaste, hair tonic or bubblegum," proceeded to employ spot announcements themselves. Their candidate, however, did not participate.

Adlai Stevenson's campaign was on a different level. Throughout he endeavored to maintain the lofty objective expressed in his acceptance speech. He recruited a battalion of writers who, as one of them later wrote, "were birds of an intellectual feather," sharing the same habits of thought, so that every man in the group was likely to arrive independently at conclusions similar to those of the others and to Stevenson's. "Consequently, nobody put alien words into his mouth. We were, so to speak, merely literary tailors, cutting and stitching materials to fit his known measurements, according to a pattern and style on which all agreed." Furthermore, Stevenson generally worked over the speeches, substituting words, phrases, sometimes entire paragraphs.

Relatively unknown to the public before the campaign, Stevenson was a stunning surprise. His appearance was not particularly impressive, with his receding hairline, slight paunch, his air of quiet reserve; but he became transformed on the platform. One observer commented that when he began to speak, it was "as if a giant switch were thrown on and Stevenson's personality and strength blazed forth in their full light." In a series of addresses he discussed in depth the issues of communism, civil liberties, foreign policy, labor legislation, agriculture, natural resources programs, and corruption in government. To the clarity and eloquence of his exposition was added the sharp thrust of a genuine wit, rare in political discourse.

In an address at Phoenix, Arizona, he satirized the split in the Republican party. The other day, he said, the General compared team play in basketball and politics and also stated that the "overwhelming majority" of federal employees were patriotic citizens, with which he certainly concurred, as did most Americans. But "the most conspicuous of those who impugn the motives and attack the integrity of our public servants are on the General's team. In fact, after last Tuesday, it looks as though some of them had been promoted to the first team. One player to whom the General gave his Republican letter—the varsity 'R'—on last Tuesday, is Senator Jenner of Indiana. And, according to Senator Jenner, the list of unpatriotic Federal employees is not only practically endless but it is headed by the revered name of General George C. Marshall, our great wartime commander and General Eisenhower's superior officer." What it all came down to, he went on, is that there was no longer one Republican party but two. "It is an ancient political vehicle, held together by soft soap and hunger, and with front-seat drivers and back-seat drivers contradicting each other in a bedlam of voices shouting to 'go right' and 'go left' at the same time."

On occasion Stevenson was outspoken to the point of being impolitic by the standards of professional politicians. He told a convention of the American Legion that if elected he would resist pressure from veterans if he thought their demands excessive or in conflict with the public interest. In Virginia he informed his audience that he was fully in accord with the civil rights platform of his party. "I should justly earn your contempt if I talked one way in the South and another way elsewhere."

Late in September, President Truman plunged into the campaign, stumping all over the country with his characteristic "give 'em hell" zest, and was soon sharing headlines with the two candidates. In his direct, earthy fashion, he attacked, counterattacked, and expounded the issues, frequently quoting the Republicans' own words and citing their actions. He suited his remarks to the locality he was in. Talking in Harlem, for instance, he derided Eisenhower's promise to eliminate racial segregation in the Army by quoting from his testimony before a Senate committee recommending segregation at the lower regimental levels.

The extensive news coverage Truman was receiving and the apparently favorable reaction of the crowds disquieted the Republicans, who organized a "Truth Squad" to follow in his wake and refute his charges. It included Senators Homer Ferguson, Bourke Hickenlooper, Francis Case, and Eugene Millikin. In press releases the President was charged with degrading the campaign, one Republican leader declaring that he had "lowered the great office of the President to the level of the cheapest politics." Senator Taft referred to his "wild talk," and the governor of Connecticut indicted his speeches as "gutter politics."

As McCarthyism continued to envenom the nation and the Republicans exploited the "Communist conspiracy" charge to the hilt, Democrats were put on the defensive. At Detroit on October 7, Stevenson devoted a major address to the internal Communist menace. For years, he said, his party had been rallying the free peoples of the world against communism. He listed the numerous measures taken by the Truman administration to cope with subversion long before McCarthy, with his wild and reckless charges, appeared on the scene. Eisenhower had recently implied that the federal government was deliberately concealing Communists, but "has offered only thundering silence about a cure. What would he do? Would he fire J. Edgar Hoover . . . General Bedell Smith, head of the Central Intelligence Agency and his own former Chief of Staff . . . Allen Dulles, the brother of his own chief advisor on foreign affairs? . . . I think we are entitled to ask, is the Republican candidate seriously interested in trying to root communists out of the Government, or is he only interested in scaring the American people to get the Old Guard into the Government?" If he were elected, Stevenson asserted, he would review the loyalty system and make whatever changes might be necessary, but police work should be "aimed at a conspiracy, and not at ideas or opinion. Our country was built on unpopular ideas, on unorthodox opinions. My definition of a free society is a society where it is safe to be unpopular."

The conviction of Alger Hiss prior to the campaign provided the Republicans with a powerful bludgeon. Richard Nixon, in particular, wielded it so often that sometimes it seemed that Hiss was one of the candidates. With variations on the theme, Nixon repeatedly charged that a Democratic victory would produce more Alger Hisses, more spies, and more crises, and attacked Stevenson as an "appeaser" and a "dupe of Hiss." Stevenson, he said in a major television address, had testified to Hiss's integrity and loyalty during the trial and "the prestige of a great state and the Governor of a state were thrown in behalf of the defendant." While he did not doubt Stevenson's own loyalty, he did question his judgment and his qualifications for leading the United States and the free world in its struggle against communism at home and abroad.

Replying two days later, Stevenson said that he had merely performed his duty as a citizen and an officer of the court by giving a deposition regarding the character of the defendant at the time he knew him. "His reputation was good. If I had said it was bad, I would have been a liar. If I had refused to testify at all, I would have been a coward." As a matter of fact, he pointed out, both General Eisenhower and John Foster Dulles had demonstrated their faith in Hiss twice. In 1946, Dulles showed his confidence in Hiss's integrity and patriotism when Hiss was appointed president of the Carnegie Endowment by the Board of Trustees of which Dulles was chairman, by dismissing a report that cast doubt on his loyalty. Two years later, when Eisenhower was a member of the same board, Hiss had been reappointed to the post. He was not suggesting, he concluded, that either Eisenhower or Dulles was "soft on communism" or even guilty of bad judgment but wished "only to make the point that the mistrust, the innuendoes, the accusations which this 'crusade' is employing threatens not merely themselves, but the integrity of our institutions."

Stalking the campaign hand in hand with communism was the emotionally charged issue of Korea, where peace negotiations had been bogged down for over a year on the question of repatriation of prisoners. At first Eisenhower had stressed the complexities of the situation, declaring that he would not put himself in the role of a "messiah" who could bring about peace. But soon he was criticizing the administration for "bungling" the nation into war; he was also lamenting the "tragic toll" of casualties, and urging that South Koreans be put in the front lines. His persistent harping on the protracted stalemate finally incensed President Truman. "Now he's been my military advisor ever since I appointed him Chief of Staff," he said angrily. "If he knows a remedy it's his duty to come and tell me what it is and save lives right now."

Then on October 24 at Detroit, Eisenhower electrified the nation. After stating solemnly that Korea, "the burial ground of 20,000 American dead," was "a damning measure of the quality of leadership we have been given," he pledged that the new administration would "forego the diversion of politics . . . and concentrate on the job of ending the Korean War. . . . That job requires a personal trip to Korea. I shall make that trip. . . . I shall go to Korea." He repeated the pledge three days later and again on October 29. Conceived by speech writer Hughes, this tour de force so mesmerized the voters that few noted it promised nothing, that no commitment had been made to any specific policy. Indignant at what he regarded blatant political opportunism, Truman demanded of Eisenhower, "Are you sure you're that much better than our old colleagues—Generals Bradley and Ridgway and Van Fleet, and Collins and Clark and Vandenberg?"

The Korean War dominated the final days of the contest. In his last address, Stevenson sought to weaken the impact of Eisenhower's dramatic pledge. Peace in Korea, he said, could be achieved by only one of four courses: complete withdrawal, enlarging the war, abandoning the moral position on forcible repatriation of war prisoners, or continuing negotiations. If the first three were untenable, then by "patience and restraint . . . the communists will be compelled to yield. . . . There is no greater cruelty, in my judgment, then the raising of false hopes; no greater arrogance than playing politics with peace and war. Rather than exploit human hopes and fears, rather than provide glib solutions and false assurances, I would gladly lose this Presidential election."

Both parties wound up their long and strenuous battle with radio and televisions programs on election eve. The Democrats presented Adlai Stevenson as the main speaker and addresses by Harry Truman, Alben Barkley, and the vice-presidential candidate, Senator John Sparkman of Alabama. Simply and concisely, Stevenson reaffirmed his faith in the Democrats as the "people's party" and declared that he had tried "diligently . . . to talk sensibly, honestly, candidly" about the nation's problems.

The script for the Republican one-hour spectacular, prepared by Batten, Barton, Durstine & Osborn, was estimated to have cost a quarter of a million dollars. The show opened with a small group of friends gathered around General and Mrs. Eisenhower in a living room to watch a television report on the campaign. During the next hour, the announcer said, the audience would be taken all over the country to see people "who have devoted months of time and labor to a Crusade led by a man with humbleness of spirit." This "spontaneous demonstration of sincere devotion" was inspired by "a matter of principle, a matter of issues!" A rapid, kaleidoscopic sequence of brief scenes followed: cash registers ringing up higher prices, Alger Hiss, Eisenhower's home, the General with Winston Churchill, with G.I.s. The camera switched from city to city: a shot of a ten-year-old child who had organized "Tykes for Ike," a Negro, a foreign-born laborer, a Korean veteran saying that "all the guys I knew out in Korea figure there's only one man for the job, General, and that's you. We've been getting kind of tired of politicians." A shot of a "Coffee with Eisenhower" meeting in Los Angeles ending with a prayer: "Almighty God bless this country at this crucial hour. As the hour approaches for all of us to assume our responsibility as voting citizens, we ask for the light of thy wisdom. . . . Protect us from callous dishonesty. . . ." The program concluded with Eisenhower cutting a victory cake.

On the following day, in unprecedented numbers, the electorate flocked to the voting booths to give Dwight D. Eisenhower a landslide victory—33,778,963 popular and 442 electoral votes. Stevenson, who received 27,314,992 votes and 89 in the electoral college, carried no state outside the traditionally Democratic South, and in that region he lost Maryland, Virginia, Tennessee, Florida, and Texas. The great farmer, labor, and middle-class coalition in the North, South, and West, which Franklin D. Roosevelt had created and which Truman had miraculously preserved in 1948, now seemingly had dissolved.

Not even seasoned political observers had anticipated the sweeping extent of the Eisenhower triumph; some had not even been sure the Republicans would win. On the day before election, a New York *Times* headline read, "Election Outcome Highly Uncertain Survey Indicates." The news item reported that, on the basis of a series of seven exhaustive surveys in various parts of the country undertaken by the paper, neither General Eisenhower nor Adlai Stevenson "can be regarded as of now as certain of election." Other public opinion polls were similarly cautious, perhaps because of what had happened in 1948. In any case, they were careful to stress the imponderable factor of the "undecided" or "independent" vote, which was appreciable, concluding that it might well divide evenly, thus making the results either way close.

Post-election surveys revealed substantial defections of Democrats who had voted for Truman among the white urban classes in the South, among Polish, Irish, and German minority groups, among Catholics, and among members of labor union families. The growing suburban sections also yielded the Republicans a considerable number of votes. Basically, however, it was a personal victory for the national hero. Ticket splitting was unusually high, with three out of five persons who voted for Eisenhower failing to support the rest of the slate. In the House, Republicans gained only enough seats for a majority of eight; in the Senate, the parties were about evenly split, 48 Republicans, 47 Democrats, and one Independent.

Eisenhower's national reputation gave him an advantage which normally accrues to a presidential incumbent candidate. That superior position was fully exploited by Republican strategists, but even without their efforts, his status would have assured him more publicity than his rival. He was warmly endorsed by sixty-seven per cent of the nation's press. While extensive newspaper coverage and support is of doubtful value in affecting the final result of a campaign —as witness the election of 1948—in this instance it strengthened the popular image of Eisenhower and underscored the issues at which the Republicans kept hammering: the Korean War, subversives in government, and corruption in high places.

According to surveys, the issues kept swelling in importance as the campaign went on. In January 1952, twenty-five per cent of those interviewed considered Korea the outstanding national problem; by September, the number increased to one third, and by late October it had risen to over fifty per cent. By a margin of four to one, those polled believed that Communist infiltration into government was a major problem with which only the Republicans could deal effectively. At the beginning of the campaign, one third of Roper's respondents believed corruption was a serious issue but that Stevenson could handle it; toward the end, a substantial majority had changed their minds as to his potential effectiveness.

By voting for Eisenhower, the electorate had not repudiated the Democratic domestic and foreign policies of the past two decades. Eisenhower's victory over Senator Taft in the preconvention battle encouraged the impression that he differed with the conservatives on public policy. During the campaign he gave every indication that he would continue along the lines the nation had been going since 1933. He definitely was not an isolationist, as evidenced by his personal involvement with NATO and his foreign policy statements. Moreover, his military and diplomatic experience made him appear more qualified than his opponent to cope with the knotty international situation.

Adlai Stevenson, as a relative newcomer on the political scene, had the formidable task not only of making himself and his views known to the public in a brief period of time but of competing with an idolized national figure. Working against him, too, was the widespread dissatisfaction with the administration's record. While he sought to establish himself as independent of the administration, his most adroit efforts did not succeed in preventing a significant number of voters who disapproved of Truman from turning against him.

Perhaps another factor contributing to his defeat was the man himself. With a personality, a mind, and a style that appealed more to intellectuals than to the average voter, and flashing wit appreciated mostly by the sophisticated—indeed, his opponent charged him (unjustifiably) with treating serious subjects frivolously—Stevenson was an exotic in American politics. He was also that exceptional candidate who regarded a presidential campaign as an opportunity for a mature dialogue to enlighten the public on national principles, programs, and purposes. A democratic government, he later wrote, is the most difficult of all systems because to succeed it depends on the good judgment and wise decisions of many people, which, in turn, depend on information and the understanding of public policy; "candidates then have the greatest responsibility of all to inform truthfully so that the people will . . . have the tools of good judgment and wise decision."

Stevenson himself did not feel that he had spoken over the heads of the electorate. Though decisively defeated, he was not discouraged by the voters' response. There were many imponderable factors, he felt, like "time for a change," Korea, and Eisenhower's great popularity, but "it is safe to say that many people voted for the Democratic candidates not because we held out any comforting hope of early tax reduction, an end to the war, peace on earth, and easy solutions for all our frustrations, but for exactly the opposite reasons, because we did not." Believing in the moral dimensions of politics, in the superiority of reason over emotion, in dialogue over slogans, Stevenson emerged out of defeat not only the undisputed leader of his party but a national leader in the world arena. The election of Eisenhower was a personal triumph; Stevenson's victory in defeat was no less impressive.

The very magnitude of Dwight D. Eisenhower's victory emphasized the narrow base on which it rested. With the Republicans still the minority party, the question was whether they would be able to convert those who had crossed party lines into confirmed supporters. If they could, the long Republican drought would be over.

10. Road to the New Frontier

THE candidate who had impressed the electorate that he was "above politics," although he spoke and acted like a politician, became the President who endeavored to remain above politics. Unfriendly critics termed Dwight D. Eisenhower "a constitutional monarch," a characterization not altogether unjustified. Those who had expected dynamic leadership on the basis of his superlative military record were to be disappointed.

Accustomed to a staff system and to delegating authority, Eisenhower carried these practices into the White House. The executive office and the White House staff were greatly enlarged, with responsibility methodically apportioned. Meetings of the Cabinet and the National Security Council were regularly scheduled, formal, and highly organized. Important policy questions were discussed with the entire group. Eisenhower's "chief of staff," Sherman Adams, technically Assistant to the President, "made decisions and performed acts which Presidents, since the establishment of the Republic, have been given to doing themselves," according to one observer. Not until Adams's resignation and the death of Secretary of State John Foster Dulles during Eisenhower's second term did the President assume personal control in the areas handled by these two men.

In his relations with Congress, Eisenhower felt that "the Chief Executive should not dominate the legislative branch," one of his friends commented. "He believes in the separation of powers. He would not bludgeon Congress even if he could because he thinks it important to preserve a balance of power." This conception of office not only discouraged a vigorous pursuit of legislative objectives but militated against keeping the right-wing extremists in his party under control.

By refusing to slap down Senator Joseph McCarthy, the President tacitly encouraged the demagogue whose reckless charges and behavior created an invidious atmosphere of suspicion throughout the country, brought the administration into disrepute, and injured American prestige abroad. McCarthy was finally hoist on his own petard when he challenged the Army. By the time he died in 1957, he was already completely discredited, but the poisonous miasma which he spread left a residue that still has not completely disappeared.

Reluctant to alienate any one group or section, Eisenhower failed to provide moral leadership in the struggle to enforce the Supreme Court's decision on school desegregation. His repeated refusals to affirm the morality of the Court's position, and his firm declaration that he would never dispatch federal troops to enforce its decision, served to embolden Arkansas's Governor Orval Faubus in 1957 to defy the order of the lower court directing that school desegregation proceed according to plan. When the situation blew up at Little Rock and mob violence threatened, the President was compelled to retreat from his position and send in troops.

Some campaign pledges were redeemed. Taxes were moderately reduced, but on balancing the budget the Republicans found themselves as helpless as the Democrats had been. Not until 1955, and then only for a brief period, was that objective attained. A truce was signed in Korea, but on terms somewhat less satisfactory than the Truman administration had been willing to settle for.

Republicans had thundered that Democratic "appeasement" of communism encouraged Russian expansion and had characterized the containment policy as "negative, futile, and immoral." In their platform they had promised to repudiate "secret understandings such as those of Yalta," and President Eisenhower in his first State of the Union message declared that the nation would "never acquiesce in the enslavement of any people." He would ask Congress, he said, for a resolution stating that the government recognized "no kind of commitment contained in secret understandings of the past . . . which would permit this kind of enslavement." Dulles and Eisenhower soon realized, however, that disavowing wartime agreements could be a two-edged sword inviting retaliatory repudiation. Moreover, they could not hope to obtain essential Democratic support for a measure that by implication stigmatized Franklin D. Roosevelt. In an effort to reach a common area of agreement, a watered-down resolution was drafted. It was unacceptable to the Taft Republicans, and an amendment submitted by them was unacceptable to the Democrats. Happily, Stalin's death provided the President with an opportunity to persuade Republican leaders to forget the whole matter.

Dulles's policy of "liberation" proved to be merely rhetoric when put to the test during uprisings against the Communist rulers in East Germany and later in Hungary. Military aid to the embattled people risked war with the Soviet Union, and neither the administration nor the American public was willing to go that far. While the revolts were being ruthlessly crushed, Congress fiddled with statements that the courage displayed by the insurrectionists would be an inspiration to the cause of freedom.

Another aspect of the "new look" in foreign policy was "massive retaliation instantly, by means and at places of our choosing." According to this strategy, the threat of nuclear warfare would so terrify the Communists that they would be deterred from instigating aggression anywhere. Moscow and Peking hardly troubled to snicker at what they regarded as another absurd slogan.

The growing threat of Communist penetration of the

Middle East, when Egypt's leader, Gamal Abdal Nasser, drew closer to the Soviet Union as a result of the Suez invasion fiasco of 1956, led to the promulgation of the Eisenhower Doctrine that the United States would, if requested, assist any nation in the area menaced by a Communist coup from internal or external sources. In July 1958, troops were sent to Lebanon to forestall a possible invasion from neighboring Syria, then a satellite of Egypt. The pro-Western regime was preserved, and by the end of the year all American troops were withdrawn.

The Middle Eastern crisis brought the Eisenhower administration full circle. Originally hopeful of pursuing a more "dynamic" policy than that of containment, it found itself compelled to employ tactics similar to those of Truman's in contending with "brush-fire" wars. Moscow was not the only source of international difficulties. The rising tide of nationalism in Asia, Africa, and Latin America posed fresh problems and dangers that were intensified by the skillful identification with nationalist sentiments of the new and more adroit leadership in the Soviet Union.

Eisenhower resolutely endeavored to bring about peace. "Any notion that 'the bomb' is a cheap way to solve things is awfully wrong," he said earnestly at a Cabinet meeting in March 1953. "It ignores all facts of world politics—and the basic realities of our allies. It is cold comfort for any citizen of Western Europe to be assured that—after his country is overrun and he is pushing up daisies—someone still alive will drop a bomb on the Kremlin."

International harmony was briefly and sporadically visible as the clouds of East-West tension lifted in between crises. One period of relative calm, following the summit conference between the President and Premier Bulganin at Geneva in the summer of 1955, elevated Eisenhower's popularity to new heights. During another phase of relaxed tensions in the fall of 1959, the new Soviet premier, Nikita Khrushchev, visited the United States and met with the President at his Camp David retreat following a cross-country tour that made daily headlines. The conference was affable and plans were made for a summit meeting to be held at Paris the following May, after which the President would make a return visit to the Soviet Union. Then, two weeks before the scheduled conclave, a U-2 espionage plane was shot down by the Russians deep in Soviet territory.

At the outset, the United States denied having had any intention to violate Soviet air space, claiming that the plane was on an ordinary weather reconnaissance and had been blown off course. The Russians then produced a very much alive pilot who had confessed to being on a Central Intelligence Agency spying mission. A blundering State Department declared first that no such flights had been authorized but later, in a complete reversal, admitted that not only had American planes been flying over Russia for a number of years but they would continue to do so. The sorry affair was climaxed with President Eisenhower's assumption of personal responsibility for the flights and his statement that, although distasteful, they were a "vital necessity" in view of the existing threat to American security.

Inevitably, the summit meeting was abortive. Khrushchev, who apparently was being accused of naïveté by his cohorts in the Kremlin for trusting the "capitalists," and under fire from Peking for his policy of peaceful coexistence, attempted to make a show of strength by demanding a personal apology from the President. Eisenhower naturally refused.

Scarcely a particle of the debris of the events touched Eisenhower. Nothing, it seemed, could shake him off the pinnacle of popularity to which he had risen almost immediately after his election. Despite a heart attack in the fall of 1955, a prolonged convalescence, a serious operation several months later, and his assertion that if he were returned to office he would be compelled to curtail his activities, Republicans gave a heartfelt sigh of relief when he consented to run again.

On the whole, the campaign of 1956 raised few hackles or elevated much blood pressure. Stevenson, again pitted

against Eisenhower, employed a more conventional electioneering style than in 1952. Noticeably absent from his
speeches, which were deliberately tailored for the average
voter, was the famed rapier wit. Neither candidate was the
target of mudslinging. Republicans relied on the shield of
peace, prosperity, and "We like Ike," against which the
Democrats battered vainly with issues of foreign policy,
farm problems, national defense. Stevenson charged Eisenhower with feeble leadership, stressed his precarious
health, and asserted that the Republicans were the party of
big business while the Democrats were for the little people.
A complacent electorate yawned and sent "Ike" back to the
White House with a plurality of over 9,500,000 and an electoral vote of 457 to Stevenson's 73, a margin almost as impressive as Roosevelt's had been twenty years before. The
Democrats, however, gained a substantial majority in Congress, upsetting the usual pattern of a presidential victor
carrying his party with him in the legislative branch.

For more than a century, the vice-presidency had been a
dead end, but Eisenhower's age and uncertain health put a
different aura about the position for Richard M. Nixon.
Furthermore, as a combination of circumstances made him
the logical candidate in 1960, he refused the President's
offer of a Cabinet post for another term as Vice-President.

Eisenhower's distaste for the grubby business of politics
had enabled Nixon to assume the role of party leader. This
position was to prove advantageous in the future, but at the
time it earned for him the reputation of being a "hatchet
man." His active role during the campaigns, his invidious
statements and slashing attacks, made Nixon the principal
target of the Democrats. In his propensity for heavy swing-
ing he was reminiscent of Harry Truman, but, as the Washington *Post* put it, the difference between the two men was
that of "a warm-hearted fellow who ploughs into a fist fight
for the sheer joy of it and the grim-minded fellow who
charges in with a pipe wrench." One of Nixon's techniques
was the use of innuendo. Without specifically calling his

opponents traitors, he skillfully manipulated language to give the desired impression. In 1954, he charged that "real Democrats are outraged by the Truman-Acheson-Stevenson gang's defense of Communism in high places," assailing the three as "traitors to the high principles in which many of the nation's Democrats believed."

Fortunately for Nixon, Eisenhower's staff system and his series of incapacitating illnesses gave him the opportunity to become a national figure and develop another image. As a roving representative of the President on numerous assignments abroad, he was constantly in the public eye. During an extended tour of South America in the spring of 1958, he comported himself with courage and dignity when he narrowly escaped death at the hands of an ungovernable anti-American mob at Caracas, Venezuela. The following year, on a visit to the International Exposition in Moscow, he turned an extemporaneous exchange with Khrushchev into a demonstration of his skill in clever repartee. A television film of the encounter showed a statesmanlike Nixon courteously but firmly replying to the provocative remarks of the Soviet premier. Numerous meetings with foreign leaders and regular attendance at sessions of the National Security Council afforded Nixon an unusual opportunity for "on-the-job" training in foreign policy and national security problems.

Republican leaders of both factions of the party throughout the country were in Nixon's debt for his contributions during the congressional campaigns, and with few exceptions they were committed to his candidacy for President in 1960. Conservative Republicans were able to regard him as one of their own, while liberals felt that he would reflect their position. Shrewdly, Nixon had also, during his travels around the country, worked to ingratiate himself with the big-business interests which supplied the essential party funds. His efforts had succeeded so well that this group was solidly behind him.

In December 1958, Nixon and a small group of friends met in Florida at the home of one of his devoted followers

to plan strategy for his nomination. All were political amateurs with the exception of Leonard W. Hall, former
chairman of the Republican National Committee and
former congressman, who had been defeated for the New
York gubernatorial nomination by Nelson Rockefeller. Also
present was Robert Finch, a thirty-five-year-old California
lawyer who was to become the most efficient and brilliant
of Nixon's aides.

The political scene they surveyed was depressing. Party
strength in both Houses had been reduced to little more
than a third, there were only fourteen Republican governors, and Republicans controlled the legislatures in only
seven states. A Gallup poll of party preferences taken sometime later was equally cheerless, revealing that forty-seven
per cent of those queried considered themselves Democrats,
thirty per cent Republicans, and twenty-three per cent independents. To win the election, Nixon needed the votes of
all the Republicans, more than half of the independent
votes, and about five million Democratic votes.

Nevertheless, the group proceeded to specific formula-
tions. Finch resigned from his law practice and moved to
Washington. Herbert Klein, editor of a newspaper in southern California, was recruited as press secretary, and Hall
made preparations to join them on a full-time basis. Before
any action could be undertaken, however, they would have
to wait for a move from Nixon's only serious possible rival,
Governor Rockefeller.

The presidential gleam brightened in Rockefeller's eye
after his surprisingly impressive victory over Governor Harriman in a year of Republican rout. His election automati-
cally made him a potential candidate, since, historically, the
governorship of the Empire State has been a launching pad
for the presidential nomination. Respected for his business
leadership and distinguished by philanthropic endeavors,
with a record of public service under three Presidents,
knowledgeable in public affairs and international problems,
handsome and engaging, he was obviously presidential
timber.

Six months after he arrived in Albany, Nelson Rockefeller set a huge machine in motion to explore the possibility of his candidacy. Command headquarters were established in two large buildings in Manhattan which he owned. A seventy-man staff was recruited and divided into a number of task forces—a political group to sound out state political leaders, a corps of speech writers, a logistics group to schedule Rockefeller's trips, and several top advertising men to work on "image."

Elaborate probings over an eight-week period revealed that "The doors were locked, barred and closed." The political and financial powers were "not only against Nelson because he was a liberal, but also committed to Nixon." If Rockefeller entered the primaries, he would be compelled to bring into the open his disagreements with the Eisenhower administration and in effect ask Republicans to repudiate the policies of their President, the most popular Chief Executive in a century. In December 1959, Rockefeller announced his withdrawal from the race, explaining that opposition to his candidacy by "those who will control the Republican convention" would require an intensive struggle in the primaries which would be to the detriment of his obligations as governor.

Early in January, Nixon officially announced his candidacy. He planned to enter all the primaries, which would not only be free of risk, in the absence of any opposition, but would demonstrate his vote-getting power. Furthermore, participation in the primaries would keep his name in the limelight at a time when it might otherwise be crowded off the news pages by the Democrats' primary battles.

During all this time, President Eisenhower had not bestowed his blessing to the Nixon candidacy. In a press conference on January 14, he said that there were "half a dozen, or ten, or maybe a dozen fine, virile men in the Republican party that I would gladly support." Finally, in mid-March, he endorsed Nixon, but in such a manner as to raise doubts about his unqualified enthusiasm.

Not long thereafter Nixon was made uneasy by the behavior of Rockefeller, who remained a considerable force in
the party, especially in the crucial urban East. When he
made it known that Rockefeller was his choice for the vice-
presidential nomination, the governor publicly refused. An
offer by the Republican National Committee to serve either
as the chairman or keynote speaker at the convention met
with the reply that he did not even plan to attend. Then, as
American relations abroad seemed steadily to deteriorate,
Rockefeller, who was deeply concerned about the nation's
security, which he believed endangered by administration
policies, flung down a challenge in a public statement issued on June 8. In a pointed reference to Nixon's failure to
announce his own policy positions beyond his identification
with the Eisenhower program, he declared that "those now
assuming control of the Republican Party have failed to
make clear where this party is heading and where it pro-
poses to lead the nation." He considered it "urgently necessary" that "the new spokesmen . . . declare now, and not at
some later date, precisely what they believe and what they
propose, to meet the great matters before the nation."

During the next six weeks, Rockefeller continued to shoot
off salvos in the press, on radio and television, and in public
addresses. Meanwhile, a draft-Rockefeller movement,
squelched by his December declaration that he would not
seek the nomination, was resuscitated. Headquarters were
opened in Chicago, and newspaper advertisements and
television appeals urged Republicans to demand that their
delegates support Rockefeller. The reaction surpassed all
expectations. A deluge of millions of letters and telegrams
descended, and innumerable telephone calls kept the wires
humming. It was, of course, too late to affect the nomination, which was already nailed down for Nixon, but the
outpouring of sentiment reinforced Rockefeller's determination to press for a stronger approach on some of the
critical issues of the day, notably civil rights and defense.

A week before the convention was to open, the Resolutions Committee, dominated by "regular Republicans,"

began to draft a platform. When Rockefeller saw the result of their efforts, he declared that the resolutions were "still seriously lacking in strength and specifics." Nixon moved to avert a floor fight which now seemed inevitable. He telephoned Rockefeller and arranged to meet secretly with him at the latter's New York apartment. From Friday evening until the early hours of the next morning they worked out what became known as the "Fourteen-Point Compact of Fifth Avenue." Published in the press on Saturday, it jolted the Platform Committee, eliciting anguished cries of outrage. Nixon was accused of "selling out to Rockefeller." Senator Barry Goldwater of Arizona denounced the statement as a "surrender," the "Munich of the Republican Party." Indignantly, the Platform Committee suspended its sessions.

When Nixon arrived in Chicago on the opening day of the convention, he found the situation chaotic. Privately, he was not displeased that his hand had been forced, since he considered it essential for the party to present a more forward-looking image if victory was to be achieved. Using all his considerable diplomatic skill and, as one of his aides put it, collecting "every political IOU we held in the country," he persuaded the committee to accept the main elements in the agreement. The platform was revised and revised again, but the final document bore a definite Rockefeller stamp.

The contest, for the most part, had been conducted out of public view. Even more significant than the issues of civil rights and national defense, over which most of the haggling took place, was the more basic struggle between opposing factions of the party for ideological representation in the platform. Republicans in the New England and mid-Atlantic states were pleased by the outcome; those in the rural areas of the Midwest and South were resentful, but their support for Nixon was in any event assured.

With everything settled beforehand, the convention devolved into little more than a disciplined gathering which listened more or less patiently to a series of generally dull speeches and cheered on cue, lustily at the beginning but with steadily diminishing enthusiasm as the time dragged on. Goldwater's name was placed in nomination, and after the ritualistic demonstration he withdrew, asking his conservative supporters to vote for Nixon. On the first ballot Nixon received every vote except the ten from Louisiana, whose delegation, in protest against the civil rights plank, cast its votes for Goldwater. Arizona then moved that the nomination be made unanimous. The balloting was over.

Selection of a vice-presidential candidate was a mere formality. Several days prior to the convention, Nixon had summoned thirty-six party leaders to discuss a running mate. Various possibilities were considered, but the final decision had been left to him. He chose Henry Cabot Lodge, Ambassador to the United Nations since 1953. Lodge fulfilled Nixon's requirements of a man with whom he could work harmoniously and who had the additional qualification of long experience in foreign affairs, which would emphasize Republican concern and competence in this area.

For the Democrats, the choice of a candidate was more involved. Congressional leaders favored the able Senate Majority Leader, Lyndon Baines Johnson, but a poll taken in the legislative body revealed that, while members of the Senate were partial to him, those in the House preferred Senator Stuart Symington of Missouri. Harry Truman and most state chairmen were for Symington. A poll of editors supported Adlai Stevenson, although he steadfastly disavowed any intention to seek the nomination. The influential Mrs. Franklin D. Roosevelt favored either Stevenson or Senator Hubert H. Humphrey, as did the liberal Americans for Democratic Action. Labor leaders were divided between Symington and Humphrey. Most governors of large Democratic states leaned toward Stevenson. When the forty-two-year-old senator from Massachusetts, John Fitzgerald Kennedy, formally announced his candidacy on January 2, 1960, seasoned politicians expressed skepticism about his chances to obtain the nomination.

Kennedy had a considerable number of assets—good

looks, intelligence, a Harvard education, a record of war heroism, and an extremely attractive wife—but they seemed to be outweighed by his liabilities. He was young, with only a limited national reputation and relatively brief political experience; he had a multimillionaire father who was a conservative and an isolationist; and an old back injury made many doubt that he could endure the rigors of a campaign. But most detrimental was his Roman Catholic religion. Even most political leaders of his own faith refused to support him at the outset because they were convinced he did not have a chance.

The youthful senator had begun reaching for the White House as early as 1956, when he was narrowly defeated for the vice-presidential nomination, after one of the longest preconvention efforts in the nation's history. He started immediately to woo party officials by serving them. That fall he campaigned for the Stevenson-Kefauver ticket, traveling more than 30,000 miles through twenty-four states. During the next three years he covered every state in the Union to rally support for national, state, and local candidates. He addressed crowds everywhere, on street corners, in theaters and armories, at airports and on fairgrounds, in restaurants and hotels, in union halls and lodge halls. He spoke before bar associations, civic groups, labor conventions, and at many colleges and universities. As early as 1958 the lowliest party official received a "personal" Christmas card from the Kennedys. To keep his name in the public eye he contributed articles to more than three dozen magazines, from *Foreign Affairs* ("A Democrat Looks at Foreign Policy") to *Living for Young Homemakers* ("Young Men in Politics") to *Life* ("Where the Democrats Should Go from Here") to *The Progressive* ("If India Falls").

Re-elected to the Senate in 1958 by the largest majority ever attained in his state, Kennedy opened headquarters for a campaign organization in the Esso Building at the foot of Capitol Hill, with his brother-in-law, Stephen Smith, in charge. To provide ideas and information, an informal group of scholars was brought together. This "Academic Advisory Committee" included Professors John Kenneth Galbraith, Arthur M. Schlesinger, Jr., Walter Rostow, and Max Millikan. When the Kennedy organization went into action, it surpassed in skill and thoroughness the operations of the legendary Roosevelt-Farley team.

After a preliminary organization meeting at the Kennedy home at Palm Beach in April 1959, a group of sixteen friends, aides, and relatives met in October at Robert Kennedy's house in Hyannis Port. Most were political amateurs and, with the exception of the candidate and one or two others, outside the professional party organization. There was Theodore Sorensen, thirty-one, whom Kennedy later called "my intellectual blood bank." Chief aide and speech writer since Kennedy entered the Senate in 1953, he now became national policy advisor and, more than anyone else, continued to influence Kennedy's thinking and literary style. Kenneth O'Donnell, thirty-five, a former Harvard classmate of Robert's, and Lawrence O'Brien, forty-two, operated as a team. Brilliant tacticians, they had been with Kennedy for eight years, during which time they had directed his senatorial campaigns. Others present included Stephen Smith, thirty-one, who would become chief administrator of finances and personnel; Louis Harris, thirty-eight, a public opinion analyst whose polls and surveys were influential in determining strategy; Pierre Salinger, thirty-four, former newspaperman and congressional investigator who became press secretary; John Bailey, Democratic State Chairman of Connecticut and a power in New England politics.

The campaign manager was Robert, but John Kennedy involved himself in all facets of the planning. He possessed an extraordinary familiarity with every aspect of the political process and, at the meeting, displayed his mastery of the political situation in each state. "He knew without notes who was friendly and who was hostile," Sorensen later related, "which states had primaries and which primaries were binding, which delegates might be governed by the unit rule, which could be instructed by state conventions and which contained wholly free agents. No one at the meeting could match his knowledge of detail."

That Kennedy also comprehended the requirements of presidential leadership for a nation compelled to be the dominant power in a perilous era was also soon apparent. Early in 1960, in an address critical of Eisenhower's approach to his office, he declared that the times demanded that the President "be the head of a responsible party, not rise so far above politics as to be invisible—a man who will formulate and fight for legislative policies, not be a casual bystander to the legislative process." A restricted concept of the Presidency, he said, was no longer adequate, for submerged beneath "the gloss of peace and prosperity" were unsolved problems that must explode to the surface; "in the challenging revolutionary sixties—the American Presidency will demand more than ringing manifestoes issued from the rear of battle. It will demand that the President place himself in the very thick of the fight, that he care passionately about the fate of the people he leads, that he be willing to serve them at the risk of incurring their momentary displeasure . . . he must above all be the Chief Executive in every sense of the word. He must be prepared to exercise the fullest powers of his Office."

With so many presidential hopefuls, the Democratic National Chairman predicted a deadlocked convention which, after five or six ballots, would settle on Stevenson or Symington as a compromise candidate. The Kennedy strategists were also sure that a deadlocked convention would spell defeat for their man; victory, if it was to be achieved, would have to come on the first or second ballot. Under the circumstances, only one path lay open to Kennedy—the primaries. The plan was for Kennedy to enter primaries in states considered strategic and win them all. He would thereby acquire delegates and a national reputation to match Stevenson's and would convince party leaders that despite his handicaps he was their best vote-getter, the only man who could defeat Nixon.

After a careful evaluation of the states where primaries were conducted, it was decided that Kennedy should enter eight, some of which would be fiercely contested. He would bypass Ohio and California; though important, they represented special problems, for his entry would generate intense factional controversies. Kennedy extracted from Ohio's Governor Michael V. DiSalle the pledge that, while DiSalle would run as a favorite son in the primary, he would deliver the state's entire delegation to him on the first ballot. His leverage was the threat to challenge DiSalle in the primary, presenting poll figures which indicated that he could easily win the state. California's Governor Pat Brown, who also wished to run as a favorite son, asked all outsiders to refrain from entering the primary. For Kennedy to oppose Brown would have meant an expensive, party-splitting fight which might even end in a victory for Hubert Humphrey, who had become his major rival. A compromise was accordingly worked out that if Kennedy won all the primaries except Oregon, where Senator Morse was a favorite son, and if the delegation contained a substantial number likely to vote for him, Brown would stay out. When the delegates were being selected, Larry O'Brien was on the scene and, through his deft operation, was able to secure a representation of about twenty-five per cent for Kennedy.

Wisconsin, where Kennedy would be involved in a direct encounter with Humphrey in the Minnesota senator's own stamping ground, was the first crucial test of strength. The Kennedy organization rolled out its artillery to capture the state. Friends, aides, the Kennedy clan, were here, there, and everywhere, making speeches and shaking hands. A Kennedy sister, brother-in-law, and even his mother visited at least once every Wisconsin town with a population of over 300. "I feel," said Humphrey, "like an independent merchant competing against a chain store." Humphrey spent as much as Kennedy, $150,000, but he could not compete with his opponent's unpaid workers. He could staff only two offices, one in Madison and one in Milwaukee, while Kennedy could bring in as many devoted friends and followers as were needed for the various centers. It was an exhausting battle for both men, who shuttled back and forth from Washington for three months, although Kennedy's logistical problems were solved by having a private plane which the family bought.

An unprecedented number of voters were drawn to the polls by the excitement generated in the campaign. Kennedy won fifty-six per cent of the votes and 20½ delegates as against 10½ for Humphrey, but his victory did not settle the religious issue. His strongest showings were mainly in the heavily Catholic districts; he carried none of the Protestant districts. No one could actually tell whether it was the concentration of working people or the preponderance of Roman Catholics that accounted for his victories; or whether Protestant majorities or agricultural populations in areas adjacent to Humphrey's Minnesota power base were responsible for his defeats. In other words, was geography or class or religion the determining factor? Many, however, read the results as a Catholic-Protestant split, which meant that more primaries were required before Kennedy would convince the political chieftains that a Catholic could win a presidential election.

As for Humphrey, he was encouraged by the meager vote in the Republican primary held that same day, which suggested to him that Republican Catholics had deserted their party and that therefore Kennedy would not fare well in predominantly Protestant states. He decided to challenge Kennedy in West Virginia, which was ninety-five per cent Protestant—a fateful decision, as it turned out, both for him and his opponent.

Most analysts believed that, because of the religious issue, Humphrey could overcome Kennedy's great financial and organizational resources, the *Wall Street Journal*, for example, predicting a 60–40 victory. Furthermore, the dreadful impoverishment resulting from widespread unemployment brought about by automation of the coal mines would seem to make a man with Humphrey's strong record of liberal legislation the more appealing candidate. Kennedy and his aides were gloomy about the prospects.

In the weeks before the balloting, the Kennedy organization marshalled all its forces. Eight main headquarters were established in the state, to which were shortly added eight subheadquarters staffed by volunteers. The total staff of Kennedy's senatorial office was mobilized, plus drivers, typists, press men, chauffeurs, television men; and these were supplemented by an army of unpaid assistants, not to mention members of the Kennedy family. A special attraction was Franklin D. Roosevelt, Jr., bearing a name which still had a magic appeal, particularly in this poverty-ridden state.

Each county was thoroughly organized. Volunteers went from door to door distributing literature; tons of printed matter were mailed; telephone campaigns were organized and receptions arranged; speakers toured the countryside. Space and time were purchased in every daily and weekly newspaper and on every radio and television station in the state. A documentary film shown over and over again throughout the state portrayed Kennedy as war hero, father, public servant, and defender of the principle of separation of church and state.

When Kennedy arrived for ten days of unremitting campaigning, the groundwork had been laid. The candidate, with his wife at his side, spoke in virtually every town and hamlet, shook every hand stretched out to him. Almost immediately it was obvious that, while unemployment and hunger were the crucial issues, the religious factor was omnipresent. Kennedy decided to meet it head on. About a week before the election, he began to include references to religion in his talks. When the Episcopal Bishop of West Virginia announced his opposition to a Roman Catholic President, Kennedy declared, "If religion is a valid issue in a Presidential campaign, I shouldn't have served in the House, I shouldn't now be serving in the Senate, and I shouldn't have been accepted by the United States Navy." The oath of office in each case, he pointed out, was practically the same—to defend the Constitution.

Finally, on the last night of the campaign, interrogated on a telecast program by Franklin D. Roosevelt, Jr., about his faith, Kennedy used ten or twelve minutes of the half hour to reply. He traced the history of church-state and state-church conflict through the centuries and said that the greatest of all decisions made by the Founding Fathers was to separate church from state. As President, he would be bound by his oath to uphold the Constitution, which meant swearing to support the separation of church and state.

Against this presentation Humphrey was helpless. There was nothing he could say without sounding bigoted, even assuming he were willing to scuttle his own principles. In practical terms it meant that the voter could demonstrate his tolerance in only one way—by voting for Kennedy. Humphrey's cup of bitterness flowed over. From the outset he was in a sadly hopeless position against the battalion of Kennedy workers—by primary day O'Brien estimated they numbered 9,000—who swarmed over the state. Moreover, he was desperately short of money. Heavily in debt for the Wisconsin campaign, he found it impossible to raise funds for the West Virginia contest. According to Theodore White, the Kennedy forces applied pressure in various places to cut off financial support for Humphrey. Governor Abraham Ribicoff of Connecticut warned Stevensonians against continued financing with the threat that otherwise Adlai Stevenson would not be considered for Secretary of State; former Connecticut Senator William Benton was warned by the political boss of the state that if he continued to aid Humphrey he would never hold another elective or appointive office. Humphrey's expenditures for the entire campaign totaled only $25,000, a mere bagatelle for a primary, whereas Kennedy reportedly spent about $100,000 for advertising alone, and over all about $250,000, excluding most staff salaries and personal expenses.

The all-out blitz culminated in a spectacular victory, Kennedy receiving over sixty per cent of the votes and carrying all but seven of the state's fifty-five counties. He had incontestably proved that a Roman Catholic could win in a predominantly Protestant state, and also that in an economically depressed area he could beat a candidate noted for his pro-labor views. Humphrey, exhausted, depressed, and drained of funds, withdrew from the race.

Nothing, as the cliché goes, succeeds like success. The Kennedy snowball, having begun to roll, never lost its momentum. From West Virginia, Kennedy went on to Oregon, where he defeated Senator Morse, receiving seventy-three percent of the votes. In the uncontested primaries in Indiana, Nebraska, and Maryland, his showing was impressive. Early in June the governor of Michigan swung the support of his delegation to Kennedy. By the latter part of the month, the Kennedy aides publicly claimed firm delegate support obtained through primaries and state conventions at 710 first-ballot votes, just 51 short of the required majority. While some considered this overly optimistic, saying that a more realistic figure was somewhere around 600, nevertheless Kennedy had more pledged delegates than any of the other candidates.

In a party oriented to liberalism, Kennedy enjoyed the additional advantage of being more closely associated with liberal programs than any of the avowed contestants. He not only pressed for a liberal platform through Paul Butler, Democratic National Chairman, and Congressman Chester Bowles, chairman of the convention's Platform Committee, but brought with him to the convention paid and volunteer staffs of experts to work out the details. While some of the delegates might have been dubious about his sincerity as a liberal or lukewarm toward him on other grounds, they could not help being affected by his efforts.

None of the other aspirants entered the primaries. The handsome, silver-haired Symington decided that his best course was to rely on the power brokers, the political bosses, to push his nomination as a compromise candidate in the event of a deadlocked convention. Also counting on a deadlock was Lyndon B. Johnson. Considered a regional candidate, he could have dispelled this image only by winning northern primaries, but, as a Southerner, to enter the contests would have been futile. With his base of power in Congress, and backed by the venerable Speaker of the

House, Sam Rayburn, he hoped to gain delegate support by cashing in on the many debts both men had accumulated over their years of service for all kinds of special favors—a bill passed, legislation brought to the floor, some benefit for state, city, or district.

The remaining contender, who flatly refused to be one, was Adlai E. Stevenson, a twice-defeated candidate, whose personality and eloquence still magnetized an unshakably devoted following. Once again a campaign was launched without his support, but this time it was run by professionals. One group operated in Madison, Wisconsin, another in New York, a third in Los Angeles, and coordinating all three was a strategy center in Washington. An official announcement of the Draft Stevenson movement was made at the beginning of June; by the end of the month clubs were operating in forty-two states. Behind the popular excitement which was generated—newspaper advertisements appealing for funds, planes towing banners across the sky emblazoned "DRAFT STEVENSON," volunteers everywhere cranking mimeograph machines and licking stamps for broadsides to be sent to politicians and delegates—plans for the convention were quietly formulated. The two leaders in the movement were Senator Mike Monroney of Oklahoma and the youthful John Sharon, a junior partner in a Washington law firm. They estimated that if Kennedy were stopped on the first three ballots the convention would inevitably turn to Stevenson, the only figure with real national stature. To entice wavering favorite sons and undecided party leaders, Monroney and Sharon covered 30,000 miles during four weeks from the end of May through June, holding up the shining vision of the ideal ticket—Stevenson and Kennedy.

Before the convention opened on Monday, July 11, it was apparent that Kennedy would be dueling with those who sought to make Stevenson the nominee. After the gavel sounded, he accelerated his pace, which had already become frenetic during the past few days, meeting with as many caucuses as time and stamina permitted, to hold delegations in line and attempt to sway others. On Monday between 8:30 A.M. and 1:30 P.M. he addressed the caucuses of Nevada, Pennsylvania, Michigan, North Carolina, Arkansas, New York, South Carolina, Florida, and Alaska. His afternoon was equally crowded, and the following day he spoke to groups from five other states. The Stevenson men were similarly busy in their own behind-the-scenes efforts.

The Kennedy machine itself was already running smoothly on well-oiled gears. About forty young men, handpicked for their poise and political know-how, had been assigned to specific state delegations. They were provided with cards listing the delegates by name, profession, hobby, children, wife, idiosyncrasies, and religion and were instructed to report back any change in mood or position to headquarters. In a cottage outside the Los Angeles Sports Arena, a communications control post was set up consisting of a switchboard with a net of lines to special telephone posts attached to the chairs of friendly delegations. Linked to the controls were walkie-talkie sets carried by eight of the forty "shepherds" as they circulated on the convention floor.

Stevenson supporters had no such elaborate set-up—indeed, their candidate had not even declared himself—but they poured into Los Angeles. By careful planning and ruse they managed to secure almost 4,000 tickets, so that they packed the galleries. Mrs. Eleanor Roosevelt received a tumultuous ovation when she addressed the convention, urging that Stevenson be given first place on the ticket. After Senator Eugene McCarthy of Minnesota ended an impassioned nominating speech, a mighty roar of "We want Stevenson" shook the hall, gold balloons rained down from the ceiling, paper banners were unfurled and waved furiously. Pleas for order from the chairman were ignored, and the chant went on and on, drowning out the band, which vainly tried to make itself heard above the shouting.

But it was a lost cause. Stevenson had responded too late to the clamor for his leadership, though it is doubtful that even had he done so earlier he could have avoided being smothered by the Kennedy avalanche. His supporters were unaware that he had attempted and failed that afternoon to secure the backing of the Illinois delegation, without which he had absolutely no chance.

Kennedy won the nomination on the first ballot. The vote was 806 to 409 for Johnson, 86 for Symington, 79½ for Stevenson. So efficient had been the Kennedy organization, so thorough its analysis of political forces, that its final estimate of the expected tally varied by only 1½ votes from the actual count.

The next consideration was the vice-presidential candidate, and the selection of Lyndon Baines Johnson was a bombshell. Kennedy had been fairly certain that the Senate Majority Leader would not want to give up his powerful position. Johnson himself had said that he would not care to trade active leadership "of the greatest deliberative body in the world for the part-time job of presiding," that the vice-presidency was a good place for a young man who required experience and training.

Not surprisingly, there are a number of versions of how Johnson finally became the nominee. All the actors in the drama were exhausted after the balloting; memory plays tricks, and the telephone calls, the back-and-forth visits, the lengthy discussions which went on undoubtedly wound up as a blur. "The confusion of that afternoon," Schlesinger writes, "defies historical reconstruction." Beginning at eight o'clock Thursday morning with a phone call by Kennedy to Johnson, the parleying was continuous until three that afternoon, when an announcement was made to the press.

The first reaction among liberal Democrats was shock and then anger, but emotions soon gave way to sober reflection. John Kenneth Galbraith pointed out, as he moved among them, "This is the kind of political expedient Franklin Roosevelt would never have used—except in the case of John Nance Garner." It was the most strategically sound choice possible, for Johnson was the one man who could secure the southern flank in 1960. Resentment was also soothed by the liberal planks in the party platform. Chester

Bowles, chairman of the Platform Committee, had appointed a twenty-man drafting panel largely composed of liberals. Aptly entitled "The Rights of Man," the platform adopted by the convention was the most progressive ever presented by a major party.

Late Friday afternoon, John F. Kennedy stood before a throng of some 80,000 people in the Los Angeles Coliseum, flanked by his mother and sisters, the unsuccessful aspirants behind him, to deliver his acceptance speech. He was weary to the bone, his face drawn with fatigue, and at times his delivery faltered, but his address was eloquent and memorable. "We are not here to curse the darkness," he said, "but to light the candle that can guide us through that darkness to a safe and sane future." The world was changing, and the old ways would not do; "we stand today on the edge of a new frontier . . . a frontier of unknown opportunities and perils. . . . But the New Frontier of which I speak is not a set of promises—it is a set of challenges. It sums up, not what I intend to offer the American people, but what I intend to ask of them. It appeals to their pride, not their pocketbook—it holds out the promise of more sacrifice instead of more security. . . . I am asking each of you to be new pioneers on that New Frontier."

Public opinion soundings taken prior to the conventions gave Kennedy a margin of fifty-two to forty-eight per cent over Nixon, but as the campaign opened in September Gallup surveys indicated a reversal in about the same ratio. In the interim, Senator Kennedy had sweated through a frustrating congressional session where all the measures he advocated—aid for schools, medicare, an increase in minimum wages—had been defeated. As the junior senator from Massachusetts, he was eclipsed by the Vice-President, who was making headlines with his forays into the South, where he was being greeted by record turnouts.

For both candidates, the campaign was to be a grueling test of endurance. In one weekend, Kennedy visited Massachusetts, New Hampshire, Maine, California, Alaska, and Michigan; in one week he covered twenty-seven states, often speaking eight or ten times each day. Nixon's pace was equally prostrating and, in addition, he was plagued at the beginning by illness, first an infected knee which sent him to the hospital for ten days and then a serious cold. But he was determined to fulfill the pledge made in his acceptance speech to carry the campaign into "every one of the fifty states." At one point, his eyes glazed with fever, he spoke at night in an open-air stadium after having made two other addresses that day and flown about 1,500 miles.

As the two youthful candidates raced frenetically around the country in pursuit of the glittering prize, talking until their voices gave out, shaking so many hands that their own swelled and spurted blood, their strategies became apparent. Nixon draped himself in the mantle of "experience" and tossed one end around Lodge. At the conclusion of one address he said modestly that it would be inappropriate to compare his experience with that of his opponent, but it was fitting to talk about that of his running mate. He was proud to have Lodge on the ticket, and he knew of no man anywhere "in the world today who has done a better job of standing up against the men in the Kremlin and representing the cause of peace and freedom."

Kennedy snapped back that Nixon was indeed experienced but "experienced in policies of retreat, defeat, and weakness." The nation, he declared, had never before suffered "such arrogant treatment at the hands of our enemy . . . such a critical decline in our prestige, driving our friends to neutralism, and neutrals to outright hostility." His campaign, he said, was "founded on a single assumption, the assumption that the American people are tired of drift in our national course . . . and that they are ready to move again."

The key word for Kennedy was "movement." Over and over he repeated, "I say we need to move again," and "Mr. Nixon says 'We never had it so good.' I say we can do better." Typical of his speeches was the one delivered at Fort Dodge, Iowa:

But if you think we can do better, if you think we can move ahead, if you think we can reverse the downward trend of agricultural prices, if you think we can build a better educational system and more security for our older people, if you think we can build a better defense, if you think that the United States should reestablish the atmosphere which existed in the 1930's of the good neighbor, if you think the power balance of the world is turning against us . . . then I want you to join with us. I want you to move with us. I want you to decide in 1960 that we say "Yes" to the next decade, and not "No"; that we want to move ahead, not stand still.

Nixon retorted that at a time when Nikita Khrushchev was at the United Nations carrying on his threatening antics, it was damaging and in poor taste to talk about America's military and economic weaknesses and the nation's declining prestige: first, because it was not true, and secondly, when the country was being attacked by an outsider, "it is up to us to point out the things that are right . . . and . . . strong about the United States." On another occasion he said that Kennedy was too "naïve and inexperienced to stand up to Khrushchev," to which his rival promptly replied that it was not naïve to call for greater strength. "It is naïve to think that freedom can prevail without it." The "most ominous sound," he said, "that Mr. Khrushchev can hear this week is not in the debates of the United Nations, but a sound of a United States on the move again, of a country ready to move."

The Democratic candidate outlined how he hoped to make the country "move" on the home front: federal aid to education for teachers' salaries and for classrooms, medical insurance for those over sixty-five through the social security system, an increase in the minimum wage to $1.25, liberalization and extension of the social security program. The Republican candidate favored similar reforms but claimed that his method of putting them into effect would cost $15 billion less than his opponent's.

For most of his campaign, Nixon relied, as one journalist commented, on "a single 'basic speech,' which he delivered in town after town day after day with hardly any change in language, or, indeed, even in the timing and movement of his gesturing hands." Kennedy dealt with a different subject or a variety of subjects in each speech, using as his springboard the theme of movement, the challenges to the nation's security, prestige, and progress. He packed his talks with facts and figures: the number of families receiving an income of less than $1,000, how many workers were not protected by minimum wages, the number of families in substandard housing, the proportion of unused steel capacity, the meager amount of loans to Africa and Latin America. He began with "I am not satisfied when . . ." or "Do you realize that . . ." and ended each one with "I think we can do better. . . . Our brightest days can be ahead." The Vice President, he said, presented a rosy and reassuring picture of America's strength, leadership, and economy, and that, he maintained, "is the basic issue that separates us." It was a contest "between the comfortable and the concerned."

Inevitably, Kennedy's religion became an issue. For a while the mutterings were subterranean; then on September 7 a group of prominent Protestant clergymen announced the formation of an *ad hoc* National Conference for Religious Freedom in Washington, D.C. Its spokesman, the highly popular columnist, author, and lecturer, the Reverend Norman Vincent Peale, issued a statement to the press that a Roman Catholic in the White House would be under "extreme pressure" from the hierarchy of his church to make his policies conform to those of the Vatican. Peale's prestige insured widespread publicity, and the item was splashed across newspapers from coast to coast.

Reaction was swift. A hundred outstanding churchmen and scholars of all denominations joined in denouncing this attempt to make religious affiliation a test for the Presidency. The New York Board of Rabbis issued an official statement that to vote for or against a presidential candidate because of his faith was "a sinister betrayal of the fundamental precepts of American democracy." Shaken by this barrage, Peale beat a hasty retreat, denying his participation in the drafting of the statement and dissociating himself from the organization.

On September 12, at the invitation of the Ministerial Association of Houston, Kennedy appeared before the group, presenting a brief but eloquent statement summing up his beliefs. He regretted, he said, that the real issues, "war and hunger and ignorance and despair," had been obscured because he was a Catholic, and that it should be necessary once more for him to explain "what kind of America I believe in." It was, he said, a country where the separation of church and state was absolute, which was "officially neither Catholic, Protestant nor Jewish . . . where religious liberty is so indivisible that an act against one church is treated as an act against all." He believed in a President "whose views on religion are his own private affair." He did not speak for his church on public matters, nor did the church speak for him. If elected, he would make his decision on any issue that came before him, "on birth control, divorce, censorship, gambling . . . in accordance . . . with what my conscience tells me to be in the national interest, and without regard to outside religious pressure or dictate." If the inconceivable should happen, a conflict between the national interest and his conscience which would require him to violate one or the other, he would resign his office.

The religious bigots were not, of course, impressed. A mammoth flood of poisonous literature poured over the country, attacking Catholicism and Kennedy's candidacy. The Fair Campaign Practices Committee estimated that tens of millions of pieces were distributed, with the cost running into hundreds of thousands of dollars. Mailing lists were compiled from the rolls of conservative Protestant churches, church directories, and other public sources. Political conservatives who opposed Kennedy helped pay the cost by contributions to churches and other Protestant organizations active in the "hate" campaign. Charles P. Taft, a Republican and prominent Protestant Episcopal layman, said, "The amounts involved in paying for millions of copies of a wide variety of leaflets are so great that they are clearly beyond the resources of the hate groups, or in the case of slightly more 'respectable' material, beyond the resources of organizations like churches and other nonprofit corporations. The religious garbage that is swamping us is clearly on the face, and often in so many words, aimed at the defeat of one of the candidates for President."

Even more significant than the emotional anti-Catholicism dispensed by the professional purveyors of intolerance were the pieces emanating from the "church and staters," represented by such groups as the National Association of Evangelicals, a conservative counterpart of the National Council of Churches, with a membership of about ten million; Protestants and Other Americans United for Separation of Church and State; and by numerous churches in the Southern Baptist Convention. The Evangelicals brought their drive to a climax on the last two Sundays in October, designating the first "Christian Conviction Sunday" and using the second, Reformation Sunday, when Protestant feeling is at its peak, for bigoted exhortation. Pastors received a letter from the president of the association stating, "If a Roman Catholic is elected President— what then? The Church of Rome will have a new great advantage, and the United States will no longer be recognized as a Protestant nation in the eyes of the world. Don't you agree that it is time for the Protestants of America to stand up and be counted?" He suggested several "very practical things" they could do, such as prayer meetings emphasizing the danger of a Catholic President and special offerings to finance the cause.

The movement against Kennedy made strange and unlikely bedfellows. Fundamentalist tracts carried stickers advertising freethinkers' magazines opposed to Catholicism, and some of these magazines carried advertisements for the fundamentalist tracts. The material sometimes exceeded all bounds of rationality: Kennedy was using his religion to gain the Presidency so that he could turn the country over to the Jews. One publication "could not decide whether Kennedy's selection was a Popish plot or a Communist conspiracy," but thought that the two worked together anyway. Another declared that "Kennedy was stirring up the religious issue to conceal the fact that he was a Communist!"

No one in the Republican leadership was guilty of raising or adding to the tide of bigotry. Nixon informed the Republican National Committee, "There should be no discussion of the religious issue in any literature prepared by any volunteer group or party organization supporting the Vice President, and no literature of this kind from any source should be made available at campaign headquarters or otherwise distributed." The national headquarters issued firm directives to state and local organizations that the Roman Catholic issue was not to be insinuated into the campaign. Unfortunately, however, these very admonitions and Nixon's frequent statements that both candidates should refrain from discussing the religious issue only drew attention to it, as did the efforts of enlightened Protestant clergymen to prevent Reformation Sunday from being made the occasion for anti-Catholic diatribes by urging their congregations not to make religion a test for the Presidency, or the Democrats' repeated use of the filmed record of Kennedy's Houston address.

A decisive factor in the outcome of the election was the confrontation between the two candidates which the nation witnessed on television. This was the first time that two presidential candidates faced each other in public debate, and for dramatic suspense, popular interest, and size of audience the four programs were unprecedented in American politics.

After Congress suspended the equal-time requirement of the Federal Communications Act for presidential and vice-presidential candidates in July 1960, Robert Sarnoff, NBC Board Chairman, offered to make eight hours of prime evening time available for what he termed "the great debate." Kennedy promptly accepted without qualifications, Nixon four days later but with the understanding that there be "a full and free exchange of views without prepared text or notes and without interruption." Details were worked out at a series of conferences. Primarily interested in a "good show" that would reach the widest possible audience, the network was persuasive in having a format accepted which placed a premium on brief generalizations on a wide variety of subjects. In the first and last debates each candidate would have eight minutes for an opening statement; two and a half minutes was the limit for direct response to questions, and one and a half minutes for rebuttal. The first debate was to be on domestic policy, the second on foreign relations, and topics for the remaining two were to be determined by the way in which the interchange had developed. Dates for the telecasts were set for September 26 from Chicago, October 7 from Washington, October 13 from Los Angeles (Nixon) and New York (Kennedy), and October 21 from New York.

For Nixon, the invitation had posed a dilemma. Most of the advantage of public exposure would accrue to his opponent, since he already had a national reputation and was established as mature and experienced. On the other hand, he might win over many undecided or independent voters and those who normally identified themselves as Democrats, a significant consideration for the candidate of a minority party. He might efface what remained of his image as "tricky Dick"—the entire country would see a "new Nixon," mellow, statesmanlike, with a firm command of public affairs. Of his skill as a debater he was completely confident. He had demonstrated this talent since high school days, had won his congressional seat from a "pro," and had outmaneuvered Khrushchev in the famous "kitchen debate." As a television performer, he was equally assured —his "Checkers" act was testimony as to his aptitude.

Kennedy had no such ambivalent feelings. On the contrary, he was most eager, for if all went well he had everything to gain. He had been striving to overcome the handicaps of being considered too young for the office and, as compared with Nixon, lacking experience. His presentation, he hoped, would dispel both impressions. Moreover, still not as well known as his opponent, he could reach more people than would be humanly possible by the most extensive travel schedule.

Both candidates arrived in Chicago a day before the debate. Kennedy, with his usual scrupulous planning, had sent ahead three members of his "brain trust," Theodore Sorensen, Richard Goodwin, and Mike Feldman. They brought with them "the portable Kennedy campaign research library—a Sears Roebuck foot locker of documents —and now, for a twenty-four-hour session . . . stretching around the clock, they operated like young men at college cramming for an exam. When they had finished, they had prepared fifteen pages of copy boiling down into twelve or thirteen subject areas the relevant facts and probable questions they thought the correspondents on the panel, or Mr. Nixon, might raise."

Early the following morning the four men began a session which lasted for several hours. The opening statements were discussed and rewritten by Kennedy; questions and answers went back and forth. After lunch, Kennedy addressed a labor organization, returned to the hotel for an almost-three-hour nap, rose about five o'clock, and for the next hour and a half went over the fact cards with his team. Then a leisurely dinner and on to the studio.

Nixon, who came in late Sunday evening, delivered a public address the following morning, after which he returned to his hotel and remained incommunicado for the rest of the day. He even refused to talk to the television technicians who wanted to discuss details of the program with him. Only during the ten-minute drive to the studio did he permit one aide to brief him quickly. Alighting from the car, he painfully struck his injured knee on the door.

At the cavernous studio, which once had been a wrestling arena, representatives of both candidates had been working since early that morning. The minutest details received assiduous attention: special lights to eliminate Nixon's deep eye shadows and cameras to be kept off his left profile, a light coating of a powder used by men with dark beards to conceal the shadow. After careful inspection, Kennedy also was given a slight trace of make-up. Then producer Don Hewitt advised him to change from his white shirt to the customary blue used on the medium. An aide sped across Chicago under police escort to the hotel and rushed back with a blue shirt.

Shortly before they went on the air, Hewitt advised the debaters, "Play to your cameras. That's where the votes are." After a brief introduction by the moderator, the dignified Howard K. Smith, the candidates locked in verbal battle before what was estimated as the largest viewing audience in television history. Kennedy began, speaking somewhat rapidly, his sentences tending to be short, staccato. "I think the question before the American people is: Are we doing as much as we can do . . . ? If we fail, then freedom fails. . . . I am not satisfied as an American with the progress that we are making. . . . This is a great country but I think it could be a greater country." He went on to list the causes for his dissatisfaction: the lowest rate of economic growth among the industrialized nations, fifty per cent of steel capacity unused, natural resources undeveloped, millions of hungry people while food rotted in storage, overcrowded schools, underpaid teachers, racial discrimination. America's deficiencies at home affected the entire world. "Can freedom be maintained under the most severe attack it has ever known? . . . I think it's time America started moving again."

Nixon both agreed and disagreed. He subscribed "completely to the spirit that Senator Kennedy has expressed . . . but our disagreement is not about the goals for America but only about the means to reach those goals." He also disputed the contention that the nation's rate of growth was unsatisfactory; the Eisenhower record was better than that of Truman, and the country had been progressing both in the public and private economic sectors at a rate unparalleled in its history.

The questions by the panel which followed—on the importance of the candidate's age, on the quality of presidential decisions, on subversion, on schools, on farms (in this hour devoted exclusively to domestic matters, civil rights was conspicuous by its absence)—appeared to be aimed more at creating headlines than probing the views of the contestants. Neither candidate had time for reflection. Kennedy sometimes ignored the direct inquiry to appeal to popular aspirations, while Nixon concentrated on scoring "debating points." Both displayed the talent for "quick recall" essential for success in a quiz competition, discussing with ease anything tossed at them in the assigned two and a half minutes.

Kennedy's relaxed manner and his physical appearance, fresh, alert, glowing with vitality and self-confidence, were in sharp contrast to that of his opponent. Nixon appeared tense and haggard. A loss of weight made his collar too large, the electronic tube was cruel to his transparent skin, the shadow of a beard giving him an unflattering dark-visaged appearance. Radio listeners when polled felt that the two men had performed about equally, but every survey of viewers' reactions indicated that Nixon came off a very poor second.

By the time of the second debate, Nixon had returned to his normal weight and his collar once more fitted properly. He also responded to advice that "I use make-up to cover my five o'clock shadow instead of the powder which had made me appear pale during the first debate." Most important, since the theme was on foreign policy, he was on more secure ground, and the result of this encounter was more favorable to him. A New York *Times* spot survey in twenty-three cities gave him a clear edge. Of the reporters who covered the event at the studio, eleven gave the contest to Nixon, four to Kennedy, and eleven rated it a draw. Many agreed with a Scripps-Howard reporter who stated that "Nixon is back in the ball game with a sharply improved national impact." Almost all observers agreed that the Vice-President had made a dramatic comeback.

Two issues of foreign policy were dominant: the Chinese offshore islands of Quemoy and Matsu and the problem of Castro's Cuba. Questioned on his position with respect to

America's responsibility toward the islands which had been under intermittent attack by the Chinese Communists, Kennedy declared that the United States should precisely define its obligations, if any. While he did not advocate revoking the nation's commitment to assist in defending the islands should they be threatened "at the point of a communist gun," he felt that they were of no strategic value and in any case ultimately could not be defended.

Nixon conceded that the islands were strategically insignificant, but he insisted that an important principle was at stake. Controlled by the Chinese Nationalists, they should not, he said, be allowed to fall to the Communists. He warned that abandoning the islands would start a chain reaction "because the Communists aren't after Quemoy and Matsu. They're after Formosa. In my opinion this is the same kind of woolly thinking that led to disaster for America in Korea."

In the interim before the next debate, Nixon charged that Kennedy's position would lead to war and surrender. Kennedy shot back that Nixon was "trigger happy." Inevitably the issue was raised again in the third debate, but this time both candidates retreated from their earlier positions. Nixon now fell back on the policy of the Eisenhower administration that the islands should be defended only if an attack on them was a prelude to an assault on Formosa. Kennedy concurred. But in the remaining weeks of the campaign, each candidate continued to beat a dead horse, each dredging up the original statements made by the other. The intention, obviously, was not to clarify a vital issue in foreign policy for the electorate but to exploit any question that showed promise of producing political capital.

The explosive issue of Cuba was injected into the last debate. Throughout the campaign Kennedy had indicted the administration for drift in its failure to cope with what he referred to as a Communist outpost ninety miles off American shores. He had outlined a four-point program, which included the statement that "we must attempt to strengthen the non-Batista democratic anti-Castro forces in exile, and in Cuba itself, who offer eventual hope of overthrowing Castro." Thus when Nixon was asked to distinguish his position from that of his opponent, he denounced Kennedy's proposals as "probably the most dangerously irresponsible recommendations" made during the campaign. He maintained that they would violate treaties with Latin American countries and the United Nations Charter, to say nothing of providing an open invitation for Russian intervention in Latin America. Kennedy retorted that the actions of the Eisenhower administration had contributed to Castroism, that Cuba marked only the beginning of our problems in Latin America.

In discussing the Cuban issue, Nixon was trapped. As a member of the administration, he knew that for months the Central Intelligence Agency had been secretly supporting and training Cuban exiles in Guatemala for an invasion of Cuba, but naturally he could not reveal this information. Later, in recalling the debates, he charged that as a candidate Kennedy had been briefed by the CIA and was taking advantage of his enforced silence to advocate a policy that many Americans would favor.*

Other issues were similarly blurred or distorted. On one occasion Nixon stated, "Now as a result of our taking the strong stand that we did on Indochina, the civil war there was ended and today, at least in the south of Indochina, the communists have moved out and we do have a strong, free bastion there"—this at a time when Vietnam was already beginning to smolder.

As an entertaining political "spectacular," the debates were a success; as a means of public enlightenment they were considerably less effective. The limitations of time in general prevented the treatment of any issue in depth, and rebuttal time was so brief that any really sound and intelligent criticism was precluded. Moreover, they undoubtedly fostered in many viewers or listeners the notion that public

---

* Ex-CIA Director Allen Dulles testified in 1962 that Kennedy had not been briefed (New York *Times,* March 21, 1962).

questions of great significance can be dealt with in 150 seconds, or the misleading impression that skill in debate necessarily qualifies a man for presidential leadership. After the first exchange, the New York *Times* commented that both candidates had been excessively concerned with "the protection of their own image."

Viewed as a personality contest, Kennedy undoubtedly was the winner. Virile, handsome, photogenic, he was especially attractive to women; the knowledge and command of facts he displayed, his rapid-fire delivery, were enormously impressive; and his quick wit struck sparks, especially in contrast to the pedantic and heavy-worded Nixon. By more than holding his own on the platform with the man who had placed a strong emphasis on his experience, Kennedy effectively dispelled a major contention of his critics that he was too young and immature for the job.

Yet, while "the great debates" were neither great nor real debates, polls indicated that their cumulative effect had been to greatly intensify electoral interest. A Roper survey conducted after the election revealed that as many as forty-four per cent of the nation's voters felt that the debates had influenced their choice, and about five per cent claimed that the debates alone had influenced their decision.

Opinion remained divided as to their fundamental significance. What can be said is that before the encounters Nixon was generally regarded as being in the lead, but afterwards the positions were reversed. One reporter noted that following the first debate the Kennedy crowds multiplied in numbers and enthusiasm, as if the sight of him on the screen "had given him a 'star quality' reserved only for television and movie idols."

Toward the end of the campaign one of those fortuitous incidents occurred that can sometimes swing the balance. On October 19, Dr. Martin Luther King was arrested in Atlanta during a restaurant sit-in, jailed, sentenced to four months at hard labor on a traffic violation technicality, and secretly removed to the Georgia state penitentiary.

As soon as Harris Wofford, director of the Kennedy cam-

paign's civil rights section, learned about the arrest, he
phoned his chief, Sargent Shriver, to suggest that the candidate call Mrs. King, who was understandably frantic
about her husband's safety. Kennedy was faced with a crucial decision. During the past week his headquarters had
been informed by three southern governors that if he inter-
fered in affairs below the Mason-Dixon line to support or
endorse Martin Luther King he could count off the South.
Nevertheless, after talking with Shriver, he promptly
picked up the phone and called Mrs. King, assuring her that
he would intervene if necessary. In New York, Robert Kennedy, informed of his brother's action, at first was concerned about the political implications, then decided on his
own to call the judge who had sentenced King.

Word of what had occurred raced through the Negro
community. King's father, a Baptist minister who earlier
had declared his support for Nixon, told reporters, "Because
this man was willing to wipe the tears from my daughter
[in-law]'s eyes, I've got a suitcase of votes and I'm going to
take them to Mr. Kennedy and dump them in his lap."
Negro leaders all over the country were similarly impressed
with the compassion Kennedy had displayed. Later, the
Kennedy organization printed a million pamphlets describing the episode, which they distributed, especially outside
Negro churches, on the Sunday before election day.

Nixon's response to the arrest seems to have been based
on what he considered the best political strategy. His warm
reception in the South early in the campaign, particularly
in Atlanta, encouraged him to believe that he might be supported by white Southerners. Would not an overt act in defense of the Negro leader jeopardize those prospects?

In any event, he remained silent. The Deputy Attorney-
General had actually written a draft statement asking for
King's release, sending one copy to the White House and
one to Nixon for approval. No action resulted from either
quarter. Nixon later claimed that he had consulted with
Attorney General William Rogers, who had joined him on
his campaign train, to ask whether King's constitutional

rights had been violated, "thus paving the way for federal action." Rogers recommended that a White House statement be issued that the Department of Justice had been requested to inquire into the situation, but apparently Nixon did not press the matter further.

Another tactical blunder on Nixon's part may have been to wait until the end of the campaign before calling on Eisenhower for his active help. Many people interpreted the President's silence as implying that he was lukewarm toward the candidate. As Eisenhower's popularity was still at its height, his support might have made a difference in the outcome. By all accounts, he was prepared to campaign for Nixon, informing the candidate several days after the Republican convention that he would do anything asked of him. Tentative arrangements were made, but Nixon did not seek help from him until the end of October. One member of Eisenhower's staff commented, "All of us expected the President would get into the campaign one hell of a lot more than he actually did." Possibly, recalling how President Truman had overshadowed Stevenson in 1952, Nixon and his aides were determined that the candidate should occupy the center of the stage. Furthermore, they probably preferred to operate without any control from the Eisenhower people, and Nixon wanted to show that he could achieve victory on his own.

Eisenhower entered the campaign on October 28 with an address at a Philadelphia rally. Several days later he toured the New York area with both Republican candidates and appeared on television that evening. On November 4, he spoke in Cleveland and made another television broadcast from Detroit. Finally, he joined Nixon on television during part of a four-hour question and answer program.

During the closing phase of the campaign, Nixon appeared to be increasingly on the defensive, hurling barbed personal epithets, accusing his opponent of "bare-faced lies." He strained to make headlines. On October 25, he promised that if elected he would place a man on the moon sometime between 1966 and 1969; he pledged a summit meeting with Khrushchev if no agreement was reached on nuclear arms control by February 1. He promised to go to eastern Europe "to carry the message of freedom into the communistic world." Two days before the election he promised that he would ask President Eisenhower to go to eastern Europe, accompanied, if possible, by former Presidents Hoover and Truman, to explore the possibilities of abating the cold war. Increasingly he echoed Kennedy: "So I say . . . there are new frontiers, new frontiers in America, new frontiers all over the universe in which we live."

As Nixon grew more tense, Kennedy became more relaxed and confident. Operating at a grueling pace, he seemed to thrive, his vitality unimpaired, even his voice growing stronger. The crowds that turned out to see him were unbelievable. Riding in an open car, he was almost smothered by the confetti and streamers which rained down over him. His motor tour through Pennsylvania cities was "like the coming of a Messiah," Governor Lawrence remarked. On occasions, the frenzy could be compared only with the mass hysteria of adolescents evoked by a popular singer. An army of police was often required to keep him from being crushed by the surging mass of people when he appeared on an open-air platform.

The effusion of money, energy, talent, and words finally came to an end. In terms of money, the cost was staggering. The Republicans spent almost two million dollars for telecasts and radio—the Nixon telethon alone cost between $200,000 (Republican estimate) and $400,000 (Democratic estimate)—and the Democrats, whose purse was not as fat, spent over a million dollars on television. The overall expenditure by both parties was estimated at about $25 million, which did not include the amounts contributed by the many state and local committees, labor, and other groups.

The two candidates, completely drained, fatigued almost beyond human endurance, returned to their homes to await the verdict of the people. With opinion surveys seesawing within a few percentage points throughout the campaign, no pollster would venture a prediction. A record number of Americans, almost seventy million, turned out to cast the closest vote in the nation's history. Kennedy won by the wafer-thin margin of 112,803 votes. In as many as eleven states, eight won by Kennedy and three by Nixon, a shift of only one per cent would have changed the electoral vote; a switch of 20,000 votes properly distributed in key states would have given the Presidency to Nixon.

Kennedy was victorious in twenty-three states with a total of 303 electoral votes; Nixon carried twenty-six states with 219 electoral votes. Despite the loss of almost the entire West and the farm states as well as several in the South, the combination of the eastern states of Pennsylvania, New York, and New Jersey, the central industrial states of Michigan, Illinois, and Wisconsin, and most of the traditionally Democratic southern states, including Texas, were more than sufficient to give Kennedy the required majority in the electoral college.

That Kennedy carried the South is ascribed to the intensive campaigning there of Lyndon Johnson, which outweighed any adverse effect of the Martin Luther King incident. As to the Negro vote in the North, Nixon may have paid heavily for his failure to respond sympathetically to King's arrest. The figures show that Kennedy carried Illinois by only 9,000 votes and that 250,000 Negroes are estimated to have voted for him; that he carried Michigan by 67,000 and an estimated 250,000 Negroes voted for him; that he carried South Carolina by 10,000 votes and that an estimated 40,000 Negroes there voted for him.

The Nixon-Lodge ticket ran strongly in the West and Midwest, winning such key states as California, Ohio, and Indiana and scoring in several southern and border states. Fourteen electoral votes representing Mississippi's slate of unpledged electors, and six from Alabama, were cast for Senator Harry Byrd of Virginia.

In a televised interview the morning after the election, Nixon rancorously attacked the press as a contributing factor in his defeat. While editorial endorsements for Nixon had been as preponderant as they usually have been for Republican candidates, Nixon's grievance was that Kennedy's popularity with the working press colored the way in which the campaign was reported. To substantiate his contention, he later cited an informal poll conducted by *Newsweek* which showed that thirty-seven of fifty top reporters who covered both candidates personally favored Kennedy. He told a Chicago *Tribune* journalist, "Republicans will get better treatment in the press only if and when more reporters, like their publishers, take a more favorable or at least a more tolerant view of Republican policies and principles and not before."

Nixon was either unaware or refused to acknowledge that his own conduct and that of his staff had antagonized the reporters. Their hostility to the press took the form of delayed transcripts of Nixon's speeches until late in the campaign, when the effectiveness of Kennedy's instant transcript policy had become unmistakably apparent. Most of the correspondents found it impossible to meet privately with Nixon and to discuss his campaign with him. Sometimes the candidate permitted the rotating pool of reporters to accompany him on his personal plane, and sometimes he denied them the privilege. Reporters, who in the beginning were evenly divided toward the candidates, were predominantly antagonistic to Nixon by the end of the campaign.

Kennedy not only respected newsmen but thoroughly enjoyed their company. Reporters especially appreciated his ready availability for quick oral exchanges while getting on or off a plane or by the side of the road when he stopped for a Coke. He asked reporters for advice, and if he particularly liked a column or article would mention this to the writer, even quoting phrases verbatim. His aides were equally warm, helpful, and considerate. By the last weeks of the campaign, the correspondents "had become more than a press corps—they had become his friends and, some of them, his most devoted admirers."

More relevant, however, than the press (which in any

case is rarely a determining factor) was the religious issue. To a large extent it accounted for the unprecedented turnout: people who had not voted for years went to the polls because they either opposed or favored a Roman Catholic in the White House. Yet how much the faith of one of the candidates determined the outcome remains inconclusive.

Most Roman Catholics voted for Kennedy. Predominantly Democratic since the Irish came to America a century ago, many adherents of that religion had deserted the party for Eisenhower. Some might not have returned to the Democratic fold to support a candidate of another faith, but in 1960 six out of every ten who had voted Republican in 1956 cast their ballots for Kennedy. The net effect was to increase the Catholic vote for the Democrats from about 50 per cent in 1956 to about 80 per cent in 1960. Furthermore, the Roman Catholic vote was concentrated in those states strategically important in the electoral college.

On the other hand, while numerous Democratic Protestants who had voted for Eisenhower returned to their party, the gains were counterbalanced by sizeable defections among those who refused to support Kennedy. Although the electorate as a whole was nearly 8 per cent more Democratic in 1960 than in the previous election, there was almost no net change at all in the Democratic percentage of the Protestant vote. Moreover, except for 1956, the Democratic showing was the poorest since the depression, when the Democrats had become the normal majority party. The Survey Research Center of the University of Michigan reported that Kennedy's overall loss nationally from Protestant Democrats was at least 4.5 million votes, far more than any Roman Catholic gains could offset. On the basis of later surveys, one prominent analyst concluded that "Kennedy won in spite of rather than because of the fact that he was a Catholic."

Perhaps what should be considered surprising is that Kennedy was victorious at all, that he succeeded in convincing about half the nation that it could rely on his leadership. There was the acknowledged handicap of his religion; there was an opponent, politically skilled, firmly endorsed by his party and supported by one of the most popular Presidents in American history; above all, there was the nature of Kennedy's approach. At a time when the country was prosperous and at peace, he was talking, Cassandra-like, of dark days ahead. When most Americans were concerned with little more than new cars and refrigerators, more and better gadgetry, he talked of the need for sacrifice. Now it would be the task of the youngest man ever elected to the Presidency to prove to those who had contributed to his triumph that their confidence had not been misplaced, and to convert the unconvinced.

11. Reaction Repudiated

$\bigstar \; \bigstar \; \bigstar \; \bigstar \; \bigstar \; \bigstar \; \bigstar$

D URING the short time that he was in the White House, John Fitzgerald Kennedy's dynamism stirred to a heightened sense of life a nation which had become lethargic and complacent. "Let the word go forth from this time and place, to friend and foe alike," he had proclaimed at his inauguration, "that the torch has passed to a new generation of Americans . . . unwilling to witness or permit the slow undoing of those human rights to which we are committed today at home and around the world." Not until he was gone, his life brutally snuffed out, did his country and the rest of the world realize with stunning impact what they had lost.

Kennedy's modernity—the "contemporary man," Adlai Stevenson called him—inspired not only youth but all who shared his ideals and goals for a civilized society concerned with the cultivation of mind and sensibility. As he said in one address, he looked toward a future for America when the country could match its military with its moral strength, its wealth with its wisdom, which would reward artistic achievements equally with those of business or statecraft and command respect for its enlightenment as well as for its material resources. His efforts toward the eradication of poverty, ignorance, bigotry, and war endeared him not only to many of his countrymen but to people everywhere, who felt his death as a personal, grievous loss. At the same time, he incurred an almost maniacal hatred from the fanatic and the fear-ridden.

The accomplishments of the Kennedy administration can be judged only as an unfinished achievement, as a potential of what might have been. With a legislature dominated by a strong conservative coalition which included members of his own party, Kennedy was balked in some of his major efforts. The strong civil rights legislation that he requested on grounds of both law and morality was turned down, as were other reforms such as medicare, federal aid to education, and a cabinet post for urban affairs. Nevertheless, he had laid the groundwork for such highly significant legislation, and all were passed in the next administration.

President Kennedy's most significant achievements were in foreign policy after the Bay of Pigs fiasco. He demonstrated an adeptness at diplomacy and made full use of presidential power during the Cuban missile crisis, was responsible for the Alliance for Progress, the Peace Corps, the Trade Expansion Act. Above all, there was the limited Nuclear Test Ban Treaty. Indicative of a slowly evolving detente with the Soviet Union, the treaty was to be important in the next election—for the first time, a Gallup poll revealed, Americans regarded the Democrats as the "peace party" and more likely to keep the country out of war.

The style of the Kennedy administration—sophisticated, intellectual, cosmopolitan, a blend of the charismatic qualities of the youthful President, his accomplished wife, the brilliant young advisors—created an aura of animation and glamour about the White House. With his successor, the winds of the Southwest's open range began to swirl about Washington.

Lyndon Baines Johnson's tastes, appetites, and performance were shaped by his native sun-parched land, where efforts to wrest a living from the soil were a daily struggle, and by the political atmosphere of home and surroundings. One grandfather had founded the city near which he was born, the other had been a member of the legislature and Secretary of State of Texas; his father had been in the state legislature, his mother was an educated woman who had put herself through college. After graduating from Southwest Texas State Teachers College, Johnson taught public speaking and debate in a Houston high school until 1932, when he went to Washington as secretary to a congressman from Texas. He was twenty-three years old, and except for a brief interlude the Capitol was henceforth to be his home. Later appointed administrator for the National Youth Administration in Texas, Johnson's exceptional performance brought him to the attention of President Roosevelt. His popularity in his state launched him on his political career in 1938, when he was elected to Congress, winning nearly double the votes of his nearest rival among ten aspirants. Eleven years later he entered the Senate.

A shrewd intelligence, extraordinary political skill, and limitless energy propelled Johnson ahead rapidly. A "politician's politician," a brilliant legislative tactician, his talent for making the political wheels spin smoothly and efficiently became legendary. Senate Majority Leader during most of the Eisenhower years, he served the Republican President in the highest tradition of a constructive head of the "loyal opposition."

As Vice-President, Johnson was restricted to the periphery of power. Normally garrulous, accustomed to dominate, and his mind churning with ideas, he must have exercised the most exacting self-discipline to sit through meetings silent for the most part as others expounded their views. Yet he was as actively involved with affairs of state as Vice-President Nixon had been. He attended meetings of the Cabinet and of the National Security Council and joined with congressional leaders in their regular White House sessions. Kennedy saw to it that he received all essential reports of military intelligence as well as those from the Joint Chiefs of Staff. With this preparation, Johnson was able to make the transition without suffering, as had Truman in his situation, the unnerving apprehension at suddenly being thrust into power.

During his first two weeks in office, the new President

gave the nation a sample of the frenetic pace at which he could operate. Pledging to complete all the unfinished legislation Kennedy had left, he did not waste a moment. Work was immediately begun on the budget. The pressing problem of civil rights was tackled. He called in for conferences every major Negro leader in the country and summoned all the legislative leaders for discussions. While many northern liberals had distrusted Johnson, their suspicions were not warranted by his record. He was the only senator from the old Confederacy who had refused to sign the "Southern Manifesto" against the Supreme Court's 1954 desegregation decision, and he was instrumental in the enactment of the civil rights legislation of 1957 and 1960.

The telephone in Johnson's hands became a potent political instrument. A staggering number of calls were made to businessmen, editors, publishers, columnists, commentators. In the course of one week after he entered the White House, Johnson met with scores of individuals and groups, held ten major meetings, and issued ten major statements.

Both parties declared a moratorium on politics during the period of national mourning, but before the year was out, Republicans, divided into two bitterly hostile camps, were deep in plans for the 1964 elections. The fragile glaze over the wide fissure between conservatives and moderates, which had cracked right after Nixon's defeat, was now completely shattered. Conservatives were firmly convinced that with the exception of Eisenhower, whom they regarded as a special case, victory had eluded the party because, having abandoned its distinctive principles and offering no real choice, Republicans in droves had stayed away from the polls. The electorate, in their opinion, was basically conservative and would rally to a candidate such as the senator from Arizona, Barry M. Goldwater. In *The Conscience of a Conservative*, which became their bible, Goldwater wrote, "I have little interest in streamlining government or making it more efficient for I mean to reduce its size. I do not undertake to promote welfare for I propose to extend freedom. My aim is not to pass laws, but to repeal them. It is not to inaugurate new programs, but to cancel old ones that do violence to the Constitution, or that have failed in their purpose, or that impose on the people an unwarranted financial burden." Among the articles of conservative faith were a doctrinaire devotion to states' rights as the last bastion of American freedom and a commitment to an all-out struggle against the demon of communism.

The other wing of the party, composed of members of the "Establishment"—the "Wall Street" and "Madison Avenue" interests—and the party leaders from metropolitan and industrialized areas of the nation together with their spokesmen in Congress, were equally certain that only a liberal would have a chance against Johnson. To win, the support of a substantial number of independents and Democrats was essential, and this could be achieved only by offering programs commensurate with the needs of a modern, industrialized society.

Chief spokesman for this group was Governor Nelson A. Rockefeller. Until the spring of 1963, polls taken throughout the country by his organization appeared to indicate that the nomination was his for the asking. Then he took a step which sent his political ambitions skittering. Though aware of the likely political consequences, Rockefeller, who had divorced his wife after a marriage of thirty years, married a woman considerably his junior, also a divorcee and the mother of four children. The results predictably were immediately apparent. A Gallup poll taken late in May revealed that Rockefeller's popularity had dropped from forty-three to thirty-five per cent while Goldwater's had risen from twenty-six to thirty.

Nevertheless, on November 7, Rockefeller announced his candidacy, probably because, as James Reston wrote, "he is unalterably opposed to the candidacy of Barry Goldwater." Having opened the door to Goldwater by his divorce and remarriage, "he now feels obliged to try to close it" although he did not really think he could win.

However Rockefeller may have assessed his prospects, many of the eastern leaders regarded his candidacy with the deepest dismay, certain that, if nominated, he would be defeated at the polls. The agonizing problem was: who else? Richard M. Nixon, who had been stopped at the very doors of the White House by a handful of votes, was tainted. Hopeful of reaping the political harvest of Eisenhower's popularity, he had emulated him by treading the middle of the road. His opportunism, however, had betrayed him, making him repugnant to both the right and the left. Moreover, his career suffered a second major setback when he was roundly trounced in the 1962 race for governor of his native state of California.

Floundering desperately, the liberal faction sought to enlist the aid of Dwight D. Eisenhower. But when the four names he suggested, including that of his brother Milton, proved unsatisfactory for one reason or another, the former President would do no more than suggest that there were at least ten other eminent Republicans who would qualify. He encouraged both Henry Cabot Lodge, Ambassador to South Vietnam, and Governor William Scranton of Pennsylvania to enter the race yet would not definitely endorse either one. Neither man professed to be interested.

Thus the situation stood when on January 3, 1964, four political amateurs announced from their headquarters in a former yarn shop in Boston's financial district that they were launching a "grass roots" campaign for Ambassador Lodge. That same day Senator Barry Goldwater declared formally that he would seek the nomination "because of the principles in which I believe and because I am convinced that millions of Americans share my beliefs in those principles."

The phenomenon that came to be known as the "Goldwater movement" evolved from an inchoate anxiety in many Americans about a world which increasingly seemed more bewildering and perilous. In their view, stable values were dissolving, respect for law and order disappearing, "creeping socialism" smothering the sturdy frontier spirit of individualism and independence, the chill of the "cold war" intensifying, and the Soviet virus of communism insidiously

infecting their own government. Most were decent if be-
fuddled men and women, but on the fringes were extreme
right-wing groups boiling with hatred against Negroes,
Jews, Roman Catholics, liberals of any persuasion, and convinced that the country was tottering on the abyss of ruin.
Commingled were the politics of paranoia with the politics
of nostalgia.

They expressed their fears by denouncing Supreme Court
decisions and advocating impeachment of the Chief Justice,
attacking the growing federal bureaucracy, demanding repeal of the income tax and other "such manifestations of
socialism," calling for abolition of foreign aid and withdrawal of the United States from the United Nations.
Yearning for an era which they refused to acknowledge had
long since vanished, they desperately sought to turn back
the clock. To these people the tall, handsome, white-
haired senator from the clean, wide-open spaces of Arizona
took on the dimensions of a Herculean figure who would
sweep away the Augean corruption and conspiracy from
the halls of government.

Barry Goldwater's own ideas were more the product of
emotional reactions than of careful study. Growing up in a
rapidly expanding western society where energy and hard
work could make dreams come true, he became a disciple
of the virtues of individualism. His formal education was
limited to a year at the University of Arizona, which he left
to enter the family merchandising business. Involvement in
public affairs was part of his family background. An uncle
whom he greatly admired, Morris Goldwater, had been instrumental in founding the Democratic party in Arizona,
had helped write the state's constitution, and was a member
of the state legislature and, for twenty-six years, Mayor of
Prescott. In 1952, Goldwater began his own political career.
Aided by the Eisenhower landslide—Goldwater described
himself as "the greatest coattail rider in history"—he won a
Senate seat against the Democratic incumbent. Six years
later he was re-elected.

At the 1960 convention, outraged at the "betrayal" of

Nixon's compact with Rockefeller, Goldwater had exhorted, "Let's grow up, conservatives! Let's, if we want to take this Party back—and I think we can some day—let's get to work." But Goldwater was an evangelist, not an organizer. The task of welding together the disaffected Republicans became the project of an organizing genius, F. Clifton White.

A dedicated conservative, White for ten years had been the controlling force in the National Federation of Young Republicans and consultant to business executives on ways and means of participating in political action. Without Goldwater's knowledge, he proceeded methodically in the summer of 1961 to lay the foundations for the senator's nomination as presidential candidate in 1964. After a series of four secret meetings during the next two years, beginning with a group of twenty-two key men, which increased to fifty-five, he succeeded in raising sufficient funds and generating enough interest to form a national Draft Goldwater committee. A rally sponsored by the committee on July 4, 1963, in Washington, D.C., was an astonishing success. Dozens of chartered buses from New York, Connecticut, Indiana, Texas, and other states brought thousands, who jammed the Armory to cheer their hero, present only in spirit.

By now, Goldwater, who had not repudiated White's efforts but had not encouraged them either, began to give serious consideration to his candidacy. He proceeded to gather a campaign staff. Victor Johnson, director of the Republican Senatorial Campaign Committee and a former Taft stalwart, became a worker for the cause, making scouting forays among Republican leaders throughout the country. In August, the senator's close friend, Denison Kitchel, although officially designated Goldwater's campaign manager for his re-election to the Senate, moved his office from Phoenix to an unmarked suite of offices one block from the Capitol. A group of conservative academicians was recruited to prepare position papers on economic policy and international affairs.

To facilitate building up local organizations, a computer was installed at headquarters for compiling lists of names and addresses of everyone who ever wrote to the senator on any subject or had ever expressed an interest in him. Kitchel proceeded to assemble a microfilm library of Goldwater's views expressed over the years in two books, 700 syndicated newspaper columns, innumerable interviews, and hundreds of public statements. To make all these words of wisdom readily available, Recordac Corporation, a subsidiary of Eastman Kodak, was employed to index the microfilm library on punch cards so that at the push of a button any public statement on any subject that he had ever made would be instantly available.

As soon as Goldwater announced his candidacy, the organization surfaced—a highly efficient operation which had already laid the groundwork for the state conventions and the seven primaries that the candidate had decided to enter. Punctilious attention was given to every detail. Two or three months before a state convention, the state chairman was requested to obtain, if possible, an estimate of the number of delegates that could be secured for Goldwater and to provide details about his precinct organizations. At a visit with a Goldwater representative which followed, he was encouraged to work among the precinct committeemen and county chairmen, urging the selection of delegates to the state convention who would be friendly to Goldwater's candidacy. Then, two or three weeks before the convention, the Goldwater man appeared again and discussed with him such matters as the chairmanship of the nominating and resolutions committees, what arrangement had been made to insure that delegates already selected would attend the convention, what could be done to have a resolution passed committing the delegates in advance. On the day of the convention, either Clifton White or Richard Kleindienst, a personal friend of Goldwater's recruited to head the national campaign, would arrive, accompanied by the regional director. Generally they asked permission to speak to the Goldwater delegates. They caucused at hotels with key leaders and distributed campaign materials, statements, buttons, bumper stickers.

In a nationwide television broadcast announcing his candidacy, Goldwater declared that he would not change his beliefs to win votes and would "offer a choice, not an echo." The campaign, he said, "will not be an engagement of personalities. It will be an engagement of principles." He stood for limited government against the increasing concentration of authority in Washington, for individual responsibility against regimentation. "I believe we must now make a choice in this land and not continue drifting endlessly down toward a time when all of us, our lives, our property, our hopes and even our prayers, will become just cogs in a vast government machine." Freedom at home and abroad could be won only by strength and determination. "And I believe that appeasement and weakness can only bring war. . . . My candidacy is pledged to a victory for principle and to presenting an opportunity for the American people to choose."

The first test of Goldwater's popular support came on March 10 when he was pitted against Rockefeller in the New Hampshire primary. Almost 90,000 Republicans slogged through snow and sleet to cast their ballots. The results confounded the most astute of political prognosticators. Both contestants were defeated by a man who was out of the country, whose name had not even appeared on the ballot, and whose entire campaign staff consisted of four amateurs operating on a shoestring—Ambassador Henry Cabot Lodge, who received an amazing 33,000 write-in votes. Goldwater, who had come into the state with the support of the machine created by the late Senator Styles Bridges, the senior Senator Norris Cotton, and the largest newspaper in the state, received 20,692 votes. Rockefeller won 19,504 votes and Nixon a write-in endorsement of 15,587.

Lodge expressed his gratification at the results but declared that he had no intention of resigning his post at Saigon. His elated quartet, however, began talking about raising a million-dollar fund to promote his cause in other states. Rockefeller, who had campaigned hard, was privately deeply disappointed; publicly he rationalized that the vote for Lodge represented support for a "favorite son" of New England as well as opposition to "extremism in the party." He pointed out that he had been a five-to-one underdog before the election, and the results only served to underscore the strength he could develop by continuing his active campaign. Goldwater, in his disarming manner, said that he had "goofed up somewhere."

Accustomed to "shooting from the lip" in the cozy intimacy of sympathetic audiences, Goldwater in New Hampshire continued to indulge in the same freewheeling statements, oblivious that now every utterance of his became public via the television cameras and newspaper reporters. Fuzzy-minded and lacking a quick wit, he frequently replied to questions in a way that distorted what he really meant. He made monumental blunders. In a state which had the fourth highest percentage of elderly and retired people in the Union, he declared that the social security system should be put on a voluntary basis. In a state where pro-United Nations sentiment was exceptionally strong, he asserted that the United States should withdraw its membership from that body if Red China were admitted. At one of the state colleges he told a student group that he had voted against federal aid to education because he did not think the colleges could possibly spend all the money they asked for. Lecturing his audience on economics, he contended that governments could not stop depressions, they only started them. And so on and on.

Commenting on Goldwater's performance, the London *Economist* observed, "Mr. Goldwater, who was joyously celebrated as Mr. Conservative by the party stalwarts only six months ago, has alienated some of his own admirers by scaring the daylights out of them." One month after the New Hampshire primary, a poll revealed that four out of ten Republicans considered the candidate too far to the right, and thirty-four per cent said they would not vote for him if he were chosen by the convention. As the Oregon primary approached, a poll in that state showed Lodge in the lead with forty-six per cent of the vote, Nixon, a poor second with seventeen per cent, and Goldwater and Rockefeller trailing with fourteen and thirteen per cent, respectively.

Goldwater decided to bypass Oregon and concentrate on California. Rockefeller, who by now felt that he had little chance of winning the nomination, hoped to stop Goldwater by proving that the Arizona senator had as little support in the West as he had in the East. He threw himself into the Oregon campaign, traveling tirelessly up and down the state, talking in urban shopping centers, in rural towns, shaking thousands of hands. The returns gave Rockefeller a striking 94,190 votes to Lodge's 79,169, Goldwater's 50,105, and Nixon's 48,000.

Greatly encouraged, Rockefeller felt that his campaign in behalf of liberal Republicanism might yet blunt the thrust of the extremists to take over the party. He was further heartened by the announcement of the Lodge people that they would support him in the forthcoming California primary. Apparently they had decided that his victory there would check Goldwater and perhaps lead to a convention deadlock from which their candidate would benefit. The encounter between the two wings of the party was now likely to prove decisive. If Goldwater could beat the combined opposition, he would surmount his poor showings in Oregon and New Hampshire and, with many delegates already committed to him, be virtually assured of the nomination.

In California, a state notorious for spawning weird, crackpot movements, where everything tends to be oversized and exaggerated, political warfare is also more intense. The rift between Republican factions in the state had been endemic since 1912, when Governor Hiram Johnson led the Progressives in their battle against the Taft wing of the party. Now the two factions reached for each other's jugular, but the right wing, which included such extremists as members of the John Birch Society, clawed with razor-sharp talons and frenzied determination.

Probably the most effective force working for Goldwater was the horde of dedicated volunteers. In Southern California, thousands were organized and marshaled by Robert Gaston, the zealous leader of the Young Republicans. Beginning in the spring, he mapped out a campaign, dividing Los Angeles County into six areas to which he sent 10,000 volunteer doorbell ringers to canvass registered Republicans. While the Rockefeller supporters had to pay their people to collect signatures for the qualifying petitions or address envelopes or man the "telephone mills," eager Goldwater followers besieged headquarters, offering their services free. Profiting from his New Hampshire experience, Goldwater escaped the hazards of impromptu remarks by avoiding press conferences and appearances at small gatherings.

Rockefeller barnstormed up and down the state, shaking hands outside of supermarkets and at organized receptions from early morning to nightfall. "On both sides," observed a New York *Times* reporter, "there is all the panoply of a full-fledged Presidential showdown—the bands, the placards . . . the fetchingly clad nymphets with plastic 'Rocky' skimmers, the collegiate folk-singers twisting 'Hello, Dolly' into 'Hello, Barry.'" But neither candidate came to grips with a single major national issue. They offered, as James Reston commented, "a bedlam of obscurities . . . whether Goldwater was reckless about the Communists and heartless about the old and poor . . . whether Rockefeller and the 'Eastern Liberal Establishment' were trying to 'buy' or 'kidnap' the Republican party."

Almost until the very end the polls showed Rockefeller with a considerable lead. Eisenhower, persuaded to define his ideal candidate, declared that Republicans, as the party of Lincoln, had "a particular obligation to be vigorous in the furtherance of civil rights." He urged "loyal support" for the United Nations and asserted that in a nuclear age there was no room for "impulsiveness." A perfect description of

Rockefeller's position, his statement by implication appeared to be directed against Goldwater. Then two things happened which tilted the balance. Three days before the California election, the birth of a son to the Rockefellers spotlighted again the candidate's divorce and remarriage. And one day before, Eisenhower in an interview declared that any inference that he was supporting one candidate against the other was completely unjustified. The convention, he said, must remain open for all contenders. "General Eisenhower camped out for the winter in Palm Springs," a columnist later wrote, "marched up the hills against Senator Goldwater two weeks before the California primary, then marched down again the day before it."

Goldwater carried California by 50,000 votes, or 51.6 per cent. His greatest strength was in the southern part of the state where, in Los Angeles and Orange counties alone, his margin was 207,000 votes. In the Bay Area counties around San Francisco, Rockefeller won by 106,000 votes. Goldwater's victory was a close one, but of sufficient psychological impact to start the band wagon. He already had about 280 delegates "locked up," whom White's organization of devoted workers had garnered at the state conventions. During the next two weeks at conventions held in various states, enough support was rounded up to give the Senator the majority of 655 required for the nomination.

The cost of the primary campaign for both contenders was the highest on record—approximately $10 million. Although the Goldwater people had continually wailed that they could not compete with the resources of their millionaire opponent, they actually exceeded Rockefeller's outlay by a half million dollars. Senator Goldwater was more than able to match Rockefeller with the support from wealthy and middle-income backers he had attracted during the years he had served as chairman of the Republican Senate Campaign Committee, and also because his staff had tapped new sources of wealth through direct-mail fundraising techniques.

Goldwater had fulfilled his promise to offer a choice and

not an echo. His position was unmistakable, even if it was often difficult to make sense of the ambiguities and contradictions with which he peppered his remarks. He could not be accused of deception in his efforts to secure the nomination.

As the convention drew near, the moderates in the Republican party were in a state of shock. The inconceivable had happened—an openly ideological candidate whose nomination would defy all the traditional rules of consensus, coalition, and brokerage politics loomed as their standard-bearer. They could foresee only disaster in November.

Those leaders who might possibly have combined to stop Goldwater failed to do so either because of their own lust for the prize or because they had been gripped by inertia. None of the potential aspirants—neither Richard M. Nixon nor William W. Scranton nor George Romney—had supported Rockefeller in California. Confident that he would win, they believed that he and Goldwater would be stalemated at the convention, leaving the way open for a compromise candidate. And Eisenhower, who might have exerted a crucial influence, persisted in remaining an immaculate figure "above the battle."

A great deal of feverish commotion that approached the farcical ensued, but little concrete progress was made on uniting behind a candidate. Rumors were abundant: Nixon was supporting Romney, Nixon was not supporting Romney; Eisenhower was supporting Scranton, Eisenhower was not supporting Scranton. Governor Scranton himself was thoroughly muddled by the ex-President's tacking, by the division and confusion among party leaders, some of whom urged that they now close ranks behind the obvious nominee, while others felt that Romney should enter the race. Finally, with considerable reluctance, Scranton decided to try for the nomination when Goldwater voted in the Senate against cloture on the Civil Rights bill, in effect voting against the bill. Scranton felt very deeply that the Republican party must not be permitted to turn its back on the

Lincoln tradition. Goldwater had made it plain that he was unequivocally opposed to the legislation, but apparently Scranton had believed he would change his position if his nomination seemed likely.

For five weeks, from June 11 to July 15, Scranton valiantly attempted to perform the miracle of luring delegates away from Goldwater. The situation was hopeless, however, despite the support of Rockefeller, Romney, Lodge, Milton Eisenhower (the former President remained inscrutably silent, as did Nixon, who still hoped to emerge as the beneficiary of a deadlock), an expenditure of $80,000, and a devoted and energetic staff. There simply was not enough time to overcome the effects of years of careful planning and laborious work. Wherever Scranton went, Goldwaterites had been there before him, and, as Senator Dirksen commented, the commitment to Goldwater was "as tight as wallpaper." All that could be done was to appeal directly to the rank and file over the heads of the delegates.

On the weekend before the convention opened at the Cow Palace in San Francisco, a number of eastern leaders, including Governor Rockefeller, Ambassador Lodge, and Senators Keating and Javits of New York, Case of New Jersey, and Scott of Pennsylvania, met with Scranton to plan eleventh-hour strategy. Seeking some means by which to crack the tightly disciplined and controlled phalanx of Goldwater supporters, they decided that the platform provided the best vehicle with which to launch an offensive. During the previous two weeks a Goldwater-dominated Resolutions Committee had succeeded in blocking every effort of the moderates to liberalize the platform, and it was decided to challenge their report on civil rights, extremism, and control of nuclear weapons. A detailed and strongly worded amendment on civil rights would be offered to substitute for "the generalities" of the approved plank. The John Birch Society would be condemned as an extremist organization, thereby bringing into the open the explosive issue of Goldwater's support by this radical right-wing group. As to nuclear weapons, it would be proposed that the President alone should control their use, an implication that Goldwater's recommendation of discretionary authority by field commanders indicated that he was "trigger happy," which raised the question of his fitness for the office he sought.

Another tactical move, which subsequently boomeranged, was that Scranton challenge Goldwater to open debate on the convention floor. Scranton, spinning from caucus to caucus to exhort and plead, had no time to attend personally to the necessary details. He gave general instructions to his staff members, who composed a letter, had it signed in his name by a secretary, and delivered it to Goldwater without even showing it to Scranton. A stinging indictment of "Goldwaterism," the request for a debate began by asking whether "the convention will choose the candidate overwhelmingly favored by the Republican voters or will it choose you?" Goldwater's organization, it went on, admitted that he was a minority candidate, "but they feel they have bought, beaten and compromised enough delegate support to make the result a forgone conclusion. With open contempt for the dignity, integrity and common sense of the convention, your managers say in effect that the delegates are little more than a flock of chickens whose necks will be wrung at will." Goldwater was accused of "casually" prescribing nuclear war as a solution to world problems, of allowing the radical extremists to use him, and of irresponsibility on the race question. "In short, Goldwaterism has come to stand for a whole crazy-quilt collection of absurd and dangerous positions that would be soundly repudiated by the American people in November."

Livid with anger, Goldwater showed the letter to his staff. Someone suggested that it be turned over to the press and photographic copies distributed to the delegates. About 4,000 copies were run off and sent out with a covering memorandum: "I am attaching a copy of a letter I received from Governor Scranton. I consider it an insult to every Republican in San Francisco. Barry." While Scranton said that he had had no part in writing the letter, he refused to disclaim responsibility for it. The only effect was to intensify an atmosphere already rancorous when the convention opened.

The keynote speaker, Governor Mark Hatfield of Oregon, began with the usual call to arms for the party to unite and the customary attack upon the opposition. But then the party cleavage surfaced when he declared, "There are bigots in this nation who spew forth their venom of hate. They parade under hundreds of labels, including the Communist party, the Ku Klux Klan, and the John Birch Society. They must be overcome." Less than half the delegates responded, their applause sounding faint in the cavernous hall. The following day Hatfield was bombarded with telegrams and letters, most of which denounced him for his "controversial" statement.

Anticipating a ruckus over the platform, the convention managers arranged for the scheduled address by Eisenhower to precede the debate, hopeful that it would reduce the tension. Eisenhower's speech was in the classic tradition of a party leader assailing the iniquities of the opponents. As an elder statesman he counseled unity, warning that only the party loses when factions are pitted against each other. Then, toward the end, he demolished everything he had tried to build up with some remarks which he had inserted into the prepared text. "Let us particularly scorn the divisive efforts of those outside our family, including sensation-seeking columnists and commentators, because, my friends, I assure you that these are people who couldn't care less about the good of our party."

The hall burst into a frenzied jeering and booing at the "enemy," the journalistic segment of the "liberal establishment," the conspirators of the press who had consistently maligned the true custodians of American patriotism. Some delegates leaped to their feet and shook their fists at the reporters in the television booths.

When the tumult had subsided, the platform was read and then the debate began on the three "stop Goldwater" amendments, each speaker being allotted five minutes.

Governor Rockefeller rose to present the one on extremism. He was greeted by a faint patter of applause followed immediately by an outburst of boos from the gallery which rocked the hall and merged into shrieks of "We want Barry! We want Barry!" Cowbells clanged wildly, trumpets and horns resounded, and a bass drum boomed. Chairman Thruston Morton pounded his gavel for some minutes before order was restored. As Rockefeller spoke he was constantly interrupted by jeers and shrieks, until at one point he interrupted his address to say icily, "This is still a free country, ladies and gentlemen," to which the ladies and gentlemen responded with derisive shouts. Trying to make himself heard above the raucous din, he recalled his experience in the California primary and that of "countless others who have also experienced anonymous midnight and early morning telephone calls, unsigned threatening letters, smear and hate literature, strong-arm and goon tactics, bomb threats and bombings, infiltration and take-over of established political organizations by Communist and Nazi methods. Some of you don't like to hear it, ladies and gentlemen, but it's the truth." More screams, shrill to the point of hysteria.

Television viewers were appalled at this treatment of one of the leading figures in the Republican party and shocked at the uninhibited malevolence. Goldwater organizational workers, moving through the galleries, tried vainly to curb the clamor, a terrifying exhibition of what fanaticism can breed.

The proposed amendment and the two that followed were quickly and overwhelmingly defeated. Eastern moderates and their supporters were decisively routed. What followed the next day was a mere formality. After seven hours of nominating and seconding speeches for eight candidates, the balloting began. Goldwater received 883 votes on the first ballot to Scranton's 214. Bedlam broke loose. While Scranton—some thought graciously, some ignominiously—appeared on the platform to urge that the nomination be unanimous, other leaders such as Rockefeller, Javits, and Keating either sat in stony silence or walked out of the hall in protest.

To add to the humiliation of the eastern liberals, Goldwater selected as his running mate the arch-conservative William E. Miller, chairman of the party's national committee and congressman from New York for fourteen years. His religion, Roman Catholic, was considered an asset in attempting to bring back to the fold those voters who had supported Kennedy in 1960. However, a tough campaigner, with the reputation of being attracted to the visceral aspect of politics, he lacked the stature that would inspire confidence in his capacity for leadership were he to become President. Goldwater was said to have remarked, "One reason I chose Miller is that he drives Johnson nuts."

In keeping with the evangelism of the Goldwater crusade, the band blared "The Battle Hymn of the Republic" as the candidate walked to the platform to give his acceptance speech. Then, like a prophet who came to deliver the nation from portending cataclysm, to destroy false idols in partnership with the Almighty, he intoned, "The Good Lord raised this mighty Republic to be a home for the brave and to flourish as the land of the free—not to stagnate in the swampland of collectivism, not to cringe before the bullying of Communism." He called on his party "to free our people and light the way for liberty throughout the world." He indicted the administration for its foreign policy and for offering the people at home "bread and circuses" instead of moral leadership—there was violence in the streets and corruption in high office.

Those who expected that in his hour of triumph the candidate would hold out the olive branch to his defeated rivals were stunned when he declared, "Anyone who joins us in all sincerity we welcome. Those who do not care for our cause, we don't expect to enter our ranks in any case. . . . I would remind you that *extremism in the defense of liberty is no vice! . . . moderation in the pursuit of justice is no virtue!*"*

* The italicized words were underlined in the candidate's text.

Goldwater had defiantly thumbed his nose at those in the party who had opposed him, reopening, as a New York *Times* correspondent observed, "the wounds inflicted on the Republican party by the contests over its platform and Presidential nomination during the national convention." Moreover, by these gratuitous remarks he emboldened the right-wing fanatics and followers of groups like the John Birch Society whom the responsible conservatives sought to keep in check. Even Eisenhower was upset, stating that "the passage conjured up a philosophy that the end justifies the means and that vigilantes and nightriders are entirely acceptable if their purpose is 'the defense of liberty' or 'the pursuit of justice.'"

The candidate, the platform, the proceedings of the 1964 Republican convention made it obvious that the party had been captured by a right-wing faction which sought the reversal of a well-established trend in the nation's domestic and foreign policies. Not even Taft conservatism, which had opposed "me tooism," urging that the voters be given a wider choice, had gone so far. On every major issue the party had abandoned or sharply modified the stand taken in the 1960 platform. The civil rights plank had been watered down by eliminating the promise of "vigorous enforcement" of civil rights legislation and, by pledging "improvements" in the statutes, seemed to suggest that the way would be opened for repeal of the sections on public accommodation and employment in the 1964 law. No mention was made, as in 1960, about expanding the unemployment insurance system or adopting a plan of federal grants for the needy. On medical care for the aged, the plank was so worded as to make the plan essentially a relief measure. In foreign policy, the earlier conciliatory position toward the Soviet Union was changed to a militant one with a repeated emphasis on "victory." Support of the United Nations was equivocal, and disarmament was viewed negatively by contrast with the 1960 approach of seeking means to negotiate and maintain peace.

This ultraconservative stand, Goldwater strategists were confident, could attract a winning coalition. They counted on 127 electoral votes from the eleven states of the Old Confederacy, where Republicans had made deep inroads in recent years among the business elements of the cities and suburbs, and in the rabidly segregationist rural areas. Traditionally Republican states such as Nebraska, Kansas, Indiana, Wyoming, Colorado, and the Dakotas should yield another 50 or so. Arizona, Kentucky, and Oklahoma, they were sure, would fall in, which meant 22 votes. If Ohio, Illinois, and California, with a total of 92 votes, could be won, Goldwater would have an electoral majority without having to score in a single one of the Atlantic seaboard states which were regarded as lost to liberalism.

The campaign strategy for the mountain and far western states was to exploit the anti-East and anti-big-government sentiments; for the Midwest, to capitalize on the traditional antagonism to big cities among small-town and rural voters; and, in cities throughout the country, to focus on fear of communism and on the "white backlash" created by resentment against Negroes, who were considered to be demanding too much. In addition, Goldwaterites were counting on the "silent vote," those millions of Americans who for years presumably had abstained from voting for a President because they had been offered only an "echo" and would jubilantly flock to the polls when given a "choice."

Before operations could be started, however, it was imperative to find some sort of balm to heal the abrasions of the party leaders that Goldwater had rubbed raw with the ill-chosen words he had flung at them in his acceptance speech. The candidate began by traveling to Gettysburg on August 6 for a conference with Eisenhower. After the meeting, he reported that the former President was "very enthusiastic" about the campaign and had already scheduled several speeches on his behalf. Three days later he released the text of letters exchanged with Nixon in which he "clarified" his "extremism in defense of liberty" statement. "If I were to paraphrase the two sentences in question in the context in which I uttered them, I would do it by saying that wholehearted devotion to liberty is unassailable, and that half-hearted devotion to justice is indefensible."

Next he called a conference of Republican leaders, which included Eisenhower, Nixon, Rockefeller, and Romney, at Hershey, Pennsylvania, on August 12. It was a chastened Goldwater, seeking to convince his listeners that he was not out of the "mainstream" of the party, who addressed the group. He pledged, if elected, a return to "the proven policy of peace through strength," that he would first consult Eisenhower or Nixon before appointing secretaries of State and Defense, and that his administration would try to repair the nation's alliances and work with America's allies for freedom and peace. He would unconditionally support the purposes of the United Nations and cooperate fully with that organization. He also reassured them "lest there be any doubt in anyone's mind," that he supported the social security system. As to the Negro problem, he pledged to execute faithfully the 1964 Civil Rights Act.

In a plea for unity, he asserted, "We seek to read no one out of this party. We seek instead to make room for all and to insure a climate . . . in which all of us will feel comfortable and at home. In this campaign we want and we need the help of every Republican if we are to win in November." Finally, he said that he did not seek the support of any extremists, whether of the left or the right. "We repudiate character assassins, vigilantes, communists, and any group such as the Ku Klux Klan that seeks to impose its views through terror or threat or violence." Conspicuous by its absence from the category of extremists was the John Birch Society.

After the meeting Eisenhower told a press conference that he would support the ticket wholeheartedly. "Any uncertainties I may have felt as to the fitness and adequacy of the political program [of the candidates] have been resolved." He had asked Goldwater to clarify his views, which he had done, and he was now fully satisfied. "I am right on his team as much as he wants me."

For some of the other Republican leaders, however, the

potion was ineffective. Governor Rockefeller made no public statements but refrained from campaigning for the ticket outside his own state. Governor Romney dissociated himself from Goldwater in his own re-election campaign. The other dissident governors maneuvered so as to avoid appearing with the candidate. Both Republican senators from New York, Kenneth Keating, who was up for re-election, and Jacob Javits, flatly refused to endorse him. Some mumbled that they would support him but went no further than feebly expressed intentions. Three southern Democratic governors, Wallace of Alabama, Johnson of Mississippi, and Faubus of Arkansas, apparently did not take Goldwater's effort to appease the moderate faction seriously, for shortly after the meeting they indicated their intention to support him in the campaign.

The choice of a candidate presented no problem for the Democrats when they convened at Atlantic City. Lyndon Baines Johnson had demonstrated his qualifications for the Presidency from the moment he entered the White House. In a brilliant display of his famed legislative leadership, he began almost immediately to move the Kennedy program through Congress. Both moderates and conservatives in the party were pleased with the new administration. Senator Richard Russell of Georgia, long the leader of the congressional southern phalanx, announced that he would back Johnson, thereby blocking prospects for an effective Dixiecrat revolt. Liberals, too, were satisfied. They were impressed by the Civil Rights Act signed into law in July, Johnson's urgent plea for enactment of the Medicare bill, and his war on poverty, which extended President Kennedy's attack on the chronically depressed situation in Appalachia to include the entire nation.

In the spring, the President announced that he would not enter any primaries. He would do the best job in office of which he was capable and let the delegates at the convention "freely" decide on a candidate. Meanwhile, he was receiving the kind of exposure from television and the press available only to the man in the White House. Almost daily the newspapers carried some item or some statistics which he supplied on the country's burgeoning prosperity. Johnson could act as though he were oblivious of the pending election, running the country rather than running for office, but his many activities and statements inevitably focused attention upon his leadership.

Except for two fund-raising dinners, engagements made prior to Kennedy's death, he made no "political" speeches. As he traveled over the country, he besought his fellow Americans to join with him in the challenging task of creating the great society and fulfilling the promise of American life. In the South, speaking as one native of the region to another, he urged that the Civil Rights Act be accepted and that the dead issues of the past be interred. The President had a good word and a promise for every segment of society. Organized labor was gratified by the easy access to the White House enjoyed by its leaders. Farmers were promised a higher income through proposed agricultural legislation. The aged and aging could anticipate relief from the nagging fear of being impoverished by high medical costs. This was the stuff from which consensus politics was made.

While the presidential nomination would be a mere formality, the convention was not to be free of controversy. Even before the scheduled opening at Atlantic City on August 24, the civil rights issue precipitated a clash. The dispute began over the seating of delegations from Alabama and Mississippi.

A law passed by the Alabama state legislature provided for a slate of unpledged electors who were obligated only to vote for a Democrat in the electoral college; they need not endorse the official nominee of the party if they did not so desire. From the other state, a predominantly Negro delegation of sixty-eight members and alternates of the newly organized Mississippi Freedom Democratic Party was challenging the legality of seating the regular delegation on the grounds that Negroes were systematically barred from the party. Throughout the South, Negroes, demanding equal treatment under the law and seeking to exercise their constitutional right of the ballot, were being beaten, arrested, and terrorized. In Alabama and Mississippi, the struggle was particularly intense, with homes and churches being bombed.

The proceedings of the Credentials Committee were telecast, and the nation watched and listened with incredulity to accounts by Negro witnesses of the barbarities to which they were subjected by law enforcement agencies to keep them from the polls. While the Freedom Democratic Party undoubtedly had morality on its side, its delegates had been chosen outside the established legal framework.

After three days of stormy wrangling, a compromise formula was adopted. Both the Alabama and Mississippi delegations would be seated provided they signed a "loyalty oath" to support the party ticket; two members of the Freedom group would be seated as delegates-at-large, and hereafter at future conventions no delegates would be admitted from states where citizens were deprived of their right to vote because of race or color. Most of the delegates from the two states promptly walked out in protest, but there was no mass exodus as had occurred in 1948. Johnson was prepared to write off the Dixiecrat elements, confident, in view of Goldwater's nomination, that the party could win handily without them.

The platform on the whole was less militantly liberal than the 1960 document. To avoid chafing the South further, the civil rights plank was moderated, pledging simply "full observance" of the recently enacted Civil Rights Act and "fair, effective enforcement if there is any default." With the advantage of meeting after their opponents, the Democrats could make a point of including planks that the Goldwater forces had rejected at San Francisco. On the use of nuclear weapons, control "must remain solely with the highest elected official in the country—the President of the United States." Extremism was condemned "whether from the right or left, including the extreme tactics of such organizations as the Communist party, the Ku Klux Klan and the John Birch Society." The nuclear test ban treaty was acclaimed as a significant and positive achievement, and renewed efforts to halt the perilous arms race were pledged. Firm resistance to the Communist danger was affirmed, but, apparently intending to underscore the image of Goldwater as reckless and impulsive, the Democrats were more restrained in their rhetoric than their opponents. The deliberations on the platform were completely harmonious: "There's no unhappiness about anything," one committeeman remarked.

The greatest excitement at the convention was occasioned by the choice of a vice-presidential candidate. The death in office of Roosevelt and Kennedy underscored the necessity for selecting the man carefully. Speculation was rife through the spring and summer as names kept bobbing up and down while the President gave no indication of his preference. As Johnson enjoyed remarkable popularity, he was not unduly concerned about the traditional requirement for balancing the ticket. The President told some key members of his staff that he was seeking the man best qualified for the office "in case I fell out of an airplane tomorrow morning."

Early in the spring, the name which appeared most frequently in the press as a possibility was that of Attorney General Robert F. Kennedy. The late President's brother had many passionately devoted partisans eager to promote him for the office, to keep alive through him the Kennedy heritage. Kennedy-for-Vice-President clubs sprouted everywhere. In an effort to put pressure on the President, a write-in campaign was launched just prior to the New Hampshire primary. It was promptly disavowed by Kennedy, who issued a statement that the President should be free to make his own choice and, therefore, he wished "to discourage any efforts in his behalf in New Hampshire and elsewhere."

By midsummer, Johnson had definitely ruled out Kennedy. The announcement was made obliquely at a news conference on July 30 when he informed the press that all members of his Cabinet had been eliminated from consideration for the vice-presidency. Two days before, at a private meeting with Kennedy, he told the Attorney General that he believed he would some day lead the country, but "this is not the year and the Vice Presidency is not the route." Johnson's decision was not surprising. The two men were temperamentally antithetical; more important, to win an election with the brother of the man about whom a mystique had already begun to develop would cloud his victory. The haunting question would persist: had he won on his own strength or because of the Kennedy name, the Kennedy glamour? Moreover, once in office, Kennedy with his devoted following would be a potential threat to his leadership of the party.

Of the two strongest possibilities now, Senators Hubert Horatio Humphrey and Eugene J. McCarthy, the former increasingly seemed the more likely choice. Humphrey, fifty-three, agreeably combined the qualities of intellectual depth and political skill. The son of a small-town pharmacist in South Dakota, he was compelled to leave the University of Minnesota during the depression. Returning after his marriage six years later, he graduated *magna cum laude*. A master's degree in political science while teaching at the University of Louisiana followed. For several years he was a college instructor until he decided to make politics his career. He was elected mayor of Minneapolis in 1945, re-elected, and, at thirty-seven, running on the Democratic-Farmer-Labor ticket, was sent to the Senate. A consistent record of support for progressive legislation, civil rights, and peace measures made him the idol of the liberals, while his pragmatic and undoctrinaire approach to politics won him the esteem of moderates and conservatives.

Initially, Humphrey, who had always been close to Johnson, believed that he was his choice, but it soon became apparent that he was only one fish in the pool. To promote his candidacy, a group of his most intimate associates began to hold weekly and biweekly strategy meetings as early as February. They conferred with politicians, labor officials, and publishers and deluged influential individuals with news articles, editorials, and public opinion polls, urging all to inform the President that Humphrey was their choice. Humphrey himself attended banquets, made speeches, and did whatever he could to bring himself to public attention.

Early in August, Johnson sent James Rowe, one of his trusted advisors, on a strange mission. He was to interrogate Humphrey on his private life, much as a man might be investigated when considered for a classified civil service post: what was his financial status, his assets, his debts; was there anything in his financial record which could be a political liability; what was his war record; had there been any romantic episodes in his past that might prove embarrassing?

Until Wednesday, the day before nominations were to be made at the convention, Johnson kept the press and the nation dangling. Starting early that morning, he was on the phone calling people all over the country for their opinions. By his own estimate he reached twenty-five to thirty governors, thirty-five senators, at least thirty-five congressmen, and innumerable newspaper publishers, editors, educators, labor leaders, and businessmen. Indefatigably he led a group of perspiring reporters trotting after him in the 89-degree heat around the White House lawn while he chatted about inconsequentials. Finally, he mentioned casually that he was asking Humphrey to come down from Atlantic City that afternoon to see him.

Actually, Johnson already had made up his mind, and all this was an attempt to wring the last drops of drama out of the occasion. When Humphrey arrived, the President took off on a lengthy monologue about the relationship between a President and Vice-President and the place of the latter in the scheme of things. Then Mrs. Humphrey was called in to hear the good news. Then a brief press conference. And then, at last, on to Atlantic City. Never before had such a grandstand effort been made to select a running mate.

Arriving at the convention, Johnson with his customary

lack of inhibition in seeking the spotlight and against all precedent marched up to the platform, took the Speaker's gavel, silenced the delegates, and announced his choice for the vice-presidency. The rest was predictable. Johnson and Humphrey were nominated by acclamation, after which the hall burst into gay pandemonium, the thousands of delegates singing, dancing, and shouting as the music blared and balloons and streamers showered down.

For the Democrats, the nomination of the ultraconservative Goldwater was a free gift, permitting them to pre-empt the politically attractive center position. In his acceptance speech, Johnson called the Democrats "a party for all Americans," and Humphrey reminded his audience that Senator Barry Goldwater, whom he labeled "the temporary Republican spokesman," had voted against such measures as the Nuclear Test Ban Treaty, the Civil Rights Act, the tax cut of 1964, and the United Nations bond issue, despite the fact that his own party had supported them.

Party strategists were confident of victory as they prepared for the campaign. Encouraged by every public and private poll, they were even optimistic about a landslide. Still, there were some imponderables which could not be measured. Continual civil rights demonstrations and race riots in northern cities could produce a "white backlash," a reaction indicated by the response to the outspokenly segregationist George Wallace of Alabama, who had come north in the spring to challenge Democratic party leadership in the primaries. In Wisconsin he had received one third of the total party vote; in Indiana, nearly thirty per cent; in Maryland forty-three per cent in a contest against the governor of the state. If the war in Vietnam escalated, if economic deterioration set in, if the President suffered a heart attack, all hopes and calculations could be wrecked.

The campaign organizations of both parties were highly efficient, but Johnson enjoyed the advantage of aides and political experts of extraordinarily high caliber, some of whom had worked for John F. Kennedy. In addition, a unique group calling itself the "Five O'Clock Club," consisting of able young lawyers and junior officials, performed valuable service by preceding or tailing the Republican candidate and providing material to the local paper or local Democratic politicians with which to refute his statements. On occasion they even managed to obtain advance copies of his talks so that the local press carried a reply to his address in the same issue in which it was reported.

Though the Goldwater operation was streamlined from the strategy board, which met regularly, down to the latest teletype machines, charts, and diagrams, it was hampered in several ways. The conservative intellectual who might have been expected to contribute ideas and suggestions or help write the speeches remained aloof, so that the burden on the few speech writers was crushing. Goldwater himself never attended any of the strategy sessions. Relying on his aides to serve as liaisons, he deprived his organization of the customary leadership.

Thousands of billboards up and down the country proclaimed, alongside the serious, handsome face of the candidate, "In Your Heart You Know He's Right." Goldwater had promised "a choice, not an echo," and that much he fulfilled. But the contents of the package he served up were either archiac, hollow, bewildering, or logically inconsistent, or perhaps, most of all, alarming.

In his opening address of the campaign, Goldwater delivered a little sermon on morality, in which the words "faith, hope, honor, purpose" kept jostling each other. He urged the voters to join him in "a good and noble cause," to purify their lives, to seek "greatness of heart and self-restraint." Then, a few paragraphs down, he called for greater military strength but for an end to the military draft.

During the following weeks he railed against what he called a dictatorial administration "that has even given you a number to replace a name." Republicans, he continued, "want to give you your freedom and your names back again" and return the government to the people. In one farming area he condoled with his listeners (better off than they had been in years) for living under this "mess of oppression." If the concentration of power could be halted, he said, their children would be able to live in freedom. In another place he thundered, "What good is prosperity if you are a slave . . . And what good is peace if you are not free?" His audience stared at him uncomprehendingly. Where were the chains about which he was speaking so passionately?

Repeatedly Goldwater decried lawlessness in the streets and the rising crime rate, suggesting that these were a direct result of the social welfare policies of the government or implying their connection with the civil rights movement. In one talk he declared that lack of leadership "has turned our streets into jungles, brought our public and private morals to the lowest state in history." His opponents were quick to respond with FBI statistics showing that his own Phoenix, where he had once served on the city council, had one of the highest crime rates in the nation.

His faculty for stomping flat-footedly on sensitive toes was a crushing liability. In the heart of the Tennessee Valley country, he repeated an earlier suggestion that the public power project should be sold to private enterprise. Not surprisingly, bumper stickers soon appeared reading, "Sell TVA? I'd rather sell Arizona." In West Virginia, the heart of the chronically depressed Appalachia poverty belt, he inveighed against the anti-poverty program, deriding President Johnson's "Great Society," in which, he declared, there would be no penalty for failure and no reward for success. "Human misery is not to be trifled with just to get votes in an election," he told the destitute people.

Goldwater raised hackles everywhere when he charged that President Kennedy had risked an atomic war with the Soviet Union for the sake of picking up votes in the congressional elections. Kennedy, he said, had deliberately timed the Cuban missile crisis for maximum domestic political effectiveness. And the present administration, he warned, was concerned about American and allied interests abroad only when it would result in votes for Johnson: "If an element of foreign policy hurts Lyndon Johnson's election chances, forget it. If it helps his election chances, assign ten press agents to it."

The Republican candidate's own position on foreign policy was unmitigatedly bellicose. He pledged militant resistance to communism, identifying disarmament with appeasement. He drew an analogy between the so-called "no win" policy in Vietnam and the defeat he claimed America had sustained in Korea. The administration, he stated, was "soft" on communism, and the Democrats were the party of "the corrupt, the power-mad and the radicals of the left."

With his views on record in three books, hundreds of columns and thousands of speeches, and the ill-considered remarks which he scattered before and after his nomination, Goldwater became indelibly etched on the public mind as "trigger happy." At a press conference in October 1963, he suggested that the supreme commander of the NATO forces be allowed more freedom in using nuclear weapons. The following June he repeated his position in an interview with the German publication, *Der Spiegel*. In August 1964, he asserted that "a way must be developed to provide NATO with its own stock of small, tactical, nuclear battlefield weapons—what may truly be called, and ultimately will be called, conventional weapons." He became identified with a policy of using atomic bombs in Southeast Asia when he responded to a question on a television program in May 1964 by recommending that "low yield atomic weapons" be employed to defoliate the forests of North Vietnam. The grim words "nuclear weapons," "holocaust," "push the button," "mass destruction" sputtered from speech after speech—one New York *Times* correspondent counted almost twenty-six in one address in as many minutes. Throughout the campaign the Democrats used with devastating effect the slogan, "In your heart, you know he might."

Goldwater had presented his opponents with a ready-made theme, his "extremism," on which a multitude of variations could be played. The Democrats denounced him as antilabor, declaring that if elected he would jeopardize gains won by the workers over the past thirty years. They spotlighted ambiguities in his statements to demonstrate that he did not know his own mind. Most important, he was portrayed as a man who made snap judgments on vital matters. "The big issue, I think, is peace—peace or war," one strategist said. "I think what most people want to know is whose hand is next to that nuclear panic button. We are going to stress responsibility versus irresponsibility in high office."

Two atrocious television "spots" were prepared to fix the image of Goldwater as reckless with the nation's welfare and ready to push the button which would plunge the world into unimaginable devastation. One showed a little girl licking an ice cream cone while a woman's gentle voice was telling her that atomic bombs used to be exploded in the air, that radioactive fallout made children die, and that the man who wanted to be President of the United States had voted against the treaty outlawing all but underground nuclear tests. "His name is Barry Goldwater," the soft voice went on, "so if he's elected, they might start testing all over again." The clicking of a Geiger counter rose to a crescendo as she concluded, and then a forceful male voice exhorted, "Vote for President Johnson on November third. The stakes are too high for you to stay at home." The other opened with a close-up of a little girl counting the petals of a daisy which she was plucking. The film gradually dissolved into a countdown at an atomic site and then the horrifying mushroom cloud flashed on the screen as Johnson's voice intoned, "These are the stakes: To make a world in which all of God's children can live, or go into the dark. We must either love each other or we must die."

Even Democrats were repelled by the blatancy of this propaganda and protested to the National Committee. Both pieces were soon withdrawn, but these "political commercials" were defended by some partisans as dramatizing the possible consequences of Goldwater's position. In fact, however, they pointed up the all too prevalent tendency in a campaign to generate fear as a substitute for rational discussion.

Johnson in his first campaign address dealt with nuclear weapons and presidential responsibility, assailing the stand his opponent had become associated with. There was no such thing, he said, as a conventional nuclear weapon. For nineteen years no nation had used the atom bomb. To delegate authority for its use now could lead to horrifying consequences. It involved "a political decision of the highest order. . . . No President of the United States can divest himself of the responsibility for such a decision." On another occasion, making a direct slap at Senator Goldwater's charges that the administration in pursuing "accommodations" was "soft" on communism, he declared, "The world's hopes for peace cannot be left with those who have no faith in the possibility of lasting agreements, and who readily predict war. . . . The future of man should not be trusted to those who would tear down the institutions and policies which a threatened world has carefully built for its own protection." At still another time he emphasized the necessity for peaceful solutions as against policies that would hurl the nation into war. "In such a world as this," he said, "a nuclear world, there is no room for bluster and bluff and belligerence. There is room only for courage, intelligence and reason." The opposition, he continued, "sound as if force or the threat of force can solve all problems, and this is dangerous."

Dealing with the American commitment in Vietnam, Johnson referred to a suggestion he said had been made by Goldwater that the war be extended into the north. "There are those that say you ought to go north and drop bombs, to try to wipe out the supply lines. . . . We don't want our American boys to do the fighting for Asian boys. We don't want to get . . . tied down in a land war in Asia." Several days later, talking to a group of New Hampshire editors, he said, "Before I start dropping bombs around the country, I would want to think about the consequences of getting American boys into a war with 700 million Chinese." He was saddened, he went on, by the rising casualty list (190 at that point), "but it's not like the 190,000 we might lose the first month if we escalated that war. We're not going north and drop bombs at this stage of the game, and we're not going south and run out and let the Communists take over either." As the campaign drew to a close, the President reiterated, "We are not about to send American boys nine or ten thousand miles away from home to do what Asian boys ought to be doing for themselves." While he was uttering these reassurances, administration plans, started months ago, were under way to escalate the war by bombing North Vietnam.* Thus on a vital issue, Johnson had created the impression that he represented a decided alternative to his "trigger-happy" opponent.

Throughout the campaign Johnson refrained from mentioning Goldwater directly. He could leave the "hatcheting" to others, such as the gifted Humphrey, a campaigner par excellence. Humphrey could tell his audiences that "what we are talking about in this election is life itself. The future of the planet. The salvation of the species." He could attack the Republican candidate as an "amateur," a "radical," an "extremist," as "irresponsible."

The President confined himself to broad generalities. Always the spokeman for the "massive middle," he was able to point to a record that was both liberal and conservative. He reached out for every hand willing to clasp his in common undertakings for achievable goals, presenting a vision of America in which its heterogeneous people marched shoulder to shoulder toward a brighter future. From the moment he took office he demonstrated the range and depth of his political virtuosity. He brought together railroad management and labor divided for years by a seemingly unbridgeable gulf. He won the trust and loyalty of busi-

---

* According to Roger Hilsman, a specialist on Far Eastern affairs in the Kennedy administration, President Johnson appointed an interdepartmental committee in February 1964 to formulate a list of bombing targets in North Vietnam. In testimony later made public, Secretary of Defense Robert S. McNamara informed the Senate Foreign Relations Committee on August 6 that steps had already been taken to dispatch large numbers of American troops to Southeast Asia. These were to include substantial contingents of ground forces for South Vietnam as well as fighter bombers to Thailand, which later became the major launching pad for the raids on North Vietnam.

nessmen by convincing them of his economy-mindedness and of labor by his "Great Society."

Johnson's basic campaign argument was exemplified in a television address. "We must," he said, "decide whether we will move ahead by building on the solid structure created by forward-looking men of both parties over the past thirty years." Now the people were being told that government "should withdraw from education, from public power, from agriculture, from urban renewal and from a host of other vital programs. We are now told that we should end Social Security as we know it, sell TVA, strip labor unions of many of their gains, and terminate all farm subsidies. . . . This is a radical departure from the historic and basic currents of American thought and action. It would shatter the foundations on which our hopes for the future rest. Too many have worked too hard and too long to let this happen. . . . The choice is yours."

With the assistance of twentieth-century gadgetry, the President revived the nineteenth-century style of political campaigning. Shouting through a bull horn while his custom-built limousine inched at a snail's pace through the humanity-choked streets, "Come down an' hear the speakin'!," or, "Bring your children and the family to hear the speakin'!," he conveyed the Jacksonian folk image of the President. Occasionally, he halted the motorcade to permit the hordes to crowd around him. Then he climbed on top of the car and bellowed that the nation needed in Washington whatever local candidate happened to be riding along with him. Or he humbly told his listeners how grateful he was "to each one of you" and, recalling the great loss the nation had sustained in the death of President Kennedy, pleaded, "Give me your help, your hand, your prayers, and I'll do the best job I can as your President." His habit of reaching out to press the hands that were extended to him kept the secret service men around him on tenterhooks.

At the ball park or outside the city hall or in the town plaza the "speakin'" sometimes went on for an hour or even two. In plain, unvarnished language, generously sprinkled with "you folks," and "I want you folks to know," he gave his audiences an "inside" view of the White House and of affairs of state. On one occasion he made vivid the confrontation between Kennedy and Khrushchev during the Cuban missile crisis. "As he and the leader of the Soviet Union came eyeball to eyeball, and their thumb started getting closer to that nuclear button, the knife was in each other's ribs, almost literally speaking, and neither of them were flinching or quivering." His own thumb moved slowly toward an imaginary nuclear button as he boomed, "Which man's thumb you want to be close to that button, what man you want to reach over and pick up that receiver on that hot line when they say, 'Moscow is calling'?"

Johnson ladled out the corn and the molasses with a lavish hand, but he also served up some tart dishes. Speaking in the South, he declared emphatically that, whatever the sentiment might be in the region, the Civil Rights Act which he had signed was the law of the land "and I'm going to enforce it." At a fund-raising dinner in New Orleans he made some remarks which for a presidential candidate, a Democrat, and a Southerner were extraordinary. Southern politicians, he said, had been exploiting the race question year in and year out, ignoring pressing social and economic problems. What they should have been talking about was the economy and what a great future the South could have if its resources were developed. Then, hitting at those obsessed with states' rights, he reminded his listeners that the greatest amount of help the South had received over the past thirty years had come from the federal government, and that it was the South which had the most to gain from federal assistance. In speech after speech he pledged himself to the eradication of poverty. "I want to wipe poverty off the face of the South—and off the conscience of the nation," he declared. However, economic progress would come about only, he said, if Southerners stopped living in the past and adopted a common-sense approach toward race relations.

Repeatedly, the Democratic candidate appealed for national unity and attempted to widen the breach between the Goldwater faction and the bulk of moderate Republicans. At one fund-raising gathering in Harrisburg he told his audience that he "had not come to Pennsylvania as a partisan." Opposing "reckless factions," he called for "a more perfect union" and denounced the Goldwaterites for being "contemptuous of the will of majorities, callous toward the plight of minorities, arrogant toward allies, belligerent toward adversaries, careless toward peace."

In his closing address, at Madison Square Garden, the President asserted that it was obvious from his opponent's position on such questions as the relationship of government to the people, TVA, social security, and education that he was seeking neither to return to the past nor maintain the status quo but rather to "shatter the tested foundations of our economy." He castigated the Goldwaterites as "radicals" who were creating an atmosphere of hate, fear, and suspicion "in which individual liberty faces its maximum danger." Then, with telling effect, he parodied his opponent. "Extremism in the pursuit of the Presidency is an unpardonable vice. Moderation in the affairs of the· nation is the highest virtue."

To many Republicans, Johnson's moderation made him appear to be the authentic "conservative" candidate who would preserve economic stability, prosperity, and world peace. Prominent financial and business leaders had no hesitation in joining the National Independent Committee for Johnson and Humphrey. Throughout the Northeast and Midwest, businessmen who had voted Republican all their lives were unabashedly supporting Johnson. "It's perfectly respectable for a businessman to be for Johnson. Nobody is shocked. You don't lose anything socially."

Even newspapers and magazines which had always been staunchly Republican switched their allegiance in numbers unparalleled in American political history. Among the defectors were the Hearst and Scripps-Howard chains, the New York *Herald Tribune*, Republican since the founding of the party, the Detroit *Free Press*, and the Binghamton (New York) *Sunday Bulletin* and the *Herald Weekly* of Camden, Maine, both Democratic for the first time since they began publishing in the early or mid-years of the nineteenth century; among the magazines, *Life* and the *Saturday Evening Post*. The latter, which never in its long history had endorsed a Democrat, editorialized: "Goldwater is a grotesque burlesque of the conservative he pretends to be. He is a wild man, a stray, an unprincipled and ruthless jujitsu artist like Joe McCarthy."

The comparison with the unspeakable McCarthy was a gratuitous insult. Goldwater was not a mountebank, but he was greatly handicapped by an inability to express himself clearly. When his supporters stormed that the press was biased against him, they were actually enraged at the reaction to Goldwater's own words in cold print. At one campaign rally a partisan shouted to the press, "Don't quote what he says, say what he means!" The best intentioned reporter, however, could not spend the time to try to ferret out what the candidate was actually trying to put across. Replying to charges of prejudice, the trade journal *Editor and Publisher* made a fitting admonition: "What the Republican nominee for the President of the United States must bear in mind before he opens his mouth is that clarity begins at home."

If Goldwater lacked press support, his followers could not complain that the amount of literature circulated on his behalf was inadequate. The country was inundated with millions of copies of cheap paperbacks written by right-wing extremists, which were either sold or given away free. They purported to show that the President was "soft on communism" and that only Goldwater could rescue the country from imminent disaster. The most widely distributed were *A Texan Looks at Lyndon* by J. Evatt Hale, *None Dare Call It Treason* by John Stormer, and *A Choice Not an Echo* by Phyllis Schafly. They were short on facts but long on rumors, insinuations, and innuendoes, packed with such phrases as "Johnson is reported to have . . . ," and

"Many people believe that . . ." Of the Stormer book, which carried on its cover the legend that it was "the carefully documented story of America's retreat from victory," the National Committee for Civic Responsibility, a nonpartisan organization, concluded, after checking 818 references, that it was "at best an incredibly poor job of research and documentation and at worst a deliberate hoax and fraud." Although the Republican National Committee had no official connection with the paperbacks, local Republican groups, the John Birch Society, and zealous individuals were energetic purveyors of this material.

Very briefly in mid-October, the Goldwaterites were buoyed by what they thought would be a devastating blow to the opposition—the disclosure that Walter W. Jenkins, the President's aide and confidante, had been arrested on a morals charge and that he had a record for a similar offense some years back. Here appeared to be a dramatic example of the decadence that Goldwater had been lashing at and which he charged reached all the way up to the White House. Furthermore, Jenkins's attendance at meetings of the National Security Council raised questions of national security, inasmuch as a sexual deviant presumably was vulnerable to blackmail by foreign powers.

The President asked for Jenkins's resignation and ordered an immediate investigation by the FBI. Several days later the Bureau issued a report that an exhaustive check revealed no information that Jenkins had "compromised the security or interests of the United States in any manner." The President himself was in no way implicated, for he had never been aware of Jenkins's earlier offense; as a matter of fact, Jenkins had been given top secret clearance as far back as 1956.

On the whole, the nation responded with compassion for the unfortunate man. Goldwater acted with commendable restraint, refusing to capitalize on the episode, though he declared that the White House had been careless in security procedures. Then, to Johnson's good fortune, the entire matter was blotted out of the public mind when headlines announced that Khrushchev had been deposed and that the Chinese had detonated a nuclear bomb.

In the last week of the campaign, Goldwater's speeches conveyed undertones of desperation, particularly in the shafts leveled at the clergy. Many churchmen had spoken out against Goldwater, motivated by concern over the direction of public policy if he should win. At Cedar Rapids on October 28, Goldwater asked how the churches could be "concentrating on morality" when clerics have become "loud advocates" of President Johnson "whose desire for power, in my opinion, represents much that is in opposition to the thinking of every church I know?" The following day Johnson neatly replied that he did not condemn clergymen "for being concerned that America meet her moral responsibility to peace" and for demanding that the United States should do "what a rich nation can and should do to wipe poverty from our land."

Two days before the election, the New York *Times* carried statements by the candidates defining the basic issues of the campaign. The central issue, Johnson said, was responsibility, which from 1789 to the present had meant seeking and achieving and maintaining "a center of unity on our nation's purposes and policies." Both parties, he continued, have always concentrated on broadening the vital center, seeking to eliminate divisions and factionalism. It was "the broadening consensus between business, labor, agriculture and government" which was under attack, for as the center of American agreement has broadened, "factions on the fringe have grown more determined in their opposition to and criticism of those in both parties who have sought, achieved, or abided by responsible consensus on our purposes and policies."

Goldwater asserted, "Either we continue the suicidal drift of the last generation away from constitutional government, away from moral order, away from freedom, and away from peace and order in the world community or we chart a new course . . . based on the wisdom of our history . . . [which] will . . . stop the spread of socialism at home and communism abroad." The constitutional system was being eroded, he warned, as the executive branch steadily expanded its power over the lives of the American people. The judiciary was subverting the Constitution and steadily expanding its power even to the point of dictating whether children should pray in local schools. The states were being reduced to so many bureaus with orders handed down from Washington. The nation, he declared, must reverse its course.

For weeks the polls had been predicting a Democratic landslide, but few anticipated the size of the avalanche. Johnson's margin was even larger than Roosevelt's in 1936, and his total vote more impressive than the stunning returns Eisenhower received in 1956—43,126,218 to 27,174,-898, or about 61 per cent for Johnson, and 486 electoral votes in forty-four states and the District of Columbia (where a presidential ballot was cast for the first time under the Twenty-third Amendment) to 52 votes in six states. It was more than a defeat for the Republicans, it was a rout.

A smaller percentage of Republicans supported their nominees than in previous elections when so-called "me-too" candidates headed the ticket, the reverse of what had been predicted by Goldwater strategists. New England, where Republicans generally made a strong showing, overwhelmingly repudiated Goldwater, backing the Johnson-Humphrey ticket by two to one. Maine, one of the two states which had supported Landon in 1936, went Democratic by 68.8 per cent, a majority exceeded by few other states. Vermont, staunchly Republican since the founding of the party in 1856, went Democratic. The farm states—Kansas, Nebraska, Iowa, North Dakota, South Dakota—which had supported Nixon by 58.8 per cent gave Johnson 57.71 per cent.

Ironically, the party of Lincoln, whose candidate in 1964 opposed civil rights legislation, received its majorities in states (except for Arizona) located in the deep South which were largely rural and segregationist. At the same time,

Goldwater's position did not produce the kind of results in the South for which his backers had hoped. The so-called "white backlash" was neutralized by a virtually solid Negro vote in Southern states for Johnson. Throughout the country, both North and South, the Negro "frontlash" crushed Goldwater. Negro precincts in New York and Maryland went Democratic by 94 per cent, in Pennsylvania by 96 per cent, and in Ohio by a fantastic 99 per cent. In Virginia, Tennessee, and Florida, which had voted Republican in the last three presidential elections, the Negro vote was a decisive factor in the Democratic triumph; in Arkansas and North Carolina, it probably swung the balance.

Goldwater's extreme conservatism had permitted Johnson to pre-empt the broad middle ground, an enviable position for a candidate. In keeping with the American pattern, Johnson had stressed consensus politics, while Goldwater, assailing the drift toward "socialism" and "tyranny," and urging a return to "conservative principles" had departed from the traditional rules of coalition politics.

By and large, Americans voted for Johnson because his opponent's policies were either confusing or completely unacceptable. The Republican candidate wished to reverse the major direction of American life to which both parties had been committed for decades—the effort by government to ameliorate the social and economic maladies of an increasingly complex society. Even before his nomination, Walter Lippmann had exposed the fatal weakness in his reasoning: the assault on governmental centralization at home while calling for a more aggressive policy abroad. "Will the Senator deny," he had asked, "that if you decide to risk war, you must prepare for war?" And to prepare for modern warfare meant not only mobilizing the armed forces but the entire national economy, which, in turn, meant enlarging the national power and influence over it. "Yet Goldwaterism at home, the longing to restore America as it was before this century, makes sense only if we can also restore the world as it was before the great wars and the great revolutions and the population explosion and the technical developments of the twentieth century."

Surveys showed that as an individual Goldwater was attractive to many voters, while Johnson was regarded as a "wheeler-dealer." But personality could not overcome the handicap of politics. Goldwater also changed the images of the parties. The Republicans, always considered the "peace party," now became the party of the "war hawks," while the Democrats, long regarded as the "war party," could now, it was felt, be trusted to maintain the peace.

One of the weakest candidates of a major party ever to seek the presidential office, Goldwater ran against the future and he also ran against himself. An estimated $17.5 million was spent on his campaign, but the election had already been lost for the Republicans at the Cow Palace in San Francisco. Goldwater's majority at the convention created an illusion of strength. In the primaries, which reflect grass-roots sentiment, his showing was negligible. Of the five he entered, he was defeated in one major contest and won in another by the narrow margin of 51 per cent. In Illinois and Indiana, he was successful against the token opposition of Senator Margaret Chase Smith of Maine and the perennial candidate, Harold E. Stassen, and in Nebraska against a write-in campaign for Richard M. Nixon. He obtained the nomination because skilled strategists were successful in enlisting partisans who might be delegates to the convention and then worked indefatigably to get them elected.

Barry M. Goldwater tried to swim against the tide and it engulfed him. Like William Jennings Bryan, who had conducted a crusade based on the politics of nostalgia, his defeat was made almost certain by his abandonment of pragmatism for "principle." If the party were to regain power in the future, it would have to nominate candidates whose solutions to domestic and international problems are relevant to the times.

12. Picking a President

O NE of the enduring myths of American politics is that the successful candidate in a presidential contest has received a mandate from the electorate to carry out specific policies. Actually, of only two or three elections could it be said that a particular program was unmistakably affirmed or repudiated at the polls.

The clearcut examples were the campaigns of 1896 and 1936. Those who voted for William Jennings Bryan saw in his plan for the free coinage of silver at a ratio of sixteen to one a panacea for their grievances and frustrations. The majority, who elected William McKinley, were persuaded in one way or another that their livelihoods or their profits would be threatened by free silver, or that the protective tariff which he advocated would solve their problems. While the Republican candidate in 1936 did not reject most of the relief and reform legislation but promised to administer it more soundly, his party had become identified with the philosophy of limited government as contrasted with the Democrats, who emphasized experimentation and innovation. In re-electing Roosevelt, the voters unequivocally expressed their desire for continuation of the New Deal.

No mandate on the most crucial issue of the day was involved in the campaign of 1860. At a time when the very life of the Republic was at stake, when the problem of slavery was tearing the nation apart, the majority of voters chose Lincoln because of his party's stand on matters of personal concern. Republican politicians had attempted to achieve maximum voter support by appealing to local economic interests—a higher tariff on steel for the iron-mongers of Pennsylvania, a homestead law for the western settlers, a national banking act for the financial elements. Ethnic, religious, and labor groups were also given special attention. Expectations on the part of those who voted for Lincoln were as varied as the range of social and economic beliefs and interests which the electorate represented.

Even when a mandate is deliberately solicited, the response of the electorate can be inconclusive as to whether it has been affirmed or denied. James M. Cox in 1920 tried to make of the election the "solemn referendum" Wilson desired for American entry into the League of Nations. Warren G. Harding, ambiguous if not hostile to the League, was elected for reasons extraneous to the issue. Businessmen expressed their dissatisfaction with wartime regulations, farmers with falling prices. German Americans resented Wilson's pro-Allied policies, Irish Americans the nation's close link with Britain. Others saw in the return to Republican rule a safeguard against "Bolshevism," while still others responded to the tranquilizing murmur of Harding's "normalcy" after two decades of moral exhortation. Many who voted for Harding undoubtedly approved of American entry into the League, and many who voted for Cox were opposed. Some newspapers editorialized that repudiation of the League had been "unmistakable," "complete," and "overwhelming," but the Republican Washington *Herald* declared that an "overwhelming majority" had endorsed it, while the Cleveland *Plain Dealer* wrote, "Millions supported Harding in the belief that he would keep his pledge for an association of nations." The League was simply not of vital concern to most voters, although Republicans chose to interpret the electoral results as a death blow to American participation.

Presidential campaigns are more likely to obscure and

distort issues than to clarify them, and candor is frequently a casualty of the electoral battle. In 1916, Woodrow Wilson was returned to the White House largely because the slogan "He kept us out of war" had been impressed on the minds of the voters. While the risk of involvement was always present, as Wilson was unhappily aware, neither he nor any of the Democratic campaigners said a word to enlighten the public on the nature of the country's stake in an Allied victory. Instead, the soporific phrase became the leitmotif, encouraging the impression that the Democratic candidate would keep the nation from becoming embroiled.

On the eve of another war, both candidates offered the hollow assurance that if elected they would keep the country out of the holocaust raging abroad. The Republican Wendell Willkie was not an isolationist, but he was running hard. President Roosevelt, he charged, was a warmonger whose meddling in international affairs had "encouraged the European conflagration." He categorically promised that he would "never send an American boy to fight in any European war." Roosevelt, in his early addresses, merely repeated the Democratic platform pledge that the nation would not go to war "except in case of attack." Democratic politicians, apprehensive about the effect of Willkie's pledge, began to pressure Roosevelt to make a more forceful statement. Finally, the President complied. At the end of October, speaking in Boston, he declared, "And while I am talking to you mothers and fathers, I give you one more assurance. I have said this before, but I shall say it again and again and again. Your boys are not going to be sent into any foreign wars." As there would be no alternative but to take up arms if an Axis victory appeared likely, the promises were flagrantly deceitful.

Consumed with desire to win, the intelligent and normally level-headed Willkie recklessly thundered that if "you return this Administration to office, you will be serving under an American totalitarian government before the long third term is finished." That this was sheer demagoguery Willkie was well aware, for he knew that the structure of the government and the deep-rooted tradition of constitutionalism virtually ruled out the possibility of a dictatorship, but it might influence the unthinking or the easily alarmed. Later he would shrug off the statement as "campaign oratory."

The tendency during a presidential campaign to treat serious issues of foreign policy and national security as political footballs not only leaves the electorate uninformed but may create serious problems with both friends and foes abroad. In the early years of the Republic, a slogan such as "All of Oregon or none," which was used to good effect in electing Polk in 1844, could be regarded with indifference by Great Britain as a harmless expression of America's youthful exuberance. In the twentieth century, however, the position of the United States as a world power makes this type of grandstand posturing hazardous.

Popular frustration over the indecisive nature of the Korean conflict and the continuing cold war offered the Republicans in 1952 an opportunity to indulge in campaign obfuscation. For highly complex and thorny problems they offered vague or simple solutions that sounded attractive. The effect was either confusion or a widespread impression that once in office Eisenhower would reverse existing trends and chart fundamentally new directions for the nation. How the Communist tide about which he inveighed was to be rolled back was never made plain, but "liberation" of the "captive" peoples made a good, appealing campaign slogan.

Relations with Castro's Cuba and the matter of the offshore islands of Quemoy and Matsu were legitimate subjects for discussion during the campaign of 1960. But in their television encounters, Kennedy exploited the first and Nixon the second to score debating points. The manner in which the subjects were handled provided no real illumination of the basic problems.

When President Johnson in the 1964 campaign referred to the steadily deteriorating Vietnam situation at all, he assured the American people that he sought "no wider war." Three months after the election, with no fundamental

factors changed, Johnson ordered a considerable enlargement of United States involvement. Those Americans who
felt duped because they had voted for the Democratic
"peace" candidate can blame the system which places a
premium upon attractive promises. If a candid assessment
of a particular problem might just possibly have an adverse
effect upon the undecided or cause some switches among
the regulars, it is simply avoided.

Political discourse intended to sharpen awareness on the
part of the electorate has rarely been employed in campaigns. A disproportionate amount of time is frequently expended on trying to demolish the opposing candidate. Lord
Bryce commented on this aspect three quarters of a century
ago and his remarks are still valid: ". . . the aim of each
party is to force on its antagonist certain issues which the
antagonist rarely accepts, so that although there is a vast
deal of discussion and declamation on political topics, there
are few on which either party directly traverses the doctrines of the other. Each pummels, not his true enemy, but
a stuffed figure set up to represent that enemy."

While technological advances in transportation and communication have affected every sector of American life, the
presidential campaign remains as long drawn out as it was
in the horse-and-buggy era. Television and radio should
make shuttling back and forth across the country unnecessary, but candidates believe that, to most effectively stimulate enthusiasm and reinforce allegiance, a "live" appearance is mandatory. (Yet what significance can be attached
to crowds when the turnouts for Nixon in Georgia and for
Kennedy in Ohio were enormous, but each man lost each of
those states respectively by a decisive margin?) A presidential candidate also feels compelled to respond to the pleas
of local and congressional office seekers throughout the
country that he endorse them in their own constituencies.
Finally, candidates who feel it necessary to enhance their
national stature want the time to make their personalities
and views more familiar to the public. On the whole, however, the electorate has made its choice weeks before the

conclusion of the campaign. Prolongation of electioneering serves only to tax the ingenuity of professional public relations men, to exhaust the candidates, to increase national tension, and, most important of all, to create an excessive "lame duck" period during which important decisions are postponed.

The basic character of the campaign also has not been altered—the appeal to the mass electorate, the emphasis upon hoop-la, the carnival atmosphere. What has been added is a professionalism which reflects the trend in other areas of contemporary society. Public relations firms have become an integral component of a candidate's strategy force, to assist him in the techniques of persuasion both before and after his nomination. Modern devices such as public opinion surveys have added a new "scientific" dimension to politics.

In seeking victory, technique and strategy may be over-emphasized. Political leaders may exaggerate the importance of such factors as party organization and unity, as though these alone could bring about triumph at the polls. In recent elections Republicans have moaned that their defeat was due to disunity, or lack of sufficient organization at the precinct and city level, or insufficient effort in bringing out the voters, or the failure of rival party leaders to subordinate their differences. In other words, they have assigned greater importance to the mechanics of campaigning than to the candidate and the party's program.

It has become apparent that, unless a candidate possesses the unique charisma of a Dwight D. Eisenhower, he must be a perceptive leader, aware of the challenges of the modern era. By addressing himself to the urgent problems of the day—poverty, urban blight, transportation, education, civil rights, health, and national security—he will mobilize the support necessary for victory more readily than by relying on the mechanics of electioneering. The candidate who responds to the nation's requirements demonstrates his fitness for office. And if his party is responsive to the changing conditions of American life, it will create the base of power upon which majorities can be built.

A candidate for the Presidency makes his appeal to a constituency that is as broad as the nation itself. In Jefferson's day it was predominantly rural. Today, it is predominantly urban, with a variety of groups and interests that constitute America's pluralistic society. The politics of presidential campaigning, therefore, is the politics of compromise, of accommodating and harmonizing, a prelude to the delicate balancing act which the victor will have to master when he enters the White House. In the battle for the Presidency, local considerations cannot take precedence over national requirements, or the parochial be emphasized at the expense of wider needs. Since people throughout the entire country vote for a President, only that candidate is likely to succeed who represents his party in terms of broadest national appeal.

The qualities required for presidential leadership have varied over the years, reflecting, to a considerable extent, the changing pattern of American life. For most of the nineteenth century, the Chief Executives, with but few exceptions, were a mediocre lot, selected for reasons other than their ability to fill the office with distinction. During the decades of bitter controversy over slavery, both parties sought innocuous candidates who could be depended upon to dodge the issue. In 1840, the Whigs turned away from men of national stature like Henry Clay and Daniel Webster in favor of a relative nonentity like William Henry Harrison, whose sole virtue was his dependability in carrying out party policies. About fifty years later, when the nation was racked by agrarian discontent and urban blight, the consequences of profound industrial and technological changes, both parties still frequently selected their candidates haphazardly. An indifferent Republican convention in 1888 gave the nomination to Benjamin Harrison, who had a minor background in politics which included one term in the Senate, because James G. Blaine, too ill to run, cabled from Scotland, "Take Harrison." A contemporary observer remarked that the political conventions of the time functioned like "the exquisite harmony of Nature, which ever strives to get into each place the smallest man that can fill it."

Nevertheless, feeble as the leadership was, the Republic prospered. Circumstances permitted the country to indulge in the luxury of mediocrity without suffering undue damage. In the present era, however, when the Chief Executive occupies a strategic place in promoting the nation's welfare at home and safeguarding its position of world leadership abroad, a Grant or a Harding in the White House would be an unmitigated disaster.

Yet there is no way an aspirant can prepare for the unique and complex role the President is required to fill. Years spent in public service, whether in Congress, administration, or a governorship, may be helpful but do not necessarily equip him for national leadership. Few men came to office with a more extensive experience in government service than James Buchanan—forty years in the legislative, executive, and diplomatic branches. But at a critical juncture in the nation's history, with North and South on a disaster course toward dissolution, he was hopelessly indecisive when the hour called for vigor and resolution. William Howard Taft's distinguished career as judge, Governor-General of the Philippine Islands, and Secretary of War greatly impressed party leaders. His legalistic approach, however, his emphasis on administrative detail, and his rigidly conservative orientation were impediments to the exercise of vigorous leadership.

If judged in terms of his background, Calvin Coolidge should have been a most effective Chief Executive. He reached the heights of political power after serving as city councilman, member of both houses of the legislature, mayor, lieutenant governor, governor, and Vice-President. Yet during his five years in the White House he offered the American people little more than a steady stream of platitudes and banalities, encouraging a perilous indifference to the stirrings at home and abroad that were portents of debacle. As his biographer said, Coolidge believed his task "was to keep the Ship of State on an even keel before a favoring wind—not to reconstruct the hull or install motive power or alter the course. . . . He won no battles, challenged no traditions, instituted few reforms." As a party and legislative leader Coolidge was completely inept—his bills were defeated and his vetoes overridden by Congress.

By contrast, Abraham Lincoln's governmental service on the national level was confined to a single term as a member of the House of Representatives a dozen years before he became President. Woodrow Wilson spent a lifetime in the academic world, his political career limited to a two-year term as governor of New Jersey before entering the White House. Yet he exerted a forceful, commanding leadership of Congress, scoring triumphs that seasoned politicians could envy. The failure that climaxed his administration was caused not by lack of political ability but to a great degree by an unfortunate flaw of personality.

How a President will cope with crises is also unpredictable. Harry S. Truman probably would not have been nominated for the vice-presidency if there had been any doubt that Roosevelt would complete his term. When he was suddenly elevated to the Presidency, the nation as a whole was appalled that its fate at that precarious period was in the hands of this unassuming man. One journalist characterized him as "a sedative in a double-breasted suit," and most informed observers were prepared to write off his administration. But the years that followed were decision-packed, with Truman demonstrating an approach to foreign relations that was unexpectedly creative and imaginative.

Is there any way, then, for the American people to determine whether a potential President will provide effective leadership? What criteria should they consider? Is there perhaps a common pattern displayed by "strong" Presidents that might provide clues?

Probably most important is a broad, expansive view of the office that permits the exercise of executive prerogative whenever public necessity requires it. Theodore Roosevelt was better prepared for leadership by virtue of his approach to the Presidency than by his years of public service. As he once said, "The most important factor in getting the right spirit in my administration was my insistence upon the theory that the executive power was limited only by specific restrictions and prohibitions appearing in the Constitution or imposed by Congress under its constitutional power. . . . I declined to adopt the view that what was imperatively necessary for the nation could not be done by the President unless he could find some specific authorization to do it."

All the outstanding Chief Executives who followed him concurred. Franklin D. Roosevelt also maintained that the Presidency is pre-eminently a place of moral leadership, and his administration was a striking example of a philosophy carried out in practice. In his view, a President must have the capacity and the imagination to adjust the national purpose to the continually changing requirements of a dynamic society while preserving the nation's heritage of humane and liberal values. John Fitzgerald Kennedy felt that the choice confronting the head of the nation was to emulate either Theodore Roosevelt or Taft. His own option was clear. "He must above all be the Chief Executive in every sense of the word . . . prepared to exercise the fullest powers of his office" whether specified or not. "He must originate action as well as study groups."

It is no coincidence that the most ineffectual Presidents were those like Taylor, Taft, Harding, and Coolidge, men firmly committed to the concept that the Chief Executive could exercise only the authority specifically granted him by the Constitution. They all carried into practice Taft's tenet: "The President can exercise no power which cannot be fairly and reasonably traced to some specific grant of power or justly implied and included within such express grant as proper and necessary to its exercise."

However rich and varied the candidate's career, he comes ill-prepared to discharge the duties and responsibilities of the presidential office if his theoretical views inhibit rather

than encourage bold, assertive leadership. In less tempestu-
ous and complex times this element in the preparation of a
President was of no great significance. The relatively un-
troubled periods in American history produced the textbook
image of the Presidency as an equal and coordinate branch
in a system of separated powers, operating strictly within
its own sphere and never trespassing beyond certain specified boundary lines. Today, however, the leader in the
White House must encompass party and legislative leadership, providing direction in economic matters and initiative
in world affairs.

Significantly, with the exception of George Washington,
all the Presidents who made a lasting impact on the nation
were men who eagerly sought the office and were avid for
leadership in public affairs. To reach the White House
would fulfill their deepest ambitions. Once in office, they
approached their tasks with zest and enthusiasm. Theodore
Roosevelt, elevated to the Presidency through an accident
of fate, probably would have achieved it eventually on his
own. He was ecstatic at the opportunity to occupy the seat
of power and found his experience a glorious adventure,
every minute of which he enjoyed. For his successor, William Howard Taft, who was persuaded to take a job he
never wanted and for which, realistically, he felt ill-suited,
it was an ordeal that he endured with outward stoicism but
inward wretchedness.

The Presidency is a lonely place—that "splendid misery,"
as Thomas Jefferson once called it—especially in times of
crisis, when the occupant of the office must repeatedly
make vital decisions for which he alone is responsible. No
one can share the burden with him, and only a man who
has confidence in his own judgment is adequately prepared
for White House leadership. Harry S. Truman's initial response to the news of President Roosevelt's sudden death
was certainly understandable. "I don't know whether you
fellows ever had a load of hay or a bull fall on you," he told
reporters, "but last night the stars and all the planets fell on
me. . . . I've got the most terribly responsible job any man

ever had." But Truman's inner core was sound and firm. Within weeks he began to demonstrate the inner security that enabled him to deal with the many grave problems that beset the nation.

Woodrow Wilson's self-confidence was of another caliber. His lack of humility, tinged with mysticism, was to prove his undoing. "God ordained that I should be the next President of the United States," he announced as he was about to enter the White House. On another occasion he said, "I am sorry for those who disagree with me because I know I am right." While the President must be firmly convinced that the course he has chosen *is* the right one, he must at the same time be flexible when circumstances require resiliency. He must have the courage of his convictions, but also the courage to change his convictions.

A significant element in a President's preparation is a plan that embodies a progressive view of the country's future. It should reflect his talent for creative innovation and display a sense of the direction in which the times are moving; it should provide ways to diagnose contemporary maladies and offer possible means for their solution. Today that plan must embrace Ghana and Ceylon as well as Georgia and Oregon. In Franklin D. Roosevelt's campaign speeches in 1932 a vision of the economic future of the nation was presented that was as bold in outline as it was imaginative. Although containing no specific blueprint, it articulated goals that were the basis of the New Deal program.

Although campaign rhetoric and political oratory can be discounted to a large extent, they provide some means for discerning the quality of a candidate. What could have been expected from Warren G. Harding on the basis of the hackneyed speeches delivered from the front porch of his home? As William G. McAdoo colorfully put it, his addresses "leave the impression of an army of pompous phrases moving over the landscape in search of an idea; sometimes these meandering words would actually capture a struggling thought and bear it triumphantly, a prisoner in their midst, until it died of servitude and overwork!" Unaware of the machinations that gave Harding the nomination, and probably indifferent had they known, Americans recklessly voted for a man whose only claim to the highest office in the land was that he *looked* like a President. A leading contemporary journal in all seriousness wrote that, whatever might be the defects of the nominee as a world statesman, Harding was "an exceedingly courteous gentleman." If he were elected, "good nature, both to political friends and to political enemies" would once again prevail in the White House. "The Senator's speeches may be properly criticized for their vagueness, for their lack of original thought, for their occasionally conflicting character . . . but they are certainly not lacking in the decencies of political controversy. And this is another case where style is the man."

Style is indeed the man. The character of the nation is influenced by the "style" of its chosen head. With "normalcy" enthroned in the White House, the nation drifted, devitalized, without elevated standards or meritorious goals. On the other hand, President Kennedy's expression of high purpose inspired a heightened sense of vitality and expectations.

Leadership in a democratic society performs an instrumental role above and beyond the functions mapped out by the constitutional system. An essential component is the President's capacity and will to influence public opinion so that necessary programs are carried out. The strong Presidents have had both an intellectual and an intuitive comprehension of this ingredient. As Theodore Roosevelt put it, "Our prime necessity is that public opinion should be properly educated." And again, "I do not desire to act unless I can get the bulk of our people to understand the situation and to back up the action; and to do that I have to get the facts vividly before them." The ineffectual Presidents were either indifferent about shaping public opinion or believed, with Calvin Coolidge, that "the people have their own affairs to look after and cannot give much attention to what Congress is doing."

The preparation of a President, then, is compounded of many intangibles. Attributes for which there is no specific training—character, convictions, and style—appear to be more basic for successful leadership than background, training, and experience. Political skill taken for granted, the effective leader captures the public imagination because he possesses moral and physical stamina, because he has a humanitarian outlook and the determination to alleviate the ills that plague our society, and because when he speaks and acts he does so not only for the moment but for the age. He has the capacity to inspire the people, to elevate them above the commonplace, to set a tone for the nation so that the vision of the future becomes the objective for the present. Such a President is a true head of state, both a politician and a statesman.

Notes

1. AN ELECTIVE KINGSHIP

Page 3. PRESIDENTIAL REACTIONS: George Stimpson, *Book About American Politics* (New York, 1952), pp. 515–17.

4. GEORGE MASON: Lucius Wilmerding, Jr., *The Electoral College* (New Brunswick, 1958), p. 5.

9. HERBERT AGAR: James MacGregor Burns, "Case for the Smoke-Filled Room," *New York Times Magazine*, June 15, 1952, p. 25.

10. H. L. MENCKEN: David S. Broder, "Despite It All, the Parties Convene," *New York Times Magazine*, June 19, 1960, p. 7.

13. ADLAI STEVENSON: New York *Times*, June 2, 1958.

14. TRUMAN: *Memoirs of Harry S. Truman* (2 vols., Garden City, 1956), II, p. 92.

14. DOUGLAS CAMPAIGNING: Stimpson, p. 400.

15. LORD BRYCE: James Bryce, *The American Commonwealth* (3 vols., London, 1888), II, p. 589.

16. CLEVELAND VS. BLAINE: Allan Nevins, *Cleveland: A Study in Courage* (New York, 1948), p. 177.

16. THE REVEREND GEORGE BULL: David S. Broder, "Why the Candidates Are Targets for Mudslingers," *New York Times Magazine*, Sept. 27, 1964, p. 124.

16. ROOSEVELT SLANDERED: James Truslow Adams, "Our Whispering Campaigns," *Harper's Magazine*, September, 1932, p. 447.

20. ELECTORAL COLLEGE REFORM: Wilmerding, p. 89.

21. SHERMAN AND HOAR: Louis Wright et al., *Democratic Experience* (Chicago, 1963), p. 257.

22. IN HIS VIEW: Theodore Roosevelt, *An Autobiography* (New York, 1924), p. 357.

2. THE PHILOSOPHER-STATESMAN AS POLITICIAN

Page 26. JEFFERSON ON POLITICAL ALIGNMENTS: William Nisbett Chambers, *Political Parties in a New Nation: The American Experience, 1776-1809* (New York, 1963), p. 75.

27. DISTRUST OF PARTIES: Noble E. Cunningham, Jr., *The Jeffersonian Republicans; The Formation of Party Organization, 1789-1801* (Chapel Hill, 1957), p. 76.

27. GEORGE WASHINGTON: James D. Richardson, *Messages and Papers of the Presidents* (11 vols., New York, 1897), I, pp. 210–11.

28. HATRED OF ADAMS: Frank Van Der Linden, *The Turning Point: Jefferson's Battle for the Presidency* (Washington, D.C., 1962), p. 137.
29. JEFFERSON: Cunningham, p. 108.
29. MARYLAND OBSERVER: *Ibid.*, p. 134.
29. ON ALIEN AND SEDITION LAWS: *Ibid.*, p. 126.
29. JEFFERSON'S BELIEFS: Paul Leicester Ford, ed., *Jefferson's Writings* (12 vols., New York, 1904), VII, pp. 327–29.
30. CIRCULATES TRACTS: Gilbert Chinard, *Thomas Jefferson, The Apostle of Americanism* (Boston, 1929), pp. 353–54.
30. ON POSTAL MAIL: Ford, p. 400.
31. PARTY ORGANIZATION IN RICHMOND: Cunningham, pp. 151–52.
32. FISHER AMES: *Ibid.*, p. 167.
32. JEFFERSON ON NEW YORK ELECTIONS: Van Der Linden, p. 157.
32. ON BURR: *Ibid.*, p. 161.
34. GALLATIN: Claude G. Bowers, *Jefferson and Hamilton, The Struggle for Democracy in America* (Boston, 1925), p. 455.
34. HAMILTON ON ELECTORAL LAWS: Henry Cabot Lodge, ed., *The Works of Alexander Hamilton* (12 vols., New York, 1904), X, p. 372.
34. HAMILTON ON ADAMS: Nathan Schachner, *Thomas Jefferson, A Biography* (New York, 1951), p. 638; Page Smith, *John Adams* (Garden City, 1962), pp. 1044–45.
35. ADAMS ON HAMILTON: Smith, p. 1046.
36. SECRETARY OF TREASURY BOMBARDED: *Ibid.*, p. 1039.
37. PROCURER CHARGE: *Ibid.*, p. 1034.
37. JEFFERSON'S RELIGION ATTACKED: Schachner, p. 641; Cunningham, p. 225.
38. PINCKNEY: Cunningham, p. 212.
38. FEDERALIST BROADSIDE: *Ibid.*, p. 223.
39. ADAMS: Smith, p. 1041.
41. JEFFERSON TO RANDOLPH: Schachner, p. 651.
41. ADAMS TO GERRY: Smith, p. 1053.
41. JEFFERSON: Cunningham, p. 241.
42. GOUVERNEUR MORRIS: Van Der Linden, p. 234.
43. ADAMS TO GERRY: *Ibid.*, p. 284.
44. WARNINGS CONVEYED TO MONROE: *Ibid.*, pp. 290–91.
44. GOUVERNEUR MORRIS: Schachner, p. 651.
45. HAMILTON ON JEFFERSON VS. BURR: Cunningham, p. 241; Van Der Linden, p. 262.
45. BAYARD TO HAMILTON: Van Der Linden, p. 266.
47. JEFFERSON TO MONROE: *Ibid.*, pp. 308–9.
47. BAYARD AT THE CAUCUS: *Ibid.*, p. 310.
48. GAZETTE: Smith, p. 1062.
49. INAUGURAL ADDRESS: Richardson, I, pp. 309–12.
50. JEFFERSON ON ELECTORAL RESULTS: Chinard, p. 51.

3. THE FOLK HERO IN POLITICS

Page 55. CORRUPT BARGAIN CHARGE: Robert V. Remini, *The Election of Andrew Jackson* (New York, 1963), p. 25.
55. CLAY'S FOLLOWERS: Florence Weston, *The Presidential Election of 1828* (Washington, D.C., 1938), p. 17.
56. ADAMS ON CLAY: Remini, p. 26.
56. JACKSON JOURNEY: *Niles Weekly Register*, July 5, 1828.

56. ADAMS AND CULTURE: James D. Richardson, *Messages and Papers of the Presidents* (20 vols., New York, 1897), II, p. 882.
58. VAN BUREN TO RITCHIE: Robert V. Remini, *Martin Van Buren and the Making of the Democratic Party* (New York, 1959), p. 120; Remini, *The Election of Andrew Jackson*, p. 57.
60. MASSACHUSETTS POLITICIAN: Remini, *Election*, p. 78.
61. WEBSTER AND QUINCY: Arthur Schlesinger, Jr., *The Age of Jackson* (Boston, 1945), pp. 38–39.
61. JACKSON AS PRESIDENTIAL ASPIRANT: *Niles Weekly Register*, XXXII, p. 400.
62. CENTRAL COMMITTEE: Remini, *Election*, p. 63.
62. JACKSON CAUTIONED: Weston, pp. 149–50; Remini, *Election*, p. 62.
62. TO INDIANA LEGISLATURE: Remini, *Election*, p. 74.
63. ADAMS'S PERSONALITY: Stefan Lorant, *The Presidency* (New York, 1951), p. 103.
64. ANTI-JACKSON ORGANIZATION PROBLEMS: Remini, *Election*, pp. 128, 134.
66. CABINET MEMBERS DENOUNCED: Weston, p. 157.
66. DUFF GREEN: Remini, *Election*, p. 101.
67. BALTIMORE BARBECUE: *Ibid.*, p. 109.
67. ADMINISTRATION EDITOR: *Ibid.*, pp. 115–16.
67. CORRESPONDENT TO CLAY: Weston, p. 165.
68. ADAMS INDICTED AS ARISTOCRAT: Remini, *Election*, p. 102.
68. ALBANY ARGUS: Weston, p. 141.
68. APPEALS TO NATIVISM: *Ibid.*, p. 164.
69. DUFF GREEN ON JACKSON: Remini, *Election*, p. 105.
69. ADAMS CALLED ANTI-CATHOLIC: Weston, p. 25.
70. ADAMS'S FAITH ATTACKED: *Ibid.*, p. 166.
70. JACKSON A DEVOUT CHRISTIAN: Remini, *Election*, p. 106; Weston, p. 171.
71. HAMMOND'S SCANDALMONGERING: Remini, *Election*, pp. 152–53.
72. COFFIN HANDBILL: Marquis James, *The Life of Andrew Jackson* (New York, 1955), p. 464.
73. NEW YORK PAPER ON JACKSON: Remini, *Van Buren*, p. 194.
73. JACKSON AS FARMER: John William Ward, *Andrew Jackson, Symbol for an Age* (New York, 1955), p. 42.
74. JACKSON NOT QUALIFIED: *Ibid.*, p. 64.
74. CORRESPONDENT TO CLAY: Weston, p. 177.
75. DUFF GREEN: Remini, *Election*, p. 181.
77. JACKSON'S MESSAGE TO CONGRESS: Richardson, III, p. 1012.
77. DANIEL WEBSTER: Remini, *Election*, p. 199.
78. SCENE AT WHITE HOUSE: *Ibid.*, p. 202.

4. THE INVINCIBLE LOG CABIN

The material in this chapter is drawn largely from Robert Gray Gunderson, *The Log-Cabin Campaign* (Lexington, Ky., 1957). Unless otherwise indicated, this title is the source for all quotations.

Page 86. BARREL OF HARD CIDER: John William Ward, *Andrew Jackson, Symbol for an Age* (New York, 1955), p. 92.
89. CARTOON: *Ibid.*, p. 96.
91. ROLLING BALLS: Rexford G. Tugwell, *How They Became President, Thirty-Five Ways to the White House* (New York, 1964), p. 115.

97. GROGGERIES: D. R. Fox, *Decline of Aristocracy in the Politics of New York* (New York, 1910), p. 424.
100. THE WHIG CHORUS: Stefan Lorant, *The Presidency* (New York, 1953), p. 160.
102. PHILADELPHIA LEDGER: *Ibid.*, p. 162.
103. TRIUMPHANT WHIGS: *Ibid.*, pp. 161–62.
103. JOURNALISTIC REACTION: *Niles Weekly Register*, Nov. 28, 1840.

5. "THE TASTE IS IN MY MOUTH . . ."

Page 106. NORTHERN DENUNCIATION: From an "Appeal of the Independent Democrats," January 24, 1854, John D. Hicks et al. (2 vols., Boston, 1964), I, p. 602.
106. PEORIA ADDRESS: Benjamin P. Thomas, *Abraham Lincoln, A Biography* (New York, 1952), pp. 149–51.
109. HOUSE DIVIDED: *Ibid.*, p. 180.
109. DOUGLAS ON LINCOLN'S CANDIDACY: *Ibid.*, p. 182.
110. DOUGLAS EXPLAINS POSITION: George F. Milton, *The Eve of Conflict* (New York, 1963), pp. 322–23.
110. DOUGLAS'S RELUCTANCE TO DEBATE: *Ibid.*, p. 329.
111. DESCRIPTION OF LINCOLN: T. Harry Williams et al., *A History of the U.S.* (2 vols., New York, 1959), I, p. 553.
112. FREEPORT DOCTRINE: William Barringer, *Lincoln's Rise to Power* (Boston, 1937), p. 25.
113. LINCOLN ON RACE AND SLAVERY: Thomas, pp. 188–89, 191.
114. LINCOLN TO SCHUYLER COLFAX: John G. Nicolay, ed., *Complete Works of Abraham Lincoln* (8 vols., New York, 1894), V, p. 132.
115. TO LYMAN TRUMBULL: Reinhard H. Luthin, *The First Lincoln Campaign* (Cambridge, 1944), p. 205.
115. TO JUDD: Thomas, p. 201.
115. COOPER UNION ADDRESS: *Ibid.*, pp. 203–4.
116. JUDD TO TRUMBULL: Luthin, p. 79.
117. DELEGATE LIST REVISED: *Ibid.*, p. 91.
118. WEED'S ACTIVITIES: Carl Schurz, *Reminiscences* (3 vols., New York, 1907), II, pp. 176–77.
119. DAVIS AND THE TELEGRAMS: Barringer, p. 295.
121. CONVENTION SCENE: Murat Halsted, *Three Against Lincoln: Caucuses of 1860* (Baton Rouge, La., 1960), p. 165.
123. NEWSPAPER COMMENT ON NOMINATION: Barringer, p. 295.
124. WILLIAM L. YANCEY: Luthin, pp. 127–28.
125. DOUGLAS'S POSITION: *Ibid.*, p. 130.
125. YANCEY TO DOUGLAS: Milton, p. 435.
125. SENATOR PUGH: *Ibid.*, p. 436.
126. BUCHANAN TO DOUGLAS: Allen Johnson, *Stephen A. Douglas: A Study in American Politics* (New York, 1908), pp. 327–28.
127. DOUGLAS TO A FRIEND: Luthin, p. 122.
127. CONGRESSMAN MONTGOMERY: Milton, p. 471.
128. CONSTITUTIONAL UNION PARTY: Kirk H. Porter, *National Party Platforms* (New York, 1924), p. 52.
129. LINCOLN TO CORRESPONDENT: Luthin, p. 119.
129. INTERVIEW WITH LINCOLN: *Ibid.*, p. 169.
130. CARL SCHURZ: Schurz, II, p. 193.
130. CAMPAIGN CLUBS: Described in Luthin, p. 174.
131. DOUGLAS AND THE TARIFF: Luthin, p. 208.
132. STRATEGY FOR ILLINOIS: *Ibid.*, p. 183.

133. DOUGLAS OPTIMISTIC: Milton, p. 487.
134. BELMONT TO DOUGLAS: *Ibid.*, p. 489.
134. ILLINOIS PAPER EDITORIAL: Marvin R. Weisbord, *Campaigning for President* (Washington, D.C., 1964), pp. 37–38.
135. "S.D.'s MOTHER": Milton, p. 490.
135. NEW HAMPSHIRE PAPER: Weisbord, p. 38.
136. DOUGLAS TO SECRETARY: Milton, p. 496.
136. URGES PRESERVATION OF UNION: *Ibid.*, p. 493.
136. SEWARD ON CONTROVERSY: Luthin, p. 188.
138. REPUBLICAN NEWSPAPER: *Ibid.*, p. 176.
138. HORACE GREELEY: New York *Daily Tribune*, June 25, 1860.
139. THURLOW WEED'S INSTRUCTIONS: Luthin, p. 218.
139. AGAR: Herbert Agar, *The Price of Union* (Boston, 1950), p. 401.

6. SILVER-TONGUED CRUSADER

Page 143. CLEVELAND ATTACKED: Matthew Josephson, *The Politicos, 1865-1896* (New York, 1938), p. 618; Stanley L. Jones, *The Presidential Election of 1896* (Madison, Wis., 1964), p. 43.
144. MORGAN LAWYER TO PRESIDENT: Allen Nevins, ed., *Grover Cleveland Letters* (Boston, 1933), p. 369.
145. TRUE AS STEEL: H. Wayne Morgan, *William McKinley and His America* (Syracuse, 1963), p. 185.
146. WILLIAM ALLEN WHITE ON HANNA: William Allen White, *Autobiography* (New York, 1946), p. 185; William Allen White, *Masks in a Pageant* (New York, 1928), p. 157.
146. MCKINLEY'S POLITICAL ECONOMY: Paul W. Glad, *McKinley, Bryan and the People* (Philadelphia, 1964), pp. 23–24.
149. SENATOR CHANDLER: Morgan, p. 189.
149. MCKINLEY REJECTS DEAL: Margaret Leech, *In the Days of McKinley* (New York, 1959), p. 70.
151. DEMOCRATIC PAPER: *Ibid.*, p. 74.
151. PLATT'S MEMORANDUM: Josephson, p. 653.
152. MCKINLEY ON PARTY PLATFORM: New York *Times*, May 18, 1896.
153. SENATOR TELLER: Morgan, p. 215.
154. JOSEPH FORAKER: George H. Mayer, *The Republican Party, 1854-1964* (New York, 1964), p. 249.
154. HANNAVERIAN DYNASTY: Jones, p. 177.
154. GOVERNOR ALTGELD: *Ibid.*, p. 177.
156. MAJORITY REPORT: Josephson, p. 673.
156. SENATOR HILL: Jones, p. 226.
156. CROSS OF GOLD ADDRESS: William J. Bryan, *The First Battle, A Story of the Campaign of 1896* (Chicago, 1896), pp. 199–206.
158. CHICAGO TRIBUNE: Jones, p. 225.
159. FUSION DILEMMA: Glad, p. 155; Jones, p. 254.
160. HENRY DEMAREST LLOYD: Martin Ridge, *Ignatius Donnelly, The Portrait of a Politician* (Chicago, 1962), pp. 356–57.
160. THE COW-BIRD: Josephson, p. 684.
161. ANGRY DEMOCRATS: Bryan, p. 356.
161. WOODROW WILSON: Josephson, p. 688.
162. WILLIAM S. OSBORNE: Glad, pp. 169–70.
163. THEODORE ROOSEVELT: Morgan, pp. 228–29.
163. FLAG PARADE: New York *Tribune*, Nov. 1, 1896.
164. PHILADELPHIA PRESS: James A. Barnes, "Myths of the Bryan Cam-

paign," *Mississippi Valley Historical Review*, XXXIV, No. 3 (December 1947), pp. 395–96.
165. TERRIFIED READER: New York *Times*, Aug. 18, 1896.
165. CLERGYMEN'S HYSTERIA: Jones, p. 388.
165. ALIENIST: New York *Times*, Sept. 27, 1896.
166. THE ENEMY'S COUNTRY: Bryan, p. 299.
167. NOT A CHRISTIAN: Marvin R. Weisbord, *Campaigning for President* (Washington, D.C., 1964), pp. 49–50.
167. GET McKINLEY ON ROAD: Morgan, p. 231.
168. REFUSES TO CAMPAIGN: *Ibid.*, p. 232.
168. McKINLEY TO SPOKESMAN: Herbert Croly, *Marcus Alonzo Hanna, His Life and Work* (New York, 1919), p. 216.
168. CANTON SCENE: Morgan, pp. 233–34.
170. TO OHIO WOOL PRODUCERS: Jones, p. 287.
170. PLEDGES TARIFF LAW: New York *Times*, Aug. 27, 1896.
171. TO PENNSYLVANIA DELEGATION: Jones, p. 289.
171. CLERGYMEN AGAINST BRYAN: New York *Tribune*, Nov. 2, 1896.
171. GLORIOUS OLD BANNER: Glad, p. 187.
171. BRYAN'S FINAL SPEECH: Bryan, pp. 594–97.
173. MONOMANIA: Richard Hofstadter, *The American Political Tradition* (New York, 1948), p. 186.
173. McKINLEY: Morgan, p. 242.
174. IGNATIUS DONNELLY: Ridge, p. 365.
174. GODKIN AND MORTON: Barnes, p. 397.
175. TRIBUNE EDITORIAL: New York *Tribune*, Nov. 4, 1896.

7. ARMAGEDDON IN CHICAGO

Page 177. A GOOD EXECUTIVE: Theodore Roosevelt, *An Autobiography* (New York, 1924), p. 282.
179. TAFT TO BROTHER: George E. Mowry, *The Era of Theodore Roosevelt, 1900-1912* (New York, 1958), p. 271.
179. TAFT'S VIEW: Henry F. Pringle, *The Life and Times of William Howard Taft* (2 vols., Hamden, Conn., 1964), II, p. 758.
180. WILD IDEAS: Mowry, p. 271.
181. ROOSEVELT TO FRIEND: Elting E. Morison, ed., *The Letters of Theodore Roosevelt* (8 vols., Cambridge, 1954), VII, p. 450.
181. FRIEND TO LA FOLLETTE: Belle and Fola La Follette, *Robert M. La Follette* (2 vols., New York, 1953), I, p. 356.
182. CONSIDERS CANDIDACY: Morison, p. 451.
182. SEEKS DRAFT: *Ibid.*, p. 485.
183. NEW YORK WORLD: La Follette, I, p. 392.
184. TOASTMASTER: *Ibid.*, I, pp. 403–4.
184. ROOSEVELT BECOMES CANDIDATE: Theodore Roosevelt, *Works* (20 vols., New York, 1925), XVII, p. 149.
185. TAFT TO SECRETARY: Pringle, II, p. 769.
186. ROOSEVELT ATTACKS TAFT: Henry F. Pringle, *Theodore Roosevelt* (New York, 1931), p. 560.
186. TAFT IN NEW ENGLAND: New York *Times*, April 26, 1912.
186. RAT IN CORNER: *Ibid.*, May 5, 1912.
188. TAFT ON ROOSEVELT: Pringle, Taft, II, p. 795.
189. WE STAND AT ARMAGEDDON: Roosevelt, *Works*, XVII, pp. 204–31.
191. HARDING: Thomas H. Russell, *The Political Battle of 1912* (L. H. Walter, 1912), pp. 191–92.

191. ROOSEVELT: George E. Mowry, *Theodore Roosevelt and the Progressive Movement* (Madison, Wis., 1946), p. 257.
193. MUNSEY: William B. Hesseltine, *Third-Party Movements in the U.S.* (Princeton, 1962), p. 74.
194. ROOSEVELT ON WILSON: Mowry, *Progressive Movement*, p. 256.
196. WESTERN PRESS ON WILSON: Arthur S. Link, *Wilson, Road to the White House* (Princeton, 1947), pp. 322–23.
196. WILSON SEEKS TO REPAIR DAMAGE: *Ibid.*, p. 340.
196. REACTION TO ATTACK ON MONEY POWER: *Ibid.*, p. 343.
197. TARIFF QUESTION: *Ibid.*, p. 344.
198. ONE OF CLARK'S SUPPORTERS: New York *Times*, Feb. 2, 1912.
198. ATTACKS BY HEARST: Link, pp. 382–83.
199. PRESS ON ILLINOIS PRIMARY: *Ibid.*, pp. 412–13.
200. WILSON NOT VERY HOPEFUL: Ray Stannard Baker, *Woodrow Wilson, Life and Letters* (8 vols., Garden City, 1927–1939), III, p. 321.
200. BRYAN RESOLUTION: Link, pp. 382–83.
201. WILSON TO McCOMBS: *Ibid.*, p. 449.
202. BRYAN EXPLAINS VOTE: *Ibid.*, p. 453.
203. WILSON ON ROOSEVELT: Baker, III, p. 390.
204. TAFT TO WIFE: Pringle, *Taft*, II, pp. 817, 815.
204. NEWSPAPER CORRESPONDENT: New York *Times*, Aug. 13, 1912.
205. ROOSEVELT TO A FRIEND: Mowry, *Progressive Movement*, p. 276.
206. ON INDUSTRIAL CONCENTRATION: Theodore Roosevelt, *Works*, XVII, p. 17.
207. BRANDEIS: Link, p. 492.
207. WILSON'S BUFFALO ADDRESS: New York *Times*, Sept. 3, 1912.
208. THE TRUST QUESTION: Link, p. 478.
208. A DREAM OF THE FUTURE: William E. Leuchtenburg, ed., *The New Freedom* (Englewood Cliffs, N.J., 1961), p. 6.
210. WROTE ONE REFORMER: Link, p. 514.
210. RELIGION AND RACE: For comments by Wilson and other Democrats see *Ibid.*, pp. 500–1, 504–5.
212. AT HARTFORD: New York *Times*, Sept. 26, 1912.
212. AT FALL RIVER: *Ibid.*, Sept. 27, 1912.
212. IN PHILADELPHIA: *Ibid.*, Oct. 29, 1912.
212. ROOSEVELT'S PRAGMATIC PHILOSOPHY: Mowry, *Progressive Movement*, p. 278.
213. GEORGE HARVEY: *Ibid.*, p. 280.
214. TAFT SHATTERED: Pringle, *Taft*, II, p. 840.

8. "I PLEDGE YOU . . . A NEW DEAL"

Page 219. SENATOR FESS: Henry B. Parkes and Vincent P. Carosso, *Recent America* (2 vols., New York, 1963), I, p. 485.
219. GIGANTIC PORK BARREL: *Ibid.*, p. 489.
220. WHITE HOUSE OBSERVER: *Ibid.*, p. 465.
220. HOOVER JOKES: Frank R. Kent, "The Next President," *Scribners*, Nov., 1932, pp. 257–59.
220. HIRAM JOHNSON: William E. Leuchtenburg, *Franklin Roosevelt and the New Deal, 1932–1940* (New York, 1965), p. 16.
221. RASKOB: Arthur M. Schlesinger, Jr., *The Age of Roosevelt: The Crisis of the Old Order, 1919–1933* (Boston, 1957), p. 276.
221. ROOSEVELT: *Ibid.*, p. 277.
222. HOWE: *Ibid.*, p. 341.

223. WILL ROGERS: Frank Freidel, *FDR: The Triumph* (Boston, 1956), p. 167.
223. ROOSEVELT TO REPORTERS: *Ibid.*, p. 169.
224. FARLEY ON LETTER CAMPAIGN: James A. Farley, *Behind the Ballots, The Personal History of a Politician* (New York, 1938), p. 71.
224. FARLEY ON HIS TOUR: Roy V. Peel and Thomas C. Donnelly, *The 1932 Campaign* (New York, 1935), p. 69.
225. ROOSEVELT TO A FRIEND: Freidel, p. 210.
225. MEDICAL REPORT: Earle Looker, "Is Franklin Roosevelt Physically Fit to be President?" *Liberty,* July 25, 1931, pp. 6–11.
226. ONE OF THE SENATORS: Freidel, p. 243.
228. GRANGE ADDRESS: New York *Times,* Feb. 3, 1932.
229. PRESS CRITICISM OF ROOSEVELT: Schlesinger, p. 291.
229. LIPPMAN: Allan Nevins, ed., *Interpretations, 1931–1932* (New York, 1932), p. 261.
230. MOLEY: Raymond Moley, *After Seven Years* (New York, 1939), pp. 10–11.
230. SWEEPING REFORMS: Franklin D. Roosevelt, *Public Papers and Addresses,* S. I. Rosenman, comp. (New York, 1938-50), I, pp. 624–47.
233. JOHN DEWEY: Leo Gurko, *The Angry Decade* (New York, 1947), p. 42.
234. IN FARLEY'S WORDS: Farley, p. 129.
236. GARNER: *Ibid.*, p. 147.
236. ROOSEVELT TO REPORTERS: Leon A. Harris, *The Fine Art of Political Wit* (New York, 1964), p. 138.
237. ACCEPTANCE SPEECH: Samuel I. Rosenman, *Working with Roosevelt* (New York, 1952), p. 78.
239. MOLEY ON BRAIN TRUST: Moley, pp. 41, 45.
240. MOLEY AND HOWE: Schlesinger, p. 422.
241. HOOVER DESPONDENT: *Ibid.*, p. 432.
241. HOOVER TO STIMSON AND PARTY WORKERS: Theodore G. Joslin, *Hoover Off the Record* (New York, 1934), p. 303.
243. INTOLERABLE FALSEHOODS: Herbert Hoover, *Memoirs* (3 vols., New York, 1952), III, p. 239.
243. THE GRASS WILL GROW: New York *Times,* Nov. 1, 1932.
244. ROOSEVELT'S ELECTION EVE ADDRESS: *Ibid.*, Nov. 8, 1932.
244. ROOSEVELT AS CAMPAIGNER: Freidel, p. 358.
245. COMMENTS BY LEADING SPOKESMEN: Schlesinger, pp. 416–17.
245. ROOSEVELT'S FIRST ADDRESS: *Ibid.*, p. 420.
246. TO REPORTER: Anne O'Hare McCormick, "Roosevelt's View of the Big Job," *New York Times Magazine,* Sept. 11, 1932, p. 2.
247. PREPARATION OF TOPEKA ADDRESS: Freidel, pp. 347–48.
248. CALLS FOR NATIONAL PLANNING: Schlesinger, p. 424.
248. IN PORTLAND: Freidel, p. 353.
249. COMMONWEALTH CLUB ADDRESS: *Ibid.*, pp. 354–55.
249. PITTSBURGH ADDRESS: *Ibid.*, p. 363.
250. WITHIN EIGHT MONTHS: Leuchtenburg, p. 11.
250. THE NATION: Nov. 9, 1932, p. 442.
250. LIPPMAN TO BORAH: Freidel, p. 368.

9. MILITARY HERO VS. RELUCTANT CANDIDATE

Page 256. DEWEY VICTORY EXPECTED: Stefan Lorant, *The Presidency* (New York, 1951), p. 710.

257. ELECTION PREDICTIONS: *Ibid.*, pp. 712, 715.
258. GERALD JOHNSON: *Ibid.*, p. 727.
258. TIMES REPORTER: Henry B. Parkes and Vincent P. Carosso, *Recent America* (2 vols., New York, 1963), II, p. 353.
261. WOMAN'S LETTER: Of 471-B, Truman Library.
264. EISENHOWER SPURNS POLITICS: Dwight D. Eisenhower, *Mandate for Change: The White House Years* (Garden City, 1963), p. 7.
266. EISENHOWER IN DALLAS: *Ibid.*, p. 39.
267. SENATOR DIRKSEN: New York *Times*, July 10, 1952.
269. PRECONVENTION COSTS: Alexander Heard, *The Cost of Democracy* (Chapel Hill, 1960), pp. 334–35.
271. AN OLD FRIEND: Walter Johnson, *How We Drafted Adlai Stevenson* (New York, 1955), p. 19.
271. STEVENSON DECLINES PRESIDENTIAL BID: New York *Times*, April 17, 1952.
271. PRESS RELEASE: Johnson, pp. 39–40.
271. LENGTHY LETTER: *Ibid.*
272. RESTON AND ALSOP: *Ibid.*, pp. 104, 109.
272. MYERS: *Ibid.*, p. 114.
273. STEVENSON NOMINATED: New York *Times*, July 21, 1952.
273. ACCEPTANCE ADDRESS: Adlai Stevenson, *The Major Campaign Speeches* (New York, 1953), pp. 7–10.
275. ADVERTISING AGENCY CAMPAIGN: Stanley Kelley, Jr., *Professional Public Relations and Political Power* (Baltimore, 1956), p. 155.
276. EISENHOWER: Sherman Adams, *Firsthand Report* (New York, 1962, paperback), p. 29.
276. PLANS FOR MAJOR ADDRESS: Kelley, p. 166.
277. "MESS IN WASHINGTON": New York *Times*, Sept. 4, 1952.
277. ON INTERNAL COMMUNISM: *Ibid.*, Oct. 6, 1952.
278. SOUNDS VERY GOOD: Emmet John Hughes, *The Ordeal of Power* (New York, 1963), p. 25.
278. REPORTERS' COMMENTS: Wilfred E. Binkley, *American Political Parties* (New York, 1964), p. 440.
278. EISENHOWER AIDE: Hughes, p. 26.
278. McCARTHY AND JENNER: Neal R. Pierce, ed., *Politics in America, 1945-1964* (Washington, D.C., 1965), pp. 17, 18.
279. TRIBUTE TO MARSHALL: Hughes, p. 42.
280. NIXON ON TELEVISION: New York *Times*, Sept. 24, 1952.
282. TV SPOTS: Kelley, pp. 190–91.
283. EISENHOWER ON SCRIPTS: Marvin R. Weisbord, *Campaigning for President* (Washington, D.C., 1964), pp. 49–50.
283. DEMOCRATS ON OPPONENTS' PROGRAMS: *Ibid.*, p. 159.
283. STEVENSON'S WRITERS: John Fisher, "A Footnote on Adlai E. Stevenson," *Harpers*, November, 1965, pp. 23, 24.
283. ONE OBSERVER: Weisbord, p. 160.
284. ADDRESS AT PHOENIX: Stevenson, pp. 123–24.
284. TO AMERICAN LEGION: *Ibid.*, p. 154.
285. STEVENSON ON LOYALTY SYSTEM: Stevenson, p. 218.
286. NIXON ADDRESS: Earl Mazo, *Richard Nixon* (New York, 1959), p. 67.
286. STEVENSON REPLIES: New York *Times*, Oct. 2, 1952.
287. TRUMAN INCENSED: Binkley, p. 444.
287. "I SHALL GO TO KOREA": New York *Times*, Oct. 25, 1952.
287. TRUMAN: *Ibid.*, Oct. 30, 1952.
288. STEVENSON'S FINAL ADDRESS: Stevenson, p. 314.

288. REPUBLICAN SPECTACULAR: Kelley, pp. 194, 195.
289. PUBLIC OPINION POLLS: *Ibid.*, p. 200.
292. STEVENSON'S COMMENTS ON ELECTION: Stevenson, p. XXV.

10. ROAD TO THE NEW FRONTIER

Page 293. CHIEF OF STAFF: Louis Koenig, *The Invisible President* (New York, 1960), p. 338.
294. COMMENT BY FRIEND: *U. S. News & World Report*, Nov. 22, 1957, p. 69.
295. STATE OF UNION ADDRESS: New York *Times*, Feb. 3, 1953.
298. WASHINGTON POST: Earl Mazo, *Richard Nixon* (New York, 1959), p. 6.
299. NIXON CHARGE IN 1954: *Ibid.*, pp. 7–8.
301. "THE DOORS WERE LOCKED": Theodore White, *Making of the President 1960* (New York, 1961), pp. 73–74.
301. EISENHOWER PRESS CONFERENCE: New York *Times*, Jan. 15, 1960.
302. CHALLENGE BY ROCKEFELLER: *Ibid.*, June 9, 1960.
306. SORENSON RELATED: Theodore C. Sorenson, *Kennedy* (New York, 1965), p. 100.
307. KENNEDY ON PRESIDENCY: *Congressional Record*, Jan. 18, 1960, p. 711.
309. WEST VIRGINIA CAMPAIGN: White, pp. 107–8.
315. JOHNSON: Sorenson, p. 165.
315. CONFUSION: Arthur M. Schlesinger, Jr., *A Thousand Days* (Boston, 1965), p. 54.
315. GALBRAITH: *Ibid.*, p. 57.
316. ACCEPTANCE ADDRESS: John F. Kennedy, "The Democratic National Convention Acceptance Address," *Vital Speeches of the Day*, Aug. 1, 1960, pp. 611, 612.
317. NIXON ON LODGE: Stanley Kelley, Jr., "The Presidential Campaign," Paul T. David, ed., *The Presidential Election and Transition 1960–61* (Washington, D.C., 1961), p. 67.
317. TIRED OF DRIFT: Senate Committee on Interstate and Foreign Commerce, *Freedom of Communications*, Part I, 87th Congress, 1st Session, pp. 44–45.
317. FORT DODGE ADDRESS: *Ibid.*, p. 319.
318. NIXON RETORTED: *Ibid.*, Part II, p. 207.
318. RIVAL PROMPTLY REPLIED: Sorenson, p. 185.
318. THE MOST OMINOUS SOUND: Kelley, p. 77.
318. SINGLE BASIC SPEECH: *Ibid.*, p. 65.
319. KENNEDY'S SPEECH STYLE: Sorenson, pp. 182, 184.
319. BOARD OF RABBIS: New York *Times*, Sept. 10, 1960.
320. KENNEDY IN HOUSTON: *Ibid.*, Sept. 13, 1960.
320. CHARLES TAFT: John Wicklein, "Vast Anti-Catholic Drive Slated Before Election," *Ibid.*, Oct. 16, 1960.
321. LETTER TO PASTORS: *Ibid.*, Oct. 17, 1960.
321. IRRATIONALITY ON RELIGIOUS ISSUE: Sorenson, p. 194.
322. NIXON TO NATIONAL COMMITTEE: Wicklein, Oct. 16, 1960.
324. CAMPAIGN RESEARCH LIBRARY: White, p. 285.
325. HEWITT: "What Really Happened Before the T.V. Debate," *Life*, Oct. 10, 1960, p. 30.
325. KENNEDY: Sorenson, pp. 198, 199.
326. NIXON—SECOND DEBATE: Richard M. Nixon, *Six Crises* (Garden City, 1962), p. 345.

327. WOOLLY THINKING: New York *Times,* Oct. 8, 1960.
327. FOUR-POINT PROGRAM: *Ibid.,* Oct. 21, 1960.
329. ONE REPORTER: White, p. 291.
330. KING'S FATHER: *Ibid.,* p. 323.
330. KING EPISODE: William B. Dickinson, "Negro Voting," *Editorial Research Reports,* Vol. II (Oct. 14, 1964), p. 759.
331. MEMBER OF EISENHOWER'S STAFF: White, pp. 308–9.
332. ECHOED KENNEDY: *Ibid.,* p. 303.
332. CAMPAIGN COSTS: Herbert Alexander, "Financing the Parties and Campaigns," David, p. 127.
334. TO CHICAGO TRIBUNE: Nixon, p. 397.
334. KENNEDY AND PRESS: White, p. 338.
335. ONE PROMINENT ANALYST: V. O. Key, Jr., "Interpreting the Election Results," David, p. 175.

11. REACTION REPUDIATED

Page 337. INAUGURAL ADDRESS: *Public Papers of the Presidents of the United States* (Washington, D.C., 1962), pp. 1–3.
340. GOLDWATER: Barry M. Goldwater, *The Conscience of a Conservative* (New York, 1960), pp. 23–24.
341. JAMES RESTON: New York *Times,* Nov. 8, 1963.
342. SEEK THE NOMINATION: *Ibid.,* Jan. 4, 1964.
343. COATTAIL RIDER: Roger Kahn, "Goldwater's Desperate Battle," *Saturday Evening Post,* Oct. 24, 1964, p. 22.
344. "LET'S GROW UP": New York *Times,* July 28, 1960.
344. GOLDWATER MEN: Activities described in Harold Faber, ed., *The Road to the White House* (New York, 1965), p. 81.
346. GOLDWATER BROADCAST: New York *Times,* Jan. 4, 1964.
347. THE LONDON ECONOMIST: March 14, 1964, pp. 991–92.
349. ROCKEFELLER BARNSTORMS: New York *Times,* May 18, 1960.
349. JAMES RESTON: *Ibid.,* June 2, 1964.
350. EISENHOWER: Faber, p. 40.
350. COLUMNIST: *Ibid.,* p. 41.
352. PRIMARY COSTS: James W. Davis, *Presidential Primaries: Road to the White House* (New York, 1967), p. 215.
353. DIRKSEN: Faber, p. 57.
354. SCRANTON LETTER AND REPLY: New York *Times,* July 13, 1964.
354. MARK HATFIELD: *Ibid.,* July 14, 1964.
355. EISENHOWER ADDRESS: *Ibid.,* July 15, 1964.
356. ROCKEFELLER: *Ibid.,* July 15, 1964.
356. GOLDWATER REMARKED: Faber, p. 96.
357. ACCEPTANCE SPEECH: New York *Times,* July 17, 1964.
357. REACTION TO SPEECH: Faber, p. 71.
357. REPUBLICAN PLATFORM: New York *Times,* July 15, 1964.
358. GOLDWATER TO NIXON: *Congressional Quarterly Weekly Report,* Aug. 14, 1964, pp. 1749–50.
359. PLEA FOR UNITY: *Ibid.,* pp. 1751–52.
359. EISENHOWER PRESS CONFERENCE: *Ibid.,* pp. 1749–50.
362. DEMOCRATIC PARTY PLATFORM: New York *Times,* Aug. 26, 1964.
363. PRESIDENT TO STAFF: *Ibid.,* Aug. 27, 1964.
363. ROBERT KENNEDY: Faber, p. 117.
364. THIS IS NOT THE YEAR: *Ibid.,* p. 119.
365. BY HIS OWN ESTIMATE: Theodore H. White, *Making of the President 1964* (New York, 1965), p. 283.

367. OPENING ADDRESS: New York *Times*, Sept. 4, 1964.
367. GIVEN YOU A NUMBER: *Ibid.*, Sept. 22, 1964.
368. WHAT GOOD IS PROSPERITY: White, pp. 326–27.
368. LAWLESSNESS IN STREETS: New York *Times*, Sept. 11, 1964.
368. STOMPING FLAT-FOOTEDLY: Faber, p. 171.
368. RAISED HACKLES: *Ibid.*, p. 165.
369. SOFT ON COMMUNISM: *Ibid.*, p. 201.
369. NUCLEAR WEAPONS FOR NATO: *Ibid.*, pp. 145, 176–77.
369. TELEVISION PROGRAM: New York *Times*, May 25, 1964.
369. TIMES CORRESPONDENT: Faber, p. 169.
370. ONE STRATEGIST: New York *Times*, Aug. 12, 1964.
370. TWO ATROCIOUS "SPOTS": Faber, pp. 167–68.
371. JOHNSON ON NUCLEAR WEAPONS: New York *Times*, Sept. 8, 1964.
371. JOHNSON ON VIETNAM: New York *Times*, Sept. 29 and Oct. 22, 1964.
372. HUMPHREY: Faber, p. 162.
373. TELEVISION ADDRESS: White, pp. 356–57.
373. "THE SPEAKIN'": New York *Times*, Nov. 2, 1964.
374. TALKS IN THE SOUTH: *Ibid.*, Oct. 11, 1964.
375. AT HARRISBURG: Neal R. Pierce, ed., *Politics in America, 1945–1964* (Washington, D.C., 1965), p. 58.
375. MADISON SQUARE GARDEN SPEECH: New York *Times*, Nov. 2, 1964.
375. PERFECTLY RESPECTABLE: Faber, p. 173.
376. SATURDAY EVENING POST: Sept. 15, 1964.
376. SHOUTED TO PRESS: Faber, p. 280.
376. EDITOR AND PUBLISHER: *Editorial Research Report*, Sept. 3, 1964, p. 648.
377. NATIONAL COMMITTEE: Faber, p. 215.
378. AT CEDAR RAPIDS: New York *Times*, Oct. 29, 1964.
378. JOHNSON'S REPLY: *Ibid.*, Oct. 30, 1964.
378. CANDIDATES' SUMMATION: *New York Times Magazine*, Nov. 1, 1964, pp. 23, 102–3.
380. WALTER LIPPMANN: Washington *Post*, July 9, 1964.
381. PARTY IMAGES CHANGED: A. Clausen, Philip E. Converse, and Warren Miller, "Electoral Myth and Reality: The 1964 Election," *American Political Science Review*, June 1965, pp. 330–332.

Selected Bibliography

Books

Alexander, Herbert E. *Financing the 1960 Election.* Princeton, N.J., 1962.
———. *Financing the 1964 Election.* Princeton, N.J., 1966.
———. *Money, Politics and Public Reporting.* Princeton, N.J., 1960.
———. *Responsibility in Party Finance.* Princeton, N.J., 1963.
Bagby, Wesley M. *The Road to Normalcy: The Presidential Campaign and Election of 1920.* Baltimore, 1962.
Bain, Richard C. *Convention Decisions and Voting Records.* Washington, D.C., 1960.
Baringer, William. *Lincoln's Rise to Power.* Boston, 1937.
Bean, Louis H. *Ballot Behavior: A Study of Presidential Elections.* New York, 1940.
Berelson, Bernard, et al. *Voting: Study of Opinion Formation in a Presidential Campaign.* Urbana, Ill., 1954.
Binkley, Wilfred E. *American Political Parties.* New York, 1962.
Blum, John M. *The Republican Roosevelt.* Cambridge, Mass., 1954.
Bowers, Claude G. *Jefferson and Hamilton: The Struggle for Democracy in America.* Boston, 1925.
Brogan, D. W. *Politics in America.* New York, 1954.
Brown, William B. *The People's Choice.* Baton Rouge, La., 1960.
Bryan, William J. *The First Battle: A Story of the Campaign of 1896.* Chicago, 1896.
Bullett, Stimson. *To Be a Politician.* New York, 1959.
Burdick, Eugene. *American Voting Behavior.* New York, 1959.
Burnham, W. Dean. *Presidential Ballots, 1836–1892.* Baltimore, 1955.

Burns, James M. *John Kennedy: A Political Profile.* New York, 1959.

Campbell, Angus, Converse, Philip, Miller, Warren, and Stokes, Donald. *The American Voter.* New York, 1954.

Chambers, William N. *Political Parties in the New Nation: The American Experience, 1776–1809.* New York, 1963.

Charles, Joseph. *The Origins of the American Party System.* Nev/ York, 1965.

Chinard, Gilbert. *Thomas Jefferson: The Apostle of Americanism.* Boston, 1929.

Coyle, David C. *Ordeal of the Presidency.* Washington, D.C., 1960.

Croly, Herbert. *Marcus Alonzo Hanna: His Life and Work.* New York, 1919.

Cummings, Milton C., Jr. *Congressmen and the Electorate: Elections for the U. S. House and the President, 1920–1964.* New York, 1966.

Cunningham, Noble E., Jr. *The Jeffersonian Republicans: The Formation of The Party Organization, 1789–1801.* Chapel Hill, N.C., 1957.

Dauer, Manning J. *The Adams Federalists.* Baltimore, 1953.

David, Paul T., ed. *The Presidential Election and Transition, 1960–61.* Washington, D.C., 1961.

———, Goldman, Ralph M., and Bain, Richard C. *The Politics of National Party Conventions.* Washington, D.C., 1960.

———, Moos, Malcolm, and Goldman, Ralph. *Presidential Nominating Politics in 1952.* Baltimore, 1954.

Davidson, J. W., ed. *Crossroads of Freedom.* New Haven, Conn., 1956.

Davis, James W. *Presidential Primaries: Road to the White House.* New York, 1967.

Davis, Kenneth S. *The Politics of Honor: A Biography of Adlai E. Stevenson.* New York, 1967.

Donald, David. *Lincoln Reconsidered.* New York, 1956.

Eaton, Clement. *Henry Clay and the Art of American Politics.* Boston, 1957.

Eaton, Herbert. *Presidential Timber: The Story of How Presidential Candidates are Nominated.* New York, 1964.

Eisenhower, Dwight D. *The White House Years.* 2 vols. *Mandate for Change, 1953–1956.* Vol. 1. New York, 1963.

Ernst, Harry W. *The Primary That Made a President: West Virginia 1960.* New York, 1962.

Evans, Rowland, and Novak, Robert. *Lyndon B. Johnson: The Exercise of Power.* New York, 1966.

Ewing, C. A. M. *Primary Elections in the South.* Norman, Okla., 1953.

Faber, Harold, ed. *New York Times Election Handbook, 1964.* New York, 1964.

———. *The Road to the White House: The Story of the 1964 Election by the Staff of the New York Times.* New York, 1965.

Farley, James. *Behind the Ballots: The Personal History of a Politician.* New York, 1938.

Felknor, Bruce L. *Dirty Politics.* New York, 1966.

Freidel, Frank. *Franklin D. Roosevelt: The Triumph.* Boston, 1956.

Glad, Paul W. *The Trumpet Soundeth: William Jennings Bryan and His Democracy, 1896–1912.* Lincoln, Nebr., 1960.

———. *McKinley, Bryan and the People.* Philadelphia, 1964.

Goldwater, Barry, *Conscience of a Conservative.* Shepherdsville, Ky., 1960.

———. *Where I Stand.* New York, 1964.

———. *Why Not Victory.* New York, 1962.

Gosnell, Harold F. *Champion Campaigner: Franklin D. Roosevelt.* New York, 1952.

Gunderson, Robert G. *The Log Cabin Campaign.* Lexington, Ky., 1957.

Handlin, Oscar. *Al Smith and His America.* Boston, 1958.

Harris, Leon A. *The Fine Art of Political Wit.* New York, 1964.

Heard, Alexander. *The Costs of Democracy.* Chapel Hill, N.C., 1960.

Henry, Laurin L. *Presidential Transitions.* Washington, D.C., 1960.

Hesseltine, Wm. B. *The Rise and Fall of Third Parties, from Antimasonry to Wallace.* Boston, Mass., 1958.

———, ed. *Three Against Lincoln: Murat Halstead Reports the Caucuses of 1860.* Baton Rouge, La., 1960.

Hofstadter, Richard. *The American Political Tradition.* New York, 1948.

Hoover, Herbert, *Memoirs.* 3 vols. *The Great Depression, 1929–1941.* New York, 1952.

Hughes, Emmet John. *The Ordeal of Power.* New York, 1963.

James, Marquis. *The Life of Andrew Jackson.* Indianapolis, 1938.

Johnson, Donald B. *The Republican Party and Wendell Willkie.* Urbana, Ill., 1960.

Johnson, Walter. *How We Drafted Adlai Stevenson.* New York, 1955.

Josephson, Matthew. *The Politicos, 1865–1896.* New York, 1938.

———. *The President Makers, 1896–1919.* New York, 1940.

Joslin, Theodore G. *Hoover Off the Record.* New York, 1934.

Kelley, Stanley, Jr. *Political Campaigning: Problems in Creating an Informed Electorate.* Washington, D.C., 1960.

———. *Professional Public Relations and Political Power.* Baltimore, 1956.

Key, V. O., Jr. *Politics, Parties and Pressure Groups.* New York, 1958.

———. *Public Opinion and American Democracy.* New York, 1961.

———. *The Responsible Electorate.* Boston, 1966.

Knoles, George H. *The Presidential Campaign and Election of 1892.* Stanford, Calif., 1942.

Kraus, Sidney. *The Great Debates.* Bloomington, Ind., 1962.

La Follette, Belle and Fola. *Robert M. La Follette.* New York, 1953.

Leech, Margaret. *In the Days of McKinley.* New York, 1959.

Link, Arthur S. *Wilson: The Road to the White House.* Princeton, N.J., 1947.

Lorant, Stefan. *The Presidency.* New York, 1951.

Lubell, Samuel. *The Future of American Politics.* New York, 1956.

Luthin, Reinhard. *The First Lincoln Campaign.* Cambridge, Mass., 1944.

Mayer, George H. *The Republican Party, 1854–1964.* New York, 1964.

Mazo, Earl. *Richard Nixon: A Political and Personal Portrait.* New York, 1959.

McCormick, Richard P. *The Second American Party System.* Chapel Hill, N.C., 1966.

Merriam, Charles E., and Overacker, Louise. *Primary Elections.* Chicago, 1928.

Miller, John C. *The Federalist Era.* New York, 1960.

Milton, George F. *The Eve of Conflict: Stephen A. Douglas and the Needless War.* New York, 1963.

Moley, Raymond. *After Seven Years.* New York, 1939.

Moos, Malcolm. *Politics, Presidents and Coattails.* Baltimore, 1952.

———. *Research Frontiers in Politics and Government.* Washington, D.C., 1955.

———, and Hess, Stephen. *Hats in the Ring.* New York, 1960.

Morgan, H. Wayne. *William McKinley and His America.* New York, 1963.

Morison, Elton E., ed. *Letters of Theodore Roosevelt.* 8 vols. *Years of Preparation.* Cambridge, Mass., 1951; *The Days of Armageddon, 1909–1914.* Cambridge, Mass., 1954.

Mowry, George E. *The Era of Theodore Roosevelt, 1900–1912.* New York, 1958.

——. *Theodore Roosevelt and the Progressive Movement.* Madison, Wis., 1946.

Myers, William S., ed. *The State Papers and Other Public Writings of Herbert Hoover.* 2 vols. New York, 1934.

Nevins, Allan. *A Century of Political Cartoons.* New York, 1944.

Nixon, Richard. *Six Crises.* New York, 1962.

Ogden, Daniel M., Jr., and Peterson, Arthur L. *Electing the President, 1964.* San Francisco, 1964.

Overacker, Louise. *Presidential Campaign Funds.* Boston, 1946.

Peel, Roy V., and Donnelly, Thomas C. *The 1928 Campaign.* New York, 1931.

——. *The 1932 Campaign: An Analysis.* New York, 1935.

Phillips, Cabel. *The Truman Presidency: The History of a Triumphant Succession.* New York, 1966.

Pierce, Neal R. *The People's President: The Electoral College and the Direct Vote Alternative.* New York, 1968.

Polsby, N. W., and Wildavsky, A. B. *Presidential Elections.* New York, 1964.

Pomper, Gerald. *Nominating the President: The Politics of Convention Choice.* Evanston, Ill., 1963.

Porter, K. H., and Johnson, D. B. *National Party Platforms, 1840–1956.* Urbana, Ill., 1956.

Presidential '68. Congressional Quarterly Report, No. 39, XXV, Sept. 29, 1967.

Pringle, Henry F. *The Life and Times of William Howard Taft.* Vol. II. New York, 1939.

——. *Theodore Roosevelt.* New York, 1931.

Ranney, A., and Kendall, W. *Democracy and the American Party System.* New York, 1956.

Remini, Robert V. *Martin Van Buren and the Making of the Democratic Party.* New York, 1959.

——. *The Election of Andrew Jackson.* Philadelphia, 1963.

Richardson, James D. *A Compilation of the Messages and Papers of the Presidents, 1789–1897.* 10 vols. Washington, D.C., 1900.

Robinson, Edgar E. *The Evolution of American Political Parties.* New York, 1924.

——. *They Voted for Roosevelt.* Stanford, Calif., 1947.

Roseboom, Eugene H. *A History of Presidential Elections.* New York, 1964.

Rosenman, Samuel I. *Working With Roosevelt.* New York, 1952.

Schachner, Nathan. *Thomas Jefferson, a Biography.* New York, 1951.

Schlesinger, Arthur M., Jr. *The Age of Jackson*. Boston, 1945.

——. *The Age of Roosevelt*. 4 vols. *The Crisis of the Old Order, 1919–1933*. New York, 1957.

Seager, Robert I. *And Tyler Too*. New York, 1963.

Smith, Page. *John Adams*. 2 vols. New York, 1962.

Stanwood, Edward. *A History of the Presidency from 1788 to 1897*. Boston, 1928.

Stein, Charles W. *Third Term Tradition*. New York, 1943.

Stevenson, Adlai E. *Major Campaign Speeches*. New York, 1953.

Stimpson, George. *A Book About American Politics*. New York, 1952.

Stoddard, Henry L. *Presidential Sweepstakes*. New York, 1948.

Stone, Irving. *They Also Ran: The Story of the Men Who Were Defeated for the Presidency*. New York, 1943.

Thomas, Benjamin P. *Abraham Lincoln*. New York, 1952.

Thomson, C. A. H. *Television and Presidential Politics*. Washington, D.C., 1956.

——, and Shattuck, F. M. *The 1956 Presidential Campaign*. Washington, D.C., 1960.

Tillett, Paul, ed. *Inside Politics: The National Conventions, 1960*. New York, 1962.

Tipple, John. *Hamilton and Jefferson: The New Order*. Cleveland, 1961.

Tompkins, Dorothy C. *Presidential Succession*. Berkeley, Calif., 1965.

Tourtellot, Arthur B. *The Presidents on the Presidency*. New York, 1964.

Tugwell, Rexford G. *How They Became President: 35 Ways to the White House*. New York, 1964.

Van Der Linden, Frank. *The Turning Point: Jefferson's Battle for the Presidency*. Washington, D.C., 1962.

Ward, John W. *Andrew Jackson: Symbol For An Age*. New York, 1955.

Weston, Florence. *The Presidential Election of 1828*. Washington, D.C., 1938.

Whicher, G. F., ed. *William Jennings Bryan and the Campaign of 1896*. Boston, 1953.

White, Clifton. *Suite 3505*. New Rochelle, N.Y., 1967.

White, Theodore H., *The Making of a President, 1960*. New York, 1961.

——. *The Making of a President, 1964*. New York, 1965.

White, William Allen. *Masks in a Pageant.* New York, 1928.

Wilmerding, Lucius, Jr. *The Electoral College.* New Brunswick, N.J., 1958.

Wilson, Woodrow. *The New Freedom.* New York, 1961.

Zornow, William F. *Lincoln and the Party Divided.* Norman, Okla., 1954.

Articles

Adams, James T., "Our Whispering Campaigns," *Harper's Magazine* (September, 1932), 447–48.

Burns, James M., "The Case for the Smoke-filled Room," *New York Times Magazine* (June 15, 1952).

"The Candidates Spell Out the Issues," *New York Times Magazine* (November 1, 1964).

Carleton, William G., "The Revolution in the Presidential Nominating Convention," *Political Science Quarterly,* VII (June, 1957), 224–240.

Clausen, A., Converse, Philip E., and Miller, Warren, "Electoral Myth and Reality: The 1964 Election," *American Political Science Review,* LIX, No. 2 (June, 1965), 321–336.

Commager, Henry Steele, "Washington Would Have Lost a TV Debate," *New York Times Magazine* (Oct. 30, 1960).

Dickinson, Wm. B., Jr., "Negro Voting," *Editorial Research Reports,* II, No. 14 (Oct. 14, 1964), 741–760.

———, "Politicians and the Press," *Editorial Research Reports,* II, No. 9 (Sept. 2, 1964), 641–660.

Dixon, Robert G., "Electoral College Procedure," *Western Political Quarterly,* III (June, 1950), 214–244.

Douglas, Paul, "Is Campaign Oratory a Waste of Breath?" *New York Times Magazine* (Oct. 19, 1958).

Hughes, Emmet John, "52,000,000 TV Sets: How Many Votes?" *New York Times Magazine* (Sept. 25, 1960).

Hyman, Sidney, "Nine Tests for the Presidential Hopeful," *New York Times Magazine* (Jan. 4, 1959).

Kallenbach, Joseph E., "Our Electoral College Gerrymander," *Midwest Journal of Political Science,* IV (May, 1960), 162–191.

Kefauver, Estes, "The Electoral College: Old Reforms Take on a New Look," *Law and Contemporary Problems,* XXVII (Spring, 1962), 188–212.

———, "Indictment of the Political Convention," *New York Times Magazine* (March 16, 1952).

———, and Shallet, Sidney, "Why Not Let the People Elect Our President?" *Collier's* (Jan. 31, 1953), 34–35.

Kelley, Stanley, Jr., "Campaign Debates: Some Facts and Issues," *Public Opinion Quarterly*, XVI, No. 3 (Fall, 1962), 351–366.

Key, V. O., Jr., "A Theory of Critical Elections," *Journal of Politics*, XVII (February, 1955), 3–18.

Kirby, James C., Jr., "Limitations on the Power of State Legislatures Over Presidential Elections," *Law and Contemporary Problems*, XXVII (Spring, 1962), 509.

Knebel, Fletcher, "One Vote For the Convention System," *New York Times Magazine* (August 23, 1964).

Phillips, Cabell, "How to Be a Presidential Candidate," *New York Times Magazine* (July 13, 1958).

Polsby, Nelson W., "Decision Making at the National Conventions," *Western Political Quarterly*, XIII, No. 3 (September, 1960), 609–617.

Reston, James, "Our Campaign Techniques Re-Examined," *New York Times Magazine* (Nov. 9, 1952).

———, The Convention System: A Five-Count Indictment," *New York Times Magazine* (July 11, 1948).

Silva, Ruth C., "State Law on the Nomination, Election and Instruction of Presidential Electors," *American Political Science Review*, XLIII (June, 1948), 523–529.

Sindler, Allan P., "Presidential Election Methods and the Urban-Ethnic Interests," *Law and Contemporary Problems*, XXVII (Spring, 1962), 221–224.

Stanton, Frank, "The Case for Political Debates on TV," *New York Times Magazine* (Jan. 19, 1964).

Warren, Sidney, "How to Pick a President," *Saturday Review* (July 4, 1964), 10–13.

Whitaker, Clem, and Baxter, Leona, "Campaign Blunders Can Change History," *Public Relations Journal*, XII, No. 8 (August, 1956), 4–6, 19.

Wicklein, John, "Religion in Politics: 1960 Election," *New York Times*, October 16 and 17, 1956.

Worsnop, Richard L., "Foreign Policy Issues in Election Campaigns," *Editorial Research Reports*, I, No. 20 (May 27, 1964), 381–400.

Index

★ ★ ★ ★ ★ ★ ★

418

DATE DUE

5/19			
NOV 5 1970			
DEC 18 1973			
NOV 24 1975			